SACRÉ-COEUR

Bᵈ MA ROCHECHOUART

M A R T R E

BOULEVARD DE LA CHAPELLE

GARE DU NORD

GARE DE L'EST

BOULEVARD DE MAGENTA

PLAN DE
PARIS

MONTMARTRE

PORTE
ST. DENIS
(ROMAN ARCH)

PORTE
ST. MARTIN
(ROMAN ARCH)

BOURSE

BOULEVARD DE SÉBASTOPOL

PLACE
DE LA RÉPUBLIQUE

AV.   DE LA RÉPUBLIQUE

BOULEVARD

Bᵈ RICHARD LENOIR

VOLTAIRE

PÈRE
LACHAISE
(CEMETERY)

RUE DE   RIVOLI

MUSÉE
CARNAVALET

PALAIS
DE JUSTICE

ÎLE
DE LA
CITÉ

NOTRE DAME

PLACE
DES VOSGES

RUE ST. ANTOINE

M A R A I S

COLONNE
DE JUILLET

PLACE
DE LA BASTILLE

PLACE
DE LA NATION

ST. MICHEL

ÎLE
SAINT-LOUIS

Bᵈ HENRI IV

Bᵈ BOURBON

Bᵈ DE LA BASTILLE

RUE DU FAUBOURG ST. ANTOINE

SORBONNE

T E R   L A T I N

UNIV. DE PARIS
FAC. DES SCIENCES

BOULEVARD DIDEROT

PANTHÉON

ÉCOLE
POLYTECH.

PICPUS
(CEMETERY)

ÉCOLE
NORMALE

JARDIN
DES PLANTES

Ioanna Tolios

Le Pont Neuf

EDWARD M. STACK

North Carolina State University

PRENTICE-HALL, INC., ENGLEWOOD CLIFFS, NEW JERSEY   07632

Le Pont Neuf
A Structural Review
Third Edition

Library of Congress Cataloging in Publication Data

Stack, Edward M
   Le Pont Neuf.

   Includes index.
   1. French language—Grammar—1950–   I. Title.
PC2112.S68 1978   448'.2'421   76-30460
ISBN 0-13-530394-X

Printed in the United States of America

10 9 8 7 6 5 4 3 2 1

The Seine River, with a view of the Pont Neuf (*Frederic Lewis*)

Cover photograph: Weidenfeld & Nicolson Ltd., London

Prentice-Hall International, Inc., *London*
Prentice-Hall of Australia Pty. Limited, *Sydney*
Prentice-Hall of Canada, Ltd., *Toronto*
Prentice-Hall of India Private Limited, *New Delhi*
Prentice-Hall of Japan, Inc., *Tokyo*
Prentice-Hall of Southeast Asia Pte. Ltd., *Singapore*
Whitehall Books Limited, *Wellington, New Zealand*

CONTENTS

Preface

Students progressing from predominantly audiolingual instruction towards literary studies will find it advantageous to bridge the transition by systematically reviewing grammatical structures and principles. This text is designed to provide that review by formulating as clearly as possible the grammatical principles already learned inductively, and by placing them in a form convenient for reading and composition. It provides a mechanism for both written practice and maintenance of oral proficiency through exercises designed for class use in French. It is recommended that a reader be used collaterally with this grammar on an alternating schedule, so that the example of authentic literature will serve both as a demonstration of grammar in action, and as a source of topics of conversation and composition.

This edition has been shortened so that it will be adaptable to one-semester courses. Each chapter contains two (sometimes three) main topics, one of which is usually a review of an important irregular verb and its associated idioms. Exercises designed for class use entirely in French include short drills for instilling a principle, longer conversationally-oriented exercises, controlled composition (*thèmes*) so that the students will all be working on the same problems of written communication, and topics of a general nature for development of original writing. Students are encouraged even in the controlled drills to attempt original additions to the minimal answer through a system of elaboration: the student answers a question calling for a relatively fixed response, then adds a supporting or collaborative thought of his own to supplement it. (Here the teacher must actively encourage the students to do this.)

The chapters are generally self-contained and independent, with adequate cross-references to other chapters. A teacher may assign a chapter out of order without adverse effect. The *passé simple*, for example, may be needed early in a course that includes a novel or historical work employing that tense. Even though this tense is dealt with in the last chapter of this grammar, it may readily be assigned earlier.

All drills, exercises, and compositions are designed for use entirely in French in the classroom. English is used for explanations of grammar to allow students to prepare their work efficiently and with full understanding at home or in the dormitory, thus preserving valuable classroom time for practice in the foreign language on topics of a general nature. The purpose is to free the teacher of the need to present grammatical material in class, other than clarification of points not fully understood. Students are expected to learn the principles from this text before arriving in class to put them into practice.

From time to time a vocabulary presentation (*révision lexicale*) appears. It groups together words and expressions common to a particular activity or location, or involves some systematic vocabulary-building explanation. These sections may serve as a source of material for composition or conversation, and may give the teacher an opportunity to provide additional information or anecdotes drawn from personal experience. The illustrations are likewise provided not only for their visual reflection of France, but as points of departure for conversation or questionnaires in class.

The end papers provide correction symbols and abbreviations for the teacher to use in checking homework. It is suggested that all work be gone over in class orally, with critical spellings being elicited in French. After students have corrected their own work and presented their alternate solutions for approval, the work is collected. Before the following class meeting the teacher may go over the papers and mark any remaining errors with a symbol from the list. Each error is underscored and the applicable symbol written at the end of the line. For example:

> 4. Les garçon arrivent à midi. *pl / Tpec*
>
> 5. La petit fille a entrée dans le salon. *ag / aux*

The papers are returned to the students for rewriting (only the sentences marked). The student identifies the kind of mistake, finds the applicable rule, and rewrites the marked sentences correctly, thus actively participating in the remedial process.

A list of the abbreviations used for convenience in the grammatical explanations appears on the following pages. Notice that irregular verbs are marked throughout the book with an asterisk (*) and stem-changing verbs with a degree mark (°). The designated position of certain words is shown in brackets thus: nouns [N], infinitives [I], and persons [P].

I wish to express my appreciation to Madame Sylvie Carduner for reviewing part of the manuscript and making many helpful suggestions, and to Hilda Tauber, Project Editor at Prentice-Hall, for her painstaking and detailed editorial supervision. I also wish to thank Mark Binn, who designed the book, and Irene Springer for photographic research.

EDWARD M. STACK

ABBREVIATIONS USED IN THE GRAMMATICAL SECTIONS

adj.	Adjective	[P]	Person appears here
adv.	Adverb	PDO	Preceding direct object
aux.	Auxiliary verb	*pl.*	Plural
[C]	Clause	*pp.*	Past participle
do	Direct object	*ps. p.*	Present participle
f.	Feminine	*s.*	Singular
FC	Future and Conditional	*tc*	Conditional tense
f.pl.	Feminine plural	*tf*	Future tense
f.s.	Feminine singular	*ti*	Imperfect tense
[I]	Infinitive appears here	*tp*	Present tense
io	Indirect object	*tpc*	Passé composé tense
m.	Masculine	*tpp*	Pluperfect tense
m. pl.	Masculine plural	*tps*	Passé simple tense
m.s.	Masculine singular	°	Stem-changing verb
[N]	Noun appears here	*	Irregular verb

A list of the abbreviations used in the vocabularies appears with the vocabulary section of the book. Abbreviations to be used for the correction of exercises and compositions appear on the inside back covers.

LE PONT NEUF

Les Champs-Élysées et l'Arc de Triomphe (*Carolyn Watson/Monkmeyer*)

1

Article défini

Aller*

ARTICLE DÉFINI *art*

~~~~~~

In French, the definite article (**le, la, l', les**) is ordinarily used with a noun or noun cluster (a noun and its accompanying modifiers) unless replaced by: (a) the indefinite article (**un, une, des**); (b) a possessive adjective (**son, mon,** etc.); (c) an expression of quantity (**beaucoup de**); or (d) a number.

la voiture	ARTICLE + [NOUN]
une voiture	(a) INDEFINITE ARTICLE + [NOUN]
ma voiture	(b) POSSESSIVE ADJECTIVE + [NOUN]
beaucoup de voitures	(c) EXPRESSION OF QUANTITY + [NOUN]
trois voitures	(d) NUMBER + [NOUN]

As a general rule, the French definite article is *always* required when the English equivalent uses "the." In addition, the French article is required in many cases where English uses no article; these cases will be indicated below.

1.01 FORMS OF THE DEFINITE ARTICLE. The French definite article has four forms:

le (*masculine singular*) before a masculine singular noun beginning with a consonant: **le professeur, le livre, le cours**. Note that most nouns ending in -*ment* are masculine.

la (*feminine singular*) before a feminine singular noun beginning with a consonant: **la faculté, la bibliothèque, la conférence.**

l' (*masculine* or *feminine singular*) before any singular noun beginning with a *vowel* sound, including mute *h* (*l'homme, l'hiver*). This is called the "elided" form, in which the vowel of *le* or *la* is replaced by an apostrophe before a vowel: **l'école, l'université, l'histoire.** All nouns ending in *-tion* are feminine.

les (*masculine* or *feminine plural*) before *any* plural noun: **les cours, les conférences, les hommes, les étudiants.**

1.02 ELISION. Elision is the dropping of **-e** in two-letter words when the next word begins with a vowel or mute *h*. Examples are:

je	j'arrive	**me**	il m'écoute
te	il t'aime	**se**	il s'est levé
le	je l'ai	**de**	il vient d'arriver
ne	ils n'ont pas	**ce**	c'est (*only form*)

One three-letter word (**que**) elides, as do its many compounds such as **jusque, lorsque, puisque, quoique, est-ce que, qu'est-ce que.** (Be careful *not* to elide **qui,** which can *never* become **qu'.**)

jusque	jusqu'au commencement
lorsque	lorsqu'elle arrivera

In addition, **si** becomes **s'il** or **s'ils** in those two forms only; **la** becomes **l'** before a vowel sound. These are the only times *i* and *a* are elided.

There are two categories of *h*, mute and aspirate. The letter *h* itself is never pronounced. When a word begins with mute *h* (the more usual), elision occurs:

l'homme	**l'hôpital**	**l'hôtel**	**l'habitation**	**j'habite**

Some words begin with *aspirate h*, marked in most dictionaries with a star or other special symbol. Treat these words as though they begin with a consonant. Neither elision (in writing) nor linking (in speech) occurs before an aspirate *h*:

le héros	**les héros** [le ero]	**la honte**	**le hibou**

1.03 CONTRACTIONS. When the preposition **à** or **de** is used before the definite article **le** or **les**, the contracted forms must be substituted:

Instead of	Use		
à + le	**au** ⎫	*to the, at the*	**au** début
à + les	**aux** ⎭		**aux** conférences
de + le	**du** ⎫	*of the, from the, some*	**du** professeur
de + les	**des** ⎭		**des** théories

No contraction is used when the article is **la** or **l'**. No contraction is used if **le** is a pronoun (*it, him*):

> Donnez-moi **de l'eau**.
> Je suis content **de le** revoir.

The meaning *some* is a function of the partitive [4.01].

1.04 USE OF THE DEFINITE ARTICLE.   The definite article is used with a noun to designate a *specific* item (for example, *the* book, as opposed to *a* book). When the English equivalent uses "the," the French uses the definite article also. In addition, the article is used in the following cases where English omits the definite article.

A.   GENERAL CATEGORIES AND ABSTRACT QUALITIES.

> **Les rayonnements cosmiques** sont dangereux.
>   *Cosmic radiation* is dangerous.
> **L'enseignement supérieur** devient coûteux.
>   *Higher education* is becoming costly.
> **Le bon jugement** est admirable.
>   *Good judgment* is admirable.

B.   GEOGRAPHICAL NAMES (EXCEPT CITIES).   Names of countries, provinces, states, continents, rivers, mountains, and other geographical names (except cities) include the definite article.

> **La France, la Suisse** et **le Portugal** sont des pays européens.
> **L'Europe** et **l'Australie** sont des continents.
> **La Seine, la Loire** et **la Garonne** sont des fleuves français.
> **Les Alpes, les Pyrénées, les Vosges** et **le Jura** sont des montagnes.

A few cities incorporate the article as part of the name:

> **Le Havre** est un port important.
> **Le Caire** est la capitale de l'Égypte.
> **La Haye** se trouve aux Pays-Bas.
> **La Havane** est la capitale de l'île de Cuba.

In these names normal contraction occurs with the masculine article **Le**:

> Pierre va **au Havre**; Hans vient **du Havre**.
>   Pierre is going *to Le Havre*; Hans is coming *from Le Havre*.

C.   MODIFIED NAMES OF PERSONS AND CITIES.   When the name of a city or person is accompanied by a modifier, the article is used:

> **Paris** est charmant.   BUT   **Le vieux Paris** est charmant.
> **Marie** est belle.   **La petite Marie** est belle.

D. TITLES. The definite article is used with titles in French, though not in English:

> Voilà **le professeur** Foulet.
> **Le colonel** Chabert fait un voyage en Égypte.
> Je vais poser une question **au commandant**.
> — Bonjour, monsieur **le maire**.

Family names are pluralized only in the definite article; do not add *-s* to the proper name:

> Nous avons vu **les Smith**.   We saw *the Smiths.*

No article is used before the titles **monsieur, madame, mademoiselle**. Notice that the noun **le monsieur** means *the gentleman* (or sometimes simply *the man*).

1.05 OMISSION OF THE DEFINITE ARTICLE. The definite article is omitted in the following instances.

A. NAMES OF PERSONS AND CITIES. No article is used with names of persons or cities (except when modified).

> **Marie, Paul** et **monsieur Dupont** sont allés à Versailles.
> J'ai visité **Paris, Londres** et **Vienne**.

B. APPOSITIVES. The article is usually omitted before an appositive (an explanatory noun showing identity, separated from the rest of the sentence by commas).

> M. Gérard Ducray, **secrétaire** d'État au Tourisme, est optimiste.
> Le Dr Henri Jarrit, **directeur** du laboratoire, a fait cette conférence.
> *Madame Bovary*, **roman** réaliste, décrit la vie d'une bourgeoise.

If "the" would be appropriate in English, as with very famous people, the article *would* be used in French:

> Einstein, **le physicien célèbre**, créa la théorie de la relativité.

C. RELIGION, PROFESSION, NATIONALITY, POLITICAL PREFERENCE. The definite article is omitted after **être*** with the name of a religion, profession, nationality, or political preference (see 5.13):

> Paul est **catholique**.   Hans est **allemand**.
> M. Masson est **médecin**.   Igor est **communiste**.
> Jean-Paul est **étudiant**.   Mme Dupont est **vendeuse**.

D.   Days of the week.   Although all the days of the week are masculine gender nouns, the article is used only when *each*, *every* is meant.

Nous sommes allés à Dijon **jeudi**.	We went to Dijon *Thursday*. (last Thursday)
Nous irons à Paris **samedi**.	We will go to Paris *Saturday*. (next Saturday)
BUT Nous allons à Paris **le samedi**.	We go to Paris on *Saturdays*. (*every* Saturday)
J'ai une classe de français **le lundi**, **le mercredi** et **le vendredi**.	I have a French class on *Mondays*, *Wednesdays*, and *Fridays*.

E.   Headings, addresses.   The article is omitted in headings and postal addresses:

Thème	place Vendôme
Dictée	34, rue Palatine
Chapitre 4	7, boulevard des Italiens
Acte 3	Paul habite rue Palatine, numéro 34.

prep   **1.06**   Prepositions replacing the definite article.   The definite article is omitted after a preposition in certain cases.

A.   Academic subjects.   After such nouns as *classe*, *cours*, *professeur*, *faculté*, and *école*, use **de (d')** alone before the name of the academic subject:

la sociologie	**Le professeur de sociologie** s'appelle M. Lebeau.
l'histoire	**Le cours d'histoire** m'intéresse.
le français	Je vais à **la classe de français**.
la médecine	**La Faculté de Médecine** se trouve là-bas.
BUT la faculté **des sciences**	
la faculté **des lettres**	

When the name of the subject is not mentioned with *la classe*, use **en classe** for "to class":

Je vais **en classe**.   BUT   Je vais **à la classe** de psychologie.

B.   Seasons.   With the three seasons beginning with a vowel sound, use **en** alone for "in" or "in the"; for *le printemps*, use **au printemps**:

L'automne me plaît.	Je fais du camping **en automne**.
L'hiver est dur.	Il fait très froid **en hiver**.
L'été est agréable.	Nous allons à la montagne **en été**.
Le printemps arrive.	Il fait très beau **au printemps**.

C. DESTINATION OR LOCATION. For geographical destination or location, use the following prepositions for *at*, *to*, or *in* (PLACE):

à [CITY]	Je vais **à Paris** et **à Genève.**
en [COUNTRY, *f.*]	Je vais **en France, en Italie** et **en Espagne.**
au [COUNTRY, *m.*]	Juan va **au Portugal**; il habite **au Portugal.**
en [CONTINENT]	Le Portugal et l'Espagne sont **en Europe.**

All European countries are feminine gender except **le Portugal, le Luxembourg,** and **le Danemark.**

States and provinces follow the rule for countries: use **en** before *feminine* names, and **au** before *masculine* names. In some cases, **dans l'État de (New York)** may be used.

la Louisiane, **la** Floride	Je vais **en Louisiane** et **en Floride.**
le Texas	Jean va **au Texas**; il habite **au Texas.**
la Normandie	Nous irons **en Normandie.**

Cities which incorporate an article as part of the name will retain the article, and contractions are made when the article is *le*:

Je vais **au Havre** et **à la Rochelle** pendant les vacances.

See Appendix E for a list of countries and languages.

rep D. REPETITION REQUIRED. Prepositions and contractions used must be repeated with each noun:

Je vais **à** Paris, **à** Rouen et **au** Havre.
Paul visitera des musées **en** Espagne et **en** Suisse.
Nous ferons un voyage **en** France, **au** Danemark et **en** Suède.

Exercice 1A L'article défini [1.01 – 1.06]

Complétez les phrases suivantes par l'article défini (si c'est nécessaire) ou par la préposition appropriée.

1. —— sports pratiqués à —— université comprennent —— tennis, —— football, —— basket et —— cyclisme.
2. —— jeune Roger Foulet suit des cours de —— mathématiques et de —— langue étrangère.
3. —— Roger demeure à Saint-Cloud avec la famille de Charles.
4. —— étudiants vont à —— université en automne, en hiver et au printemps.
5. Tout le monde préfère les cours pratiques et utiles.
6. Le campus est très moderne: les bâtiments, les arbres et les gazons sont magnifiques.
7. Il y a des problèmes budgétaires: les crédits ne suivent pas l'augmentation du coût de la vie.

8. <u>La</u> décentralisation de l'université a séparé <u>la</u> faculté <u>des</u> sciences de <u>la</u> faculté <u>des</u> lettres.
9. —— Charles et —— Roger font —— devoirs à —— maison le soir.
10. Ils vont toujours —— théâtre —— jeudi soir.
11. M. Chamard, —— professeur —— anglais —— Paris, a fait une conférence au sujet de George Orwell.
12. —— père de —— Charles est —— directeur d'une grande maison de détail.
13. Il est —— catholique; —— petite Françoise est —— protestante.
14. —— camarade de chambre de Charles est —— étudiant en économie: il proteste contre —— coût de la vie et —— augmentation brutale —— prix.
15. —— fanatiques de football vont aussi en classe de temps en temps.

VERBE IRRÉGULIER aller*

Review **aller*** [*to go*] in the *présent*, *imparfait*, and *passé composé*. (See Appendix C, verb table 1.) Notice that this verb uses *être** as auxiliary, hence the past participle agrees with the subject in gender and number [16.02].

1.07 PREPOSITIONS USED WITH MEANS OF TRAVEL. For travel by foot, bicycle, or horseback (the three slowest means of travel) use the preposition **à**:

Il va en ville **à pied**.
    à bicyclette.
    à cheval.

For other conveyances, use the preposition **en**:

Il va à Londres **en auto** (= en voiture).
    en autocar.
    en avion.
    en bateau.
    en chemin de fer.
  BUT **par le train.** } (*by train*)

The verb **prendre*** [*to take*] may be used with the name of the conveyance, as in English.

Il prend un taxi	He is taking a taxi.
Il a pris le métro.	He took the subway.
Il prendra l'avion.	He will take the plane. (He will fly.)
Il prenait le train.	He used to take the train.

1.08 **aller*** **en** [CONVEYANCE] *to fly, to drive.*

Il **est allé** à Londres **en avion**.	He flew to London.
Il **est allé** au cinéma **en auto**.	He drove to the movies.
Nous **allons** à Dijon **en voiture**.	We are driving to Dijon.

The person actually at the controls of an automobile would say, "J'ai conduit" (*I drove*). The verb *conduire** does not apply to the passengers.

1.09 VERBS OTHER THAN **aller*** EXPRESSING *to go.*

to go in	entrer (dans)	Il **entre dans** le salon.
to go out	sortir (de)	Ils **sortent du** laboratoire.
to go up (stairs)	monter (à)	Il **monte au** premier.
to go down (stairs)	descendre (à)	Il **descend à** la cuisine.
to go with	accompagner	Il **accompagne** sa mère.
to go (do) without	se passer de	Il **se passe de** voiture.
to go across	traverser	Il **traverse** la rue.
to go by [PLACE]	passer par	Il **passe par** la librairie.
to go to bed	se coucher	Il **se couche** à onze heures.
to go to sleep (fall asleep)	s'endormir*	Il **s'endort** tout de suite.

1.10 IMMEDIATE FUTURE. Use **aller*** + INFINITIVE to indicate imminent future action, as in English. Notice that if the action is *not* expected to happen rather soon, the future tense is preferred [21.01].

	Je **vais lire** le journal.	I am going to read the paper.
	Nous **allons partir** maintenant.	We are going to leave now.
BUT	Nous **partirons** mardi.	We will leave Tuesday. (Action not imminent)

In the imperfect tense, **aller** [I][1] is used for "*was going [to do something]*" an intended action in the past that for some reason was not carried out:

J'**allais étudier**, mais j'ai dû accompagner mon père en ville.
I *was going* to study, but I had to go downtown with my father.

1.11 USE OF THE VERB **visiter**. Use **visiter** [PLACE] without a preposition before the name of the place:

J'ai **visité la France**; Paul **a visité Paris** et **la Normandie**.

By contrast, **aller*** is followed by one of the prepositions required [1.06C, 1.07]:

Je **suis allé en** France; Paul est allé **à** Paris et **en** Normandie.

[1]The notation [I] means that an infinitive should appear at that location in the sentence.

*Verbe irrégulier
aller**

Do not use **visiter** for visiting people. The structure used for people is **faire*
une visite à** (*someone*) or **rendre visite à** (*someone*):

> J'ai **fait une visite à** mon oncle.   Paul **a rendu visite** à son ami.

Exercice 1B   Locutions avec *aller* [1.07]

Remplacez les mots en italique par des locutions employant *aller*:

MODÈLE: Je *prends ma bicyclette* pour aller en classe. (**pour** [ɪ] = in order to)
Je *vais* en classe *à bicyclette.*

1. Le directeur *prend l'avion* pour aller à Berlin.
2. Je *prends le train* pour Lyon.
3. Les commerçants *prennent le bateau* pour Londres.
4. J'*ai pris l'autocar* pour aller à l'aéroport.
5. Les Dupont *ont pris un taxi* pour aller à l'opéra.
6. Roger *a pris sa bicyclette* pour aller à l'université.
7. Je *prenais* toujours *l'autobus* pour aller à la bibliothèque.

Exercice 1C   [1.01 – 1.09]

NOTE: In exercises calling for a personal answer on your part, your response
should consist of (a) a reply to the question, and (b) a second sentence in which you
explain or elaborate on your reply. If you forget to continue on with a second
sentence, your teacher might remind you to do so by saying something like "Tiens!"
which means approximately "Well, that's interesting! Tell me more!" For example:

> Q: Quel temps fait-il aujourd'hui?
> A: Il fait beau aujourd'hui. Il fait du soleil.
> Q: Très bien. Quelle ville voudriez-vous visiter en France?
> A: Je voudrais visiter Paris.
> Q: Tiens!
> A: Je voudrais bien voir la Tour Eiffel.

Later on, after you have become accustomed to adding one statement, your teacher
may ask for two or even three additional statements in such exercises.

Répondez aux questions suivantes par des phrases complètes. Employez les
réponses indiquées; ensuite ajoutez une phrase d'explication.

MODÈLE: Quel continent voudriez-vous visiter? (*Je voudrais aller . . .*)
Europe
Je voudrais aller **en Europe**. J'ai des parents en Allemagne.

1. Quel continent voudriez-vous visiter?
   Europe / Amérique du Sud / Asie / Australie
2. Quelle ville voudriez-vous visiter . . .
   en France? (Je voudrais aller à . . .) / en Espagne? / au Canada? / en
   Angleterre? (Londres?) / en Italie? / en Russie? (Moscou?)

3. Comment iriez-vous . . .

en France? (*J'irais en France* par le train.) / en Angleterre? / à Marseille? / de Paris à Genève? / à Santa Fe? / au dortoir? / au sixième étage? (*en ascenseur*)

4. Quelle langue parleriez-vous . . .

en France? (*Je parlerais* . . .) / en Russie? / en Suisse? / au Canada? / au Brésil?

5. Où parle-t-on . . .

français? (*On parle français* en France, au Canada, en Suisse, au Maroc.) / espagnol? / portugais? / anglais? / allemand? / arabe?

6. Où vont . . .

les professeurs? (*Ils vont* à la bibliothèque. Ils consultent des livres.) / les étudiants? (*en classe?*) / les touristes? / les millionnaires? / les dames (*le marché? les grands magasins?*)

7. Est-ce que vous connaissez . . .

Londres? (*Je connais bien* Londres ou *Je ne connais pas* Londres.) / vieux Londres? / France? / belle France?

8. Quels cours suivez-vous?

français (*Je suis un cours* de français. Le professeur s'appelle ——) / anglais / histoire / mathématiques / physique / (*autres?*)

Exercice 1T Thème français

NOTE: In preparing a *thème français* (translation into French)[1] remember that there are not necessarily the same number of words in the translation as in the original, and the word order often differs. Concentrate on the material presented in the chapter, and just do your best with what has not yet been reviewed. Words you are not sure of should be looked up in the English-French vocabulary at the back of the book. If you find a reference number in brackets such as [1.06], it is a good idea to look at that section before going on.

1. The Antoines flew to London last Friday. They are going to visit France next week.
2. Jacques Duplessis, a student at the university, takes the subway to [*jusqu'à*] the Place de la République; then he walks to his home.
3. I was going to read the paper, but I had to write a thème.
4. François lives in the United States. He visits Switzerland every summer.
5. He flies to Geneva, then he takes the train to Lugano.
6. My mother and aunt are going to Italy, Spain, Portugal, and France.
7. In the spring the Duponts are going to Vienna, Venice, Cairo, and Le Havre.
8. In Marseilles [spelled *Marseille* in French] we are going to go sight-seeing by bus.
9. Professor Leblanc, a scientist at the School of Medicine, is going to do some research on the application of computers to medical diagnosis.
10. Jean-Paul is taking courses [*suivre* un cours. Il suit des cours*] in English, history, mathematics, and physics.

[1]All *thèmes* carry the Exercise letter "T" in this text.

La Maison Internationale à la Cité Universitaire (*French Government Tourist Office*)

2

ARTICLES
défini et
indéfini

POSSESSION

ÊTRE *

ARTICLE DÉFINI (suite) *art*

2.01 NAMES OF LANGUAGES.   The masculine definite article **le** is used with all languages, except after **parler**.

Le français est une langue vivante.	French is a modern [i.e. living] language.
Mes amis comprennent **l'allemand**.	My friends understand German.

Omit the article when the language immediately follows **parler** (positive *or* negative):

Roger **parle français**.	BUT	Roger parle *bien* le français.
Henri **ne parle pas** italien.		Henri ne *comprend* pas l'italien.

When *in* is meant, use **en** with the name of a language:

Il a composé une lettre **en anglais**.
Le conférencier a parlé parfois **en allemand**.

Notice that names of languages are not capitalized, nor are adjectives designating nationality. When the capital letter is used, it shows that a *person* is referred to:

le français	French (*language*)	NOUN
le Français	the Frenchman	NOUN
une auto française	a French automobile.	ADJECTIVE

See Appendix E for names of languages and countries.

2.02 ACADEMIC SUBJECTS. Like other nouns, academic subjects are used with their definite articles:

Je suis des cours intéressants: **la psychologie, la sociologie** et **la physique.**

But after **cours, classe, professeur, école, faculté,** use **de** without an article:

Je suis un **cours de biologie.**
Voilà mon **professeur de français.**
L'École de Médecine est à Paris.

Distinguish between **le professeur de français** and **le professeur français**: the first teaches French (but is not necessarily a Frenchman), and the second is a Frenchman who is a teacher (we do not know what subject he teaches). The academic subject is introduced by **de.**

Students in a particular specialization are indicated by **en**:

un étudiant **en médecine**	a medical student
un étudiant **en économie**	an economics student

rep   **2.03** REPETITION OF ARTICLE REQUIRED. Unlike English usage, the article must be repeated with each noun:

La porte et **la** fenêtre sont ouvertes.
La France et **la** Suisse considèrent la question.
Le cahier et **les** stylos sont sur la table.
Un homme et **un** petit garçon sont arrivés.
Les frères et **les** sœurs de Pierre vont partir.

Contrast this with English, in which the second article can often be omitted: *The door and window are open.*

ARTICLE INDÉFINI

The indefinite article **un**, **une**, **des** (meaning *a, an, some*) is used when a person or thing is first mentioned. It indicates a previously unspecified thing, as in English.

> **Un étudiant** entre dans la salle. *Il* s'appelle Jean-Paul.
> Voilà **une Fiat**. *Elle* est petite.
> Il y a **des clients** qui attendent. *Les clients* sont dans la salle d'attente.

2.04 USE OF **C'est un**(e). When a noun is accompanied by the indefinite article, the subject of the verb *être* is *ce*, giving the form **C'est** (see also 5.13). Notice that **c'est** means *he is, she is,* or *it is,* according to the antecedent.

> Voilà Georges Masson. **C'est un** professeur d'anglais. (*He's an* English teacher.)
> Voilà Mme Dupont. **C'est un** professeur d'économie. (*She's an* economics teacher.)
> Voilà ma voiture. **C'est une** Ford. (*It's a* Ford.)

When a plural noun is used, substitute **Ce sont** (*they are*):

> Voilà trois hommes en uniforme. **Ce sont des** agents. (*They are* policemen.)

The inverted (question) form of **C'est** is **Est-ce**:

> **Est-ce** une Renault ?   Is it a Renault ?
> **Est-ce** un professeur d'anglais ?   Is he an English teacher ?

Exercice 2A   Emploi de l'article défini (langues) [2.01 – 2.04]

Combinez les fragments de la liste A avec les noms de la liste B à tour de rôle, selon le modèle suivant.

> PROFESSEUR: français. Je parle . . .
> 1ᵉ ÉTUDIANT: Je parle **français.**
> PROFESSEUR: Je ne parle pas . . .
> 2ᵉ ÉTUDIANT: Je ne parle pas **français.**
> PROFESSEUR: Albert parle bien . . .
> 3ᵉ ÉTUDIANT: Albert parle bien **le français.**
> PROFESSEUR: Je comprends . . .
> 4ᵉ ÉTUDIANT: Je comprends **le français.**
> PROFESSEUR: Je ne comprends pas . . .
> 5ᵉ ÉTUDIANT: Je ne comprends pas **le français.**
> PROFESSEUR: Voici une lettre composée . . .
> 6ᵉ ÉTUDIANT: Voici une lettre composée **en français.**

PROFESSEUR: Voilà mon professeur . . .
7ᵉ ÉTUDIANT: Voilà mon professeur **de français.**
PROFESSEUR: C'est un professeur . . .
8ᵉ ÉTUDIANT: C'est un professeur **français.** etc.

A	B
(a) Je parle . . .	(1) français
(b) Je ne parle pas . . .	(2) espagnol
(c) Albert parle bien . . .	(3) allemand
(d) Je comprends . . .	(4) anglais
(e) Je ne comprends pas . . .	(5) italien
(f) Voici une lettre composée . . .	(6) russe
(g) Voilà mon professeur . . . [MATIÈRE]	(7) chinois
(h) C'est un professeur . . . [NATIONALITÉ]	(8) portugais
(i) Je suis un cours . . .	
(j) J'aime bien . . .	

POSSESSION

pa **2.05** POSSESSIVE ADJECTIVES. As the table shows, possessive adjectives agree in gender and number with the noun modified. Notice that the choice of gender of the adjective depends entirely upon the gender of the noun, and not of the person possessing.

	BEFORE FEMININE SINGULAR NOUNS BEGINNING WITH A CONSONANT	BEFORE MASCULINE SINGULAR NOUNS *AND* FEMININE SINGULAR NOUNS THAT BEGIN WITH A VOWEL SOUND	BEFORE ALL PLURAL NOUNS (PRONOUNCE FINAL -S AS [Z] BEFORE NOUNS STARTING WITH A VOWEL SOUND)
my	**ma** table	**mon** {livre (*m.*) / école (*f.*)	**mes** {livres (*m. pl.*) / écoles (*f. pl.*)
your	**ta** table	**ton** {livre (*m.*) / idée (*f.*)	**tes** {livres (*m. pl.*) / amis (*m. pl.*) / idées (*f. pl.*)
his } her } its }	**sa** {table / maison	**son** {livre (*m.*) / ami (*m.*) / école (*f.*)	**ses** {livres (*m. pl.*) / amis (*m. pl.*) / écoles (*f. pl.*)
	BEFORE ALL SINGULAR NOUNS		
our	**notre** table		**nos** livres
your	**votre** livre		**vos** tables
their	**leur** ami		**leurs** amis

Notice the use of the masculine forms **mon, ton, son** with feminine singular nouns beginning with a vowel sound. This makes for ease of pronunciation. Students often forget to use the masculine possessive adjective with a feminine singular noun that begins with a vowel sound:

une école	**mon** école (*not* "ma école")
une amie	**mon** amie (*not* "ma amie")

EXAMPLES

Voilà Lucien. **Son** livre et **sa** montre sont sur la table.
  His book and *his* watch are on the table.
Voilà Marie. **Son** livre et **sa** montre sont sur la table.
  Her book and *her* watch are on the table.
—Va chercher **tes** cahiers, dit le père.
  "Go and get *your* notebooks," said the father.

rep **2.06** REQUIRED REPETITION OF POSSESSIVE ADJECTIVES. Unlike English, which permits "My father and brother are coming," French requires that the possessive adjective be repeated before *each* noun modified:

Mon père et **mon** frère arrivent.
Ma tante et **mon** oncle voyagent.
Vos cahiers et **votre** stylo se trouvent sur la table.

2.07 **De** + [NOUN] FORMS THE POSSESSIVE. French has no device quite so convenient as the English apostrophe and *-s* (John*'s*, the teacher*'s*, etc.) to indicate ownership. Instead, French employs a prepositional phrase: **de** + name of possessor. If the name of a person or the title *monsieur, madame* or *mademoiselle* [1.04D] is used, there is no article:

Voilà la maison **de Paul.**	There is Paul's house.
Le livre **de Suzanne** est là.	Susan's book is there.
C'est l'amie **de madame Antoine.**	She is Mrs. Antoine's friend.

If a common noun is used after *de*, the article is included. Contractions are required when the article is *le* or *les*.

l'appartement **de l'**ami	the friend's apartment
la maison **du** professeur	the teacher's house
l'intelligence **des** étudiants	the students' intelligence

When a family name is used in the plural sense, the article *les* is contracted with *de* to form *des*. You will recall [1.04D] that no *-s* is added to the family name in French:

l'auto **des Dupont**	the Duponts' car

2.08 **être* à** [NOUN] OR [DISJUNCTIVE PRONOUN]. Possession may also be expressed by using **être à** and the noun or disjunctive pronoun (discussed in 28.07).

Ce chien **est à** monsieur Martin.	This is Mr. Martin's dog.
Cette voiture **est à** moi.	That is my car.

2.09 PARTS OF THE BODY, ARTICLES OF CLOTHING. When it is obvious that the arm, leg, hand, or article of clothing mentioned belongs to the subject of the sentence, use the definite article (instead of *mon, son, sa, leur*, etc.) to indicate posession:

Robert a **les** mains dans **les** poches.	Robert has his hands in his pockets.
J'ai mal à **la** tête.	I have a headache. (My head aches.)
Pierre a **les** yeux bleus.	Pierre has blue eyes.
Tu as **les** pieds sur la chaise.	You have your feet on the chair.

The part of the body is singular in French even when several people are indicated, provided each individual uses only one:

Les étudiants lèvent **la main**.	The students raise *their* hand*s*.

Exercice 2B   Possession [2.05 – 2.09]

Complétez en ajoutant les adjectifs possessifs appropriés.

MODÈLE: Jean a fermé (porte et fenêtres).
            Jean a fermé *sa* porte et *ses* fenêtres.

1. Jean a fermé (porte et fenêtres).
2. Paul ouvre (livre et cahiers).
3. Je fais une visite à[1] (oncle et tante).
4. (beau-père et belle-mère) habitent à Vichy.
5. (père et mère) vont souvent au bord de la mer en été.
6. Nous sommes fiers de[1] (bibliothèque et musée).
7. Cette petite voiture est à moi. C'est (voiture).
8. Ce stylo bleu est à toi. C'est (stylo).
9. Cette maison est à nous. C'est (maison).
10. Voilà la famille de Marie et de Jean. C'est (famille).

Récrivez les phrases suivantes pour y incorporer le nom du propriétaire indiqué entre parenthèses. Ajoutez une seconde phrase selon le modèle.

MODÈLE: (Charles) Voilà le dictionnaire.
            Voilà le dictionaire **de Charles. C'est son dictionnaire.**

[1]Répétez la préposition *à* ou *de* avec chaque nom.

11. (Marie)   Voilà *le stylo.*
12. (Robert)   La jeune fille là-bas est *sa petite amie.*
13. (mon oncle)   *L'appartement* se trouve rue de la Grenouille.
14. (votre père)   *La voiture* est dans le parking.
15. (the Dupont's) Nous allons à *la soirée.*

Complétez en ajoutant l'article ou l'adjectif possessif, selon le cas. Ajoutez une second phrase personnelle.

MODÈLE: Albert se brosse (dents.)
          Albert se brosse **les dents. Je me brosse les dents après chaque repas.**

16. Albert se lave (mains et figure).
17. Il a (chapeau sur tête).
18. Le professeur a (main dans poche).
19. Marie a (yeux bleus).
20. Alexandre a (cheveux blonds).

VERBE IRRÉGULIER être*

2.10 Review **être*** [*to be*] in the *présent* and *imparfait*. (Appendix C, verb table 13). Note the following meanings of these two tenses:

PRÉSENT: I am, you are, he is, we are, you are, they are
IMPARFAIT: I was, I used to be

Learn the following idioms:

être (très) bien	to be comfortable (used only for people)
être d'accord (avec [P])	to agree with [P]
être de bonne (mauvaise) humeur	to be in a good (bad) mood
être de retour	to be back
être en train de [I]	to be engaged in [I]; [*doing something*] right now
être à [P] = **appartenir* à** [P]	to belong to [P]

EXAMPLES

Le patron est **de mauvaise humeur** aujourd'hui.
    The boss is in a bad mood today.
Je **suis très bien** sur cette chaise; elle est très confortable.
    I am quite comfortable in this chair; it is very comfortable.
Robert dit que ce film est mauvais; je **suis d'accord** (avec lui).
    Robert says this film is bad; I agree (with him).

Jean est parti à midi; il **est de retour** maintenant.

Jean left at noon; he is back now.

Marie ne peut pas sortir; elle **est en train d'**étudier.

Marie can't go out; she is studying right now.

Cette voiture **est à** moi.

This car belongs to me. (This is my car.)

Exercice 2C Idiotismes avec *être* [2.10]

Complétez en employant un idiotisme avec **être***:

MODÈLE. Le patron est très gai aujourd'hui; il . . .

Le patron est très gai aujourd'hui; il **est de bonne humeur.**

1. La salle est confortable; nous . sommes bien
2. Mon ami Albert a les mêmes opinions politiques que moi; nous . sommes d'accord
3. Le patron s'irrite aujourd'hui; il . . .
4. D'ordinaire il ne s'irrite pas; il . . .
5. Janine était en Italie pendant les vacances; maintenant elle . est de retour
6. En ce moment j'étudie; je . suis en train d'étudier
7. Ce dictionnaire n'est pas à toi; il . . .
8. J'espère que cette chaise est confortable; êtes-vous bien . . . ?

Exercice 2T Thème français

1. Albert's father and sister speak Italian. They are going to fly to Italy.
2. Do you agree that a Swedish car is good? The Saab over there is mine.
3. Little Marie went to England with her uncle, but they are back now.
4. She has blue eyes and blond hair; right now she is washing her hair.
5. The Duponts drove to Rouen with Dr. Petit and our English teacher.
6. They saw the sights of the city; they agree that it's impressive.
7. At the university I am taking courses in mathematics, history, English, and economics.
8. Right now I am engaged in writing a paper on budgetary problems of cities.
9. My roommate is a Frenchman who is always in a good mood.
10. I am taking the express train (*le rapide*) to Dijon; I am going to pay a visit to my aunt and uncle.

Aux Galeries Lafayette (*Helena Kolda/Monkmeyer*)

3

Pluriel des noms

Quantités

Avoir*

PLURIEL DES NOMS *pl*

3.01 Sign of the plural is **les**; noun + **s**. To form the plural of a noun, the singular article **le**, **la**, or **l'** is changed to **les**, pronounced [le] before consonant sounds (including aspirate *h*) and [lez] before vowel sounds (including mute *h*):

la fille	**les** filles
la dame	**les** dames
le livre	**les** livres
le héros	**les** héros [1.02]
l'église	**les** églises
l'homme	**les** hommes

Most nouns add -*s* to the singular form, and the resulting plural form is pronounced in exactly the same way as the singular. Nouns ending in -*u*, -*al* or in -*s*, -*x*, -*z* in the singular are exceptions.

3.02 Nouns ending in -**u**.

A. Add -*x* to all endings (except -*ou*).

Unité 3, Leçon 4 Vocabulaire

les animaux domestiques

un animal

un chat

un chien

un cheval

un oiseau

le château	les châteaux	*castles*
le neveu	les neveux	*nephews*
le bateau	les bateaux	*boats*
le vœu	les vœux	*wishes, vows*
le feu	les feux	*fires, (traffic) lights*
le jeu	les jeux	*games*
l'eau	les eaux	*waters*

B. Add -*s* to -*ou*.

le sou	les sous	sous
le clou	les clous	nails
le matou	les matous	tomcats

Except the following, which add -*x:*

le genou	les genoux	knees
le hibou	les hiboux	owls
le caillou	les cailloux	pebbles
le chou	les choux	cabbages
le bijou	les bijoux	jewels
le joujou	les joujoux	toys
le pou	les poux	lice

memorize

Notice that there is no change in the pronunciation between the singular and the plural forms of the noun itself in any of the nouns ending in -*u*. Only the pronunciation of the article *les* tells the listener that a plural is being uttered.

3.03 NOUNS ENDING IN **-al** CHANGE TO **-aux**.

le journal	les journaux	newspapers
les cheval	les chevaux	horses
le général	les généraux	generals
l'animal	les animaux	animals
l'hôpital	les hôpitaux	hospitals

3.04 NOUNS ENDING IN **-s**, **-x**, OR **-z** DO NOT CHANGE IN THE PLURAL.

le héros   les héros

le **fils** [fis]	les **fils** [fis]	sons
le **nez**	les **nez**	noses
le **choix**	les **choix**	choices

3.05 IRREGULAR PLURALS.

l'**œil**	les **yeux**	eyes
le **ciel**	les **cieux**	sky, heavens
le **pneu**	les **pneus**	tires

monsieur	messieurs	gentlemen; Messrs.
madame	mesdames	plural of Mrs.
mademoiselle	mesdemoiselles	plural of Miss

Exercice 3A Pluriel des noms [3.01 – 3.06]

Mettez les noms suivants au pluriel.

1. le billet / le musée / l'étage / le ruisseau
2. le palais / le Français / la Française / le héros
3. l'eau / le chapeau / le cheveu / le cheval
4. l'animal / un animal / l'autobus / le bateau
5. le pays / un cours / un bruit / le facteur
6. la bouteille / un œil / un avocat / un joueur
7. une sœur / la tasse / la qualité / une voiture
8. un ingénieur / un château / un chapeau / un feu
9. un général / un pneu / le livre / le neveu
10. le conte / le genou / le journal / un fils

Exercice 3B Pluriel des noms [3.01 – 3.06]

Mettez au pluriel les mots en italique, en faisant les autres changements nécessaires, selon le modèle.

MODÈLE: *Mon neveu* est à Paris.
Mes neveux sont à Paris.

1. Jean-Paul voudrait voir *le château.*
2. *L'homme* du bureau parle très lentement.
3. *Le héros* du voyage dans la lune est très modeste.
4. Fermez *l'œil.*
5. Ma voiture a *un pneu* usé.
6. *Le général* va à Londres en avion.
7. Complétez *le travail* aussitôt que possible.
8. *Le journal* annonce le mariage de ma cousine.
9. *Le bateau* part de Bâle.
10. *Le fils* de M. Leduc est très habile.

QUANTITÉS

q **3.07** ADVERBS OF QUANTITY FOLLOWED BY **de** (**d'**) AND NO ARTICLE. The following adverbs of quantity are used before a noun, and should be learned together with the **de** as a unit (**beaucoup de**). *No article* is used with the noun, so contractions never appear with these words:

ADVERB	MEANING	EXAMPLE
assez de [N]	enough	**assez d'argent**
beaucoup de [N]	much, many, lots of	**beaucoup de** café
trop de [N]	too much, too many	**trop de** chats
moins de [N]	less, fewer	**moins d'argent que** vous
peu de [N]	very little, few	**peu de** livres
un peu de [N]	a little	**un peu d'eau**
plus de [N]	more	**plus de** cigarettes **que** moi
autant de [N]	as much, as many	**autant de** livres **que** vous
combien de [N]?	how many?	**combien de** disques?

3.08 EXPRESSIONS OF QUANTITY OR MEASUREMENT. After expressions of quantity such as the following, use only **de (d')** before the noun, and *no article*:

QUANTITY	DE + NOUN	MEANING
un verre	**de** vin	a glass of wine
une tasse	**de** thé	a cup of tea
une bouteille	**d'eau** minérale	a bottle of mineral water
un morceau	**de** gâteau	a piece of cake
une bouchée	**de** fromage	a mouthful of cheese
deux kilos	**de** pommes	two kilogrammes of apples

3.09 De REPEATED, ADVERB OF QUANTITY "UNDERSTOOD." An adverb of quantity (*beaucoup de* and others listed in 3.07) may modify *several* following nouns. It is not necessary to repeat the adverb, but the preposition **de** must be repeated.

Il a *beaucoup* **de** livres et [*beaucoup*] **de** disques.
He has many books and records.
Combien **de** bicyclettes et **d'**autos avez-vous vues?
How many bicycles and cars did you see?

3.10 EXPRESSIONS USED ALONE. No article or preposition is used after **plusieurs, quelques,** or a number.

plusieurs amis — several friends
quelques livres — a few books
dix-huit étudiants — eighteen students

3.11 **Quelque chose de, rien de** [+ *m.s.* ADJECTIVE]. These expressions are followed by an adjective in the masculine singular form.

Voilà **quelque chose de nouveau!** — There's something new!
Je ne vois **rien d'intéressant.** — I don't see anything interesting.

Exercice 3C   Expressions de quantité [3.07 – 3.11]

Dans une phrase complète, combinez l'expression de quantité de la liste A avec les noms de la liste B.

MODÈLE: beaucoup / châteaux
Il y a **beaucoup de châteaux** en Espagne.

	A	B
1.	beaucoup	châteaux / leçons / animaux / vin
2.	assez	vin / bière / argent / soldats
3.	trop	soldats / devoirs / travail / chats
4.	pas	chats / argent / chance / cigarettes
5.	plusieurs	cigarettes / phrases / amis / disques
6.	moins	disques / intelligence / café / eau
7.	une bouteille	eau / bière / vin / citronnade
8.	quelques	amis / étudiantes / livres / francs
9.	un peu	argent / vin / sucre / difficulté
10.	peu	difficulté / argent / chance / amis

VERBE IRRÉGULIER avoir*

3.12   Review **avoir*** [*to have*] in Appendix C, verb table 2, paying special attention to the present and imperfect tense forms. Learn the idioms below.

avoir besoin de [I] ou [N]	to need [TO DO] or [SOMETHING]
avoir envie de [I]	to feel like [DOING SOMETHING]
avoir faim	to be hungry
avoir soif	to be thirsty
avoir raison	to be right
avoir tort	to be wrong
avoir sommeil	to be sleepy
avoir mal à [PART OF BODY]	to have a pain in [PART OF BODY]
avoir beau [I]	to [DO SOMETHING] in vain
avoir de la chance	to be lucky
avoir l'air [ADJ. *m.s.*]	to seem [ADJECTIVE]

EXAMPLES

J'ai envie d'aller au cinéma.	I feel like going to the movies.
Paul **a besoin d'**argent.	Paul needs money.
J'ai mal aux dents.	I have a toothache.
J'ai mal à la tête.	I have a headache.
J'ai beau étudier: je n'apprends rien.	There's no use in my studying; I'm not learning anything.
Marie **a l'air** fatigué.	Marie seems tired.

3.13 AGE. Age is expressed by **avoir** [NUMBER] **ans**. The word **ans** may not be omitted.

J'**ai** dix-huit **ans**.	I am nineteen (years old).
Papa **a** quarante-trois **ans**.	Dad is forty-three.
Quel **âge avez-vous**?	How old are you?

VOCABULARY NOTE: Use **d'un certain âge** for "middle-aged":

C'est une dame **d'un certain âge**.	She's a middle-aged lady.

3.14 IMPERSONAL EXPRESSION **il y a**, *there is, there are.*

A. STATEMENT OF EXISTENCE. **Il y a** is used with the general meaning *there is, there are* to designate something that cannot be pointed to by the speaker; a phrase telling where the object is located is usually added:

Il y a un bon dictionnaire *dans la bibliothèque.*
There's a good dictionary in the library.
Il y a des étudiants *devant le café.*
There are some students in front of the café.

When the speaker can point out the thing about which he is talking, he would use **voilà** [N], and point to it, or nod in its direction:

Voilà le dictionnaire.	There's the dictionary.

If the speaker is able to point out the thing he is talking about, but does not wish to do so, he would use **voilà** and add a phrase telling where to look:

Voilà le professeur, derrière la table.
Voilà le chat, dans le coin.

B. INTERROGATIVE FORM. **Y a-t-il,** *is there, are there?*

Y a-t-il assez de place pour tout le monde?
Is there enough room for everyone?
Y a-t-il de bons dictionnaires dans la bibliothèque?
Are there some (any) good dictionaries in the library?

C. TIME AGO **il y a** [TIME].

il y a une semaine (huit jours)	a week ago
il y a trois ans	three years ago
Il est arrivé **il y a huit jours**.	He arrived *a week ago.*
Je l'ai vue **il y a dix ans**.	I saw her *ten years ago.*

3.15 avoir lieu, *to take place.*   This idiom is used for important events such as *une cérémonie, une réunion, une fête, un concert, une conférence.* The place is usually indicated.

> La fête **aura lieu** à Cannes.
> The festival will take place in Cannes.
> Le concert **a eu lieu** au Conservatoire.
> The concert took place at the Conservatory.
> Les Jeux Olympiques **ont lieu** tous les quatre ans.
> The Olympic Games take place (are held) every four years.

Exercice 3D Quantités [3.07 – 3.11]

Répondez aux questions suivantes en employant l'équivalent français des indications anglaises.

1. Avez-vous des cousins? (*Mais oui, j'ai plusieurs cousins.*)
   several / too many / more . . . than Paul / very few
2. Avez-vous des disques de Johnny Hallyday?
   many / enough / very few
3. Avez-vous des devoirs à faire?
   many / several / too many
4. Que prenez-vous comme boisson? (*Je prends . . .*)
   a cup of coffee / a glass of wine / a bottle of beer
5. Qu'est-ce qu'il y a dans le journal?
   something amusing / nothing new / something new / something interesting

Exercice 3E Verbe irrégulier **avoir*** [3.12 – 3.13]

Employez l'idiotisme approprié avec **avoir** en répondant aux questions suivantes.

1. (soif)   Pourquoi cherchez-vous un bar? (*C'est que j'ai . . .*)
2. (faim)   Pourquoi voulez-vous manger si tôt?
3. (tort)   Paul dit que Londres est votre ville favorite. A-t-il raison?
4. (sommeil) L'enfant a l'air fatigué. Qu'est-ce qu'il a?
5. (mal)   J'ai besoin d'une aspirine. Pourquoi? (*C'est que . . .*)
6. (chance)   Comment Alain a-t-il vendu sa vieille voiture?
7. (beau)   Jeanne étudie beaucoup, mais elle n'apprend pas. Que pensez-vous de cela?
8. (ans)   Mon frère est né en 1966. Quel âge a-t-il?
9. (envie)   Il y a un bon film au cinéma. Veux-tu y aller?
10. (air)   Papa a travaillé toute la journée. Comment est-il?

Révision lexicale **La famille**

1. **les parents:** le père et **la mère** (on les appelle familièrement "papa" et "maman").

un **parent** ou des **parents**: toute personne qui fait partie de la famille est un (*ou* une) parent.

2. **un** (ou **une**) **enfant**: Paul est **le fils** de M. et Mme Dupont. C'est **le frère** de Jeanne. Jeanne est **la fille** de M. et Mme Dupont. C'est **la sœur** de Paul.

3. **les grands-parents**: le père de papa, c'est **mon grand-père** (du côté paternel); la mère de papa, c'est **ma grand-mère** (du côté paternel). J'ai aussi des grands-parents du côté maternel.

4. **un oncle**: c'est le frère de papa ou de maman; ou bien le mari de ma tante.
   une tante: c'est la sœur d'un de mes parents; ou bien la femme de mon oncle.

5. **le cousin**: c'est le fils de mon oncle et de ma tante.
   la cousine: c'est la fille de mon oncle et de ma tante.

6. **le neveu**: le fils de mon frère ou de ma sœur.
   la nièce: la fille de mon frère ou de ma sœur.

7. **le beau-père** et **la belle-mère** sont les **beaux-parents** [*in-laws*].

Exercice 3T Thème français

polite form (use conditionel)

1. My grandmother is sixty-three; I am eighteen.
2. I feel like going to a movie on Saturdays. *J'ai envie d'aller au cinéma le samedi.*
3. Do you have many nephews and nieces?
4. I am going to visit one of my relatives in Belgium.
5. George has lots of cousins. There is his cousin Marguerite, over there.
6. No matter how much I work, I don't earn enough money.
7. My mother-in-law is in the doctor's office. She has a headache. *dans le bureau de médecin.*
8. You are right; the concert takes place Tuesday. *a lieu mardi*
9. There is something interesting in the papers today. *d'aujourd'hui*
10. We are going to Rouen. We would like to visit some relatives.
11. How many glasses of wine are there on the table? *combien de verres y a-t-il sur la table?*
12. I need a pencil and some paper. *J'ai besoin*
13. Dominique's cousin seems very intelligent. Do you agree? *a l'air*
14. Are there enough pencils for everybody?

Exercice 3F Conversation ou composition

1. Parlez de votre famille. Combien de membres y a-t-il, comment s'appellent-ils, où demeurent-ils?
2. Décrivez la famille du président des États-Unis.

Conférence à l'université (*Helena Kolda/Monkmeyer*)

4

ARTiclES
pARTiTif ET
géNéRAl

liRE,
écRiRE

ARTICLE PARTITIF (**de** + Article général)   *p*

4.01   USE.   The partitive article (**le partitif**) means *some*. It is used to differentiate between a *whole category* of objects [4.02] and merely a *part* (or personal share) of the objects. Notice the distinction between the following:

I **like** coffee. [= *the whole category*]   J'aime **le café**.   GENERAL ARTICLE
I **am having** (some) coffee. [= *a share*]   Je prends **du café**.   PARTITIVE

When the English equivalent contains "the," use the general article (**le, la, les**); when it contains or implies "some," use the partitive (**du, de la, des**).

4.02   GENERAL CLASS.   The general class (designated by the definite article and the plural noun of countable items) means "in general." It is found after statements of *liking*, *disliking*, or other generalities. Suppose we represent the general class by a circle:

J'aime { les livres	la viande	le café	l'eau
pl.	*f.*	*m.*	initial vowel

31

As the speaker can have an attitude towards a whole class of things, he can say "I like books (in general)," or "I like meat (in general)." If the words "in general" can be added to your statement, the general article should be used.

If, however, only a part of the general class could be involved, as would be the case with any form of consumption by an individual, use the partitive. Verbs of *having, taking, eating, looking at,* and the like, obviously could not apply to *all* of a class. The partitive is formed by prefixing **de** to the general class, resulting in the partitive article ("some"), just an individual *share* of the whole:

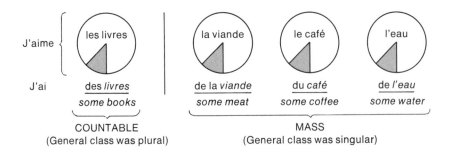

COUNTABLE	MASS
(General class was plural)	(General class was singular)

4.03 PERSONAL OWNERSHIP OR CONSUMPTION: PARTITIVE REQUIRED.

A. USE. After verbs indicating personal ownership or consumption (that is, where *some* rather than *all* would be appropriate before the noun), use the partitive.

GENERAL ○	J'aime les disques.	I like records.
PARTITIVE ▲	J'*ai* **des** disques.	I have (some) records.
GENERAL ○	Il s'intéresse aux films.	He is interested in movies.
PARTITIVE ▲	Il *a vu* **des** films.	He has seen (some) movies.
GENERAL ○	Il déteste les chats.	He hates cats.
PARTITIVE ▲	Sa mère *a* **des** chats.	His mother has (some) cats.

B. CUES. The partitive is usually expected after such verbs as *avoir** (*il y a*), *acheter*, apporter, boire*, commander, demander, dépenser, donner, porter, regarder, voir**.

J'ai vu **des** actrices admirables.
Nous regardions **des** animaux.

When the noun after such verbs is followed by some qualifier that identifies the noun as a *specific* one, the definite article is used.

J'ai vu **les** actrices | *dont vous m'avez parlé.* | [RELATIVE CLAUSE]

Nous regardions **les** animaux $\boxed{\textit{dans le jardin zoologique.}}$ [PREPOSITIONAL PHRASE]

Henri cherche **l'argent** $\boxed{\textit{qu'il a perdu.}}$ [RELATIVE CLAUSE]

Since *les actrices*, *les animaux*, and *l'argent* are all specific things (not generalities) identified by the clauses that follow, the definite article is used. The clauses need not be expressed, but may be understood or clearly required by the context.

4.04 CUES FROM ENGLISH. If "the" appears in the English equivalent, the reference is specific, hence the French requires the definite article **le, la, l', les.**

I like **the** meat. Give me **the** meat, please.
J'aime **la** viande. Donnez-moi **la** viande, s'il vous plaît.

If "the" does *not* appear in English, the problem in French becomes that of selecting the general or partitive. Test yourself on the following examples.

1. **He wants coffee.** General or partitive?

   He wants [*some*] coffee. PARTITIVE.
   Il désire **du café.** (He would not want *all* the coffee there is.)

2. **Give me orange juice,** please. General or partitive?

   Give me [*some*] orange juice, please. PARTITIVE.
   Donnez-moi **du jus d'orange,** s'il vous plaît.

3. **Books are useful.** Is *books* general or partitive?

   Books [*in general*] are useful. GENERAL.
   Les livres sont utiles.

If you want to say "*Some* books are useful," begin with **Il y a** (which calls for the partitive):

   Il y a **des livres** qui sont utiles.
   There are (some) books which are useful.
   Il y a **du café** que j'aime.
   There is some coffee that I like.
   = I like *some* coffee (not other coffee).

(The relative pronouns **qui** and **que** are dealt with in Chapter 23.)

Article partitif

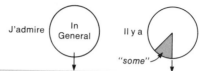

PLURAL IN THE GENERAL CLASS (countable nouns)			
Item (with *the*)	General Class (without *the*)	Partitive ("some")	Form of Partitive
le soldat	**les** soldats	**des** soldats	
le frère	**les** frères	**des** frères	
le château	**les** châteaux	**des** châteaux	
la maison	**les** maisons	**des** maisons	
la forme	**les** formes	**des** formes	**des** *(plural partitive for* COUNTABLE *nouns)*
la bouteille	**les** bouteilles	**des** bouteilles	
l'école	**les** écoles	**des** écoles	
l'homme	**les** hommes	**des** hommes	
l'avion	**les** avions	**des** avions	
SINGULAR IN THE GENERAL CLASS (mass or uncountable nouns)			
le vin	**du** vin		
le café	**du** café		**du** *(m.s.)*
le sucre	**du** sucre		
la viande	**de la** viande		**de la** *(f.s.)*
la bière	**de la** bière		
l'eau	**de l'** eau		**de l'** *(m.* or *f.) (before vowels)*
l'argent	**de l'** argent		

Generally, French and English are identical with regard to whether a noun is singular or plural when the general class is designated. The majority of nouns are plural in the general class, and the French partitive for them always uses **des**. Other nouns, most of which are names of liquids, granular material (*le sucre*), or other items not thought of as a collection of individual items, are singular in the general class. These "mass," or "uncountable" nouns add **de** before the singular article to form the partitive, resulting in the partitives **du** (*m.*), **de la** (*f.*), or **de l'** (for mass nouns beginning with a vowel sound).

dd   **4.06** PARTITIVE BECOMES **de** AFTER A NEGATIVE VERB.

A.   PARTITIVE ARTICLE.   After a negative verb, the partitive article (**des, de la, du, de l'**) is reduced to **de** (**d'**).

Article partitif

	POSITIVE		NEGATIVE	
J'ai acheté	**de la** viande	Je n'ai **pas** acheté	**de** viande
Nous avons	**des** livres	Nous n'avons **pas**	**de** livres
Georges a	**de l'**argent	Georges n'a **pas**	**d'**argent
Donnez-moi	**du** café	Ne me donnez **pas**	**de** café

FULL PARTITIVE   **de** ONLY

B. GENERAL OR DEFINITE ARTICLE IS UNCHANGED. When a noun with the definite article follows a negative verb, use the same article as after a positive verb. Notice that there is never **de** in this construction.

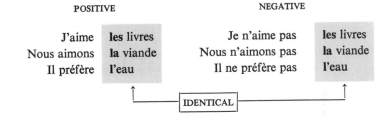

	POSITIVE		NEGATIVE	
J'aime	**les** livres	Je n'aime pas	**les** livres
Nous aimons	**la** viande	Nous n'aimons pas	**la** viande
Il préfère	**l'**eau	Il ne préfère pas	**l'**eau

IDENTICAL

Exercice 4A Article partitif et article général [4.01 – 4.06]

Combinez les fragments de la liste A avec les noms de la liste B à tour de rôle, selon le modèle.

PROFESSEUR: le livre. J'aime . . .
1ᵉ ÉTUDIANT: J'aime **les livres**. [4.02]
PROFESSEUR: Je n'aime pas . . .
2ᵉ ÉTUDIANT: Je n'aime pas **les livres**. [4.06B]
PROFESSEUR: J'ai . . .
3ᵉ ÉTUDIANT: J'ai **des livres**. [4.03]
PROFESSEUR: Je n'ai pas . . .
4ᵉ ÉTUDIANT: Je n'ai pas **de livres**. [4.06A]

(Après avoir épuisé la liste A, le professeur recommencera en utilisant le second nom de la liste B, et ainsi de suite.)

A	B
J'aime . . .	(1) le livre
Je n'aime pas . . .	(2) la pomme
J'ai . . .	(3) le disque
Je n'ai pas . . .	(4) le café
J'ai beaucoup . . .	(5) le vin
Donnez-moi . . .	(6) les petits pois
Ne me donnez pas . . .	(7) le timbre-poste
	(8) la viande
	(9) le gâteau
	(10) l'argent

Exercice 4B   Le Partitif et les expressions de quantité [Revoir 3.07]

Remplacez les tirets par *l'article partitif, l'article général, l'article défini* ou **de**, selon le cas.

1. Il y a _des_ étudiants qui ont toujours raison.
2. Mon cousin adore _des_ autos, mais il attrape souvent _des_ contraventions [*tickets*], beaucoup _de_ contraventions.
3. _Les_ médecins d'un grand hôpital ont trop _de_ malades à visiter.
4. Il y a _des_ avocats habiles qui ont _des_ maisons élégantes.
5. Au restaurant j'ai commandé _du_ vin mais je n'ai pas commandé _d'_ eau. En plus, j'ai pris _de la_ soupe (*f.*), _de la_ salade (*f.*), _du_ rosbif (*m.*), _des_ pommes frites (*f.*), _des_ petits pois, et, comme dessert, _des_ fruits.
6. Je préfère _les_ restaurants où il y a _de la_ musique (*f.*).
7. Nous aimons _du_ vin, aussi [*therefore*] buvons-nous beaucoup _de_ vin.
8. Vous autres Américains aimez _l'_ eau (*f.*); eh bien, commandez _de l'_ eau.
9. _Les_ dictionnaires sont _des_ livres très utiles.
10. Les chats sont _des_ animaux familiers.

VERBES IRRÉGULIERS lire*, écrire*

4.07   Review the forms of **lire*** [*to read*] in Appendix C, verb table 16, paying particular attention to the following tenses: present (abbreviated *tp*), imperfect (*ti*), passé composé (*tpc*), and future (*tf*). Examples:

tp   Jean **lit** un roman policier.
        Jean **est en train de lire** un roman policier [2.10].
ti   Jean **lisait** un roman la semaine passée.
tpc Jean **a lu** un des romans de Gide.
tf   Jean **lira** un roman historique la semaine prochaine.

4.08   Review the forms of **écrire*** [*to write*] in Appendix C, verb table 11. Pay particular attention to the *tp, ti, tpc,* and *tf* forms. Examples:

tp   Paul **écrit** une lettre à une amie en Suisse.
        Paul **est en train d'écrire** une composition.
ti   Paul **écrivait** une poésie quand je suis entré.
tpc Paul **a écrit** son nom sur la fiche.
tf   Paul **écrira** une composition demain.

Révision
lexicale

La lecture

1. **Un poète** est un écrivain qui fait de **la poésie**. *La poésie symboliste*; **un poème** de Baudelaire. Le contraire de la poésie c'est **la prose**.

[handwritten: novels]

2. **Un romancier (une romancière)** est un écrivain qui compose des **romans** (*m.*). *Un roman historique, un roman d'amour, un roman d'aventures, un roman policier.* Un roman d'Albert Camus.

3. **Un auteur dramatique** fait **des pièces** (de théâtre). (*f.*). Une pièce en trois actes. *La Folle de Chaillot* est une pièce de Jean Giraudoux. Il y a **la comédie, la tragédie, le drame.**

4. Il y a aussi **le critique**, qui juge les œuvres littéraires, **l'historien**, qui transmet la connaissance du passé, **le journaliste**, qui écrit des articles de journaux.

5. La personne qui profite de **la lecture** (l'action de lire), c'est **le lecteur** ou **la lectrice**.

6. On lit **un livre, un chapitre, un paragraphe, une phrase** [*sentence*]**, une locution** [*phrase*]**, une proposition** [*clause*]**.**

7. D'autres **genres littéraires** sont: **le conte**—un récit de faits, d'aventures imaginaires, pour amuser; **la nouvelle** [*short story*]—les nouvelles de Marcel Aymé; **un essai**—les *Essais* de Montaigne.

[handwritten: plus-que parfait (long time ago)]
[handwritten: passé composé (closer to present)]

Exercice 4C   *lire** et *écrire**

Mettez la forme appropriée du verbe indiqué:

1. Cette semaine nous [*lire*] un conte d'Alfred de Vigny.
2. Vigny [*écrire*] ce conte il y a plus d'un siècle. *[handwritten: avait écrit]*
3. En ce moment nous [*être*] en train de [*lire*] une poésie de Charles Baudelaire.
4. Baudelaire admirait énormément Edgar Poë: il [*écrire*] des poésies sous l'influence des idées de Poë.
5. Demain Paul [*écrire*] une composition au sujet de Marcel Aymé.
6. Paul [*lire (tpc)*] une nouvelle qui s'appelle "Le Passe-Muraille." *[handwritten: same tense]*
7. Il [*lire (ti)*] un conte pendant que je [*écrire*] quelques phrases en italien.
8. C'est avec grand plaisir que nous [*lire*] les comédies de Molière; la semaine prochaine nous [*lire*] *Le Médecin malgré lui.*
9. Qu'est-ce que vous [*lire*] quand je suis entré?
10. Je vais [*écrire*] mon nom dans ce livre: il est à moi.

Exercice 4T   Thème français

1. Reading is amusing. I have some novels by Balzac. In my collection there are also many other novels and a few short stories.
2. At the university we are reading novels, poems, short stories, and plays.
3. Mary and her boy friend are reading some tragedies by Racine, but they are not reading any comedies.
4. In our economics class we are in process of writing a report on the financial situation of schools in the United States.
5. In our French class we have read some magazines and newspapers on the subject of international sports.
6. In sociology class we wrote a report concerning crime and the problems of the police.
7. In history class we used to read accounts of battles, crusades, explorations, and kings of the Middle Ages.

[handwritten in left margin: le mal du pays / HOME SICK]

8. We went to a restaurant near the Louvre. There are lots of cafés in Paris; I prefer the sidewalk cafés [*la terrace*].
9. Paul asked for wine. He likes wine, but he doesn't like water.
10. Jeanne ordered beer, meat, potatoes, salad, and, for dessert, some apples.

Exercice 4D   Sujets de composition

Écrivez une composition d'au moins cinq phrases simples sur l'un des sujets suivants. (Attention à l'ordre logique de vos phrases.)

1. Ce que nous sommes en train d'étudier dans nos cours de littérature.
2. Ce que je commande au restaurant.
3. Mes lectures favorites.

La Seine et le pont Bir-Hakein; au fond, les nouveaux édifices de la Rive gauche (*Bill Raftery/Monkmeyer*)

5

Accord
des adjectifs

C'est
ou il est

ACCORD DES ADJECTIFS

An adjective must agree in gender and number with the noun or pronoun it modifies. Adjectives normally *follow* the noun (exceptions will be covered in Chapter 6).

5.01 AGREEMENT: MASCULINE AND FEMININE; SINGULAR AND PLURAL. An adjective must agree in gender and number with the noun it modifies, so there are usually four possible forms:

	MASCULINE	FEMININE
Singular	intéressant	intéressante
Plural	intéressants	intéressantes

The masculine singular form (*m.s.*) is converted to feminine singular (*f.s.*) by adding -*e*. Either masculine *or* feminine singular is made plural by adding -*s*.

The main exceptions to this rule are: (1) adjectives already ending in -*e* in the masculine singular form (*facile*, *jeune*, etc.), to which nothing is added for the feminine singular; (2) adjectives ending in a consonant which is doubled before adding the feminine ending -*e* (*actuel*, *actuelle*); (3) adjectives ending in -*er* and -*ier*, which add a grave accent before adding the feminine -*e* (*dernier*, *dernière; premier, première*); and (4) adjectives ending in -*x* in the basic (*m.s.*) form, which remain the same in the masculine plural, but which change -*x* to -*se* in the feminine (*heureux, heureuse*).

PRONUNCIATION NOTE: In spoken French, it is helpful to learn the feminine form first. Then, by dropping the final consonant sound, the sound of the masculine form is obtained (compare the phonetic transcriptions below).

FEMININE	MASCULINE	DROPPED SOUND
évidente [evidãt]	évident [evidã]	[t]
curieuse [kyrjøz]	curieux [kyrjø]	[z]
étroite [etrwat]	étroit [etrwa]	[t]
blanche [blãʃ]	blanc [blã]	[ʃ]

There are a number of exceptions to this general principle of pronunciation. For example *bonne, bon* [bɔn] [bɔ̃] *brune, brun* [bʀyn] [bʀœ̃] in which nasalization occurs in the masculine form; and *dernière, dernier, première, premier* with the pronunciations [jɛʀ] (*f.s.*), [je] (*m.s.*).

5.02 ADJECTIVES ENDING IN -*e* IN THE MASCULINE SINGULAR. These adjectives have only one pronunciation, and only two written forms.

	MASCULINE	FEMININE
Singular	facile	facile
Plural	faciles	faciles

Here are some common adjectives of this type (the dagger indicates adjectives which *precede* the noun modified):

facile	easy	**difficile**	difficult, hard
riche	rich	**pauvre**	poor
agréable	pleasant	**ridicule**	ridiculous
jeune†	young	**admirable**	admirable
malade	ill	**faible**	weak
moderne	modern	**utile**	useful
même†	same	**autre†**	other
célèbre	famous	**possible**	possible
rouge	red	**jaune**	yellow
large†	wide	**politique**	political

5.03 ADJECTIVES ENDING IN -**el, -ul; -en, -on; -et, -s.** With these adjectives the final consonant is doubled before adding -*e* to form the feminine.

actuel, actuelle	current, present
cruel, cruelle	cruel
nul, nulle† [+ NOUN]	no, not any [N]
ancien, ancienne	ancient; former [6.04]
bon, bonne†	good
net, nette	neat, clean
bas, basse†	low
épais, épaisse	thick
naturel, naturelle	natural
spirituel, spirituelle	witty

5.04 ADJECTIVES ENDING IN **-ier** AND **-er.** These adjectives add a grave accent on the *-e* before the final *-r*, then add *-e* for the feminine.

premier, première†	first
dernier, dernière†	last
léger, légère†	light, slight
cher, chère	dear, expensive

5.05 ADJECTIVES ENDING IN **-x.** These adjectives usually change the *-x* to *-s*, then add *-e* for the feminine.

	heureux, heureuse	happy, fortunate
	généreux, généreuse	generous
	jaloux, jalouse	jealous
BUT	**vieux, vieille†**	old
	doux, douce	sweet

5.06 A. ALTERNATE MASCULINE FORMS. **Bel, vieil, nouvel** [6.01] are *masculine singular* only, and are used (instead of *beau, vieux, nouveau*) only in front of a masculine singular noun beginning with a *vowel* sound. These alternate forms are pronounced just like the feminine forms.

SINGULAR	PLURAL
un **bel** arbre	de **beaux** arbres
un **vieil** homme	de **vieux** hommes
un **nouvel** avion	de **nouveaux** avions

Notice that the *regular* plural form is used with plural nouns, regardless of the sound they begin with.

B. IRREGULAR ADJECTIVES.

neuf, neuve	(brand) new
blanc, blanche	white

5.07 DEMONSTRATIVE ADJECTIVE **ce.** The demonstrative adjective **ce** (**cet, cette, ces**) precedes the noun. Like *beau, nouveau,* and *vieux,* it has an alternate masculine form (*cet*) for use before a masculine singular noun beginning with a vowel sound (*cet arbre, cet homme*):

	MASCULINE	FEMININE	MEANING
Singular	ce / cet	cette	this, that
Plural	ces	ces	these, those

Ce livre est très intéressant.
Cet homme habite à Lyon.
Cette pièce est très longue.
Ces garçons et **ces jeunes filles** habitent à Genève.

The appropriate form of **ce** is repeated with each noun, just as the article or possessive adjective must be repeated:

Ce stylo et **ce** crayon sont bleus.
Ce garçon et **cette** jeune fille sont heureux.
Ces messieurs et **ces** dames dansent bien.

5.08 SUFFIXES **-ci, -là.** Some ambiguity exists with such a phrase as *ce livre*, which may mean either *this book* or *that book*. In conversation it would be clear from the speaker's distance from the book. To eliminate doubt in writing, add a suffix to the noun (attached with a hyphen).

-ci (from *ici*)	this	ce livre-**ci**	this book
-là	that	ce livre-**là**	that book
		cette maison-**là**	that house

EXAMPLES

J'aime **ce livre-ci**, mais je n'aime pas **ce livre-là**.
    I like *this* book, but I don't like *that* book.
Cette maison-ci est chère; **cette maison-là** est bon marché.
    This house is expensive; *that* house is cheap.

Notice that without these suffixes, there would be no way to distinguish between the identical nouns (*ce livre . . . ce livre*).

Exercice 5A   Accord des adjectifs [5.01 – 5.08]

Employez l'adjectif entre parenthèses avec les noms qui le suivent.

MODÈLE: (distingué)   Un monsieur / une dame / des savants
C'est un monsieur **distingué**.
C'est une dame **distinguée**.
Ce sont des savants **distingués**.

1.	(intéressant)	un article / une peinture / des livres / des dames
2.	(neuf)	un livre / une robe / une voiture / des maisons
3.	(actuel)	la situation / son emploi / le gouverment
4.	(spirituel)	un homme / une dame / un ouvrage / des auteurs
5.	(cher)	un livre / une maison / un hôtel / des voitures
6.	(heureux)	un étudiant / une jeune fille / un événement
7.	(blanc)	un éléphant / une rose / une voiture / des maisons
8.	(facile)	un devoir / une leçon / une solution / des examens
9.	(étroit)	une rue / un chemin / une porte / des portes
10.	(large†)	une salle / un boulevard / un cercle

EMPLOI DE c'est ou de il est

5.09 C'est + MODIFIED NOUN. C'est is used to precede a noun accompanied by its article, an adjective, or any other modifiers. It may mean *he is*, *she is*, or *it is*:

MODIFIED NOUN

$$\text{C'est} \begin{cases} \textbf{le } \text{professeur} \\ \textbf{mon } \text{livre} \\ \textbf{un bon } \text{étudiant} \\ \textbf{un } \text{médecin} \\ \textbf{celle de mon } \text{père} \end{cases}$$

C'est is also used before disjunctive pronouns [28.09].

C'est **moi** qui ai fait cela.

5.10 ANY TENSE OF être* MAY BE USED.

C'était mon père.	It was my father.
Ce sera un long voyage.	It will be a long trip.
Je doute que **ce soit** un bon étudiant.	I doubt that he's a good student.

5.11 Ce sont + PLURAL MODIFIED NOUN. When the modified noun following the verb **être*** is plural, use the plural **ce sont.**

Ce sont mes professeurs.	They are my teachers.
Ce sont de bons étudiants.	They are good students.
Ce sont des catholiques.	They are Catholics.

5.12 Il est + ADJECTIVE ALONE. When an adjective alone (or with *très* or *bien*) follows a form of *être**, use the personal pronoun as a subject (instead of *ce*):

C'est ou Il est

. . . Georges	**Il**	est	**très grand.**
. . . Marie	**Elle**	est	**intelligente.**
. . . le patron	**Il**	est	**fatigué.**
. . . vos amis	**Ils**	sont	**charmants.**

However, if the adjective is part of a **noun group** (that is, noun + adjective) use **c'est** as indicated in 5.09:

C'est un homme grand.	He's a tall man.
C'est une femme intelligente.	She's an intelligent woman.
Ce sont des savants distingués.	They are distinguished scientists.
C'est une voiture laide.	It's an ugly car.

Exercice 5B   Accord des adjectifs [5.01 – 5.04] [5.09]

Répondez aux questions suivantes selon le modèle, en employant l'adjectif entre parenthèses:

MODÈLE: (facile)   Comment trouvez-vous cette leçon?
            Elle est facile. **C'est** une leçon facile.

1.	(difficile)	Comment trouvez-vous ce devoir? / cette leçon?
2.	(agréable)	Comment trouvez-vous cet appartement? / cette maison?
3.	(cruel)	Comment trouvez-vous cette femme? / ce soldat?
4.	(épais)	Comment est ce mur? / cette planche [*plank*]?
5.	(utile)	Comment est ce dictionnaire? / cette leçon?
6.	(léger)	Comment est cette machine? / ce livre?
7.	(incroyable)	Comment est ce récit? / cette histoire?
8.	(formidable)	Comment était le film? / la soirée?
9.	(confortable)	Comment est votre chambre? / ce fauteuil?
10.	(intéressant)	Comment était la conférence? / le compte-rendu?

5.13 Il est + ONE-WORD "HONORARY ADJECTIVE." Designations of religion, profession, nationality, and political persuasion may be classed as "honorary adjectives." When they consist of a single, unmodified word, follow the rule for adjective alone [5.12]: Use the personal pronoun **il, elle,** etc. as subject.

Il est + | ONE WORD (Adjectival) |

Il est	**catholique.**	RELIGION
Elle est	**française.**	NATIONALITY
Il est	**médecin.**	PROFESSION
Il est	**communiste.**	POLITICAL PERSUASION

But if any modifier (such as indefinite article, possessive adjective, etc.) is used, **il est** is replaced by **c'est**, and names of nationalities are capitalized as nouns:

C'est + MODIFIED NOUN

C'est	**un bon** catholique.
C'est	**une** Française.
C'est	**un** médecin **distingué**.
C'est	**mon** professeur **de français**.
Ce sont	**des** avocats **renommés**.

5.14 IMPERSONAL STATEMENTS WITH **Il est** or **C'est**.   Impersonal statements (beginning with *It is* [*interesting, possible, easy, hard, probable*, etc.]) are of two kinds in French. The choice depends upon whether the statement is self-sufficient or not. Self-sufficient impersonal statements begin with **Il est**; other statements which depend on a previous remark to make sense begin with **C'est**.

A.   **Il est** BEFORE INFINITIVE PHRASE or **que**-CLAUSE.   Self-sufficient statements use the structure **Il est** [ADJECTIVE] + **de** [INFINITIVE]. By "self-sufficient" we mean that the statement is complete and comprehensible by itself, without reference to any previous conversation or statement:

FORMAT: **Il est** ADJECTIVE **de** INFINITIVE STRUCTURE

Il est intéressant	**d'étudier** l'archéologie.
Il est facile	**de comprendre** l'espagnol.
Il est difficile	**de lire** cette poésie.

FORMAT: **Il est** ADJECTIVE + **que**-CLAUSE

Il est vrai	**que** Robert viendra ce soir.
Il est probable	**que** Suzanne prend le train.
Il est possible	**que** le train soit[1] en retard.

5.15 **C'est** WITH DEPENDENT IMPERSONAL STATEMENTS.   When an impersonal statement (one beginning with *It is*) is not self-sufficient, use **C'est** for "It is." A statement is not self-sufficient if it depends upon some previous mention or reference. When such a statement is uttered alone, it raises a question immediately as to what it refers:

C'est facile.   (QUESTION: *What* is easy?)
C'est difficile à expliquer.   (QUESTION: *What* is difficult to explain?)

---

[1]It should be noted that some **que**-clauses require the verb following to be in the subjunctive, depending upon the nature of the **Il est** portion of the sentence (see 25.02).

A. **C'est** + ADJECTIVE.   Before a single word use **C'est** for *It is*:

C'est intéressant.	It is interesting.
C'est difficile.	It is difficult.

B. **C'est** + ADJECTIVE + **à** + INFINITIVE.   When an infinitive is added, the preposition à is required before it:

C'est intéressant **à faire.**	It is interesting to do.
C'est difficile **à croire.**	It is difficult to believe.
C'est facile **à voir.**	It is easy to see.

These dependent impersonal statements make sense only in the context of a foregoing conversation or remark. Sometimes these remarks are combined with the impersonal statement:

Étudier les langues, **c'est intéressant.**
Aller plus vite, **c'est possible.**
Le train n'arrive pas: **c'est étonnant.**

Exercice 5C   Emploi de *c'est un / il est* [5.09 – 5.13]

Faites une phrase complète en commençant par **C'est, Ce sont, Il est, Elle est** ou **Ils (Elles) sont.**

MODÈLE: le facteur
            C'est le facteur.

1. mon professeur	11. mathématicien
2. une dame élégante	12. bon étudiant
3. Française	13. petit chat
4. un Français	14. petit
5. un soldat allemand	15. maisons magnifiques
6. soldat	16. charmante
7. un bon catholique	17. élégants
8. intelligent	18. médecin
9. un homme bien connu	19. avocat célèbre
10. très spirituelle	20. mon frère qui habite à Lyon

Exercice 5D   *C'est facile à / Il est facile de* [5.14 – 5.15]

Complétez la phrase en commençant par **C'est facile à** ou par **Il est facile de,** selon le cas.

MODÈLE: voir
            C'est facile à voir.

48

1. flatter une personne peu intelligente
2. faire
3. comprendre cette leçon
4. comprendre
5. répondre aux questions du professeur
6. croire
7. croire que René est très habile
8. trouver l'entrée du métro
9. trouver
10. oublier un numéro de téléphone

Exercice 5T   Thème français

1. In my room there are two blue chairs, a comfortable bed, a low table, and a wide armoire. (*Omit the comma before* "and" *in French.*)
2. We live in a modern apartment house in Paris: it is a white building near the Place de la République.
3. Our apartment has five rooms: a large living room, a small kitchen, a bathroom, and two charming bedrooms. It's great!
4. This room is yellow; that room is white. It's obvious.
5. There is my physics teacher. He's a good teacher. He's very pleasant.
6. Marcel is a salesman. He's a Frenchman, and he's a good Catholic.
7. To go to his office, Jacques always takes the green bus. It is convenient [*commode*] to take the bus.
8. Today his boss is in a good mood; that is hard to believe.
9. It is easy to write a long letter; to write a short letter—that is difficult.
10. This table and bed are mine; they are comfortable pieces of furniture.

Exercice 5E   Sujets de composition

Écrivez une composition d'au moins cinq phrases sur l'un des sujets suivants.

1. Décrivez votre maison, votre appartement ou votre chambre, en signalant les meubles qui s'y trouvent, les formes et les couleurs, etc.
2. Nommez cinq personnes que vous connaissez, en indiquant leur profession et leur qualité.
3. Décrivez un endroit que vous avez visité; ou bien décrivez la photographie en face.

La banlieue de Paris se transforme (*Ministère de l'Agriculture-Verney*)

6

Place de l'adjectif

METTRE*

PLACE DE L'ADJECTIF

wo   **6.01** PRECEDING ADJECTIVES. Most French adjectives *follow* the noun they modify. The adjectives in the list below are exceptions, because they usually precede the noun, as in English. Learn them well, because they are very commonly used, and because if you are very familiar with this list, you will know that any adjective that does *not* appear on it will normally come *after* the noun.

To aid in memorization, these adjectives are grouped according to meaning (similar, opposite, or related meanings) insofar as possible. When two forms are shown, the first is the "basic" *m.s.* form, and the second is the *f.s.* form. If only one form is given, the masculine and feminine forms are identical. Notice the four adjectives which have an alternate masculine form.

bon, bonne	good	**mauvais, mauvaise**	bad
grand, grande	big	**petit, petite**	small
long, longue	long	**court, courte**	short
haut, haute	high	**bas, basse**	low
joli, jolie	pretty	**beau [bel], belle** [5.06]	beautiful, fine

50

jeune	young	vieux [vieil], vieille	old
nouveau [nouvel], nouvelle	new	[5.06]	
[5.06]			

Not grouped by meaning are these preceding adjectives:

ce [cet], cette [5.07]	this, that
autre, un(e) autre	other, another
même [N]¹	same [N]
large	wide
propre [N]	own [N] (my *own* book)
cher, chère	dear
premier, première	first (*All numbers precede*)
dernier, dernière	last

EXAMPLES

Elle a une **nouvelle** robe.	She has a new (= another) dress.
J'ai une **nouvelle**² voiture.	I have a new car.
C'est une **longue** rue.	It's a long street.
Voici ma **dernière** cigarette.	Here is my last cigarette.
On a construit **un autre** pont.	Another bridge has been built.

6.02 TWO ADJECTIVES WITH A SINGLE NOUN. Place each adjective in its normal position if one precedes and one follows.

un **petit** livre **rouge**	a small red book
une **nouvelle** revue **française**	a new French magazine

If two or more *preceding* adjectives are used, the adjectives most likely to be closest to the noun are **jeune, vieux,** and **nouveau.** Those likely to be farthest from it are **même** and **autre**:

une autre **jeune fille**	another girl
une autre belle **jeune fille**	another beautiful girl
le même **vieil homme**	the same old man
le même **petit vieil arbre**	the same little old tree

Notice that certain [ADJECTIVE + NOUN] groups may be considered a single word: **une jeune fille** (*a girl*), **les petits pois** (*peas*).

If two following adjectives are used, they are joined by **et** (if similar in nature) or **mais** (if contrasting in nature).

¹[N] indicates that a NOUN appears in this location in the sentence.
²**une nouvelle voiture** might be a 1935 model, but if I just bought it, it is "new" to me. When "brand new" is meant, however, use the adjective **neuf, neuve,** which *follows* the noun:

J'ai une voiture **neuve**.	I have a brand-new car.

| une dame **charmante et spirituelle** | a witty and charming lady |
| un monsieur **riche mais malheureux** | a rich but unhappy gentleman |

It is, however, poor style to accumulate too many adjectives with a single noun, and this should be avoided.

dd **6.03** INTERVENING ADJECTIVE: **des > de**. When an adjective (usually one in 6.01) comes between **des** and the noun, **des** becomes **de (d')**.

des tables	**de** *petites* tables
des jeunes filles	**de** *belles* jeunes filles
des maisons	**de** *grandes* maisons
des garçons	**d'***autres* garçons

wo **6.04** WORD ORDER AND ALTERNATE MEANINGS. Certain adjectives may be placed either before or after the noun modified. Care must be taken with these adjectives, because the meaning differs depending on the position.

ADJECTIVE	MEANING BEFORE NOUN	MEANING AFTER NOUN
ancien, -ne	former	old, ancient
brave	good, worthy, fine	brave
certain, -e	particular	unquestionable
cher, chère	dear (*cherished*)	expensive
dernier, dernière	last (*of a series*), final	last (*most recent*)
grand, -e[3]	great, large	tall
même	same	very, itself
pauvre	poor (*unfortunate*)	poor (*no money*)
propre	own	clean

Compare the following examples:

mon **ancien** professeur	my old (former) teacher
l'histoire **ancienne**	ancient history
un **brave** garçon	a fine boy
un homme **brave**	a brave man
un **certain** monsieur	a certain (particular) gentleman
une chose **certaine**	a sure thing
ma **dernière** cigarette	my last cigarette
la semaine **dernière**	last week
un **grand** homme	a great man
un homme **grand**	a tall man

---

[3]**Grand** means *great, important* only when applied to people, particularly with **un homme, une dame, un général**, etc. Otherise **grand** simply means *big, large*.

le **même** livre	the same book
le livre **même**	the book itself
la **pauvre** victime	the poor victim
un étudiant **pauvre**	a poor (impoverished) student
ma **propre** chemise	my own shirt
une chambre **propre**	a clean room

Exercice 6A Accord et place de l'adjectif [6.01]

Combinez l'adjectif (ou les adjectifs) avec les noms indiqués.

MODÈLE: (petit) une maison / un chat / des voitures
une **petite** maison / un **petit** chat / **de petites** voitures

1. (mauvais) un garçon / une note / des films
2. (facile) une leçon / un travail / des exercices
3. (beau) un château / un arbre / une jeune fille
4. (vieux) un soldat / un ami / une dame / un homme
5. (ce) garçon / dame / étudiant / professeurs
6. (même, jeune) le professeur / la femme / les gens
7. (long) un boulevard / une rue / une leçon / des exercices
8. (étroit) une porte / une rue / des fenêtres
9. (grand) un appartement / une maison / des familles
10. (dernier) la leçon / la semaine / l'exemple

Exercice 6B Deux adjectifs [6.02]

Employez les adjectifs entre parenthèses avec les noms indiqués.

MODÈLE: (autre, intéressant) un livre
C'est un **autre** livre **intéressant**.

1. (même, spirituel) la dame / le monsieur / les professeurs
2. (agréable, petit) une soirée / une maison / un appartement
3. (beau, intelligent) un chien / un homme / une dame
4. (vieux, riche) un monsieur / un homme / une dame
5. (petit, blanc) des maisons / des chats / une voiture
6. (court mais difficile) un exercice / une leçon / des instructions
7. (pauvre mais heureux) un homme / une dame / des jeunes gens
8. (sympathique et spirituel) un ami / une amie / un conférencier

VERBE IRRÉGULIER **mettre***

6.05 Review the forms of **mettre*** [*to put, to place*] in Appendix C, verb table 17, paying particular attention to the following tenses:

tp Jean **met** son livre sur la table. [*is putting*]
Jean est en train de **mettre** son livre sur la table. [2.11]

ti　Jean **mettait** son livre sur la table quand je suis entré.　[*was putting*]

tpc　Jean **a mis** une lettre *à la poste* hier à midi.　[*mailed*]

tf　Jean **mettra** une heure à faire ses devoirs.　[*will take*]

Idioms with **mettre***:

mettre* la table	to set the table
mettre* une lettre **à la poste**	to mail a letter
mettre* [*une heure*] **à** [ɪ]	to take [*an hour*] to [DO SOMETHING]
se mettre* à [ɪ]	to begin to [DO SOMETHING]
= **commencer à** [ɪ]	
se mettre* en route (pour [N])	to set out (for [PLACE])
se mettre* en colère (contre)	to get angry (at)
= **se fâcher** (contre)	

EXAMPLES

Marie est en train de **mettre la table**.

Jeanne **se met à** étudier la leçon.

Nous **nous sommes mis en route** pour Dijon.

Le soldat **s'est mis en colère** contre le lieutenant.

6.06　VERBS CONJUGATED LIKE **mettre***.　The following verbs are conjugated in the same way as **mettre***, the only difference being in the prefix, which remains the same throughout each verb. Knowing **mettre***, you also know the following compounds:

permettre* (à [N] **de** [ɪ])	to permit (*someone*) to [DO SOMETHING]
promettre* (à [P] **de** [ɪ])	to promise (*someone*) to [DO SOMETHING]
remettre* [N] **à** [P]	to give (*something*) to (*someone*); to hand back; to hand in (*homework*)
transmettre* [N]	to transmit (*something*)

EXAMPLES

Le professeur **permet aux** étudiants **de** parler en classe.

　The teacher allows the students to talk in class.

J'ai promis à papa **de** travailler dur.

　I promised Dad to work hard.

Les élèves **remettent** leurs copies **au** professeur.

　The pupils are handing in their exercises to the teacher.

Nous **transmettons** sa lettre par avion.

　We are forwarding his letter by air mail.

Exercice 6C   Le verbe *mettre** [6.05 – 6.06]

Récrivez la phrase en ajoutant le mot entre parenthèses. Faites attention au temps du verbe.

MODÈLES: (demain)   Jeanne **met** la table.
Jeanne **mettra** la table *demain*.
(autrefois)   Papa me **permet** de conduire la voiture.
Autrefois papa me **permettait** de conduire la voiture.

1. (demain)   Elle **se met au** travail.
2. (hier)   Paul **mettra** votre lettre **à la** poste.
3. (autrefois)   Je **mets** toujours une heure à déjeuner.
4. (demain)   Nous **nous mettons en route** pour Chartres.
5. (en ce moment)   **J'ai mis** mes devoirs sur le bureau.
6. (hier)   Nous **remettons** ces devoirs au professeur.
7. (la semaine passée) Nous **promettons** de travailler dur.
8. (hier)   Ils **mettent** deux heures **à** faire le voyage.
9. (autrefois)   Je **mets** la table pour ma mère.
10. (hier)   Je **permets à** mon camarade **de** conduire mon auto.

Exercice 6D   Conversation

Répondez à la question; ajoutez ensuite une ou plusieurs phrases pour expliquer votre réponse.

MODÈLE: Mettez-vous longtemps à étudier le français?
Mais oui, je **mets** deux heures à étudier le français.
Les leçons sont intéressantes, vous savez.

1. Combien de temps mettez-vous à écrire un thème français?
2. Est-ce que vous remettez vos devoirs à temps tous les jours?
3. Le professeur permet-il aux étudiants de chanter en classe?
4. À quelle heure vous mettez-vous en route pour votre premier cours?
5. Est-ce que le professeur se met quelquefois en colère?
6. Avez-vous promis à quelqu'un de bien travailler ce semestre?
7. En rentrant à la maison où mettez-vous vos livres?
8. À quelle heure vous mettez-vous à étudier le soir?

Révision lexicale

Les édifices (*m.*)

1. **un immeuble:** un grand bâtiment d'habitation en ville, à plusieurs étages. Il contient de nombreux appartements.
2. **un appartement:** l'équivalent d'une maison, composé de plusieurs pièces dans un immeuble; *un appartement de trois pièces.*
3. **un gratte-ciel** (*pl.* **des gratte-ciel**) un immeuble à très nombreux étages qui atteint une grande hauteur. *La Tour Montparnasse est un gratte-ciel.*
4. **une maison:** habitation d'une famille; on emploie ce mot aussi en parlant d'une société commerciale, par exemple *la Maison Freschède.*

5. **une pièce** est **une salle**, terme général. Dans une maison il y a plusieurs pièces : **le salon** (on dit aussi **le living-room**), **la salle à manger, la cuisine, la salle de bains, la chambre** (à coucher), **la cave** [*basement*].

6. **un monument** : un édifice public. Il y a la bibliothèque, le musée, la cathédrale, la gare, l'hôtel de ville, la préfecture de police, l'université, les écoles, les théâtres. Les monuments sont des édifices importants. (Attention ! Ici *important* veut dire *grand*.)

7. **le magasin, la boutique, le restaurant, l'hôtel** (*m.*), **le cinéma** sont d'autres bâtiments commerciaux.

8. **un étage** [*floor*]. Attention à la désignation des étages :

le rez-de-chaussée	ground floor	= U.S.	1st floor
le premier (étage)	first floor	=	2nd floor
le second (étage)	second floor	=	3rd floor
le troisième (étage)	third floor	=	4th floor
le grenier	attic		
la cave / le sous-sol	basement		

Mon bureau se trouve **au troisième**.   My office is *on the fourth floor*.

On emploie la préposition **au** (*au premier, au second, au rez-de-chaussée, au sous-sol*, etc.), mais on dit **dans** *la cave*.

Exercice 6T   Thème français

1. My parents live in a small but comfortable apartment.
2. It is on the same narrow street as the Smiths' house.
3. Our present apartment house is in a charming old section of Paris.
4. There is an enormous skyscraper on the site of our old apartment house.
5. In the country there are various kinds of houses : there are elegant châteaux, farms, cottages ; and in Switzerland there are chalets.
6. My sociology teacher lives in a villa in the suburbs of Paris ; he is lucky.
7. My father allows my sister to have her own television [set] in her room.
8. Another student in my English class lives on a farm ; he sets out for the university very early every morning.
9. He takes two hours to make the trip by bus.
10. In my first class another student took my last cigarette.
11. In literature class we read novels, short stories, and plays, but no poetry.
12. We were beginning to discuss a tragedy by Racine when you entered.

Exercice 6E   Sujets de composition ou de conversation

1. Parlez des divers bâtiments de votre ville, en signalant l'aspect, la situation et l'emploi de ces édifices. (Employez des adjectifs !)
2. Comparez deux voitures, deux personnes, ou deux édifices, en employant des adjectifs pour insister sur les différences entre les deux.

Un 2 CV attrappe une contravention (*Helena Kolda/Monkmeyer*)

7

Adverbes

Locutions avec de

PLACE DE L'ADVERBE *adv*

7.01 USUAL POSITION IN SENTENCE. Certain adverbs (mostly short, common ones) follow strict rules of word order. Other longer adverbs may be rather freely positioned.

A. ADVERBS LIKE **déjà**. The common adverbs listed in 7.06 (there are others) directly follow a simple verb. In compound tenses, they follow the auxiliary verb, that is, they *precede the past participle.*

SIMPLE TENSE	COMPOUND TENSE
Il parle **bien**.	Il a **bien** parlé.
Elle arrive **déjà**.	Elle est **déjà** arrivée.
Il paie **toujours**.	Il a **toujours** payé.

B. ADVERBS ENDING IN **-ment**. The ending **-ment** is equivalent to *-ly* in English. Adverbs in **-ment** [7.07] may be placed at the beginning or end of a sentence. Sometimes they are placed in other locations so as to precede the word modified (examples 3, 4 below):

(1) Il est entré **lentement**. He entered *slowly*.
(2) Elle parlait **rapidement**. She used to speak *rapidly*.

| (3) Paul a **complètement** oublié la clé. | Paul *completely* forgot the key. |
| (4) Ce rectangle est **légèrement** irrégulier. | This rectangle is *slightly* irregular. |

7.02 ADVERBS OF TIME AND PLACE. The adverbs **aujourd'hui, demain, hier, ici, là, partout, tôt, tard, de bonne heure, à l'heure, en retard, d'abord** come *after the past participle* in a compound tense.

Il sera parti **demain**.	He will have departed tomorrow.
Il est arrivé **hier**.	He arrived yesterday.
Vous êtes rentrée **tard**.	You came home late.
Nous sommes arrivés **en retard**.	We arrived late.
Ils se sont levés **de bonne heure**.	They got up early.

Some adverbs (such as **aujourd'hui, demain, hier,** and **d'abord**) often appear at the beginning of a sentence or clause:

Aujourd'hui nous allons au bord de la mer.
D'abord nous irons au musée.

7.03 DAY PRECEDES TIME. When both a *day* (**hier, demain, aujourd'hui, lundi,** etc.) and a *time* (hour) are mentioned, *day precedes time*.

Lucien est arrivé **hier à trois heures**.

7.04 ADVERBS MODIFYING ADJECTIVES OR ANOTHER ADVERB. An adverb *precedes* an adjective or adverb that it modifies.

Georges est **très** *intelligent*.
La porte était **partiellement** *ouverte*.
Le professeur parle **trop** *vite*.
Pourquoi es-tu **si** *fatigué*?

The adverb of quantity **beaucoup** may *not* be modified by *si*, *très*, or *trop*. The superlative of this word is **énormément**.

| Cela me plaît **beaucoup**. | That pleases me *a lot*. |
| Cela me plaît **énormément**. | That pleases me *very much indeed*. |

7.05 WORDS REQUIRING INVERSION. The following words require inversion of subject and verb when used *at the beginning* of a clause or sentence: **aussi** [*therefore, so*], **peut-être** [*perhaps, maybe*], and **à peine . . . que** [*scarcely . . . when*]:

Marie est née à Paris, **aussi** | parle-t-elle | français.

Marie was born in Paris, so (therefore) she speaks French.

Jean n'est pas arrivé aujourd'hui; **peut-être** | viendra-t-il | demain.

John didn't arrive today; perhaps he will come tomorrow.

À peine $\boxed{\text{était-il}}$ entré **que** Gérard sortit.

Scarcely had he come in when Gérard left.

When positioned after the verb, **aussi** means *also*; **peut-être** retains the meaning *perhaps*.

Marie parle français et elle $\boxed{\text{parle}}$ **aussi** l'anglais.

Jean $\boxed{\text{viendra}}$ **peut-être** demain.

7.06 COMMON ADVERBS THAT FOLLOW THE INFLECTED VERB. The adverbs listed below follow a simple verb, or (in compound tenses) precede the past participle:

beaucoup	Il parle **beaucoup**.	Il a **beaucoup** parlé.
trop	Il parle **trop**.	Il a **trop** parlé.
assez	Il souffre **assez**.	Il a **assez** souffert.
déjà	Il part **déjà**.	Il est **déjà** parti.
bientôt	Il arrivera **bientôt**.	Il sera **bientôt** arrivé.
souvent	Elle écrit **souvent**.	Elle avait **souvent** écrit.
toujours	Nous comprenons **toujours**.	Nous avons **toujours** compris.

Notice that **assez** before an adjective or adverb means *rather, quite*:

Cette leçon est **assez** difficile.   This lesson is *rather* difficult.

Le soldat marche **assez** vite.   The soldier walks *quite* fast.

FORMATION DE L'ADVERBE

7.07 A. REGULAR FORMATION. Many adverbs are formed from the feminine adjective, to which **-ment** is added:

ADJECTIVE	FEMININE	ADVERB	MEANING
actuel	actuelle	**actuellement**	currently
complet	complète	**complètement**	completely
doux	douce	**doucement**	softly
égal	égale	**également**	also, likewise
léger	légère	**légèrement**	slightly
malheureux	malheureuse	**malheureusement**	unfortunately

B. IRREGULAR FORMATION. The following adverbs have a slight spelling change from the normal formation:

poliment	politely
absolument	absolutely
assurément	certainly
énormément	greatly, tremendously
forcément	necessarily, inevitably
précisément	precisely, exactly
notamment	notably, particularly
récemment	recently
évidemment	obviously

7.08 ADVERBIAL EXPRESSIONS USING **avec**. Certain prepositional phrases with **avec** are the equivalents of adverbs. Only a few are given below. They usually appear at the end of a sentence or clause.

PHRASE	ADVERB	MEANING
avec élégance	**élégamment**	elegantly
avec grâce	**gracieusement**	gracefully, graciously
avec soin	**soigneusement**	carefully
avec patience	**patiemment**	patiently
avec bruit	**bruyamment**	noisily
avec douceur	**doucement**	gently, softly
avec vigueur	**vigoureusement**	vigorously

7.09 REVIEW OF ADVERBIALS OF TIME

A. With relation to a fixed appointment or habitual time of an event:

en avance	in advance	
de bonne heure	early	
à l'heure	on time	FOR AN APPOINTMENT
en retard	late	

NOTE: **tard** means *late* with regard to a usual time:

Il s'est levé **tard**.   He got up late.

tôt means *early* with regard to a usual time:

Vous êtes rentré **tôt**.   You came home early.

The adverbs **tôt** and **tard** may be modified by **très, trop, assez:**

Vous arrivez **trop tard**.   You are arriving too late.

B. Days with relation to *today*:

hier	yesterday
aujourd'hui	today
demain	tomorrow

Days with relation to any named day:

le lendemain	the next day
la veille	the day before

C. Synonyms, antonyms, distinctions:

parfois = **quelquefois**	sometimes
ensuite = **puis**	then, next (*order of events*)
≠ **alors**	then (*at that time in the past*)
tout de suite = **immédiatement**	immediately, at once
tôt ≠ **tard**	early / late
souvent ≠ **rarement**	often / rarely
d'abord ≠ **enfin**	first (of all) / finally
toujours ≠ (ne) . . . **jamais**	still, always[1] / never

Exercice 7A   Place de l'adverbe [7.01 – 7.06]

Ajoutez à la bonne place dans la phrase l'adverbe donné.

MODÈLE: (déjà)   Il part. / Il est parti.
          Il part **déjà**. / Il est **déjà** parti.

1. (déjà)   La pièce commence. / La pièce a commencé.
2. (bien)   Paul parle. / Il a parlé.
3. (trop)   Vous travaillez. / Vous avez travaillé.
4. (en retard)   Nous arrivons. / Nous sommes arrivés.
5. (demain)   Ma tante partira. / Georges va partir.
6. (assez)   Ils travaillent. / Ils ont travaillé.
7. (doucement)   Il ferme la porte. / Il a fermé la porte.
8. (très)   Mon cousin est intelligent. / Il parle vite.
9. (avec bruit)   Il entre. / Il est entré.
10. (beaucoup)   Ma belle-mère parle. / Elle a parlé.
11. (à midi)   Mon oncle est arrivé hier.
12. (aujourd'hui) Le train arrivera à sept heures.
13. (légèrement)   C'est un dessin irrégulier.
14. (si)   Pourquoi le patron est-il irrité?
15. (peut-être)   Il est de mauvaise humeur.
16. (aussi)   Elle est malade; elle reste à la maison.
17. (hier)   Le journal a annoncé le mariage de ma cousine.
18. (entièrement) Vous avez raison.
19. (hier)   La conférence a eu lieu à vingt heures.
20. (à l'heure)   Le professeur arrive. / Je suis arrivé.

---

[1]The surrounding context indicates whether **toujours** means *still* or *always*: Elle a toujours faim = *She is always hungry;* BUT Elle vient de manger un sandwich mais elle a toujours faim = *She is still hungry.*

LOCUTIONS AVEC de

7.10 EXPRESSIONS OF QUANTITY. Use **de** + [NOUN] without the article in expressions of quantity [3.07]:

beaucoup de vin	a lot of wine
assez de livres	enough books
une tasse de thé	a cup of tea
une bouteille de vin	a bottle of wine
une douzaine d'oranges	a dozen oranges
une boîte de petits pois	a can of peas

The two quantities **plusieurs** (several) and **quelques** (a few) appear *directly* before the noun. The article *is* used with **bien de** + [article + NOUN] (many), and **la plupart de** + [article + NOUN] (most):

J'ai **quelques** disques.	I have *a few* records.
Il a **plusieurs** dictionnaires.	He has *several* dictionaries.
Nous avons **bien des** journaux.	We have *many* newspapers.
La plupart de ces étudiants sont français.	**Most of these** students are French.

7.11 THE **de**-PHRASE AS EQUIVALENT OF AN ADJECTIVE. When a **de**-phrase is the equivalent of an *adjective*, no article is used with the noun [1.06A]:

une maison **de bois**	a *wooden* house
une robe **de laine**	a *woolen* dress

Academic subjects mentioned after *classe, cours, professeur* and the like use only **de** [1.06A]:

la classe **de français**	the *French* class
le cours **de mathématiques**	the *mathematics* course (class)
le professeur **d'anglais**	the *English* teacher

NOTE: **le professeur anglais** means a teacher whose *nationality* is British, but who may be teaching some other subject, such as French, mathematics, or physics. The use of **de** makes it clear that an academic subject is being mentioned.

7.12 De MEANING *from* [FEMININE SINGULAR COUNTRY]. No article is used.

Il arrive **de France.**	He is arriving *from* France.
Il revient **de Suisse.**	He is returning *from* Switzerland.
Il vient **de Suède.**	He comes *from* Sweden.

This rule does not apply to *masculine* singular countries, to plural names, nor to compound names:

Il arrive **du Canada**.	He is arriving from Canada.
Il vient **de la Nouvelle-Zélande**.	He comes from New Zealand.
Il arrive **des États-Unis**.	He is arriving from the United States.

7.13   De MEANING *with* OR *by* AFTER CERTAIN VERBS.   In the following verb structures, nouns following **de** omit the article:

charger (de [N])	to load (with [*something*])
écraser (de [N])	to overwhelm (with [N])
entourer (de [N])	to surround (with [N]) by [N])
fournir (de [N])	to furnish (with [N])
remplir [OBJECT] (**de** [N])	to fill [*something*] (with [N])

EXAMPLES

Le camion est **chargé de** bois.	The truck is loaded with wood.
Le jardin est **entouré de** maisons.	The garden is surrounded by houses.
Le garçon a **rempli** les verres **d'eau**.	The waiter filled the glasses with water.

Exercice 7B   Révision

Répondez aux questions suivantes en employant les mots signalés.

MODÈLE: Aimez-vous la musique?
beaucoup / énormément / toujours
Mais oui, j'aime **beaucoup** la musique.
Mais oui, j'aime **énormément** la musique.
Mais oui, j'aime **toujours** la musique.

1. Avez-vous des disques?
   beaucoup / plusieurs / trop
2. Aimez-vous les disques de Johnny Hallyday?
   beaucoup / bien / enormément
3. Connaissez-vous des avocats à Paris?
   plusieurs / quelques / très peu
4. Lisez-vous des romans policiers?
   souvent / énormément / parfois
5. Voudriez-vous du vin?
   un verre / une bouteille / un peu
6. Aimez-vous le vin?
   un peu / beaucoup / parfois
7. Combien de vos amis sont partis en vacances?
   plusieurs / beaucoup / la plupart

8. Quel cours suivez-vous maintenant?
   français / psychologie / physique
9. Est-ce que vous étudiez le soir?
   toujours / parfois / rarement
10. Comment préparez-vous vos devoirs?
    avec soin / patiemment / lentement
11. D'où vient-il?
    France / Canada / États-Unis [7.12]
12. De quoi le verre est-il rempli?
    vin / eau / fleurs [7.13]

Exercice 7C   Adverbes temporels [7.09]

Complétez la phrase en vous servant des locutions suivantes: **en avance, de bonne heure, en retard, à l'heure, tôt** ou **tard.**

1. Mon train part de la gare à cinq heures du matin. J'arrive à la gare à 5 h 05. Le train part très —— le matin, mais je suis arrivé ——.
2. Je suis arrivé trop —— pour prendre le train.
3. J'ai un rendez-vous avec mon professeur de sociologie à dix heures. J'arrive à son bureau à dix heures précises: je suis donc ——.
4. J'arrive à ma classe d'histoire à dix heures et demie, mais elle a déjà commencée. Je suis —— pour la classe, malheureusement.
5. Jean est arrivé à cette même classe à dix heures vingt. Il est arrivé plus —— que moi. Mais nous sommes tous les deux ——.

Complétez en vous servant de la liste suivante: **aujourd'hui, demain, hier, le lendemain, la veille.**

6. —— je suis en train de travailler dans mon jardin; —— j'ai fait une visite à mon oncle qui habite à Courbevoie; —— je vais visiter le musée.
7. Le lundi 6 juin nous avons quitté Paris pour aller à Genève; —— nous sommes arrivés dans cette ville magnifique en Suisse. C'était le 7 juin.
8. J'ai passé un examen d'anglais le 31 mars, donc j'ai beaucoup étudié ——.

Révision lexicale

Voitures

1. **une voiture: une auto.** Toutes les marques sont féminines: une Renault, une B.M.W., une Fiat, une Ford. La **2 CV**[2] est une petite Citroën. Il y a aussi **la berline** [*sedan*] à deux ou à quatre portes; **le break** [*station wagon*].
2. **le camion:** un gros véhicule pour transporter des marchandises. **Le fourgon** [*delivery van*] est plus petit; **le poids-lourd** [*tractor-trailer*] est le plus grand des camions.
3. **la motocyclette,** 'la moto': petit véhicule à deux roues.
4. **la bicyclette, le vélo.** On *monte* à bicyclette, on *roule* à bicyclette, on *fait du vélo*. Une bicyclette à moteur s'appelle **un cyclomoteur.**

---

[2] **CV** stands for **chevaux vapeur** [*horsepower*].

5. **le trajet** [*trip*]: Je fais le trajet d'Enghien à Paris par le train. **Le voyage** n'est pas limité à la mer comme en anglais: on *fait le voyage* entre Paris et Berlin en avion, en auto ou par le train.

6. **Un autobus** fait des trajets à l'intérieur d'une ville. **Un autocar** fait des trajets entre des villes: on l'appelle aussi **le car. Un car de ramassage scolaire** transporte les écoliers à l'école.

Exercice 7T   Thème français

1. Recently my parents bought a truck. Obviously it is not a tractor-trailer rig.

2. At present we have a small French sedan; actually [*en réalité*] I like very much to drive a big American car.

3. Yesterday I drove to Chartres with some friends from Sweden. We left quite early in the morning.

4. A big rig passed our car noisily; it was loaded with heavy machines.

5. I intended to turn left, but I completely forgot to turn on my directional signal [*mettre le clignotant*].

6. Unfortunately I got a ticket. Perhaps I was wrong.

7. We are going to enter a beautiful town soon. Then we can go to a restaurant. I am hungry.

8. My math teacher comes from Switzerland, therefore he speaks German fluently. He's interesting, and he's an excellent teacher.

9. There's a Renault. It's beautiful. It's an excellent car, but it is quite expensive.

10. Hardly had we arrived at the house than my brother filled some glasses with beer.

La Tour Eiffel vue des Tuileries (*Bernard Silberstein/Monkmeyer*)

8

Comparaison des adjectifs et des adverbes

TOUT

faire*

COMPARAISON DES ADJECTIFS ET DES ADVERBES

8.01 COMPARATIVE FORMS.   To obtain the comparative form of adjectives and adverbs, place **plus** [*more*], **moins** [*less*], or **aussi** [*just as*] before the adjective or adverb, and **que** after it.

ADJECTIVES

Louise est **plus intelligente** que Paul	$+$ PLUS
Paul est **moins intelligent** que Louise.	$-$ MOINS $\}$ [ADJ] **que**
Jean est **aussi**[1] **intelligent** que Suzanne.	$=$ AUSSI

ADVERBS

Ce train marche **plus vite** que l'autocar.	$+$ PLUS
L'autocar marche **moins vite** que le train.	$-$ MOINS $\}$ [ADV] **que**
Ma voiture marche **aussi vite** que la voiture de Jean.	$=$ AUSSI

[1]**si** may be used instead of **aussi** after a negative verb:

Jean n'est **pas si intelligent** que Suzanne.

*Comparaison des
adjectifs et des
adverbes*

J'ai **plus de livres** que vous.

Tu as **moins d'argent** que moi.

Il a **autant de talent** que Jean.

+ PLUS **de** [N]
− MOINS **de** [N] }que
= AUTANT **de** [N]

8.02 SUPERLATIVES.   The superlative is formed by adding the appropriate definite article (**le, la, les**) to the comparative of the adjective. The superlative of adverbs is formed by prefixing invariable **le** to the comparative form. Either **plus** or **moins** may be used.

	UNCOMPARED FORM	COMPARATIVE	SUPERLATIVE
ADJECTIVES	intelligente (*f.s.*)	**plus** intelligente **moins** intelligente	**la plus** intelligente **la moins** intelligente
	belles	**plus** belles **moins** belles	**les plus** belles **les moins** belles
ADVERBS	vite	**plus** vite **moins** vite	**le plus** vite **le moins** vite

EXAMPLES

WITH A FOLLOWING ADJECTIVE

Voici un livre **intéressant**.

Voici un livre **plus intéressant**.

Voici **le** livre **le plus intéressant**.   Note repeated article **le**.

C'est une robe **chère**.

C'est une robe **plus chère**.

C'est **la** robe **la plus chère**.   Note repeated article **la**.

WITH A PRECEDING ADJECTIVE [6.01]

Voilà une **grande** maison.

Voilà une **plus grande** maison.

Voilà **la plus grande** maison du quartier.

WITH AN ADVERB

Notre voiture marche **vite**.

Notre voiture marche **plus vite** que celle de Jean.

Notre voiture marche **le plus vite**.

rep   **8.03** REPETITION OF DEFINITE ARTICLE WITH ADJECTIVES.   The definite article is repeated when the superlative adjective follows the noun.

Voici **le** livre **le** plus intéressant.   Here is *the most interesting* book.

8.04 GENERAL CLASS. After a superlative, *de* is used for "in" or "of" when the general class is mentioned.

> Voilà **la plus grande** maison <u>de</u> la ville.
> Marie est la jeune fille **la plus intelligente** <u>de</u> la classe.
> Henri marche **le plus vite** <u>de</u> **tous les élèves.**

8.05 WITH NUMBERS. When a number follows the words *plus* or *moins*, use *de* rather than *que*.

J'ai **plus de deux** dollars.	I have more than two dollars.
Il a **moins de seize** ans.	He is less than 16 years old.

8.06 IRREGULAR COMPARISONS. Learn the following irregular comparisons:

ADJECTIVE	COMPARATIVE	SUPERLATIVE
bon (*m.*) ⎱ good **bonne** (*f.*) ⎰	**meilleur** ⎱ better **meilleure** ⎰	**le meilleur** ⎱ the best **la meilleure** ⎰

ADVERB	COMPARATIVE	SUPERLATIVE
bien, well	**mieux,** better	**le mieux,** the best
mal, badly	⎰**plus mal** worse ⎱[**pis,** worse	**le plus mal,** the worst [REGULAR] **le pis,** the worst] [IRREGULAR]
beaucoup, much	**plus,** more	**le plus,** the most
peu, little	**moins,** less	**le moins,** the least

EXAMPLES

Voici **le meilleur roman** de la saison. [ADJECTIVE]
>   Here is the best novel of the season.
Voilà **les meilleures maisons** de la ville.
>   There are the best houses in (of) the city.
Jean parle **bien**; Paul parle **mieux**; Robert parle **le mieux.** [ADVERB]
>   John speaks well; Paul speaks better; Robert speaks the best.
Je gagne **peu**; Jean gagne **moins**; Hans gagne **le moins.**
>   I earn (very) little; John earns less; Hans earns the least.

Exercice 8A Comparaison des adjectifs [8.01]

Comparez les deux noms en vous référant à la qualité signalée entre parenthèses. Faites attention à l'accord de l'adjectif [5.01] avec le *premier* nom mentionné.

MODÈLE: (la beauté: beau) la rose et le mimosa
>   La rose est **plus belle que** le mimosa.
>   Le mimosa est **moins beau que** la rose.

1. (la douceur: doux)   une orange et un citron
2. (l'intelligence: intelligent) un homme et un chien
3. (l'âge: jeune / vieux)   un fils et son père
4. (la force: fort / faible)   un éléphant et un cheval
5. (la grandeur: grand)   une maison et un hôtel
6. (la vitesse: vite / lent)   une Renault 16 et une 2 CV
7. (l'excellence: bon)   le cinéma et la télévision
8. (l'épaisseur: épais / mince) le mur et une planche
9. (la taille: grand / petit)   Napoléon et de Gaulle
10. (la difficulté: difficile / facile) un thème et une version

Exercice 8B   Superlatif des adjectifs [8.02 – 8.06]

Employez le superlatif de l'adjectif. Ajoutez la locution avec **de** [8.04] pour indiquer la classe générale.

MODÈLE: Cet appartement est **bon.** (quartier)
           Cet appartement est **le meilleur du quartier.**

1. Cette maison est bonne. (quartier)
2. Cette école est grande. (ville)
3. Cette femme est généreuse. (village)
4. Ce boulevard est long. (Paris)
5. Ce spectacle est intéressant. (saison)
6. Ce grand magasin est commode. (ville)
7. Ces stylos sont bons. (établissement)
8. Ces tables sont bonnes. (restaurant)
9. Cette frontière est longue. (pays)
10. Cette robe est chère. (collection)

Exercice 8C   Comparatif de l'adverbe [8.01]

Répondez aux questions suivantes en employant le comparatif de l'adverbe.

MODÈLE: Lucille travaille **beaucoup.** Et vous?
           Moi, je travaille **plus que** (*ou* **moins que**) Lucille.

1. Le président voyage *beaucoup.* Et vous?
2. Le chien mange *peu.* Et le chat?
3. L'étudiant écrit *bien.* Et le journaliste?
4. Votre père prend *souvent* la voiture. Et vous?
5. Mon professeur parle *fort.* Et ce comédien?
6. Votre bicyclette roule *vite.* Et le cyclomoteur?
7. Un chat comprend *bien.* Et un chien?
8. Une infirmière étudie *longtemps.* Et un médecin?
9. Antoine regarde *peu* la télévision. Et son frère?
10. Georges conduit *lentement.* Et cette vieille dame?

8.07 FORMS OF THE ADJECTIVE **tout.** As an adjective, **tout** precedes the noun it modifies, and agrees with it in gender and number. Notice that the meaning of the singular (**tout, toute**) varies with the addition or omission of the article. The article **les** (or a possessive like **mes**) *must* be used with the plural.

	MASCULINE	FEMININE	MEANING
SINGULAR	tout	toute	any (every) [N] NO ARTICLE
	tout le	toute la	the whole [N] WITH ARTICLE
PLURAL	tous les	toutes les	all (of) the [N] WITH ARTICLE

EXAMPLES

MASCULINE

Tout soldat est brave.   Any (Every) soldier is brave.
Tout le cours est bon.   The whole course is good.
Tous les livres sont utiles.   All of the books are useful.
Tous mes livres sont utiles.   All my books are useful.

FEMININE

Toute saison est belle.   Any (Every) season is beautiful.
Toute la saison est belle.   The whole season is beautiful.
Toutes les saisons sont belles.   All of the seasons are beautiful.

8.08 ADVERBIAL **tout.** Used as an adverb, **tout** is invariable and means *quite, very*:

Ce livre est **tout** usé.   (*m.s.*) This book is quite worn.
Elle est **tout** effrayée.   (*f.s.*) She is quite frightened.
Elle est **tout** émue.   (*f.s.*) She is very moved.
Cela est **tout** décidé.   (*m.s.*) That is completely decided.
Ce chat est **tout** jeune.   (*m.s.*) That cat is very young.

EXCEPTION: Before a *feminine* adjective beginning with a *consonant*, the feminine forms **toute** or **toutes** are used to retain the feminine sound (final *t* sound).

Elle est **toute** prête.	She is quite ready.
Elles sont **toutes** neuves.	They are quite new.

8.09   EXPRESSIONS WITH **tout**.   The following expressions are invariable:

(pas) du tout	(not) at all
tout à fait	completely, entirely
tout à l'heure	just a moment; in a moment
tout de suite	immediately, at once
tout le monde	everybody
tout à coup	suddenly
tout d'un coup	in one try, all at once
tout de même	anyway, all the same

EXAMPLES

Je ne comprends **pas du tout**.	I don't understand *at all*.
Je l'ai vu **tout à l'heure**.	I saw him *just a moment ago*.
Il reviendra **tout à l'heure**.	He will be *right* back.
À **tout à l'heure**!	See you *soon*.
La porte s'ouvrit **tout à coup**.	The door *suddenly* opened.
Le vent emporta **tout d'un coup** le toit.	The wind carried off the roof *in one fell swoop*.

Exercice 8D   Emploi de l'adjectif *tout* [8.07]

Remplacez le singulier de **tout** par la forme appropriée du pluriel.

MODÈLE: **Toute langue** vit, travaille, respire.
          Toutes les langues viv*ent*, travaill*ent*, respir*ent*.

1. Tout homme est mortel.
2. Tout travail mérite un salaire.
3. Toute vérité n'est pas bonne à dire.
4. La nuit, tout chat est gris.
5. Tout Français admire Napoléon.

Exercice 8E   Emploi de *tout* au sens d'*entier* [8.07]

Remplacez **une partie de** par le singulier de **tout**, suivi de l'article approprié.

MODÈLE: **Une partie de la saison** est belle.
          Toute la saison est belle.

1. Une partie de cette maison est blanche.
2. Une partie de ce cours est difficile.
3. Une partie de la route est dangereuse.
4. Une partie de la collection a été vendue.
5. Une partie de ce roman est intéressante.

Exercice 8F Emploi de l'adverbe *tout* (= *très*) [8.08]

Répondez aux remarques suivantes en ajoutant **tout** à l'adjectif employé.

MODÈLE: Le ciel est **bleu** aujourd'hui.
Mais oui, il est **tout bleu**.

1. Votre verre est plein de vin.
2. Cette bouteille est pleine de cognac.
3. Ces garçons sont seuls.
4. Cette jeune fille est contente.
5. Ce petit garçon est heureux.
6. Cette petite fille est heureuse.
7. Ma leçon de français est prête.
8. Ces pneus sont usés.
9. Ces voitures sont neuves.
10. La jeune fille est émue.

VERBE IRRÉGULIER faire*

8.10 Review the forms of **faire*** [*to make, to do*] in Appendix C, verb table 14, paying particular attention to the following tenses:

tp Je **fais** mes devoirs de français maintenant.
Je suis en train de **faire** mes devoirs.
ti Je **faisais** mon propre lit quand j'étais jeune.
tpc J'**ai fait** un voyage en Italie l'été passé.
tf Je **ferai** du camping cet été.

The verb **faire*** is used in connection with many activities, some of which are listed below.

A. DOMESTIC TASKS (*le travail domestique*).

faire la cuisine	to cook, to do the cooking
faire la vaisselle	to wash the dishes
faire le lit	to make the bed

B. TRIPS AND TRANSPORTATION (*les voyages et le transport*).

faire une promenade	to take a walk
. . . à bicyclette	to go bicycle riding
. . . à cheval	to go horseback riding
. . . en auto	to go for a ride (in a car)
faire un voyage	to take a trip
faire le trajet de X à Y	to make the trip from X to Y

C. SOCIAL EVENTS (*la vie mondaine*).

Verbe irrégulier
faire*

faire la connaissance de [P]	to meet [P]; to make the acquaintance of [P]
faire une visite à [P] = rendre visite à [P]	to visit [P] (*do not use* visiter)[1]
faire semblant de [I]	to pretend to [I]
faire attention à [N]	to pay attention to [N]

D. WEATHER (*le temps qu'il fait*)

Il fait beau / mauvais.	The weather is nice / bad.
Il fait chaud / froid / frais.	It is warm / cold / cool.
Il fait du soleil / du vent.	It is sunny / windy.

Note these other weather conditions:

Il pleut.	It is raining.
Il neige.	It is snowing.

E. SPORTS AND AMUSEMENTS (*les sports et les divertissements*)

faire du sport	to go in for sports
faire du football[2] / du basket	to play soccer / basketball
faire du tennis / du ski	to play tennis / to ski
faire du camping	to go camping
faire de l'auto-stop	to hitch-hike

Note the nouns used with **faire*** for certain sports and other activities:

faire un match de football	to play a game of soccer
faire une partie de tennis	to play a tennis match
faire un voyage d'agrément	to take a trip (for pleasure)
faire un voyage d'affaires	to go on a business trip

EXAMPLES

Je **ferai le trajet** de Paris à Londres en avion.
I will make the trip from Paris to London by plane.
Hier **j'ai fait la connaissance d'**une jolie jeune fille suédoise.
Yesterday I met a pretty Swedish girl.
Mon chien **fait semblant de** dormir.
My dog is pretending to sleep.

[1]Un médecin **visite les malades.** = A doctor *attends* the sick.
Le douanier **visite les bagages.** = The customs official *inspects* the baggage.
[2]*football* (U.S.) is **le football américain.**

—**Quel temps fait-il?** —**Il fait très beau.**

"How's the weather?" "It's very nice."

—Est-ce que **tu fais du sport**? —Mais oui, je **fais** souvent **du tennis.**

"Do you go in for any sports?" "Sure, I play tennis quite often."

NOTE: Causative **faire*** is dealt with in section 17.01. Never use **faire** for *to make someone happy, sad*, etc. In this sense use *rendre*:

Il **rend** sa mère **heureuse.**   He makes his mother happy.

Exercice 8G   Emploi de *faire**

Répondez aux questions suivantes en employant une locution avec **faire*.**

MODÈLE: Comment aidez-vous votre mère?
           Je **fais mon lit**, et quelquefois je **fais la vaisselle** après les repas.

1. Que fait-on pour préparer les repas?
2. Avez-vous fait de longs voyages?
3. Comment faites-vous le trajet de la maison à l'université?
4. Faites-vous souvent des promenades?
5. Quels sports faites-vous?
6. Faites-vous du camping?
7. Avez-vous fait la connaissance d'une personne sympathique cette année?
8. Ferez-vous une visite à quelqu'un (ou à quelqu'une) pendant les vacances?
9. Quand vous ne savez pas la réponse en classe, que faites-vous semblant de faire?
10. Faites-vous souvent de l'auto-stop?

Exercice 8T   Thème français

1. The most interesting play of the season is rather long.
2. In the last scene there is a religious ceremony: it takes place on the square in front of the cathedral.
3. The author is famous: he is just as famous as another French playwright, Jean Cocteau.
4. He writes less well than Mr. Cocteau, but his best plays are masterpieces.
5. Almost everybody goes in for sports: every sport has its enthusiasts.
6. I feel like taking a bicycle ride. I will make the trip from here to the Place de la Concorde.
7. When the weather is nice, I often go camping, especially in the summer.
8. Sometimes I hitch-hike to Berlin to visit a German friend. He's the most famous mathematician in the university.
9. Two years ago we took a trip to Spain. I speak Spanish poorly, but I understand Spanish better than my roommate.
10. I took a whole month to make the trip from Italy to Sweden. I hitch-hiked, but when I got back home I was completely broke [*fauché*].

Attendant l'autobus (*Helena Kolda/Monkmeyer*)

9

Temps présent | Imperatif | prendre*

EMPLOI DU PRÉSENT *tp*

9.01 ACTION AT THE PRESENT MOMENT.

— Que **faites-vous**?   "What are you doing?"
— Je **prépare** mes devoirs.   "I'm doing my homework."

9.02 HABITUAL ACTION STILL IN EFFECT.

— Que **faites-vous** le dimanche?   "What do you do on Sunday(s)?"
— Je **vais** toujours à l'église.   "I always go to church."

9.03 CONDITIONAL SENTENCES WITH **si**.   In conditional sentences, when the result clause is in the *future* or *imperative*, use the present after **si**:

Si vous **parlez** français, je vous comprendrai.
    If you speak French, I will understand you.   [FUTURE] [21.03]
Si vous **allez à pied**, partez de bonne heure.
    If you are walking, leave early.   [IMPERATIVE]

The **si**-clause need not be first in the sentence:

Je vous comprendrai *si* vous **parlez** français.

9.04 A. BEFORE A **depuis**-PHRASE. The word **depuis** means *since* literally, and is used to show how long an action currently in progress has been going on. Inasmuch as the action is actually occurring at the moment, the present tense is used:

Je **suis** ici **depuis** dix minutes.   I *have been* here *for* ten minutes.

The word **depuis** is best translated by *for* [TIME] in such sentences. The literal meaning is "I am here (and have been here) *since* (a point in time) ten minutes back." The logic of using the present tense is good: the action or state of being exists at the moment of the utterance.

Notice that the position of the **depuis** + [TIME]-phrase is always at the *end* of the sentence.

Georges **travaille** | depuis une semaine. |
George has been working for a week.

Ambiguity sometimes arises when the **depuis**-phrase can be interpreted either as a specific clock time or as a span of time. For example, "Je suis ici **depuis deux heures**" has two possible meanings:

I have been here *since two o'clock.*
I have been here *for two hours.*

To avoid ambiguity, if you mean *for two hours*, use **Il y a . . . que** [9.06].

B. COMPLETED AND FUTURE ACTION. When the action is *not* continued into the present, use **pendant** or **pour** to express *for* [TIME].

(1) **pendant** for completed action of some duration in the past:
Nous sommes restés en France **pendant trois semaines.**
We stayed in France *for* three weeks.

NOTE: Here the preposition **pendant** can be omitted, as can *for* in English.

(2) **pour** for future actions:
Jean-Paul va en Suisse **pour un mois.**
Jean-Paul is going to Switzerland *for* a month.

9.05 QUESTIONS WITH **depuis**. To inquire how long something has been going on, the present tense is used after one of the following forms:

(1) **depuis quand** + [*tp*] to elicit a DATE or indication of day (*hier, ce matin*)

(2) **depuis combien de temps** + [*tp*] to find out DURATION

EXAMPLES

Depuis quand étudiez-vous le français? ["*since when?*"]
   Je l'étudie **depuis** le 20 septembre (deux heures et demie; ce matin).
Depuis combien de temps étudiez-vous le français? ["*how long?*"]
   Je l'étudie **depuis** trois ans (vingt minutes, un mois, etc.)

Notice that the answers as well as the questions use the *present tense (tp)* to indicate that the activity is still going on.

9.06 **Il y a** [TIME] **que** / **Voilà** [TIME] **que** + PRESENT TENSE. These two expressions are used before a present tense verb to express exactly the same idea as a **depuis**-construction. However, they appear at the *beginning* of a sentence. Compare:

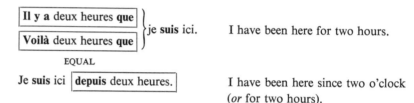

I have been here for two hours.

I have been here since two o'clock (*or* for two hours).

9.07 ACTIONS IN THE IMMEDIATE FUTURE. The present tense may be used to indicate future actions, as in English:

Demain **je pars** pour Rouen.

Tomorrow I am leaving for Rouen.

Je passe l'examen demain.

I am taking (will take) the exam tomorrow.

The adverb of time makes the future context clear.

FORMATION DU PRÉSENT

Regular verbs can be formed mechanically, by rule. The present tense of *irregular* verbs should be memorized because of their lack of consistency in the stems (and occasionally also in the endings).

9.08 PRESENT TENSE, REGULAR VERBS. The present tense of regular verbs is formed by (1) dropping the infinitive ending and (2) adding the present tense endings.

	VERB TYPE		
	-er	**-re**	**-ir**
je	-e	-s	-is
tu	-es	-s	-is
il (elle, on)	-e	-	-it
nous		-ons	-issons
vous		-ez	-issez
ils (elles)		-ent	-issent

EXAMPLES:

	parler	*vendre*	*finir*
je	parl e	vend s	fin is
tu	parl es	vend s	fin is
il	parl e	vend	fin it
nous	parl ons	vend ons	fin issons
vous	parl ez	vend ez	fin issez
ils	parl ent	vend ent	fin issent

9.09 MEANINGS OF THE PRESENT TENSE. There are two main meanings in English which are equivalent to the present tense in French. In most instances the two-word equivalent is appropriate. If it does not sound right, try the one-word equivalent. In English, the two-word present is for action going on *right now*, the one-word present is for *habitual* action.

PRESENT TENSE (French)	PRESENT TENSE (English)	
	TWO-WORD ("right now")	ONE-WORD ("usually")
il **travaille**	he is working	he works
elle **étudie**	she is studying	she studies
nous **arrivons**	we are arriving	we arrive
il **va**	he is going	he goes

The two-word English equivalent (*present progressive form*) is not usable for certain verbs, such as **il comprend**, **il sait**, **il est**, which must be given the one-word equivalents *he understands*, *he knows*, *he is*.

The distinction between an immediate action and a habitual action is determined by the context or by adverbial expressions used:

Il travaille *maintenant*.   He **is working** now.   IMMEDIATE

Il travaille *tous les jours*.   He **works** every day.   HABITUAL

When a **depuis**-phrase completes the sentence, you must use the English equivalent *have been / has been —ing*.

Il travaille depuis dix minutes.

He **has been working** for ten minutes.

Exercice 9A   Formation du présent

Composez une phrase en employant les mots donnés. Ajoutez une seconde phrase d'explication.

MODÈLE: (je)   travailler—bibliothèque
     { **Je travaille** à la **bibliothèque** tous les soirs.
     { J'étudie mes leçons dans la salle de lecture.

1.	(nous)	travailler—université	16.	(ils)	gagner—argent
2.	(vous)	préparer—devoirs	17.	(il)	penser (à)—voiture
3.	(ils)	étudier—leçon de français	18.	(je)	habiter—banlieue (*f.*)
4.	(tu)	visiter—musée	19.	(vous)	écrire—lettre
5.	(elle)	assister—conférence	20.	(nous)	lire—roman
6.	(je)	jouer (à)—tennis	21.	(il)	finir—travail
7.	(tu)	jouer (de)—guitare (*f.*)	22.	(nous)	obéir (à)—agent
8.	(Paul)	aller—théâtre	23.	(ils)	bâtir—maison
9.	(nous)	aller—cinéma	24.	(vous)	réussir (à)—examen
10.	(Marie)	faire—camping	25.	(Jean)	vendre—auto
11.	(elles)	parler—italien	26.	(Marie)	faire—cuisine
12.	(je)	être de retour	27.	(tu)	rendre—devoirs
13.	(Pierre)	fermer—fenêtres	28.	(je)	perdre—patience (*f.*)
14.	(elle)	trouver—dictionnaire	29.	(nous)	attendre—professeur
15.	(tu)	passer—examen	30.	(Alain)	échouer (à)—examen

Conversation à la ronde

Posez à votre voisin ou à votre voisine une question basée sur les mots de l'exercice précédent, par exemple:

— Travaillez-vous souvent à l'université le soir?

La personne qui répond ajoutera une seconde phrase d'explication:

— Mais oui, je travaille souvent à l'université le soir.

Je prépare mes devoirs pour le lendemain.

Ensuite cette personne posera à l'étudiant suivant (ou à l'étudiante suivante) une question basée sur numéro 2 de l'exercice, et ainsi de suite.

L'IMPÉRATIF *imp*

9.10 USE OF THE IMPERATIVE. The imperative (command) forms of a verb are used for giving directions or orders. They are derived from the present tense *tu-*, *vous-* and *nous-* forms. The three imperative forms are:

A. The *tu*-form (*Familiar form*), used for giving orders to *one* individual who is a member of the family, a close friend, a child, or an animal. (If an order is directed to *more than one* individual in these categories, the *vous*-form is used.)

B. The *vous*-form, for giving orders to one or several people not in the categories above; or to more than one individual in the familiar category.

C. The *nous*-form, for suggesting that something be done by the speaker along with others addressed.

Finis le travail, mon petit.	Finish the work, young fellow.	(*tu*)
Finissez le travail, monsieur.	Finish the work, sir.	(*vous*)
Finissons le travail, mes amis.	Let's finish the work, my friends.	(*nous*)

9.11 FORMATION OF THE IMPERATIVE. The imperatives consist of the *tu-*, *vous-*, and *nous*-forms of the present tense, after dropping the personal pronouns.

IMPERATIVE	DERIVED FROM	MEANING
parle	tu parle*s*	speak!
parlez	vous parlez	speak!
parlons	nous parlons	let's speak!

Notice that the final *-s* is dropped from the *tu*-form when the preceding letter is *e* or *a*. (An exception is made before the pronouns *y* and *en*, where final *-s* is retained in the *tu*-form of the imperative: **Vas-y**; **Penses-y**; **Cherches-en**.)

9.12 IMPERATIVE OF IRREGULAR VERBS. Irregular verbs form the imperative in the same ways as regular verbs, with the exception of **avoir***, **être***, and **savoir***.

	TU-FORM	*VOUS*-FORM	*NOUS*-FORM
faire*	**fais**	**faites**	**faisons**
mettre*	**mets**	**mettez**	**mettons**
prendre*	**prends**	**prenez**	**prenons**

EXCEPTIONS: **avoir*** and **être*** form their imperative from the present subjunctive forms:

avoir*	aie	ayez	ayons
être*	sois	soyez	soyons

The imperative of **savoir*** is as follows:

savoir*	sache	sachez	sachons

EXAMPLES

N'**ayez** pas peur.	Don't be afraid.
N'**aie** pas peur, mon enfant.	Don't be afraid, my child.
Soyons diligents.	Let's be diligent.
Sache la vérité, mon fils.	Know the truth, my son.

Exercice 9B   Impératif [9.10 – 9.12]

Complétez les idées suivantes en ajoutant un impératif.

MODÈLE: Vous voudriez *traverser* la rue?
          Traversez la rue.

1. Vous voudriez *entrer dans* le musée?
2. Tu voudrais *accompagner* maman?
3. Nous voudrions *visiter* le Louvre.
4. Vous avez envie de *parler* français?
5. Tu as envie d'*étudier* ce soir?
6. Nous avons envie d'*apprendre* l'allemand.
7. Vous désirez *faire* une promenade?
8. Tu désires *chercher* ton dictionnaire?
9. Nous désirons *aller* en Suisse.
10. Tu veux *prendre* le train?
11. Tu préfères *commander* du vin?
12. Vous voudriez *lire* un roman historique?
13. Nous voulons *quitter* la conférence.
14. Tu voudrais *être* spirituel?
15. Vous voudriez *attendre* le facteur?
16. Nous voudrions *répondre à* la question.
17. Tu voudrais *poser* une question au professeur?
18. Vous voudriez *faire la cuisine* ce soir?
19. Tu as envie de *faire du tennis*?
20. Nous avons envie d'*entrer dans* cette boutique.
21. Vous voulez *savoir* la vérité?
22. Tu veux *être* sage?

Exercice 9C   Impératif

Dites à votre voisin ou à votre voisine de …

1. ... fermer la porte
2. ... être le bienvenu
3. ... répondre à la question
4. ... faire la vaisselle
5. ... aller à la fenêtre

VERBE IRRÉGULIER prendre*

9.13 Review the forms of **prendre*** [*to take*] in Appendix C, verb table 23. Pay special attention to the following tenses:

tp   Je **prends** un stylo dans le tiroir.
      Je suis en train de **prendre** un stylo dans le tiroir.
ti   Paul **prenait** les billets quand je suis arrivé.
tpc   Marie **a pris** le petit déjeuner de bonne heure.
tf   Le directeur **prendra** une décision.

9.14 IDIOMATIC USES OF **prendre***.

prendre* un billet (pour [N])	to buy a ticket (for [N])
prendre* la décision (de [I])	to make a decision (to [DO SOMETHING])
prendre* la parole	to take the floor (to speak)
prendre* quelque chose	to have something to eat (or drink)
prendre* le petit déjeuner	to have breakfast

EXAMPLES

Robert **a pris** deux **billets** au guichet.	Robert bought two tickets at the ticket-window.
J'ai pris une décision importante.	I made an important decision.
Le doyen **a pris la parole.**	The dean spoke.
Prenons quelque chose au café.	Let's have something at the café.
J'ai pris le petit déjeuner à l'hôtel.	I had breakfast at the hotel.

9.15 TRANSLATION DIFFICULTIES. Be careful to avoid using **prendre** when translating *to take* in the following expressions:

to **take** a walk	**faire*** une promenade [8.10B]
to **take** [time] to do something	**mettre*** [heures, minutes] **à** [I] [6.05]

     J'ai mis une heure à préparer ma leçon de français.
       I took an hour to prepare my French lesson.

9.16 COMPOUNDS OF **prendre***. The following verbs are compounds of *prendre** and are conjugated in the same way:

apprendre* [N] à [P]	to learn; to teach [*something*] to
comprendre*	to understand; to include
entreprendre*	to undertake (a task)
reprendre*	to take back; to resume
surprendre*	to surprise

Exercice 9D Le verbe *prendre**

Répondez aux questions en employant **prendre***, **faire***, ou **mettre***, selon le cas.

MODÈLE: Les touristes —— le petit déjeuner à l'hôtel. Et vous?
Les touristes **prennent le petit déjeuner** à l'hôtel.
Moi, je prends toujours **le petit déjeuner** chez moi.

1. Jean est toujours généreux: il —— les billets quand nous allons au cinéma. Et vous?
2. François —— la parole quand il a une idée. Et vous?
3. Mes amis —— quelque chose après le film. Et vous?
4. Les touristes —— une promenade dans le Jardin du Luxembourg. Et vous?
5. Les garçons —— souvent du camping. Et vous?
6. Alain —— trois heures à faire ses devoirs. Et vous?
7. Le directeur —— des décisions importantes tous les jours. Et vous?
8. Les touristes —— le petit déjeuner à l'hôtel. Et vous?
9. Ils —— une demi-heure à manger. Et vous?
10. Georges —— toujours quatre billets pour le match de football. Et vous?

Exercice 9T Thème français

1. I am still (in process of) reading a long novel for my English course.
2. I'm hungry. Let's go and get a bite to eat.
3. We are playing tennis tomorrow. I play some tennis every day, and this afternoon I am teaching a friend to serve the ball correctly.
4. Let's go into this department store. I have decided to buy several shirts, a few neckties, and lots of handkerchieves.
5. I have been writing these French sentences for fifteen minutes. Obviously, I started writing them fifteen minutes ago.
6. A month ago I learned some irregular verbs and in addition some verbs that are slightly irregular. I am still studying them.
7. I feel like going to the movies this evening. Let's take the bus to town. The bus is slower than the subway, but I like it better.
8. The first show is at 2:30. We will take an hour and a half for the trip and we will be on time.

9. Is there a bank near the movie theater? I need to get (obtain) some money, and then I will buy the tickets.
10. At the present moment I am finishing the translation from English to French. I always finish my work early.
11. How long have you been waiting for the bus?
12. I have been waiting for the bus for half an hour. I am already tired.

Accès aux quais, gare de Strasbourg (*Sybil Shelton/Monkmeyer*)

10

Négation ⟩ Chronologie

NÉGATION *neg*

10.01 VERB UNIT IDENTIFICATION.   It is helpful for negation (and for interrogation) to be able to identify the verb unit. The verb unit consists of the inflected verb[1] together with all preceding pronouns except the subject.

Il ⌐les lui **donne**⌐.   Il ⌐les lui **a**⌐ donnés ce matin.

⌐**Fermez**⌐ la porte.   Aussi ⌐**est-elle**⌐ restée chez elle.

Notice that a hyphenated form is treated as an inseparable verb unit.

10.02 SIMPLE NEGATION: **ne** [VERB UNIT] **pas**. To make a statement, question, or command negative, place **ne** in front of the verb unit, and **pas** after it.

---

[1]An *inflected verb* is a verb form other than the infinitive. The dictionary form of the verb (the infinitive) has to be changed to agree with a particular subject (*je, nous, ils*, etc.) and to indicate tense. These changed forms are inflected verbs, for example **nous allons** (from *aller*). In compound tenses, only the auxiliary verb is inflected: **il a vu, nous avons vu** (from *voir*).

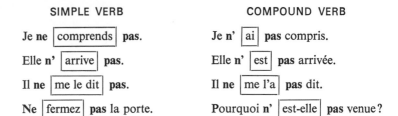

SIMPLE VERB	COMPOUND VERB
Je ne comprends pas.	Je n' ai pas compris.
Elle n' arrive pas.	Elle n' est pas arrivée.
Il ne me le dit pas.	Il ne me l'a pas dit.
Ne fermez pas la porte.	Pourquoi n' est-elle pas venue?

10.03 ALTERNATE NEGATIVES REPLACING **pas.** To obtain other negative meanings, **ne ... pas** is replaced by one of the following expressions:

ne ... jamais	never	Il **ne** parle **jamais.**
ne ... rien	nothing	Il **ne** dit **rien.**
ne ... plus	no longer	Il **ne** travaille **plus.**
ne ... guère	scarcely	Il **n'**étudie **guère.**
ne ... pas encore	not yet	Il **n'**a **pas encore** compris.

Notice that **pas encore** stays together as a negation element.

10.04 ALTERNATE NEGATIVES THAT FOLLOW THE PAST PARTICIPLE. With certain negative expressions, the second element of the negation follows the *past participle* when used with a compound tense:

ne ... personne	nobody, not ... anyone
ne ... que	only [N]; not ... except [N]
ne ... aucun(e) [N]	not ... any [N]; no [N] (*use singular noun*)
ne ... ni [N] ... ni [N]	neither [N] nor [N]

EXAMPLES

Il **n'**a trouvé **personne.**	He did not find anyone.
Je **ne** cherche **personne.**	I am not looking for anyone.
Il **ne** parle **à personne.**	He does not talk to anyone.
Il **n'**a **que** trois dollars.	He has only three dollars.
Je **n'**ai **aucun** billet.	I don't have any ticket.
Il **n'**y a **aucune** exception.	There is no exception.
Il **n'**a **ni** le stylo **ni** le crayon.	He has neither the pen nor the pencil.
Il **n'**a écrit **ni** roman **ni** poème.	He wrote neither a novel nor a poem.
Il **n'**a vu **ni** sa sœur **ni** son frère.	He saw neither his sister nor his brother.

Notice the omission of the indefinite article with **ni ... ni,** but the inclusion of possessive adjectives and definite articles.

When using **ne . . . que** you should place the word **que** at the location in the sentence where it shows the limitation of *only*. It need not appear directly after the verb unit:

Nous **n'**avons trouvé dans ce livre **que** trois photos.
We have found *only* three photos in this book.

10.05 **Rien** AND **personne** AS SUBJECTS. When **rien** [*nothing*] or **personne** [*nobody*] is the subject of a clause or sentence, it is placed at the beginning. The word **ne** is an essential part of the meaning, and appears in the usual place in front of the verb.

Rien ne me trouble.   Nothing bothers me.
Personne n'a compris.   Nobody understood.

The words **rien**, **personne**, **jamais** and **plus** may also be used *alone* as answers to questions.

— Qu'est-ce qui se passe?   What's going on?
— **Rien.**   Nothing.
— Qui est entré?   Who came in?
— **Personne.**   Nobody.
— Allez-vous à l'opéra?   Do you go to the opera?
— **Jamais.**   Never.

10.06 INFINITIVES NEGATED. Infinitives are made negative by placing both **ne** and the accompanying negative word *together* before the infinitive.

— Je vous demande de **ne pas** *sortir*. I am asking you not to go out.
— Il s'amuse à **ne rien** *faire*.   He is having fun doing nothing.

The negative expressions in section 10.04 straddle the infinitive:

Il a promis de **ne** *voir* **personne**. He promised to see *nobody*. (or):
                                            He promised *not* to see *anybody*.

Exercice 10A   Négation [10.02]

Mettez les phrases suivantes à la forme négative. Imaginez une seconde phrase pour compléter la pensée.

MODÈLE: Jean étudie sa leçon.
           Jean **n'**étudie **pas** sa leçon. Il regarde la télévision.

1. La première représentation a commencé. (Elle commence à . . .)
2. Paul prend les billets. (C'est Robert qui . . .)

3. Paul a pris son billet.
4. Le film est français.
5. La vedette du film était Paul Newman.
6. Il y a beaucoup de monde dans la salle.
7. Mon père va souvent à Londres.
8. Il fait le trajet en bateau.
9. Ma mère prend le petit déjeuner à six heures.
10. Mon frère fait la cuisine.
11. Je fais la vaisselle.
12. Est-ce que vous faites la cuisine ?
13. Fermez la porte, s'il vous plaît.
14. Écrivez une longue lettre au maire.
15. Nous arrivons en retard.
16. Nous avons posé des questions difficiles. [4.06]
17. Le directeur est de retour.
18. Vous avez fini le travail.
19. J'ai envie de faire une promenade.
20. Cette jeune fille est toute seule.

Négation de l'infinitif [10.06]. Mettez à la forme négative les infinitifs en italiques.

21. Être ou *être*, voilà la question.
22. Elle demande aux étudiants de *faire* du bruit.
23. On nous demande de *fumer*.
24. Le professeur demande aux étudiants d'*écrire* des phrases compliquées.
25. Il est difficile de *comprendre* ces phrases simples.

Exercice 10B   Autres termes de la négation [10.3 – 10.5]

Répondez aux questions suivantes en employant le terme de la négation entre parenthèses.

MODÈLE: (pas encore)   Allez-vous en ville maintenant ?
   Pas encore. Je **ne** vais **pas encore** en ville.

1. (pas encore)   Vous allez déjeuner maintenant ?
2. (jamais)   Vous jouez au tennis ?
3. (aucun, -e)   Adolphe a-t-il beaucoup d'amis ?
4. (rien)   Que faites-vous ?
5. (plus)   Allez-vous souvent au cinéma ?
6. (guère)   Est-ce que le film est amusant ?
7. (personne)   Qui cherchez-vous ?
8. (plus)   Est-ce que vos parents visitent toujours l'Italie ?
9. (ni)   Avez-vous des sœurs et des frères ?
10. (pas encore)   Écrivez-vous votre composition ?
11. (jamais)   Avez-vous fait la connaissance de cet auteur ?
12. (aucun, -e)   Y a-t-il une exception à la règle ?

CHRONOLOGIE

10.07 TIME DIVISIONS. Review the following **divisions du temps.**

le siècle	century
au XIXᵉ siècle	in the 19th century
l'an,² l'année	year
le mois	month
quinze jours	two weeks
la semaine, huit jours	week
la semaine prochaine	next week
la semaine passée	last week
le jour,² la journée	day
le matin	morning
midi, minuit	noon, midnight
l'après-midi (*m.* ou *f.*)	afternoon
le soir	evening
la nuit	night
une heure	hour
une minute	minute
une seconde	second

10.08 DAYS OF THE WEEK. Review **les jours de la semaine.**

lundi	Monday	**vendredi**	Friday
mardi	Tuesday	**samedi**	Saturday
mercredi	Wednesday	**dimanche**	Sunday
jeudi	Thursday		

REMINDER: Do not use the article with the name of a day when a *specific day* is meant. For habitual action ("on Mondays," "Saturdays," etc.) use the singular article **le.** [1.05D]

10.09 MONTHS. Review **les mois de l'année.**

janvier	January	**mai**	May	**septembre**	September
février	February	**juin**	June	**octobre**	October
mars	March	**juillet**	July	**novembre**	November
avril	April	**août**	August	**décembre**	December

²Use the masculine forms **an, jour** when a number (other than *one*) precedes:
Jean habite à Paris depuis **trois ans.**
Il a passé **une année** en Suisse.
Nous avons passé **une journée** agréable à la plage.

To say "in [*month*]" use **en** or **au mois de**:

> **En** juillet, nous ne serons plus à la maison.
> Je fais du ski **au mois de** janvier.

10.10 Dates.   In writing dates (**la date**), no capital letters are used for the days of the week or the months of the year. The definite article is often dropped:

> **le 14 novembre 1978**   *or, informally,*   **14 november 1978**

In stating the year, one can say either *nineteen hundred seventy-eight* or *one thousand nine hundred seventy-eight*.

> dix-neuf cent soixante-dix-huit.
> mil neuf cent soixante-dix-huit } 1978

To ask the date:

	Quel jour sommes-nous aujourd'hui?	What is today's date?
	Nous sommes le 23 novembre.	It's the 23rd of November.
or	**Quelle est la date aujourd'hui?**	What is today's date?
	C'est aujourd'hui le 3 avril.	It's the 3rd of April.

Notice that only cardinal numbers are used in French (with the one exception of the *first*), whereas the ordinal numbers are commonly used in English.

> C'est aujourd'hui **le premier avril.**   Today is April 1st.

To ask the day of the week:

> **Quel jour de la semaine est-ce?**   What day of the week is it?
> C'est aujourd'hui mardi.   Today is Tuesday.

For a complete review of numbers, see Appendix A.

10.11 Clock time (**l'heure** *f.*).   The general way of stating the time (o'clock) is "Il est — heures."

A.   The half-hour is expressed by "Il est — heures **et demie**" (*f.*). Notice how this is abbreviated numerically.

> Il est sept heures **et demie** (7 h 30).

The masculine form **et demi** is used after **midi** [*noon*] and **minuit** [*midnight*]:

> Il est **midi et demi** (12 h 30).
> Il est **minuit et demi** (0 h 30).

B. The quarter-hour is expressed by **et quart**.

Il est deux heures **et quart** (2 h 15).

C. The quarter *before* the hour is expressed by **moins le quart**.

Il est dix heures **moins le quart** (9 h 45).
   It is *quarter of ten.* or It is *nine forty-five.*

The number of minutes *before* the hour is **moins** [*number of minutes*]:

Il est midi **moins vingt** (11 h 40).
Il est huit heures **moins cinq** (7 h 55).

D. The number of minutes *past* the hour is expressed:

Il est dix heures **trois** (10 h 03).
Il est onze heures **seize** (11 h 16).

E. To indicate A.M. and P.M. add **du matin** for morning hours, and **du soir** to indicate evening hours (if it is not obvious from the context).

Il arrivera à huit heures vingt **du soir**.
   He will arrive at eight-twenty P.M.
Il est sept heures **du matin**.
   It is seven o'clock in the morning (A.M.).

F. The twenty-four-hour system is used by railroads, airlines, theaters, military services, etc. This system makes the indicators A.M. and P.M. superfluous. For example, here is a typical schedule of departure times for trains from Paris to Le Havre:

Départ		Departures
9 h 11	*that is:*	9:11 A.M.
11 h 10		11:10 A.M.
14 h 11		2:11 P.M.
16 h 44		4:44 P.M.
19 h 56		7:56 P.M.

G. "Exactly" and "Approximately"

Il est neuf heures **précises**.   It is *exactly* nine o'clock.
Il arrivera **vers** dix heures.   He will arrive *around* ten o'clock.

Exercice 10C Divisions du temps [10.07, 10.08]
   Répondez aux questions suivantes.

MODÈLE : Quel jour est-ce aujourd'hui ?
C'est aujourd'hui mardi le 7 novembre.

1. Quel jour est-ce aujourd'hui ?
2. Quelle heure est-il ?
3. Quels sont les mois de l'année ?
4. Combien de mois y a-t-il ?
5. Combien de jours y a-t-il dans une semaine ?
6. Quels sont les jours de la semaine ?
7. Quel est le jour de congé des étudiants en France ?
8. Combien d'années font un siècle ? (*Employez* **ans** *dans la réponse.*)
9. Quelle est la date du commencement du vingt-et-unième siècle ?
10. Quels sont les trois parties de la journée ?
11. Quand dormez-vous ?
12. Combien de secondes y a-t-il dans une minute ?
13. Quelle heure est-il à midi ?
14. Quel est l'équivalent de "deux semaines" ?
15. Quel est l'équivalent de "huit jours" ?
16. Quelle heure est-il maintenant ?
17. Quel temps fait-il en hiver ? [8.10D]
18. Quel sport faites-vous en automne ?
19. Quel temps fait-il en été ?
20. Que faites-vous depuis cinq minutes ?

Exercice 10D   La date et l'heure [10.09 – 10.11]

Répondez aux questions suivantes.

A. **Quelle heure est-il?**
(6 h 00)   Il est **six heures précises**.

1. 7 h 00	11. 8 h 35	21. 2 h 06
2. 7 h 15	12. 8 h 40	22. 14 h 07
3. 7 h 30	13. 8 h 45	23. 14 h 15
4. 7 h 45	14. 8 h 50	24. 14 h 45
5. 8 h 00	15. 8 h 55	25. 15 h 00
6. 8 h 05	16. 9 h 00	26. 17 h 09
7. 8 h 10	17. 9 h 03	27. 18 h 17
8. 8 h 15	18. 12 h 00	28. 20 h 20
9. 8 h 20	19. 24 h 00	29. 22 h 30
10. 8 h 30	20. 0 h 05	30. 23 h 35

B. **Quel est la date aujourd'hui?**
(January 23)   **C'est aujourd'hui le 23 janvier.**

1. September 3rd	7. December 5th
2. June 9th	8. February 22nd
3. April 1st	9. July 14th
4. May 19th	10. March 30th
5. October 10th	11. December 25th
6. November 7th	12. January 1st

Exercice 10T   Thème français

1. The Duponts rarely go to the movies, because they don't like present-day films.
2. I never fly to London because I am always afraid of planes.
3. Nobody takes the boat to [*pour*] Paris; nobody has the time.
4. I have only two days for the trip to London. I am going on Wednesday.
5. Nothing is more important than money and friends.
6. There is nothing in this dictionary except words; there is no map.
7. Nobody is looking for this newspaper; the date is July 21, 1948.
8. John is taking three difficult courses, but he scarcely studies.
9. My sister never washes the dishes: she is always tired.
10. Don't spend [*passer*] a week in Bordeaux; go to the seashore and you'll feel like spending two weeks there.

Exercice 10E   Sujets de conversation ou de composition

1. Parlez des choses que vous préférez ne pas faire, en indiquant pourquoi vous n'aimez pas les faire.
2. Comparez les occupations [*activities*] de deux de vos connaissances, en signalant les différences remarquables. (*Employez la négation.*)

La Cité Universitaire avec le stade Charléty (*Sodel-M. Brigaud/Interphototèque*)

11

Infinitif

VENIR*

TENIR*

INFINITIF *inf*

~~~~~~

11.01 PREPOSITIONS FOLLOWED BY INFINITIVE.   When a verb occurs after a preposition use the infinitive. (When the preposition is **après** or **en**, special structures are required, as indicated in 11.07 and 11.08.)

> Le professeur quitte la salle **sans dire** au revoir.
> > The teacher leaves the room without saying goodbye.
> Il est facile **de faire** des fautes de grammaire.
> > It is easy to make grammatical errors.
> Nous promettons à Paul **de conduire** avec soin. [6.06]
> > We promise Paul to drive carefully.

Use the preposition **pour** to indicate purpose [*in order to*]:

> Nous étudions **pour apprendre** le français.
> > We are studying (in order) to learn French.

g inf   **11.02** GOVERNMENT OF INFINITIVES: NOTHING, **à**, OR **de** BEFORE AN INFINITIVE.   When an inflected verb is followed by an infinitive, one must decide whether to insert NOTHING, **à**, or **de** before that infinitive. This decision depends upon the inflected verb, *not* upon the infinitive. For example, if the inflected verb *commence* is followed by the infinitive **lire**:

$$\text{Je commence} \begin{cases} \text{(—)?} \\ \text{(à)?} \\ \text{(de)?} \end{cases} \text{LIRE le journal.}$$

the selection of the correct structure depends upon **commencer.** An examination of the lists below (11.03 for verbs followed directly by the infinitive, 11.04 for those requiring **à** before a following infinitive, and 11.05 for those requiring **de**) shows that **commencer à** is the correct solution. The only correct way to make the statement is therefore:

Je commence à LIRE **le journal.**

There is no evident logic involved in the selection of **à**, except that commencer **à** [I] *sounds* right to a French speaker, just as an English speaker finds certain combinations correct (to comply *with*, to engage *in*, to infer *from*) and others incorrect (to comply *at*, to be oblivious *from*). The choice of the correct preposition is based on practice and familiarity with the structures. Concentrate on those in the lists below, using them frequently. A more complete reference list, for use when you are in doubt, is given in Appendix D.

11.03 VERBS FOLLOWED DIRECTLY BY AN INFINITIVE. Certain inflected verbs may be followed directly by an infinitive.

Je **vais** ÉTUDIER ce soir.   (ÉTUDIER follows **vais** directly)

Among the verbs that may be followed directly by an infinitive are:

aimer	to like	Paul **aime** jouer au tennis.
aller*	to go	Nous **allons** faire un voyage.
désirer	to desire	Ils **désirent** visiter le musée.
entendre	to hear	J'ai **entendu** arriver le taxi.
faire*	to have (done)	Jean **a fait** fermer la porte.
falloir*[1]		
il faut	one must	**Il faut** étudier ce soir.

[1]**falloir*** is a "defective" verb, in that it exists only with the impersonal subject *il*. The following meanings should be noted:

tp	**il faut**	one must [I], it is necessary [I]
	il ne faut pas	one must not [I]
ti	**il fallait**	it was (used to be) necessary [I]
tpc	**il a fallu**	it was necessary [I]
tc	**il faudrait**	it would be necessary [I]

The meaning "it is necessary" must be changed in the negative to "must not":

Il **ne faut pas** fumer.   You *must not* smoke.

laisser	to allow, let	L'agent **laisse** passer le touriste.
venir*	to come	Robert **vient** voir le professeur.
vouloir*	to want	**Voudriez-vous** voir ce film?

11.04 Verbs requiring **à** before a following infinitive. Certain verbs may be followed by an infinitive only if **à** is placed before the infinitive.

Nous **apprenons à** PARLER français.

Some of these verbs are listed below (see Appendix D for a more complete list).

apprendre* à	to learn	**J'apprends à** écrire le russe.
avoir* à	to have	**J'ai à** étudier ce soir.
chercher à	to try	Paul **cherche à** ouvrir cette porte.
commencer° à²	to begin	Ils **commencent à** travailler.
continuer à	to continue	Alain **continue à** lire.
hésiter à	to hesitate	Hans **hésite à** parler français.
penser à	to think (about —ing)	Mon père **pense à** faire un voyage.
tenir* à [11.12]	to be eager	Je **tiens à** voir le Moulin Rouge.

11.05 Verbs requiring **de** before an infinitive. Certain verbs may be followed by an infinitive only when **de** is inserted before the infinitive.

Jean-Paul **refuse de** faire la vaisselle.

Among the verbs in this category are:

accepter de	to agree	Il **accepte de** nous aider.
cesser de	to cease	Il **cesse de** travailler à quatre heures.
décider de	to decide	Nous **avons décidé de** voir ce film italien.
éviter de	to avoid	Ma mère **évite de** conduire la 2 CV.
essayer° de	to try	Philippe **essaie de** fermer la fenêtre.
finir de	to stop	**J'ai fini de** lire le journal.
oublier de	to forget	Marie **a oublié de** lire cette poésie.
refuser de	to refuse	Georges **refuse de** sortir.
tâcher de	to try	Philippe **tâche de** fermer la fenêtre.
venir* de [11.10]	to have just	Le professeur **vient d'**entrer dans la salle.

11.06 After **avant de** [*before —ing something*]. The infinitive is used after **avant de**, according to the general rule that the verb after a preposition must be in the infinitive form. Special attention to this structure is required because of its contrast with the English equivalent. In English the expression "Before *we* closed the door, *we*. . ." uses an inflected verb with "before." In French the structure is "Before closing the door, we. . .": **avant de** + INFINITIVE.

---

²The symbol ° indicates a stem-changing (slightly irregular) verb, discussed in 30.01. Verbs marked with an asterisk (*) are irregular.

Nous étudions **avant de** QUITTER la maison.
We study before leaving [before we leave] the house.
Avant d'aller au cinéma, Marie fera la vaisselle.
Before she goes to the moves, Marie will do the dishes.

11.07 AFTER **après**: INFINITIVE **avoir*** OR **être*** + PAST PARTICIPLE. The preposition **après** cannot be followed by a personal pronoun, as is the case in English. Instead, use **après avoir** + PAST PARTICIPLE [15.03A]:

Après avoir fini mes devoirs, je suis allé au cinéma.
After having finished my homework, I went to the movies.
or
After I finished my homework, I went to the movies.

Verbs using the auxilary **être***, including all reflexive verbs, require the structure **après être*** + PAST PARTICIPLE. In addition, the past participle must then agree in gender and number with the subject [16.02]:

Après être arrivée, Marie a regardé la télévision.
After Mary arrived, she watched television.
(After having arrived, Mary watched television.)

11.08 AFTER **en**: PRESENT PARTICIPLE. After the preposition **en** [*by, while*] the present participle [31.02] is used instead of the infinitive:

On apprend le français **en parlant.**
One learns French by speaking.
Jean écoute la radio **en lisant** le journal.
John listens to the radio while reading the paper.

For NEGATION OF INFINITIVES refer to 10.06.

Exercice 11A Emploi de l'infinitif après une préposition [11.01]

Complétez les phrases suivantes en employant la form appropriée des locutions entre parenthèses.

MODÈLE: (Elle va au cinéma.) Marie fait la vaisselle avant . . .
Marie fait la vaisselle **avant d'aller** au cinéma.

1. (Il fait ses devoirs.)   Jean-Paul joue au tennis avant . . .
2. (Nous apprenons.)   Nous sommes à l'université pour . . .
3. (Il ne comprend pas.)   Lucien lit beaucoup sans . . .
4. (Je prends mon billet.)   Je cherche de l'argent pour . . .
5. (J'ai pris mon billet.)   J'entre dans la salle après . . .
6. (Il ne fait pas ses devoirs.)   Gaston quitte la maison sans . . .
7. (Il écrit une lettre.)   Albert cherche un stylo pour . . .
8. (Je regarde la télévision.)   Je fais mes devoirs avant . . .
9. (Je regarde la télévision.)   Je fais la vaisselle après . . .
10. (Nous étudions la leçon.)   Nous comprenons bien après . . .

Emploi de l'infinitif [11.03 – 11.05]

Terminez chaque phrase avec *parler français*.

MODÈLE: Je commence . . .
           Je **commence à** parler français. [11.04]

1. Nous aimons bien . . .
2. Paul et Marie vont . . .
3. Je ne refuse pas . . .
4. Il faut . . .
5. Tout le monde apprend . . .
6. Vous commencez . . .
7. Je n'oublie jamais . . .
8. On nous laisse . . .
9. Est-ce que vous hésitez . . . ?
10. Nous venons . . .

Continuez de même en terminant chaque phrase avec *étudier*.

11. Désirez-vous . . . ?
12. Je pense . . .
13. J'ai décidé . . .
14. Nous allons . . .
15. Maintenant je commence . . .
16. Jacques voudrait . . .
17. Il faut certainement . . .
18. On ne cesse jamais . . .
19. Mon camarade de chambre évite . . .
20. Continuez . . .

VERBES IRRÉGULIERS venir* et **tenir***

11.09   REVIEW **venir*** [*to come*] in Appendix C, verb table 30; and **tenir***
[*to hold*] verb table 29. Notice the similarity of these two verbs, whose irregularity lies in the "L-AREA" forms (*je, tu, il, ils*). The *nous-* and *vous-* forms
conform to the stem of the infinitive. The present tense:

venir*

je **viens**	nous **venons**
tu **viens**	vous **venez**
il **vient**	ils **viennent**

L-AREA: IRREGULAR STEM

tenir*

je **tiens**	nous **tenons**
tu **tiens**	vous **tenez**
il **tient**	ils **tiennent**

L-AREA: IRREGULAR STEM

11.10   IDIOMS WITH **venir***

venir* [I]   **to come** [for the purpose of DOING SOMETHING]
           Jean-Jacques **vient voir** le professeur.
           Jean-Jacques *has come to see* the teacher.

venir* de [I]   **to have just** [DONE SOMETHING]
           Jean **vient de** VOIR le professeur.
           Jean *has just* seen the teacher.

In the imperfect tense, **venir* de** [I] means **had just** [I]

Jean **venait de** VOIR le professeur quand je suis arrivé.
    Jean *had just* seen the teacher when I arrived.

NOTE: *Only* the present and imperfect tenses can be used with this idiom.

11.11 VERBS CONJUGATED LIKE **venir***

revenir*	to come back	Il **revient** demain.
devenir*	to become	La situation **devient** difficile.
se souvenir* (**de**)	to remember	Je **me souviens de** votre sœur.

CAUTION: Distinguish between the following meanings:
    to *come* back   **revenir***   (The subject is *approaching* the speaker)
    to *go* back   **retourner**   (The subject is *going away from* the speaker)

Les Beatles **viennent** aux États-Unis. (Speaker is in the U.S.)
Plus tard ils **retournent** en Angleterre.
Les Beatles **reviennent** (deuxième voyage) aux États-Unis.
Ils **retournent** ensuite en Angleterre.

    If the speaker were in England, the account of the trips would be as follows:

Les Beatles **vont** aux États-Unis.
Ils **reviennent** en Angleterre.
Ils **retournent** aux États-Unis.
Ils **reviennent** ensuite en Angleterre.

Notice the special use of **devenir*** for *become of:*

— Et Georges Brun, qu'**est-il devenu**?   "And what has become of
                                                    George Brun?"
— Il a déménagé.   "He moved."

11.12 IDIOMS WITH **tenir***

tenir* à [I]   to be eager (anxious) to DO SOMETHING
tenir* à [N]   to value [N] highly; to prize [N]

Je **tiens à** OBTENIR une bonne note en physique.
    I am eager to get a good grade in physics.
Jean-Paul **tient à** *sa voiture.*
    Jean-Paul thinks so much of his car [*that he would never part with it*].

Verbes irréguliers
venir et tenir

retenir*	to remember; to retain
obtenir*	to obtain
contenir*	to contain
appartenir* (à)	to belong (to)
maintenir*	to maintain

Il est difficile de **retenir** tout cela.
    It is difficult to remember all that.
J'obtiendrai le dictionnaire que tu désires.
    I will obtain the dictionary you want.
Ce livre **appartient à** Marie.
    This book belongs to Marie.

Exercice 11C   *venir** et *tenir** [11.09 – 11.13]

Répondez à la question et ajoutez une deuxième phrase.

MODÈLE: Pourquoi est-ce que le professeur vient en classe?
        Il **vient** en classe pour apprendre le français aux étudiants.
        Les étudiants **tiennent à** parler une langue étrangère.

1. Pourquoi venez-vous en classe?
2. Comment venez-vous à l'université?
3. Est-ce que vous venez en classe le samedi?
4. Est-ce que les autres étudiants viennent en classe tous les jours?
5. À quelle heure retournez-vous à la maison?
6. Est-ce que votre mère est contente de voir revenir son fils (ou sa fille)?
7. Quand revenez-vous à la classe de français?
8. Combien d'étudiantes viennent en classe tous les jours?
9. À quelle heure faut-il revenir en classe?
10. Est-ce que vous retenez bien la poésie?
11. Est-ce que ce livre appartient au professeur?
12. Avez-vous envie de devenir riche?
13. Tenez-vous à obtenir une bonne note en français?
14. Qu'est-ce que vous tenez à la main en ce moment?
15. Qu'est-ce que vous venez de faire en classe?

Exercice 11T   Thème français

1. We want to see a new French play tomorrow evening.
2. One of my friends is going to buy all the tickets.
3. At present we are thinking of taking the bus.
4. My father refuses to drive his new car downtown.
5. He has just left the house (in order) to go to his office.
6. There is a good play Saturday, but there is a better play next week.
7. Don't forget to come to the house before you start out.

8. After attending Professor Coindreau's lecture on Tuesdays, I go back to the library to read.
9. I must study after I finish this letter to my former psychology teacher.
10. Sometimes I completely forget to hand in my homework to the professor.

Révision systématique

Starting with this lesson, each chapter will provide an exercise reviewing important structures and idioms from previous lessons.

1. We are going to visit France, Portugal, Spain and the United States. [1.04]
2. John is in process of studying mathematics right now. [2.11]
3. Professor Brun's sons are visiting the castles in Germany. [2.07] [3.02] [3.04]
4. My mother needs sugar, peas, bread, meat and apples. [3.12] [4.04]
5. The concert of the Orchestre de Paris takes place tomorrow evening at eight. [3.15] [10.11]

L'Église de la Madeleine (*Batchelder/Monkmeyer*)

12

INTERROGATION

PRONOMS possessifs

INTERROGATION

Questions may be divided into two categories: (1) those in which a complete sentence is made into a question, and (2) those in which the subject, direct object, or object of a preposition is unknown to the questioner, and is what he is trying to find out. The first type is discussed in 12.01–12.07, the second in 12.08–12.10.

12.01 **Est-ce que** + [COMPLETE SENTENCE]. By placing **est-ce que** in front of a complete sentence in *normal word-order*, a question is formed:

STATEMENT	Paul étudie l'anglais.	Paul is studying English.
QUESTION	**Est-ce que** ⎡Paul étudie l'anglais⎤ ?	Is Paul studying English?
	COMPLETE SENTENCE	

Elision occurs before a sentence beginning with a vowel:

Est-ce qu'il finit son travail avant cinq heures?

12.02 [QUESTION WORD] + **est-ce que** + [STATEMENT]. Additional information may be elicited about the complete statement by placing one of the

108

following words in front of **est-ce que**:

Pourquoi
Comment
Quand } est-ce que | Paul étudie l'anglais | ?
À quelle heure   NORMAL STATEMENT
Où

Thus one can find out *why* (**pourquoi**), *how* (**comment**), *when* (**quand**), *at what time* (**à quelle heure**) or *where* (**où**) for any situation.

If **est-ce que** is omitted, invert subject and verb:

Pourquoi Paul **étudie-t-il** l'anglais?

12.03 INVERSION OF PRONOUN SUBJECT AND VERB. Another way of forming a question is to exchange the positions of subject and verb in the sentence, and join them with a hyphen. This method can be used only with pronoun subjects, not including **je** [12.05].

Nous partons à neuf heures.	We are leaving at nine o'clock.
Partons-nous à neuf heures?	Are we leaving at nine o'clock?

When the verb form ends in a written vowel, the letter **-t-** is inserted before **il** and **elle**. This happens with regular **-er** verbs and with some irregular verbs.

Elle travaille à la librairie.	**Travaille-t-elle** à la librairie?
Il a fini le devoir.	**A-t-il** fini le devoir?
Il arrivera demain.	**Arrivera-t-il** demain?
	NO INSERTED **-t-**:
Elle est partie à midi.	**Est-elle** partie à midi?
Ils arrivent demain.	**Arrivent-ils** demain?

12.04 NOUN SUBJECT: INVERSION OF SUPPLIED PRONOUN. A noun subject and its verb cannot be inverted to form a question. Instead the sentence is left in *normal word-order*, and the appropriate pronoun (corresponding to the subject) is added after the verb, and hyphenated to it:

Marie travaille à la librairie.	Marie travaille-**t-elle** à la librairie?
Paul a fini le devoir.	Paul **a-t-il** fini le devoir?
Pierre arrivera demain.	Pierre arrivera-**t-il** demain?
Les étudiants font l'exercice.	Les étudiants font-**ils** l'exercice?

12.05 INVERSION NOT USED WITH **je**. With the pronoun **je**, use **Est-ce que** to form a question.

Je dois revenir demain.	**Est-ce que je** dois revenir demain?
I must come back tomorrow.	Must I come back tomorrow?

12.06 QUESTIONS BY INTONATION. Another way to indicate interrogation is by giving a rising intonation to a statement (shown in writing by the question mark). This is the most frequent way of asking questions in conversation.

Je dois revenir demain?
Marie travaille à la librairie?
Vous cherchez le professeur?

INTONATION

12.07 USE OF **n'est-ce pas?** To get confirmation of a statement (spoken or written), add **n'est-ce pas?** at the end.

Ces arbres sont beaux, **n'est-ce pas?**	. . . aren't they?
Paul est parti, **n'est-ce pas?**	. . . hasn't he?
Tu comprends, **n'est-ce pas?**	. . . don't you?

12.08 MISSING SUBJECT: **qui** [*who*]; **qu'est-ce qui** [*what*]. If the blank in your information is the subject of a sentence representing the answer, use

PERSON	**Qui** + VERB	who
THING	**Qu'est-ce qui** + VERB	what

Qui a une cigarette?	Who has a cigarette?
Qui va faire la vaisselle?	Who is going to wash the dishes?
Qui arrive?	Who is arriving?
Qu'est-ce qui arrive?	What is happening?
Qu'est-ce qui fait ce bruit?	What is making that noise?

Notice that the **qui** before the verb (in all the examples above) signals the *subject* of the sentence, whether for persons or things.

12.09 MISSING DIRECT OBJECT: **qui** [*whom*]; **que** [*what*].

A. SHORT FORM. Inversion is required after **Qui** (PERSONS) or **Que** (THINGS)

Qui regardez-vous?	Whom are you looking at?
Qui avez-vous vu au café?	Whom did you see at the café?
Qui cherchez-vous?	Whom are you looking for?
Que cherchez-vous?	What are you looking for?
Qu'avez-vous vu en ville?	What did you see downtown?
Que regardez-vous?	What are you looking at?

B. LONG FORM. Normal word-order is used after forms containing **est-ce**. Notice that a long form beginning with **qui** refers to a person; if it begins with qu' it refers to a thing. (The short form is preferred when the subject is a pronoun.)

PERSON	**Qui** est-ce que + NORMAL ORDER	**whom**
THING	**Qu'**est-ce que + NORMAL ORDER	**what**

Qui est-ce que vous regardez?	Whom are you looking at?
Qu'est-ce que vous regardez?	What are you looking at?
Qui est-ce que le chien déteste?	Whom does the dog hate?
Qu'est-ce que tu désires faire?	What do you want to do?

Observe that the word order (subject, then verb) is normal rather than inverted when the long form is used. This is particularly helpful when the subject is a noun (which cannot be inverted):

Qu'est-ce que |le nouveau professeur| a dit aux étudiants?

Qui est-ce que |vos parents| ont rencontré au bord de la mer?

12.10 MISSING OBJECT OF A PREPOSITION. When the information sought is the object of a preposition ("... *with whom* did you go down town?"), the following forms are available:

		EXAMPLE
preposition + WHOM	**qui**	avec qui
preposition + WHAT	**quoi**	de quoi

Avec qui allez-vous au concert?	With whom are you going to the concert?
De qui parlez-vous?	Whom are you talking about?
De quoi parlez-vous?	What are you talking about?
À quoi pensez-vous?	What are you thinking of?
Pour qui ton père a-t-il fait cela?	For whom did your father do that?
Sur quoi Jean a-t-il posé la boîte?	What did John place the box on?

Notice the use of inversion throughout.

Exercice 12A   Interrogation [12.01] [12.03]

Mettez les phrases suivantes à la forme interrogative, d'abord avec **est-ce que**, ensuite par l'inversion du sujet.

MODÈLE: Elle est catholique.
Est-ce qu'elle est catholique?
Est-elle catholique?

1. Il est médecin.
2. Elle va en France.
3. Il fait beau aujourd'hui.
4. Vous faites du camping en hiver.
5. Il y a un taxi devant l'immeuble.
6. Ils descendent à l'hôtel Lutèce.
7. Il a vingt-deux ans.
8. Nous faisons le voyage en avion.
9. On parle français au Canada.
10. Vous avez une voiture suédoise.

Exercice 12B Interrogation quand le sujet est un nom [12.01] [12.04]

Mettez les phrases suivantes à la forme interrogative selon le modèle.

MODÈLE: Ma tante arrive à midi.
Est-ce que ma tante arrive à midi?
Ma tante **arrive-t-elle** à midi?

1. Monsieur Lefort comprend l'anglais.
2. Madame Masson donne sa conférence à 14 h 20.
3. Ma cousine déclare qu'elle a mal à la tête.
4. Pierre et Jean ont envie de faire du tennis.
5. Cet élève a les pieds sur la chaise.
6. Ta petite amie a les yeux bleus.
7. Les employés ferment les portes maintenant.
8. Francine est en train d'étudier.
9. Notre professeur est de bonne humeur en ce moment.
10. Ces livres appartiennent à ma nièce.

Exercice 12C Interrogation employant *pourquoi, quand,* etc. [12.02]

Mettez les phrases suivantes à la forme interrogative, en ajoutant le mot entre parenthèses.

MODÈLE: Jeanne écrit une lettre au maire. (Pourquoi?)
Pourquoi est-ce que Jeanne écrit une lettre au maire?
Pourquoi Jeanne **écrit-elle** une lettre au maire?

1. Paul étudie la littérature russe. (Pourquoi?)
2. Michel parle anglais. (Comment?)
3. Le directeur part pour Vienne. (Quand?)
4. François prend le petit déjeuner. (À quelle heure?)
5. Vous étudiez tous les soirs. (Où?)

Exercice 12D   Interrogation [12.08 – 12.10]

Formez la question à laquelle répond la phrase. Imitez les modèles.

MODÈLES: (*Gérard*) met son dictionnaire sur la table
Qui met son dictionnaire sur la table?
Gérard met (*son livre*) sur le bureau.
Qu'est-ce que Gérard met sur le bureau?
Gérard met son stylo (*sur le bureau*).
Où Gérard met-il son stylo?
Gérard écrit avec (*un crayon*).
Avec quoi Gérard écrit-il?

1. (*Le professeur*) arrive toujours à l'heure.
2. (*Paul*) commande souvent du vin au restaurant.
3. Vos amis commandent toujours (*du vin*) au restaurant.
4. Auguste regarde (*la belle jeune fille*).
5. Marc écrit une composition avec (*un stylo à bille*).
6. Marguerite écrit (*son thème*) sur la machine à écrire.
7. (*Le professeur*) écrit des phrases au tableau.
8. Le professeur écrit (*des phrases*) au tableau.
9. Le professeur écrit des phrases (*au tableau*).
10. Le professeur écrit des phrases au tableau avec (*un morceau de craie*).

PRONOMS POSSESSIFS

12.11 USE. A possessive pronoun may replace a noun group beginning with a possessive adjective (like *son livre*, *ma table*). It may also replace a noun group showing possession by a *de*-phrase (*le livre de mon père*) [2.07].

The possessive pronoun must agree in gender and number with the noun group it replaces.

Avez-vous   **mon dictionnaire français**? (*m.s.*)
Avez-vous   **le mien**? (*m.s.*)

As with all pronouns, the noun replaced must have been mentioned so recently that it is fresh in the hearer's mind as the main topic of discussion. In the foregoing example, **le mien** could not be used intelligibly unless someone had been talking about **mon dictionnaire français** just previously.

The essential criterion for the use of possessive pronouns is the idea of *ownership*. Compare the following:

NO POSSESSION	Est-ce que vous regardez **la maison**?
POSSESSION	Est-ce que vous regardez **ma** maison?
POSSESSIVE PRONOUN	Est-ce que vous regardez **la mienne**?

12.12 WORD ORDER.   Possessive pronouns are located in the same "slot" vacated by the replaced noun structure. The order is generally the same as English.

Il a vendu **sa maison**.	He sold *his house*.
Il a vendu **la sienne**.	He sold *his*.
J'ai gardé **ma maison**.	I kept *my house*.
J'ai gardé **la mienne**.	I kept *mine*.

12.13 FORMS OF THE POSSESSIVE PRONOUNS.   A possessive pronoun must agree in gender and number with the possessive noun group it represents, that is, with the antecedent. (The *antecedent* is merely the previous mention of the noun group being replaced.) The possessive pronoun always requires two words: (1) the appropriate definite article, and (2) the pronoun itself.

ag

	GENDER OF THE REPLACED NOUN GROUP		
	Masculine	Feminine	Meaning
SINGULAR	**le mien** [lə mjɛ̃]	**la mienne** [la mjɛn]	mine
	le tien [lə tjɛ̃]	**la tienne** [la tjɛn]	yours
	le sien [lə sjɛ̃]	**la sienne** [la sjɛn]	his, hers
	le nôtre [lə notrə]	**la nôtre** [la notrə]	ours
	le vôtre [lə votrə]	**la vôtre** [la votrə]	yours
	le leur [lə lœr]	**la leur** [la lœr]	theirs
PLURAL	**les miens** [le mjɛ̃]	**les miennes** [le mjɛn]	mine
	les tiens [le tjɛ̃]	**les tiennes** [le tjɛn]	yours
	les siens [le sjɛ̃]	**les siennes** [le sjɛn]	his, hers
	les nôtres [le notrə]		ours
	les vôtres [le votrə]		yours
	les leurs [le lœr]		theirs

Pronunciation: The masculine forms rhyme with **bien**, using the nasal sound [ɛ̃]. The corresponding feminine forms end in [ɛn] with no nasal sound.

EXAMPLES

(1)   Vos fenêtres sont fermées mais **nos fenêtres** sont ouvertes.
      Vos fenêtres sont fermées mais **les nôtres** sont ouvertes.
      Your windows are closed but *ours* are open.

(2)   Jean apprend sa leçon et Paul apprend **sa leçon**.
      Jean apprend sa leçon et Paul apprend **la sienne**.
      John is learning his lesson, and Paul is learning *his*.

(3) Mes devoirs sont courts; **leurs devoirs** sont longs.

Mes devoirs sont courts; **les leurs** sont longs.

My homework is short; *theirs* is long.

(4) Notre maison est petite, mais **la maison des Morel** est grande.

Notre maison est petite, mais **la leur** est grande.

Our house is small, but *theirs* is big.

In each example, the first sentence contains a repetitious noun with a possessive adjective. This noun structure [*poss. adj.* + N] is the only kind replaceable by a possessive pronoun. The second sentence in each example illustrates this substitution.

Exercice 12E   Pronoms possessifs [12.11–12.13]

Remplacez les mots en italique par le pronom possessif approprié.

MODÈLE :   ma voiture et *ta voiture*

ma voiture et **la tienne**

1. mon cousin et *ton cousin*
2. ma cousine et *votre cousine*
3. ta mère et *ma mère*
4. mon livre et *votre livre*
5. mes classes et *leurs classes*
6. vos leçons et *nos leçons*
7. votre appartement et *l'appartement des Smith*
8. ta tante et *ma tante*
9. vos amies et *mes amies*
10. votre voiture et *la voiture de Paul*
11. Sa voiture est bleue, *ma voiture* est jaune.
12. Votre appartement est petit, *notre appartement* est assez grand.
13. La bicyclette de Pierre est toute neuve, *ta bicyclette* est vieille.
14. Mes professeurs sont sympathiques, et *tes professeurs*?
15. Je vais au théâtre avec les Brun. J'ai mes billets et *leurs billets*.

Exercice 12T   Thème français

1. Who is working in the store right now?
2. What are you doing in the kitchen?
3. To whom are you writing that long letter?
4. Are you looking for Paul's dictionary or mine?
5. What is behind that little round table?
6. Who is doing the dishes after dinner, your sister or mine?
7. What are those policemen looking for?
8. Why are you making the trip to Dijon by bus? The train arrives in that city earlier.
9. My motorcycle is behind the building. Where is yours?
10. Are you still hungry? Let's get a bite to eat at my house.

Révision systématique

1. We have been reading this play for two days. [9.04]
2. There's my old English teacher over there. She's very nice. [5.09]
3. It is probable that your parents and mine are at the movies. [5.14]
4. Look at the little old lady in front of the store. She's a very interesting person. [5.09]
5. Do you really want to learn to write Russian? It's difficult to do. [5.15]

L'aéroport Charles de Gaulle, avec ses sept satéllites (*J.J. Moreau*)

13

PRONOM complément d'objet direct

PRONOM EN

PRONOM COMPLÉMENT D'OBJET DIRECT *do*

~~~~~~

13.01 Identification of direct object.   To determine the direct object, quote the subject and verb, then ask "what?" The noun that answers this question is the direct object. (Notice that a prepositional phrase cannot be the answer.)

> Paul rend ses devoirs au professeur.
>
> Test: **Paul rend** [WHAT?]   Answer: **ses devoirs** = direct object

The prepositional phrase **au professeur** is an *in*direct object [14.01].

13.02 Position of the direct object pronoun.   (**La place du pronom complément d'object direct**)

A.   Pronouns appear before the inflected verb.

> Paul **rend** *ses devoirs* au professeur.
> Paul *les* **rend** au professeur.   (Before a simple verb)
> Paul *les* **a** rendus au professeur.   (Before the auxiliary verb)

B.   Before a dependent infinitive.   When the meaning is most closely attached to an infinitive, the pronoun precedes the infinitive.

Nous allons **voir le professeur**.
Nous allons *le* **voir**.
Je commence à **comprendre la leçon**.
Je commence à *la* **comprendre**.

C.   BEFORE A NEGATIVE IMPERATIVE.   When a command is negative, the pronoun appears in the usual place, before the verb.

Ne fermez pas **les fenêtres**.
Ne *les* **fermez** pas.

D.   AFTER A POSITIVE IMPERATIVE.   This is the only time the object pronoun follows a verb. It is attached to the verb with a hyphen.

Fermez **les fenêtres**.
Fermez-*les*.

E.   BEFORE **voilà, voici**.

Voilà la porte.   **La voilà.** (There it is.)
Voici le professeur.   **Le voici.** (Here he is.)

13.03   TABLE OF DIRECT OBJECT PRONOUNS.

(1)	**me (moi)**	me	**nous**	us
(2)	**tu (toi)**	you	**vous**	you
(3)	**le (l')**	it, him	**les**	them
	la (l')	it, her		

(1)   **moi** is used only after a positive imperative.

Regardez-**moi**.   Cherchez-**moi**.

When the command is negative, **me** is used before the verb.

Ne **me** regardez pas.   Ne **me** cherchez pas.

(2)   **toi** is used only after a positive imperative. In all other cases **te** is used in front of the verb.

Lève-**toi**.   Couche-**toi**.

(3)   **l'** is used when the following word begins with a vowel sound.

J'aime la musique.   Je **l'**aime.
J'apprends le proverbe.   Je **l'**apprends.

13.04 Neuter direct object supplied. The neuter direct object pronoun **le** is used when the verb demands a direct object, and none is in evidence other than a general idea. It may represent a noun, an adjective, or a whole clause.

— Monsieur Dupont va arriver demain.	
— Je **le** sais.	I know (**it**).
— Êtes-vous fatigué ?	
— Je **le** suis.	I am. (I am **it** = tired)
— Êtes-vous étudiant ?	
— Je **le** suis.	I am.
— Est-elle contente ?	
— Elle **l'**est.	She is.

13.05 Verbs requiring a direct object. The following verbs are followed directly by a noun in French. This contrasts with English, where a prepositional structure (*for*, *to*, *at* [N]) is used.

attendre [N]	to wait *for* (= to await [N])
chercher [N]	to look *for*
demander [N]	to ask *for*
écouter [N]	to listen *to*
envoyer° **chercher** [N]	to send *for*
payer° [N]	to pay (*for*)
regarder [N]	to look *at*

EXAMPLES

J'attends l'autobus.	I am waiting *for* the bus.
Il **cherche** son cahier.	He is looking *for* his notebook.
Il **demande** un journal.	He is asking *for* a newspaper.
Nous **écoutons** la radio.	We are listening *to* the radio.
Jean **paie** le repas.	Jean is paying *for* the meal.
Papa **a payé** la bonne.	Dad has paid the maid.
Envoyez chercher le médecin.	Send *for* the doctor.
Je **regarde** la télévision.	I am looking *at* (watching) television.

Pronoun substitution. The direct object pronoun may replace the direct object [N]:

Je **l'**attends.	I am waiting *for it*. [l'autobus]
Il **le** cherche.	He is looking *for it*. [le cahier]
Il **le** demande.	He is asking *for it*. [le journal]
Nous **l'**écoutons.	We are listening *to it*. [la radio]
Jean **le** paie.	Jean is paying *for it*. [le repas]

*Pronom complément
d'objet direct*

13.06 VERBS REQUIRING A PREPOSITION. Certain verbs cannot take a direct object in French, although they can in English.

A. Requiring **à** [N]:

obéir à [N]	to obey	J'**obéis à** mon père.
jouer à [N: game]	to play	Henri **joue au** tennis.
plaire* à [N]	to please	Cela **plaît à** ma mère.
promettre* à [N]	to promise	Il **a promis à** Jean d'étudier.
répondre à [N]	to answer	Je **réponds à** la lettre.
ressembler à [N]	to resemble	Vous **ressemblez à** votre frère.
écrire* à [N]	to write	J'**ai écrit à** mon oncle.

B. Requiring **de** [N]:

s'apercevoir* de [N]	to perceive	Je m'**apercevais de** sa timidité.
s'approcher de [N]	to approach	Il **s'approche de** la table.
douter de [N]	to doubt	Je **doute de** son succès.
se douter de [N]	to suspect	Je ne me **doute de** rien.
jouer de [N: instrument]	to play	Elle **joue de** la guitare.
se souvenir* de [N]	to remember	Je me **souviens de** votre oncle.
se servir* de [N] [16.07]	to use	Il **se sert d'**un stylo à bille.

Exercice 13A Pronom complément d'objet direct [13.02 – 13.05]

Répondez aux questions suivantes (a) affirmativement et (b) négativement, en remplaçant les mots en italique par le pronom complément d'objet direct approprié.

MODÈLES: Comprenez-vous *cette leçon*?
(a) Oui, je **la** comprends. (b) Non, je ne **la** comprends pas.
Est-ce que vous lisez *ce roman de Balzac*?
(a) Oui, je **le** lis. (b) Non, je ne **le** lis pas.

1. Comprenez-vous *l'allemand*?
2. La nuit fermez-vous *toutes les fenêtres*?
3. Aimez-vous regarder *la télévision*? [13.02B]
4. Regardez-vous souvent *la télévision*?
5. Vos amis écoutent-ils *la musique de Gounod*?
6. Le soir demandez-vous *la permission de sortir*?
7. Est-ce que vous trouvez *cette leçon* difficile?
8. Est-ce que les étudiants visitent *le musée*?
9. Est-ce que vous cherchez *le bureau du professeur*?
10. Avez-vous *les livres pour vos cours*?
11. Êtes-vous *fatigué* après vos classes?
12. Votre camarade (compagne) de chambre est-il (-elle) *sympathique*?
13. Avez-vous envie de voir *le nouveau film italien*?
14. Avez-vous besoin d'étudier *la grammaire*?

Exercice 13B   Pronom complément d'objet direct avec l'impératif [13.02 C, D]

Répétez les impératifs suivants (a) affirmativement et (b) négativement, en remplaçant le complément d'objet direct par le pronom approprié.

MODÈLE: Fermez *la porte de la salle de classe.*
(a) Fermez-**la**.   (b) Ne **la** fermez pas.

1. Fermez *les fenêtres.*
2. Cherchez *le dictionnaire français-anglais.*
3. Visitez *la cathédrale de Notre-Dame.*
4. Prenons *la voiture de votre père.*
5. Regardons *ces étalages.*
6. Étudions *les règles de grammaire.*
7. Finissez *le travail.*
8. Accompagnons *ma mère* en ville.
9. Lisez *cet article dans le journal.*
10. Mettez *la lettre* sur la table.

PRONOM en

13.07   USE.   **En** replaces a previously mentioned noun governed by a form of **de** (**du, des, de la, de l'**). The English meaning depends upon the context.

Il arrive	**de Paris.**		Il	**en**	arrive. (1)
Jean parle	**de la leçon.**		Il	**en**	parle. (2)
Il voit	**des soldats.**		Il	**en**	voit. (3)
Elle a	**des livres.**		Elle	**en**	a. (4)

de-PHRASE   **en**

The various contextual meanings for the examples are, in order, (1) *from there*, (2) *about it*, (3) and (4) *some*, replacing partitives [4.01].

A.   If **de** + [N] represents a *thing*, the whole prepositional unit may be replaced by **en** before the verb:

Il s'est approché *de la table.*   He approached the table.
Il s'**en** est approché.   He approached *it*.

Je doute *de votre sincérité.*   I doubt your sincerity.
J'**en** doute.   I doubt *it*.

Je me souviens *de cette gare.*   I remember this station.
Je m'**en** souviens.   I remember *it*.

B.   If **de** + [N] represents a *person*, do not use **en**. Instead, retain the **de** and add the appropriate disjunctive pronoun [28.07]:

Paul s'approche **de l'agent**.	Paul is approaching *the policeman*.
Paul s'approche **de lui**.	Paul is approaching *him*.
Je parle **de mon amie**.	I'm talking about *my girlfriend*.
Je parle **d'elle**.	I'm talking about *her*.

However, if the partitive (*some*) is used, **en** may replace even persons:

Je cherche **des agents**.	I'm looking for *some policemen*.
J'**en** cherche.	I'm looking for *some*.

13.08   **En** REQUIRED.   When a French sentence ends with a *number* or *expression of quantity*, **en** is required before the verb.

Il a deux autos.	Il **en** *a* deux.	He has *two*.
Elle a plusieurs chats.	Elle **en** *a* plusieurs.	She has *several*.
Il a vu trois amis.	Il **en** *a* vu trois.	He saw *three*.
Il lui reste une bouteille.	Il lui **en** *reste* une.	He has *one* left.

13.09   **Quelques** [N] > **en** [VERB]. . . **quelques-un(e)s.**   If the expression of quantity is **quelques**, add **-uns** or **-unes** when it is at the end of the sentence, and replace the [N] by **en**:

J'ai vu **quelques** acteurs.	I saw a few actors.
J'**en** ai vu quelques-**uns**.	I saw some.
Michel a **quelques** amies.	Michael has a few friends.
Michel **en** a quelques-**unes**.	Michael has a few.

13.10   WORD ORDER WITH **en**

A.   INFLECTED VERBS.   The pronoun **en** precedes the inflected verb. This means that **en** comes before the auxiliary in compound tenses.

Il voit **des soldats**.	Il **en** voit.
Il a vu **des soldats**.	Il **en** a vu.

B.   MAIN VERBS FOLLOWED BY DEPENDENT INFINITIVE.   When the main verb is followed by a dependent infinitive, **en** precedes the infinitive rather than the inflected verb.

Il *veut* ACHETER des livres.	He wants to buy some books.
Il *veut* **en** ACHETER.	He wants to buy some.

C.   NEGATION AND INVERSION.   In negatives and inversions, **en** clings to the verb, and becomes part of the verb unit.

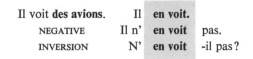

	Il voit **des avions.**	Il	**en voit.**	
	NEGATIVE	Il n'	**en voit**	pas.
	INVERSION	N'	**en voit**	-il pas?

VERB UNIT

	Il a vu **des avions.**	Il	**en a**	vu.
	NEGATIVE	Il n'	**en a**	pas vu.
	INVERSION	N'	**en a**	-t-il pas vu?

VERB UNIT

Exercice 13C   Le pronom *en* [13.07 – 13.10]

Remplacez les mots indiqués par le pronom **en**.

MODÈLE: L'argent? Pierre a beaucoup *d'argent.*
          L'argent? Pierre **en** a beaucoup.

1. La France? Ce vin vient *de France.*
2. Les marchandises? Ce camion-là est chargé *de marchandises.*
3. Vous m'offrez du café? Je prends *du café.*
4. Les étudiants? Il y a toujours *des étudiants* qui ont raison.
5. L'argent? Je n'ai pas *d'argent* actuellement.
6. Le vin? Albert a commandé beaucoup *de vin.*
7. Les poèmes? Nous sommes en train de lire *des poèmes.*
8. L'économie? Le professeur a parlé *de l'économie* en classe.
9. Des contes fantastiques? Aymé a écrit *des contes fantastiques.*
10. Des éléphants? Il a y plusieurs *éléphants* dans le jardin zoologique.

Exercice 13D   Le pronom *en* en conversation

Répondez aux questions suivantes: (a) en employant le nom complément
d'objet direct et (b) en le remplaçant par le pronom approprié.

MODÈLE: Cherchez-vous des stylos?
          (a) Je cherche des stylos.   (b) J'**en** cherche. (*ou négativement*)

1. Désirez-vous du café?
2. Attendez-vous des amis après la classe?
3. Avez-vous des disques de rock?
4. Est-ce qu'il y a de bons étudiants dans cette classe?
5. As-tu donné de l'argent à la Croix Rouge?
6. Est-ce que tu écris des lettres au président des États-Unis?
7. Votre livre de français vient-il de France?
8. Votre bureau est-il chargé de bouteilles?
9. Avez-vous des cigarettes?
10. Écrivez-vous beaucoup d'exercices?

L'aéroport

1. **un aéroport.** Il y a trois aéroports qui desservent Paris: l'aéroport Charles de Gaulle, situé à 27 kilomètres au nord-est de la capitale, est le plus grand et le plus moderne. Orly au sud et Le Bourget au nord desservent aussi Paris.

2. **l'aérogare** (*f.*). Les bâtiments réservés aux voyageurs et aux marchandises composent l'aérogare. Les passagers arrivent le plus souvent en autocar. Les voyageurs qui arrivent dans leurs propres voitures peuvent les laisser dans le parking. Les **salles d'attente** sont agréables et spacieuses. Pour aider les voyageurs à passer le temps il y a toutes sortes de boutiques à leur disposition: une librairie, un restaurant, une pharmacie, un bureau de poste, et d'autres.

3. **le personnel.** Dans l'aérogare se trouvent des représentants des divers compagnies (Air France, SAS, Lufthansa, British Airways, etc.) qui contrôlent les billets et s'occupent des bagages des passagers. **L'équipe** (*f.*) de l'avion comprend le pilote, le copilote, le navigateur, les hôtesses et d'autres.

4. **le vol.** On annonce les vols qui arrivent et qui partent. —Mesdames et messieurs: Air France annonce l'arrivée du vol 437 en provenance de Barcelone. Le vol 345 à destination de Marseille est prêt à partir.

5. **la piste.** Les avions **atterrissent, roulent au sol**, et **décollent** de la piste. L'avion qui est prêt à décoller attend le signal de la tour de contrôle, qui assure la sûreté des avions.

6. **la douane et l'immigration.** Les passagers internationaux qui débarquent passent aux postes de la douane et de l'immigration pour le contrôle des bagages et des passeports.

Exercice 13T Thème français

1. There are three important airports near Paris. Charles de Gaulle airport located at Roissy is the most modern.
2. All the airports have terminal buildings where the passengers wait for their flights.
3. At this moment there is a large jet liner for Barcelona at the end of the runway.
4. The pilot is waiting for the signal from the control tower.
5. Air France's flight 542 leaves Roissy at 12:35 P.M., and the plane is ready to take off when the runway is clear (free).
6. Lufthansa's flight 237 from London is landing right now; it is on time, and many passengers in the terminal are watching it begin to taxi.
7. Obviously most of the passengers have baggage [*use plural*] and they go to look for it before they pass through customs and immigration.
8. That young Englishman beside the soldier has one suitcase; his wife has two.
9. Some of the travelers are waiting for a connecting flight (*la correspondance*) and they pass the time in the shops or in one of the restaurants.
10. Our car is in the parking area. We have been looking for it for ten minutes.

Révision systématique

1. The whole family is visiting Nice and several other big cities in France. [8.07] [1.04] [3.10]
2. Before we have lunch we are going to see a seventeenth-century chateau. [11.06]
3. After we visit that historic building we are going to have something to eat. [11.07]
4. We are beginning to be acquainted with France and to meet some interesting Frenchmen. [11.04] [8.11]
5. My little brother is pretending to read a Russian book; actually he is not doing anything. [8.11]

Le Concorde, avion supersonique (*Photo Aérospatiale*)

14

Pronom complément d'objet indirect

Pronom y

PRONOM COMPLÉMENT D'OBJET INDIRECT

io **14.01** IDENTIFICATION OF INDIRECT OBJECT NOUN. To determine the indirect object, quote the subject and verb of the sentence, and then ask "*to whom*?" (**à qui**?). The indirect object *noun* will invariably be preceded by the preposition **à** (**au, aux**).

> Paul rend ses devoirs au professeur.
> TEST: Paul rend [**à qui**?]   ANSWER: **au professeur** = indirect object

In English the preposition *to* is often omitted, but by inserting it with the various nouns following the verb, the indirect object can be found:

> I gave my father the newspaper.
> TEST: I gave [**to whom**?] **to** the newspaper? **to** my father?

Obviously the indirect object is "my father" is this sentence. Remember that in French, **à** is *always* present in front of the *indirect object noun*.

14.02 POSITION OF THE INDIRECT OBJECT PRONOUN. The indirect object pronoun is placed before the verb.

A. In front of the INFLECTED VERB:

SIMPLE TENSE: Je ⏐parle⏐ à cette dame.   Je lui ⏐parle⏐.

COMPOUND TENSE: J' ⏐ai⏐ parlé à cette dame.   Je lui ⏐ai⏐ parlé.

B. In front of a DEPENDENT INFINITIVE:

Je voudrais ⏐parler⏐ à cette dame.   Je voudrais lui ⏐parler⏐.

C. In front of a NEGATIVE COMMAND (Negative Imperative):

Ne ⏐répondez pas⏐ à l'agent.   Ne lui ⏐répondez pas⏐.

D. After a POSITIVE COMMAND, joined by a hyphen:

⏐Répondez⏐ à l'agent.   ⏐Répondez⏐-lui.

14.03 TABLE OF INDIRECT OBJECT PRONOUNS (*io pn*).

me (moi)	to me	**nous**	to us
te (toi)	to you	**vous**	to you
lui	to him / to her	**leur**	to them

(1) The forms **moi** and **toi** are used instead of **me** and **te** following a positive command [14.02D]:

Le professeur **me** parle.   *but*   Parlez-**moi**.
Tu **te** lèves.   *but*   Lève-**toi**.

(2) The form **leur** [*to them*] is invariable, unlike the possessive adjective **leur** (*m.* and *f. s.*), **leurs** (*m.* and *f. pl.*), which agrees with a following noun.

Je parle **à mes amis**.   Je **leur** parle.

14.04 STRUCTURES REQUIRING AN INDIRECT OBJECT. The following verbal structures take an indirect object in French. (The word *to* may be omitted in English and could cause you to miss the structure in French.)

poser une question à [P]	to ask (*someone*) a question
obéir à [P]	to obey (*someone*)
répondre à [P]	to answer (*someone*)
dire* (*quelque chose*) **à** [P]	to say (*something*) to someone
dire* **à** [P] **de** [I]	to tell (*someone*) to (DO SOMETHING)

demander (*quelque chose*) **à** [P]	to ask (*someone*) for (*something*)
demander à [P] **de** [I]	to ask (*someone*) to (DO SOMETHING)
écrire* à [P]	to write ([*to*] *someone*)

The designation of a person would appear at the symbol [P], which is an indirect object, since it is preceded by **à** in all these structures.

EXAMPLES

L'avocat pose une question **au témoin**.	Il **lui** pose une question.
The lawyer asks the witness a question.	He asks him a question.
Le pilote obéit **aux directeurs**.	Il **leur** obéit.
The pilot obeys the executives.	He obeys them.
La tour répond **au pilote**.	Elle **lui** répond.
The tower answers the pilot.	It answers him.
Elle dit **au pilote** de décoller.	Elle **lui** dit de décoller.
It tells the pilot to take off.	It tells him to take off.
Je demande **à maman** de lire.	Je **lui** demande de lire.
I ask mother to read.	I ask her to read.
Paul demande un billet **à l'agent.**	Il **lui** demande un billet.
Paul asks the agent for a ticket.	He asks him for a ticket.

14.05 TWO PRONOUNS BEFORE VERB. When there are two object pronouns before the verb, the order is as follows:

1	2	3	4	5
me				
te	⎧le	⎧lui		
se before	⎨la before	⎨leur	+ [y + en] +	VERB
vous	⎩les	⎩leur	[14.07]	
nous	L'S LINKED TO VERB			

As an informal memory aid, it may be noted that (disregarding **y** and **en**) when two of the pronouns begin with the letter *l*, the order is alphabetical (*la lui, les leur*). When only one begins with *l*, it comes closest to (*l*inked to) the verb.

Il **me la** donne.   On **nous les** donne.

This same order applies to negative imperatives [14.02C]:

Ne donnez pas les livres à Pierre.
Ne **les lui** donnez pas.
Ne rendez pas cette machine à ces messieurs.
Ne **la leur** rendez pas.

14.06 POSITIVE IMPERATIVES: PRONOUN ORDER. When both a direct and an indirect object pronoun are used with a positive command (imperative) [14.02D], the direct object precedes the indirect object. The word order for pronouns is therefore as follows:

	1	2
IMPERATIVE VERB (**Donnez-**)	$\begin{cases}\text{-le}\\\text{-la}\\\text{-les}\end{cases}$	$\begin{cases}\text{-moi}\\\text{-lui}\\\text{-nous}\\\text{-leur}\end{cases}$

Notice that hyphens are used to join all the pronouns to the imperative.

Donnez les livres à Pierre.
Donnez-**les-lui**.   Give them to him.
Rendez cette machine à ces messieurs.
Rendez-**la-leur**.   Give it to them.
Donnez-**moi** ce livre.
Donnez-**le-moi**.   Give it to me.

Exercice 14A   Pronom complément d'objet indirect [14.01 – 14.04]

Remplacez le complément d'objet indirect par le pronom approprié.

MODÈLE: Lucien obéit *à ses parents.*
Lucien **leur** obéit. / Il **leur** obéit.

1. François obéit toujours *à son père.*
2. Obéissez tout de suite *à l'agent de police.*
3. Obéissons *aux agents de police.*
4. L'agent répond poliment *au touriste.*
5. Paul pose une question technique *au pilote de notre avion.*
6. Robert désire poser des questions aux députés.
7. Michel est un étudiant excellent: il plaît à ses professeurs.
8. Jean-Paul demande de l'argent à sa mère.
9. M. Lefort demande à cet étudiant de lire un paragraphe.
10. Le pilote dit aux passagers de rester assis.

Exercice 14B   Place des pronoms multiples [14.05 – 14.06]

Remplacez les noms soulignés par les pronoms appropriés.

MODÈLE: Charles écrit des lettres à des amis en Angleterre.
Charles **leur en** écrit.
1. Les étudiants posent des questions difficiles aux ingénieurs.
2. Les passagers demandent des renseignements à l'employée.
3. Le professeur demande à cette étudiante de lire la poésie.
4. Le facteur nous apporte une lettre recommandée [*registered*].

5. Le jeune architecte nous parle <u>des problèmes techniques</u>.
6. Nous rendons <u>nos devoirs</u> <u>au professeur</u> tous les jours.
7. Remettez <u>cette lettre</u> <u>à l'avocat</u>, s'il vous plaît.
8. N'apportez pas <u>le journal</u> <u>au patron</u> en ce moment.
9. Apportez-moi <u>les billets</u> demain, s'il vous plaît.
10. Ne dites jamais <u>la vérité</u> <u>aux espions</u>.

PRONOM y

14.07 Use. The pronoun **y** replaces (a) a prepositional phrase indicating location, (b) an **à**-phrase generated by a verbal structure, or (c) **là**. It is used *only* for things, never for persons. It appears before the inflected verb or dependent infinitive, like object pronouns.

(a) Jean est **dans la maison.**   Jean **y** est.   LOCATION
(b) Il répond **à la question.**   Il **y** répond.   VERBAL STRUCTURE
(c) Il reste **là.**   Il **y** reste.   [**là**]

When the prepositional phrase to be replaced by **y** follows an infinitive, **y** appears before that infinitive instead of before the inflected verb:

Je $\boxed{\text{vais}}$ **en ville.**   J'**y** $\boxed{\text{vais}}$.   INFLECTED VERB

Je voudrais $\boxed{\text{aller}}$ **en ville.**   Je voudrais **y** $\boxed{\text{aller}}$.   INFINITIVE

If the object of a prepositional phrase to be replaced is a PERSON, regular indirect object pronouns must be used [14.03] rather than **y**:

Jean répond **à cette lettre**.   Jean **y** répond.   THING
Jean répond **à son amie**.   Jean **lui** répond.   PERSON

In some cases such as **penser à** [PERSON], the prepositional phrase is retained, and a disjunctive pronoun is substituted for the noun [28.09B]:

Jeanne pense **à son grand-père.**
Jeanne pense **à lui.**   (**à** + disjunctive pronoun)

14.08 Locations replaced by **y**. Prepositional phrases designating locations may be replaced by **y**. Such prepositional phrases may begin with *à*, *dans*, *en*, *devant*, *derrière*, *sur*, etc.

Nous entrons **dans la salle.**   Nous **y** entrons.
Il retourne **en ville.**   Il **y** retourne.
L'autocar est **devant la gare.**   L'autocar **y** est.
La tasse est **sur la table.**   La tasse **y** est.

It is assumed that the location has already been mentioned, so that the meaning of **y** will be clear to the hearer.

14.09   **y** AND **là**.   These two words are synonymous only if *there* is meant. Word order is different, in that **là** comes at the end of a sentence.

> — Est-elle dans la cuisine?
> — Mais oui, elle est **là**.   (Elle **y** est.)

Informally, **là** sometimes means *here*, as in the following telephone conversation:

> — Est-ce que Marie est **là**?   "Is Marie *there*?"
> — Oui, mademoiselle, elle est **là**.   "Yes, she is (*here*)."

R   **14.10**   VERBAL STRUCTURES REQUIRING **à** (*Régimes*).   The following verbal structures include **à** + NOUN. If the noun refers to a thing (and has been mentioned already as an antecedent), the pronoun *y* may replace that prepositional phrase (**à** + NOUN). If the noun is a person, use the indirect object pronouns [14.03]:

assister à	to attend [*a function*]
jouer à[1]	to play [*a game*]
obéir à	to obey [*a person* or *thing*]
renoncer° à	to give up; to renounce
répondre à	to answer [*a person* or *thing*]
réussir à [un examen]	to succeed in; to pass [*an exam*]

The following may replace **à** [N] by the pronoun **y**; but if a PERSON is involved, the prepositional phrase cannot be replaced. Instead, keep **à** and use a disjunctive pronoun after it [28.09B].

faire attention à	to pay attention to
s'intéresser à	to be interested in
penser à	to think about
songer° à	to think about

EXAMPLES

Je m'intéresse **à la langue française**.	Je m'**y** intéresse.
Je m'intéresse **à cette actrice**.	Je m'intéresse **à elle**.
Pierre obéit **à la loi**.	Pierre **y** obéit.
Pierre obéit **à sa mère**.	Pierre **lui** obéit.
Gérard répond **à la question**.	Gérard **y** répond.
Gérard répond **au professeur**.	Gérard **lui** répond.

[1]**jouer de:** to play [*a musical instrument*]

Pronom y

y être*	to understand; to be "with it"
Y êtes-vous?	Do you follow me?
	Are you with me?
Vous y êtes!	You've got it!
Ah, j'y suis!	Now I understand!
y compris [N] (*fixed form*)	including [N]

J'ai étudié des langues, **y compris le russe**.
I have studied languages, including Russian.

Exercice 14C   Pronom *y* [14.07 – 14.10]

Remplacez par le pronom *y* une partie de chacune des phrases suivantes :

MODÈLE: Le patron répond *à la lettre du candidat*.
Le patron y répond.

1. Pierre va *au Havre*.
2. Je prends toujours l'autobus pour aller *à l'université*.
3. Nous allons *à Londres* en avion.
4. Son livre et sa montre sont *sur la table*.
5. J'ai envie d'aller *au Bois de Boulogne*.
6. Nous regardons les animaux *au jardin zoologique*.
7. *Au restaurant*, Roger a commandé du vin.
8. Il est commode d'aller *en ville* par le train.
9. Le bureau de mon père se trouve *dans un gratte-ciel*.
10. Il faut faire attention à la leçon.
11. Lucien obéit à la loi.
12. Je réponds poliment aux questions du touriste.
13. Mon camarade de chambre joue au tennis tous les jours.
14. Hier soir nous avons assisté à un concert de Mozart.
15. Est-ce que vous pensez aux prix qui montent?
16. Je renonce complèment aux cigarettes.
17. Suzanne Masson s'intéresse aux grands magasins de Paris.
18. Mes livres sont dans la bibliothèque [*bookcase*].
19. Je réussis toujours à mes examens.
20. La grand-mère du Petit Chaperon Rouge demeurait dans une chaumière.

Exercice 14D   Pronoms *y, en,* et pronoms complément d'objet direct et indirect

Remplacez les mots soulignés par les pronoms appropriés :

MODÈLE: Les passagers demandent des renseignements à l'agent.
Les passagers **lui en** demandent. / Ils **lui en** demandent.

1. Paul répond tout de suite à la question.
2. Paul répond au professeur sans hésiter.
3. Est-ce que vous avez besoin de mon dictionnaire?

4. Je n'ai plus de cigarettes, je regrette.
5. Pierre donne des cigarettes à ses amis.
6. Paul met les livres sur le bureau du professeur.
7. Voilà la jeune fille anglaise. Je voudrais parler à cette jeune fille.
8. Je vais à l'aéroport en autocar. Voilà l'aéroport.
9. J'ai beaucoup de valises; j'ai trois valises.
10. Envoyez chercher le médecin tout de suite!

Exercice 14T Thème français

1. Do you like the theater? There's a good play tonight, and Jean and Marie are going to see it.
2. Give the tickets to your father; don't give them to me.
3. Where is the employee? There he is. I am going to ask him some questions about [au sujet de] the display.
4. I am going to the airport. I need information [des renseignements] on flights for Geneva because I am going there next week.
5. Why don't you telephone? Ask your questions and the employee will answer them. It's easy.
6. "Look out! [Attention!] There's a tractor-trailer behind our car. Do you see it?" "No, I don't see anything there."
7. The boss asked me to answer these letters, so I am answering them immediately. I always obey him.
8. Tell your roommate to go to the dean's office as soon as possible. He wants to talk to him as soon as he arrives there.
9. When I return to my room, John always asks me if I am tired, and I say, "I am."
10. "How many connecting flights for London are there this afternoon?" "There are three. At what time do you want to arrive there?"

Révision systématique

1. Mr. Brun is a poor but happy man. [6.02]
2. There are some interesting new books in the bookcase. [6.02] [6.03]
3. There are several English boys in my class, and they are good students. [6.03]
4. Napoleon was a great man, but he wasn't a tall man. [6.04]
5. Jean-Paul gave his last cigarette to his old (former) German teacher. [6.04]

Vitrines de la Maison Cartier, rue de la Paix ; au fond, la colonne Vendôme (*Photo Cartier*)

15

Passé composé (auxiliaire AVOIR)

OUVRIR*

Passé composé avec l'auxiliaire **avoir*** tpc

15.01   GENERAL.   The *passé composé* is a verb tense dealing with events in the past; the form consists of two parts (it is *composé*), as distinguished from the *passé simple* which is a single-word form. The two parts of the *passé composé* are the auxiliary verb (**avoir** or **être**) plus the past participle:

Il **a posé** des questions.	He *asked* questions.	(aux. **avoir**)
Il **est arrivé** à l'heure.	He *arrived* on time.	(aux. **être**)

Most verbs use the auxiliary **avoir**; those using **être** are listed in section 16.03.

15.02   USE OF THE PASSÉ COMPOSÉ.   This tense is used to indicate actions that happened in the past, are fully completed, and occurred only once at a time specifically indicated or strongly implied.

L'employé **a ouvert** la porte à midi.	The employee opened the door at noon.
L'avion **a atterri** ce matin à 10 h.	The plane landed this morning at ten.

Notice that habitual past actions or actions in progress when something else happened are *not included* in the scope of the *passé composé*. Such actions are described using the imperfect [20.01].

15.03 FORMATION OF THE PASSÉ COMPOSÉ. Regular verbs form their past participles in a standard way shown below; irregular verbs must be learned individually.

A. FORMATION OF THE PAST PARTICIPLE (**le participe passé**). Drop the infinitive ending (**-er, -ir,** or **-re**) and substitute the past participle endings as follows:

VERB TYPE	DROP	ADD **PP** ENDING	EXAMPLE	MEANING
parler	-er	-é	il **a parlé**	he spoke
finir	-ir	-i	il **a fini**	he finished
vendre	-re	-u	il **a vendu**	he sold

The past participle must not be used alone as a verb, but always in conjunction with the appropriate form of the auxiliary verb.

Please turn to Appendix B (Model Regular Verbs) for a display of the complete *passé composé* of the three model conjugations: for **-er** verbs, **travailler** (verb 1); for **-ir** verbs, **remplir** (verb 4); and for **-re** verbs, **vendre** (verb 5).

pp B. PAST PARTICIPLES (*pp*) OF IRREGULAR VERBS. Learn the past participles of the following irregular verbs that use the auxiliary **avoir***. The complete *passé composé* is displayed in Appendix C.

VERB	PP.	EXAMPLE	MEANING
avoir*	eu	J'**ai eu** faim.	I got hungry.
être*	été	Il **a été** bâti en 1976.	It was built in 1976.
faire*	fait	Il **a fait** une promenade.	He took a walk.
lire*	lu	Il **a lu** la lettre.	He read the letter.
mettre*	mis	Elle **a mis** la table.	She set the table.
prendre*	pris	Il **a pris** les billets.	He bought the tickets.
savoir*	su	Il **a su** la nouvelle.	He found out the news.
pouvoir*	pu	Il **a pu** le faire.	He was able to do it.
voir*	vu	Il **a vu** ce film.	He saw that movie.
devoir*	dû	J'**ai dû** étudier.	I had to study.
écrire*	écrit	J'**ai écrit** la phrase.	I wrote the sentence.
dire*	dit	Il m'**a dit** de partir.	He told me to leave.
ouvrir*	ouvert	J'**ai ouvert** la fenêtre.	I opened the window.
tenir*	tenu	Il **a retenu** le livre.	He kept the book.

ag **15.04** AGREEMENT OF THE PAST PARTICIPLE (**Accord du participe passé**). The past participle for verbs compounded with **avoir*** is invariable, unless a direct object stands before it. In that case, the past participle agrees with that preceding direct object (PDO). The only words that can affect the ending of the past participle as preceding direct objects are the direct object pronouns (**le, la, les, l', me, te, se, nous, vous** [13.03]), the relative pronoun used as a direct object (**que** [23.03]), the interrogatives **combien de, quel** [21.07], **lequel** [21.08], and the exclamatory **que de** [17.05].

Agreement is made with a PDO in gender and number, using the same method as for agreement of adjectives [5.01]. Add **-e** to the basic form to make it feminine; add **-s** to the basic form to make it masculine plural; add **-es** to the basic form to make it feminine plural. Since the past participle agrees only with a direct object that stands before it in the sentence, the participle is invariable when a direct object *follows* it.

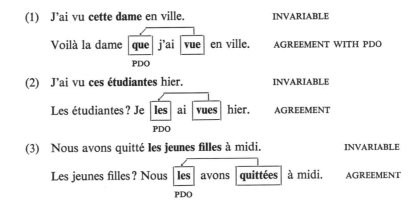

(1) J'ai vu **cette dame** en ville. INVARIABLE

Voilà la dame ⎡que⎤ j'ai ⎡vue⎤ en ville. AGREEMENT WITH PDO
PDO

(2) J'ai vu **ces étudiantes** hier. INVARIABLE

Les étudiantes? Je ⎡les⎤ ai ⎡vues⎤ hier. AGREEMENT
PDO

(3) Nous avons quitté **les jeunes filles** à midi. INVARIABLE

Les jeunes filles? Nous ⎡les⎤ avons ⎡quittées⎤ à midi. AGREEMENT
PDO

Other examples of preceding direct objects:

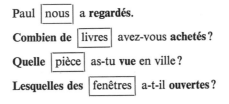

Paul ⎡nous⎤ a **regardés**.

Combien de ⎡livres⎤ avez-vous **achetés**?

Quelle ⎡pièce⎤ as-tu **vue** en ville?

Lesquelles des ⎡fenêtres⎤ a-t-il **ouvertes**?

Review the method of identification of a direct object [13.01].

TEST YOURSELF. Agreement of the Past Participle.
Supply the correct form of the past participle in the following problems. Cover the answer that appears on the line below each problem until you have written the necessary form.

1. Jean a ⎡trouver⎤ la lettre.
    TEST: Jean found what? DO is **la lettre**. It follows the verb, so there is *no* agreement: Jean **a trouvé** la lettre.

2. Les lettres ? Je les ai ⌐finir⌐.

TEST: I finished *what*? **les** is the DO, and since it comes before the verb, there *is* agreement: Je les **ai finies.**

3. Voilà la lettre que Jean a ⌐écrire*⌐.

TEST: Jean wrote what? DO is **la lettre**. Since it appears *before* the participle, there *is* agreement: Voilà la lettre **que Jean a écrite.**

15.05 INVARIABLE PAST PARTICIPLE.   In addition to the rule that past participles using the auxiliary *avoir* agree only if there is a PDO, notice the following two cases.

A.   Agreement is never made with **en**, even though it may be a PDO:

Il a vu *de belles statues.*	Il *en* a **vu.**
He saw some fine statues.	He saw some.
J'ai acheté *des tables.*	J'*en* ai **acheté.**
I bought some tables.	I bought some.

B.   When the past participle is completed by an infinitive (expressed or implied), there is no agreement (cf. [17.03]):

La dame **que** nous avons **entendu** *chanter* s'appelle Madame Brun.
Voilà la voiture **que** le soldat **a laissé** *passer*.

Exercice 15A   Formation du passé composé [15.03]

Terminez la phrase en y ajoutant la locution entre parenthèses. Mettez le verbe au passé composé.

MODÈLE: (*parler* avec le pilote) Hier Paul . . .
Hier Paul **a parlé** avec le pilote.

1. (*composer* une lettre) Ce matin je . . .
2. (*donner* une conférence intéressante) Monsieur Brun . . .
3. (*poser* une question) Le professeur . . .
4. (*avoir* mal à la tête) Hier soir je . . .
5. (*fermer* la porte) Jean . . .
6. (*écrire* une composition) Pour ma classe d'anglais je . . .
7. (*avoir* lieu hier soir) Le concert . . .
8. (*voir* des amis) Ce matin je . . .
9. (*finir* la leçon à 11 h) Le professeur . . .
10. (*commander* du vin) Les garçons . . .
11. (*attraper* une contravention) Le chauffeur de cette voiture . . .
12. (*visiter* les bagages) Le douanier à l'aéroport . . .

13. (*lire* un roman historique) Notre classe . . .
14. (*mettre* votre lettre à la poste) Votre cousin . . .
15. (*remettre* leurs copies au professeur) Tous les étudiants . . .
16. (*comprendre* l'explication de l'ingénieur) Tout le monde . . .
17. (*promettre* de ne pas fumer) Je . . .
18. (*faire* mes devoirs) Je . . .
19. (*assister* au concert) Nous . . .
20. (*réussir* à l'examen) Paul . . .

Exercice 15B   Accord du participe passé [15.04 – 15.05]

Remplacez les mots en italique par le pronom approprié.

MODÈLE :   J'ai appris *la leçon.*
              Je l'ai **apprise.**

1. Nous avons vu *cette pièce.* (Nous l' . . .)
2. Paul a écrit *cette poésie.*
3. Tous les étudiants ont préparé *leurs devoirs.*
4. Vous avez déjà lu *ce roman.*
5. Mes parents ont appris *la nouvelle.*
6. Pierre a fait *des fautes de grammaire.*
7. Les Dupont ont bâti *cette maison magnifique.*
8. Nous avons accepté *les livres* avec plaisir.
9. Le petit Robert a demandé *la permission de ses parents.*
10. J'ai su *la vérité.*

Exercice 15C

Répondez aux questions suivantes (a) en employant tous les noms, et (b) en remplaçant les noms par les pronoms appropriés. Faites attention à l'accord du participe passé.

MODÈLE :   Avez-vous préparé *la leçon*?
           (a) Mais oui, j'ai préparé *la leçon.*
           (b) Je l'ai **préparée.**

1. Avez-vous visité *la capitale*?
2. Est-ce que vos parents ont vu *votre école*?
3. Avez-vous fait *des exercices*?
4. Avez-vous fermé *la porte de votre chambre*?
5. Avez-vous regardé *les tableaux*?
6. Avez-vous donné *la réponse à la question précédente*?
7. Avez-vous conduit *la voiture de vos parents*?
8. Avez-vous passé *les examens de français*?
9. Avez-vous mérité *les notes que le professeur vous a données*?
10. Est-ce que vous avez compris *cette leçon*?

VERBE IRRÉGULIER ouvrir*

The following verbs are completely regular except in the present indicative and the past participle:

ouvrir*	*to open*	rouvrir*	*to open . . . again*
couvrir*	*to cover*	découvrir*	*to discover; to reveal*
offrir*	*to give, to offer, to present*		

15.06 PRESENT TENSE (**-er** ENDINGS). These **-ir** verbs are irregular in that they use the present tense endings for **-er** verbs.

*ouvrir**		*couvrir**		*découvrir**	*offrir**
j'**ouvr**	e	couvr	e	découvre	offre
tu **ouvr**	es	couvr	es	découvres	offres
il **ouvr**	e	couvr	e	découvre	offre
nous **ouvr**	ons	couvr	ons	découvrons	offrons
vous **ouvr**	ez	couvr	ez	découvrez	offrez
ils **ouvr**	ent	couvr	ent	découvrent	offrent

15.07 PAST PARTICIPLE. These verbs form the past participle in **-ert**. All are conjugated with *avoir**.

VERB	PP.	EXAMPLE
ouvrir*	ouvert	Il **a ouvert** les fenêtres.
couvrir*	couvert	Il **a couvert** son visage.
découvrir*	découvert	Il **a découvert** ce procédé.
offrir*	offert	Il m'**a offert** une cigarette.

Exercice 15D   *ouvrir** et verbes apparentés

Mettez les verbes en italique au passé composé.

1. On *ouvre* les portes maintenant. (hier à midi)
2. On *couvre* cent kilomètres en une heure et demie.
3. Georges *découvre* des fautes dans ses phrases.
4. Les élèves *offrent* un livre au meilleur professeur.
5. Nous *offrons* un cadeau à notre père pour son anniversaire.

Mettez les verbs en italique au présent.

6. Nous *avons rouvert* les yeux. Nous les *avons rouverts*.
7. Les savants *ont découvert* leurs projets au public. Ils les *ont découverts*.

8. Le garçon *a couvert* le plat d'un couvercle.
9. Je lui *ai offert* une place près de la porte.
10. Mon oncle nous *a offert* ses billets pour l'opéra.

Exercice 15T Thème français

1. My former roommate took a trip to Japan last year.
2. Columbus, the great explorer, discovered America over four hundred years ago.
3. You told me the truth, and you told it to the policeman, too.
4. I took the blue Peugeot this morning; I took it in order to go to the post office.
5. Your brother understands this fable. In fact he understood it when you read it to him the first time.
6. You put the typewriter on the floor. Why didn't you put it on the desk as usual?
7. Three Swissair flights took off for London this morning; my English friend saw them when they landed at Heathrow airport.
8. The books that you put on the bookshelf around noon are detective novels; I looked at them this afternoon.
9. I have eaten too much meat, and I drank three glasses of wine; how many apples did you eat for [*comme*] dessert? I had two [13.08].
10. Nobody has bought the tickets for the play yet; I ordered two, and Marguerite is going to bring them to us tomorrow.

Révision systématique

1. Jeanne is slightly absent-minded: she completely forgot to buy sugar, coffee, bread, and vegetables. [7.01] [4.01]
2. Perhaps she is going shopping later today and is planning [*penser à*] to buy them then. [7.05] [11.04]
3. The girls had to study their Spanish lessons, so they decided to stay home today. [7.05] [11.05]
4. At present we are absolutely certain that we are right: this thick door has been closed for several hours, and nobody has opened it. [7.06] [9.04] [10.05]

Révision lexicale

Matière et emploi d'objets

1. MATIÈRE. On emploie **de** ou **en** pour indiquer la matière dont un objet est fait:

une maison **de bois** *ou* une maison **en bois**	a wooden house
une robe **de soie** *ou* une robe **en soie**	a silk dress
une montre **en or** (massif) *ou* une montre **d'or** (massif)	a (solid-) gold watch

2. EMPLOI DES OBJETS. On emploie **à** + INFINITIF pour indiquer l'usage de certains objets:

la **salle à manger**	the dining room
la **machine à écrire**	the typewriter
la **machine à coudre**	the sewing machine

On emploie **à** ou **de** pour d'autres objets:

des moteurs **à essence**	gasoline engines
une lampe **à huile**	an oil lamp
un animal **à quatre pattes**	a four-footed animal
une salle **de réunion**	a meeting room, assembly room
une galerie **de peinture**	an art gallery

Attention! Distinguez entre **de** et **à**:

une tasse **à thé**	a teacup	PURPOSE
une tasse **de thé**	a cup of tea	CONTENTS

Montmartre et la Basilique du Sacré-Cœur (*Sodel-M. Brigaud/Interphototèque*)

16

Passé composé (auxiliaire ÊTRE) · Distinctions de vocabulaire · PARTIR*

PASSÉ COMPOSÉ AVEC L'AUXILIAIRE être* *tpc*

16.01 FORMATION. The fifteen intransitive verbs of motion listed in 16.03 form the *passé composé* with the present tense of the auxiliary verb être* plus the past participle. (All reflexive verbs also form their passé composé with *être*, as shown in chapter 19.)

Past participles are formed in the regular way [15.03A] for all these verbs except **venir*** [*venu*] and its compounds, **mourir*** [*mort*], and **naître*** [*né*].

The rule for agreement of past participles differs from that for verbs using **avoir*** as the auxiliary: verbs using the auxiliary être* have the past participle agree in gender and number with the SUBJECT.

The verb **aller*** forms its *passé composé* as follows:

je **suis allé(e)**	I went, I have gone
tu **es allé(e)**	you went, you have gone
il **est allé**	he went, he has gone
elle **est allée**	she went, she has gone
nous **sommes allé(e)s**	we went, we have gone
vous **êtes allé(e)(s)**	you went, you have gone
ils **sont allés**	they went, they have gone
elles **sont allées**	they went, they have gone

NOTE: The letters added to the past participle **allé** in parentheses indicate the various possibilities of agreement (**l'accord du participe passé**) with the gender and number of the subject. Notice that final **-s** is obligatory with the **nous** form since it is plural. Agreement with the **tu** form depends on the sex of the person being addressed. When writing French, select the one appropriate agreement. (In practicing writing full paradigms you might benefit by indicating all the possibilities as shown above.)

Examine Appendix C for further paradigms (displays of the forms) of verbs using **être*** listed in 16.03. Good examples are **venir*** (*vt* 30) and **partir*** (*vt* 20).

ag

16.02 AGREEMENT OF THE PAST PARTICIPLE, VERBS COMPOUNDED WITH **être***. When *être** is the auxiliary, the past participle agrees with the SUBJECT in gender and number. Agreement is made as though the participle were an adjective: add **-e** for feminine singular, **-es** for feminine plural, **-s** for masculine plural. The basic form is masculine singular.

Il est **arrivé**.	(*m.s.*)	Ils sont **arrivés**.	(*m.pl.*)
Elle est **arrivée**.	(*f.s.*)	Elles sont **arrivées**.	(*f.pl.*)

ATTENTION! This rule does *not* apply to *reflexive verbs* [18.01], nor to *monter, descendre, rentrer* and *sortir** when used with direct objects [16.05].

16.03 VERBS COMPOUNDED WITH **être***. The fifteen intransitive verbs listed below use the auxiliary *être** in compound tenses; compounds of these verbs (such as *repartir* from *partir**) also use this auxiliary.

All reflexive verbs are compounded with *être** also, but the rule for agreement of past participles is that pertaining to verbs using **avoir*** as an auxiliary [19.02].

If you learn these verbs, you will never be in doubt as to the correct auxiliary verb to use; any verb *not* learned as part of this group may be considered to use *avoir**. Notice the irregularly formed past participles shown in brackets.

Verbs compounded with **être***:

{ **aller***	to go
{ **venir*** [*pp.* **venu**]	to come
revenir*	to come back
devenir*	to become
{ **arriver**	to arrive
{ **partir*** (**de**)	to depart (from)
{ **entrer** (**dans** PLACE)	to enter
{ **sortir*** (**de** PLACE)	to go out
{ **monter** (**dans**)	to go up; to get into, on (*a vehicle*)
{ **descendre** (**de**)	to go down; to get off, out of (*a vehicle*)

⎰ **naître*** [*pp.* **né**]	to be born
⎱ **mourir*** [*pp.* **mort**]	to die
rester	to remain, to stay
tomber	to fall
retourner	to go back

prep **16.04** PREPOSITIONS REQUIRED AFTER **entrer, sortir*, partir*.** If a location is named after one of these verbs, the indicated preposition must be used.

Paul entered │ the house │.   Paul **est entré dans** │ la maison │.

He left │ his room │.   Il **est sorti de** │ sa chambre │.

He left │ the library │.   Il **est parti de** │ la bibliothèque │.

If no location is mentioned, there is no preposition:

Il est entré.   He went in.

16.05 TRANSITIVE USE OF **monter, descendre, rentrer,** AND **sortir*.** When used with the auxiliary **avoir*** these four verbs may take a direct object with the meanings listed below.

monter [N] (**avoir***)	to take [*something*] up(stairs)
descendre [N] (**avoir***)	to take [*something*] down(stairs)
sortir* [N] (**de** [N])	to take [*something*] out (*of* [N])
rentrer [N]	to bring [N] back

EXAMPLES

J'ai monté *le journal* à mon père.   I took the paper up to my father.

Les touristes ont descendu *leurs valises.*   The tourists brought their suitcases down.

J'ai sorti *un stylo* du tiroir.   I took a pen out of the drawer.

Paul **a descendu** le journal.   Paul has brought the paper downstairs.

J'ai rentré *les chaises* du jardin.   I brought the chairs back in from the garden.

DISTINCTIONS DE VOCABULAIRE *v*

16.06 SEMANTIC DIFFERENCES. Learn to distinguish among the meanings of **partir*, sortir*, quitter, laisser,** so that you may use them appropriately.

A. **partir*** (**de** [N]) means *to depart* (*from a place*), *to leave* (*a place*). If the place is mentioned, the preposition **de** is necessary.

| Il **part** à six heures. | He is leaving at six o'clock. |
| Il **part de Paris** à six heures. | He is leaving Paris at six o'clock. |

B. **sortir*** (**de** [N]) means *to leave, to go out of* (*a place*). This verb is used only for *to leave* in the sense of *going out* of some "container" like a house or room. If the place is mentioned, **de** must precede it.

| Il **est sorti.** | He has gone out. |
| Il **est sorti de la maison.** | He has left the house. |

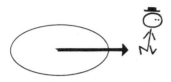

C. **quitter** [N] means *to leave* (*a person or place*), *to go away from* (*a person or place*). This verb cannot be used alone like **partir*** or **sortir***; the person or place left must be mentioned. No preposition is used.

Il **a quitté son ami** à la gare.	He left his friend at the station.
J'ai **quitté mon hôtel** à midi.	I left my hotel at noon.
Nous **l'avons quitté** à midi.	We left it (*or* him) at noon.

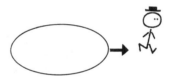

D. **laisser** [N] means *to leave* (*something*). This verb indicates that some object has been placed and left behind. That object must be mentioned (it is the direct object).

| J'ai **laissé mon livre** sur la table. | I left my book on the table. |
| Robert **laisse le pourboire.** | Robert is leaving the tip. |

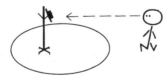

The structure **laisser** [I] + [N] means *to allow* (*something* [N]) (*to be done* [I]). Notice the reversal of order from the English equivalent.

Le professeur **a laissé partir** *les étudiants.*
    The teacher allowed the students to leave.
Le douanier **laisse passer** *les voyageurs.*
    The customs officer allows the travelers to pass.

Some common combinations of **laisser** and an infinitive lend themselves to simpler translation. For example, **laisser tomber** [N] may be given the equivalent *to drop*:

> La dame **a laissé tomber** *son sac.*
> The lady **dropped** her handbag. (The lady *let* her handbag *fall*.)

This structure may be compared with *causative* **faire*** [17.01].

Exercice 16A   Formation du passé composé [16.01]

Mettez le verbe au passé composé.

MODÈLE :   Elle *reste* à la maison.
            Elle **est restée** à la maison. Elle est fatiguée.

1. Je *vais* en ville.
2. Elle *vient* nous voir.
3. Ils *deviennent* riches.
4. Nous *arrivons* en retard.
5. Elles *partent* déjà.
6. Nous *partons* de l'école.
7. La jeune fille *entre*.
8. Nous *sortons* du cinéma.
9. Elle *entre* dans la salle.
10. Jean et moi, nous *montons* dans l'autocar.
11. On *descend* de la voiture.
12. Napoléon *naît* à Ajaccio.
13. Il *meurt* à Sainte-Hélène.
14. Nous *restons* longtemps à la soirée.
15. Richard *tombe* amoureux d'Elisabeth.
16. Les Beatles *retournent* en Angleterre.
17. Je *monte* le journal à mon père.
18. Il *descend* la machine à écrire.
19. Vous *sortez* une pièce de la poche.
20. Nous *arrivons* à la fin de l'exercice.

Exercice 16B   Le passé composé [15.01][16.01]

Mettez les verbes en italique au passé composé. Faites attention au choix d'auxiliaire (**avoir** ou **être**), et à l'accord du participe passé.

MODÈLE :   Nous *allons* à la Gare du Nord. Nous *prenons* le train de 6 h.
            Nous **sommes allés** à la Gare du Nord. Nous **avons pris** le train de 6 h.

1. Je *pars* de la maison à midi, et après le travail je *quitte* le bureau vers cinq heures.
2. — Je *vais* à la bibliothèque, dit-elle, pour consulter des œuvres de référence.

3. Elle *reste* dans la salle de lecture pendant une heure; elle *met* ses livres sur une table.

4. Elle *consulte* l'article intitulé «Italie» parce qu'elle cherchait des renseignements sur Venise, ville bâtie sur un groupe d'îlots.

5. En 1834, George Sand *tombe* amoureuse d'Alfred de Musset. Ils *voyagent* à Venise où ils *restent* pendant un certain temps.

6. Après avoir lu cet article, j'*arrive* à l'article sur Vienne, la capitale de l'Autriche.

7. Je *sors* de la bibliothèque et je *trouve* que la circulation devenait intense.

8. Des voyageurs *entrent* dans la gare; d'autres en *sortent* au moment où j'y *arrive*.

9. Ma grand-mère *vient* à Paris nous rendre visite, mais elle *retourne* chez elle dans l'après-midi.

10. Heureusement elle *revient* une seconde fois, et elle *descend* de l'autocar près de notre immeuble.

Verbes irréguliers de la famille de **partir***

16.07 PRESENT TENSE. **Partir*** may be grouped with six other **-ir** verbs having the same irregularity in common. All of them use only the first three letters of the infinitive as the stem for singular forms (except *courir**, which uses the full regular stem). In addition, these verbs use the present-tense endings for **-re** verbs, like *vendre*: **-s, -s, -t / -ons, -ez, -ent**.

INFINITIVE	MEANING	SINGULAR STEM	PLURAL STEM	PP.	(AUX)
partir*	*to depart*	je **par**-s	nous **part**-ons	**parti**	(être)
sortir*	*to go out*	**sor**-s	**sort**-ons	**sorti**	(être)
sentir*	*to feel*	**sen**-s	**sent**-ons	**senti**	(avoir)
servir*	*to serve*	**ser**-s	**serv**-ons	**servi**	(avoir)
dormir*	*to sleep*	**dor**-s	**dorm**-ons	**dormi**	(avoir)
mentir*	*to lie*	**men**-s	**ment**-ons	**menti**	(avoir)
courir*	*to run*	**cour**-s	**cour**-ons	**couru***	(avoir)

Examine the complete paradigm in Appendix C: **partir*** *vt* 20, **courir*** *vt* 6.

EXAMPLES

Je **pars** maintenant pour Londres.
  I am leaving now for London.
Nous **sentons** les effets de l'augmentation du coût de la vie.
  We are feeling the effects of the increase in the cost of living.
Cette machine **sert** à plier des feuilles de papier.
  This machine is used to fold sheets of paper.

Avez-vous bien **dormi**?

Did you sleep well?

Le garçon est entré **en courant**. [31.01]

The waiter ran in.

Exercice 16C *partir** [16.07]

Remplacez le présent par le passé composé.

MODÈLE: Paul *part* à midi.

Paul **est parti** à midi. Il est allé au cinéma.

1. Nous *partons* à midi.
2. Je *sors* de la salle à une heure.
3. Tu *sens* un courant d'air?
4. Le garçon *sert* la viande.
5. Le chat *dort* dans une boîte.
6. Martin ne *ment* jamais.
7. Le pilote *court* un grand danger.
8. Nous *partons* de l'immeuble avant 8 heures du matin.
9. Vous *sortez* un stylo du tiroir.
10. Les étudiants *dorment* tard.

Mettez le verbe au présent:

11. Alexandre *est parti* à huit heures.
12. Marie *est sortie* avec Albert.
13. Nous *sommes partis* avant midi.
14. Giovanni *a menti* au douanier.
15. Tu *as senti* que Jean avait raison.
16. J'*ai dormi* jusqu'à dix heures.
17. Tout le monde *a couru* voir ce film.
18. Évidemment ce flatteur *a menti*.
19. Tu *es sortie* de ta chambre?
20. Les Dupont *sont partis* pour la campagne.

Exercice 16T Thème français

1. My uncle and aunt left Paris yesterday: they drove to Lausanne. [1.08]
2. My girlfriend went into the library after she left us. [16.06C]
3. She went up to the third floor to find some history books.
4. Then she brought the books down to the reading room and put them on a table.
5. My cousin, a law student in Vienna, flew to Paris. She arrived at Roissy this morning.
6. She stayed in Paris for [9.04B] a week, and she returned to Vienna by train yesterday.
7. Then she came back to Paris in order to attend a lecture at the university.
8. Gertrude Stein, the famous writer, was born in Pennsylvania and she died in Paris several years ago.

9. Before they went to the station, the girls had something to eat.
10. I took some pencils out of the drawer and gave them to the students.

Exercice 16E   Sujets de conversation ou de composition

1. Décrivez un voyage que vous avez fait, en employant le passé composé des verbes utilisant l'auxiliaire *être* et quelques idiotismes choisis parmi ceux déjà étudiés.
2. Racontez l'histoire du Petit Chaperon Rouge (*Little Red Riding-Hood*) en la modernisant si vous le voulez.

Révision systématique

1. Our black dog is more intelligent than yours, but yours runs faster. [8.01] [12.13]
2. Your school is good, but ours is the best school in the neighborhood. [8.04] [8.06]
3. John writes well, but your cousin Marguerite writes better. She wrote an excellent poem recently. [4.08] [8.06]
4. All the short stories in our reader are interesting; each story has a complicated plot and there is lots of action. [8.07] [8.08]
5. Our pilot for this flight is very young, but he has been a pilot for six years. [8.09] [9.04]

L'École Militaire et le Champ-de-Mars ; au fond, la tour Maine-Montparnasse (*Bill Raftery / Monkmeyer*)

17

faire* causatif | laisser + infinitif | Exclamations

faire* CAUSATIF

17.01 Review **faire*** [8.10 – 8.11] and its forms in Appendix C, verb table 14. When this verb is followed by an infinitive, indicating that the action is accomplished by someone other than the subject, it is known as *causative* **faire.**

Je **fais** *bâtir* une maison.	I am having a house built.

Here, *fais bâtir* means "I *am causing* to be built" rather than that I am doing the actual building myself. In English, "I am building a house" generally means that I am having a house built for me by a contractor. In French, a differentiation is made by using the *faire* [I] structure whenever the subject is not the actual doer of the activity.

Notice that the inflected form of *faire* is immediately followed by (1) the INFINITIVE showing the kind of activity, then (2) the NOUN:

(1) (2)	(2) (1)
Elle **fait** *planter* des arbres.	She **is having** some trees *planted*.

This is quite different from English word order, where the noun follows the form of "have" being used. Because of the distinctive word order, you must pay special attention to the structure.

Il **fait** *chanter* Marie.	He has Marie sing.
Il **fait** *chanter* la chanson.	He has the song sung.
Il **fait** *lire* l'histoire.	He has the story read.
Il **fait** *lire* les élèves.	He has the pupils read.

17.02   OBJECT NOUNS AND PRONOUNS WITH **faire** [I].   When there is both a direct object and an agent (the person actually doing the work), the agent may be made into an indirect object, or **par** [AGENT] may be used:

Il **fait** *chanter* la chanson **par Marie** (ou **à Marie**).
   (He **causes** the song *to be sung* by Marie.) = He has Marie sing the song.
Il **fait** *lire* la phrase **par** l'étudiant.
   He has the student read the sentence.

Since the substitution of *à l'étudiant* for *par l'étudiant* in the above sentence would cause some ambiguity, it is better to use **par** [AGENT], remembering that since an **à**-phrase is possible, the agent may be replaced by the *indirect object* pronoun [14.03]:

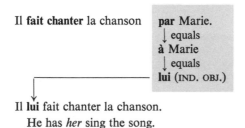

Il **lui** fait chanter la chanson.
   He has *her* sing the song.

The *direct* object may also be replaced by a direct object pronoun [13.03]; [*word order* 14.05]:

Il **la** lui fait chanter.   He has her sing **it**.

   The **faire** [I] structure is inseparable. Noun objects follow it; pronoun objects precede it.

TEST YOURSELF
Try the following, in writing. Cover the answer under each problem until you have written your solution.

   1.   I am having a house built.
        Je **fais bâtir** une maison.

2. I am having a sentence read.
   Je **fais lire** une phrase.
3. I am having the teacher read a sentence.
   Je **fais lire** une phrase **par** le professeur (or **au** professeur)
4. I am having him read a French sentence.
   Je **lui fais lire** une phrase française (une phrase en françai
5. Mary is having her car repaired [*réparer*].
   Marie **fait réparer** sa voiture (son auto).
6. She is having it repaired by a mechanic [*le mécanicien*].
   Elle **la fait réparer** par un mécanicien.
7. She is having a dress made.
   Elle **fait faire** une robe.

Exercice 17A *faire** causatif

Remplacez le verbe par **faire** causatif en y ajoutant l'agent entre parenthèses. Ensuite remplacez l'agent par le pronom approprié.

MODÈLE : **J'ai fermé** la porte. (à Robert).
(a) **J'ai fait fermer** la porte **à** (**par**) **Robert.**
(b) Je **lui** ai fait fermer la porte.

1. J'ai choisi un dictionnaire. (par mon professeur)
2. Le professeur a lu une poésie. (par Jacques)
3. Ma mère a mis la table. (à ma sœur)
4. Le patron a écrit une lettre au général. (par la dactylo)
5. J'ai nettoyé le garage. (par mon cousin)
6. Le ministre a bâti une maison magnifique. (par Brissac et Cie)
7. Avez-vous monté les valises ? (par le chasseur)
8. Le professeur a remarqué une faute. (aux étudiants)
9. Ma mère a fait une robe de soie. (à la couturière)
10. Le metteur en scène [*director*] a répété le dialogue. (aux acteurs)

Exercice 17B *faire** causatif

Remplacez *demander de* ou *dire de* par **faire*** causatif. Notez la cohésion de l'infinitif au nom suivant dans l'original et dans votre réponse.

MODÈLE : Le professeur demande aux étudiants de ⏐ lire une phrase. ⏐

Le professeur **fait** ⏐ lire une phrase ⏐ (par les) (aux) étudiants.

1. Le professeur dit à Paul de fermer la porte.
2. Papa demande à son ami de prendre trois billets.
3. Le douanier dit au conducteur de la voiture d'ouvrir le coffre.
4. Le douanier dit au passager de montrer son passeport.
5. J'ai demandé au mécanicien de réparer ma voiture.

6. Le patron dit à l'employé de mettre une lettre à la poste.
7. Ta mère demande à ta sœur de laver la vaisselle.
8. Les Dupont disent à leur architecte de bâtir une maison magnifique.
9. Le directeur demande à une secrétaire de polycopier plusieurs pages.
10. Le touriste demande au chasseur de monter ses bagages.

Exercice 17C   Thème français

1. Geneviève had a silk dress made.
2. The manager had three typewriters taken (*transporter*) to another office.
3. My father had the newspaper brought up to our room.
4. He had the bellhop (*le chasseur*) bring a few magazines up, also.
5. The boss had one of the secretaries write a letter to the mayor.
6. Jean-Paul had the waiter bring us two bottles of red wine.
7. We had two rooms reserved (*retenir**) for May twenty-third.
8. I had my new shirts washed by the hotel laundry. (*la blanchisserie*)
9. Then I had my secretary write a long letter to professor Legrand.
10. You had the concierge call a taxi, didn't you?

laisser + INFINITIF

17.03 laisser [I]. The verbs **laisser, entendre, voir***, and **regarder** may be followed immediately by an infinitive, forming an inseparable unit when the English equivalent *ends in a verb*:

Le soldat │ a laissé PASSER │ le fermier.

    The soldier *let* the farmer *pass.*

Nous │ avons entendu CHANTER │ Mlle Sills.

    We *heard* Miss Sills *sing.*

Je le │ vois VENIR │.

    I *see* him *coming.*

Nous │ avons regardé JOUER │ le chat.

    We *watched* the cat *playing.*

English speakers must be careful *not* to place the noun directly after these four verbs; to do so would break up the inseparable verbal unit.

    On the other hand, if the English equivalent does not end in a verb, but instead *ends in a noun*, the word order is the same in French as English:

    The soldier let the farmer cross the *border.*

    Le soldat │ a laissé │ le fermier │ **passer** │ **la frontière.**

We heard Miss Sills ̑sing *at the Paris opera.*

Nous │ avons entendu │ Mlle Sills │ chanter │ à l'Opéra.

I see the teacher ̑coming *into the room.*

Je │ vois │ le professeur │ entrer │ dans la salle.

Exercice 17D *laisser, entendre, voir* + [I] [17.03]*

Donnez l'équivalent français des phases suivantes:

1. We let Jacques buy the tickets.
2. I hear the lecturer speaking.
3. Do you see the teacher coming?
4. I have heard that said.
5. My father let my little brother drive.
6. I heard the policeman shout to the driver.
7. Did you see the train leave?
8. We heard the pilot speak to the crew.
9. The employee allowed us to pass.
10. He let the passengers go into the air terminal.

EXCLAMATIONS

A sentence may be converted into an exclamation by prefixing **que** [*How . . . !*]. Any noun may be converted into an exclamation by prefixing **Que de** [*What a lot of . . . !*] or **Quel** [*What . . . !*] to call attention to the quantity or the quality.

17.04 Que [COMPLETE SENTENCE]!; **Comme** [COMPLETE SENTENCE]!; [*How . . . !*]

	COMPLETE SENTENCE	
Que	ce monsieur est charmant!	How charming this gentleman is!
Que	cette leçon est longue!	How long this lesson is!
Que	ce voyage est difficile!	How difficult this trip is!
Comme	ce voyage est difficile!	

17.05 QUANTITY.   **Que de** [NOUN ONLY]! [*What a lot of . . . !*]

	NOUN	
Que de	livres!	What a lot of books!
Que de	soldats!	What a lot of soldiers!
Que de	café!	What a lot of coffee!

Exclamations

	NOUN	
Quel	général!	What a general!
Quels	soldats!	What soldiers!
Quelle	belle femme!	What a beautiful woman!
Quelles	maisons!	What houses!

Exercice 17E   Exclamations

Changez en exclamations les fragments ou les phrases suivants.

MODÈLES: Cette dame est charmante.
   Que cette dame est charmante! **Comme** cette dame est charmante!
   livres (*beaucoup de*)
   Que de livres!

1. Cette aérogare est grande.
2. Ce pilote est jeune.
3. Il est beau.
4. Cette étudiante est intelligente.
5. Elle est intelligente.
6. Ce gratte-ciel est énorme.
7. un bâtiment (*étonnant* [*quality* emphasized])
8. livres (*beaucoup de*) [*quantity* emphasized]
9. livres (*beaux*)
10. la musique (*délicieuse*)
11. La voiture est chère.
12. le prix (*trop coûteux*)
13. des fleurs (*belles*)
14. des fleurs (*beaucoup*)
15. Les fleurs sont magnifiques.

Exercice 17T   Thème français

1. Our psychology professor had us observe some experiments with rats. What unfortunate animals!
2. The director asked the secretary to bring in some coffee for his visitors.
3. Then he had her type a letter to the mayor. What a long letter!
4. She let him read it before she put it in an envelope.
5. Napoleon had his generals prepare plans for an invasion of Russia.
6. He let them work slowly and carefully. What preparations!
7. In Russia during the winter of 1812 he saw the soldiers suffer.
8. What a catastrophe! The Russian winter caused the French to be defeated.
9. We heard the tower tell the pilot to take off.
10. The English teacher let the students leave. He let them leave early.

1. I need your car (in order) to go to the bookstore. [3.12]
2. If you buy the tickets, I will go get the girls. [9.03] [9.14]
3. "How long have you been watching television?" "For half an hour." [9.05]
4. Don't be afraid. Answer all the doctor's questions carefully. [9.10] [8.07] [7.08]
5. What did you take out of that black box? [12.09]

Architecture moderne près de la Gare Montparnasse (*Helena Kolda/Monkmeyer*)

18

VERBES
PRONOMINAUX:
PRÉSENT
ET IMPÉRATIF

INFINITIF
PRONOMINAL

VERBES PRONOMINAUX

Reflexive verbs are called *pronominaux* in French because they require an extra pronoun before the verb. A reflexive verb has *two* pronouns: the subject pronoun and the reflexive pronoun, always in the same combinations (**je me, tu te, il se,** etc.). The action is said to be *reflexive* because it is reflected upon the doer: **il se lave** = he is washing *himself.* Sometimes the action is reciprocal: **ils se parlent** = they are talking *to each other*; **ils se battent** = they fight *with each other*; **ils s'entendent** = they get along *together.*

Many reflexive verbs also can be used non-reflexively, but the meaning is altered: **se lever°** means *to get up*, whereas the non-reflexive **lever°** means *to raise.*

> Il **se lève** vers sept heures du matin.   REFLEXIVE
> He gets up around seven o'clock in the morning.
> Il **lève** la table.   NOT REFLEXIVE
> He raises the table.

Some verbs exist only reflexively, although no reciprocal or reflexive action is involved. They simply require the reflexive form. Among these are s'en aller* (*to go away*), se souvenir* de (*to remember*), and s'écrier (*to exclaim*).

Il s'en va.   Je me souviens de lui.
He goes away.   I remember him.

18.01 COMMON REFLEXIVE VERBS. Listed below are some of the commonly used reflexive verbs, grouped by -er, -ir, and -re systems.

REFLEXIVE -er VERBS

s'adresser (à [P])	to address oneself (to someone)
s'amuser (bien)	to have a good time
s'appeler° [29.04]	to be named
s'approcher (de [N])	to approach (*sthg*); to go up to
s'arrêter (de [I])	to stop (*doing sthg*)
se composer de	to be composed of
se contenter de	to content oneself with
se coucher	to go to bed
se couper	to cut oneself
se débarrasser de [N]	to get rid of (*sthg*)
se décourager° [30.02]	to become discouraged
se demander (si)	to wonder (whether)
se dépêcher (de [I])	to hurry (*to do sthg*)
se douter (de [N]) or (que)	to suspect (*sthg*) or (*that*)
s'écrier	to exclaim
s'éloigner (de)	to move farther away (*from*)
s'en aller*	to go away
s'exprimer	to express oneself
se fâcher (de [N])	to get angry (*about sthg*)
s'habiller	to get dressed
s'habituer à [N]	to become accustomed to (*sthg*)
se déshabiller	to get undressed
s'installer	to settle down
s'intéresser à [N]	to be interested in (*sthg*)
se laver [N] [2.09]	to get washed
se lever° [29.02]	to get up
se marier (avec [P])	to marry (*sbdy*)
s'occuper de [N] or [I]	to take care of (*sthg*); to be busy with (*sthg*)
se passer (= arriver)	to happen
se passer de [N]	to get along without (*sthg*); to do without (*sthg*)
se peigner	to comb one's hair
se presser (= se dépêcher)	to hurry
se procurer [N]	to obtain, to procure, to get (*sthg*)
se promener° [29.02]	to take a walk (ride)

Verbes pronominaux

REFLEXIVE **-er** VERBS (cont'd)

se **réveiller**	to wake up
se **reposer**	to rest
se **tromper de** [N]	to be mistaken (about); to have the wrong [N]
se **trouver** (= être situé)	to be; to be located

REFLEXIVE **-ir** VERBS

s'**endormir***	to go to sleep; to fall asleep
se **servir*** de [16.07]	to use; to make use of
se **réunir**	to meet (*a prearranged gathering*)
se **souvenir*** de [11.09]	to remember (*sbdy, sthg*)
s'**asseoir*** (*pp.* assis)	to sit down
Il s'**agit de** [N] or [I] *invar.*	It concerns (*sthg*) or (*doing sthg*)

REFLEXIVE **-re** VERBS

se **rendre à** [N]	to go to (*place*)
se **rendre compte de** [N] or (**que**)	to realize (*sthg*) or (*that*)
se **plaindre*** (**de** [N]) [29.05]	to complain (*about sthg*)

18.02 REFLEXIVE PRONOUNS. The double pronoun combinations required with reflexive verbs are shown below. (In the third person, the subject pronouns *il(s)* and *elle(s)* can be replaced by nouns.)

je	**me**	demande	**nous**	**nous**	demandons)	
tu	**te**	demandes	**vous**	**vous**	demandez	} *I wonder, you wonder*, etc.
il	**se**	demande	**ils**	**se**	demandent)	

↑————REFLEXIVE PRONOUNS————↑

Elision occurs with reflexive pronouns before a vowel sound.

Je m'adresse à Jean.	Nous nous adressons à Jean.
Tu t'adresses à Jean.	Vous vous adressez à Jean.
Il s'adresse à Jean.	Ils s'adressent à Jean.

imp **18.03** IMPERATIVE FORMS OF REFLEXIVE VERBS. Review the use of the imperative [9.10]. In the command forms the subject pronoun is dropped and the reflexive pronoun is attached after the verb by a hyphen. In the *tu*-form, *te* is replaced by **toi**, and the verb ending **-s** is dropped if the preceding letter is **-e** or **-a**.

IMPERATIVE	DERIVED FROM	MEANING
Lève-toi.	tu te lèves	Get up.
Levez-vous.	vous vous levez	Get up.
Levons-nous.	nous nous levons	Let's get up.

IMPERATIVE	DERIVED FROM	MEANING
Repose-toi.	tu te reposes	Rest.
Reposez-vous.	vous vous reposez	Rest.
Reposons-nous.	nous nous reposons	Let's rest.
Dépêche-toi.	tu te dépêches	Hurry up.
Dépêchez-vous.	vous vous dépêchez	Hurry up.
Dépêchons-nous.	nous nous dépêchons	Let's hurry.

18.04 Negative imperatives. Reflexive verbs follow the general rule for imperatives [13.02C]. Normal pronoun order is restored in the negative form: the reflexive pronoun appears before the verb.

POSITIVE	NEGATIVE
Dépêchez-**vous.**	Ne **vous** dépêchez pas.
Lève-**toi.**	Ne **te** lève pas.
Approchons-**nous.**	Ne **nous** approchons pas.

neg **18.05** Negation of reflexive verbs. The verb unit for purposes of negation (and interrogation) consists of the reflexive pronoun plus the verb itself. Place **ne** before the verb unit, and **pas** (or alternate negative term) after it:

	VERB UNIT
POSITIVE	Nous	**nous levons**	de bonne heure.
NEGATIVE	Nous ne	**nous levons**	pas de bonne heure.

18.06 Possession or ownership with reflexive verbs. When the subject of the verb is also the owner of the body part or article of clothing mentioned, use the definite article alone (rather than a possessive adjective) to show possession [2.09].

Il se lave **les** mains.	He is washing *his* hands.
Van Gogh s'est coupé **l'**oreille.	Van Gogh cut off *his* (own) ear.
Elle se peigne **les** cheveux.	She is combing *her* hair.

18.07 Interrogative forms of reflexive verbs.

A. **Est-ce que** method. Place **Est-ce que** in front of a statement in normal order to create a question [12.01]:

Est-ce que | Van Gogh s'est coupé l'oreille | ?

Did Van Gogh cut off his ear?

Est-ce que | vous vous rendez compte de cela | ?

Do you realize that?

B. INVERSION. The verb unit (the inflected verb and all preceding pronouns except the subject) is placed first, the subject pronoun second. The verb unit is joined to the subject pronoun by a hyphen [12.03]:

VERB UNIT

NORMAL ORDER: **Vous** | vous levez | de bonne heure.

INVERSION: | Vous levez |**-vous** de bonne heure?

NORMAL ORDER: **Elle** | s'est | amusée à la plage.

INVERSION: | S'est |**-elle** amusée à la plage?

When the subject is a noun, leave the sentence in normal order and supply the appropriate subject pronoun after the verb unit, joined by a hyphen [12.04]:

VERB UNIT

STATEMENT: Alain | se passe | de voiture cet été.

QUESTION: Alain | se passe |**-t-il** de voiture cet été?

↑
SUPPLIED SUBJECT PRONOUN

INFINITIF PRONOMINAL APRÈS UNE PRÉPOSITION

18.08 REFLEXIVE PRONOUN IN INFINITIVES. When the infinitive form of a pronominal verb is used after a preposition [11.01], the reflexive pronoun *se* is changed to agree with the person involved in the action of the infinitive (if other than third person):

INFINITIVE

Nous sommes allés à Tivoli **pour** | nous amuser |.

We went to Tivoli to have a good time.

Il nous demande **de** | nous lever |.

He asks us to get up.

Vous êtes parti **sans** | vous procurer | les matériaux?

You left without getting the materials?

Exercice 18A   Verbes pronominaux [18.02]

Répondez aux questions suivantes.

MODÈLE: Nous nous amusons bien. Et vous?
Moi, je **m'amuse** bien aussi.

1. Nous nous adressons au professeur. Et vous?
2. L'étudiante s'approche de la table. Et vous?
3. Les autres s'arrêtent de parler. Et vous?
4. Paul se demande si le professeur le comprend. Et vous?
5. Nous nous dépêchons de finir le repas. Et vous?
6. Le professeur ne se fâche jamais. Et vous?
7. Paul se lève à sept heures du matin. Et vous?
8. Nous nous habillons à sept heures et quart. Et vous?
9. Nous nous dépêchons de prendre le petit déjeuner. Et vous?
10. Nous nous excusons de notre hâte. Et vous?
11. Nous nous occupons de nos leçons. Et vous?
12. Nous nous reposons un peu pendant l'après-midi. Et vous?

Mettez les phrases ci-dessus (excepté N° 6) à la forme négative [18.04].

1. Nous **ne** nous adressons **pas** au professeur.
   Je **ne** m'adresse **pas** (non plus) au professeur.

Exercice 18B   Verbes pronominaux

Complétez les phrases suivantes en ajoutant les mots entre parenthèses; mettez l'infinitif à la forme appropriée.

MODÈLE: Quand je suis en retard, je (*se dépêcher*).
          Quand je suis en retard, je **me dépêche**.

1. Quand je suis fatigué, je (*se reposer* un peu).
2. Hier les étudiants (*se réunir* à deux heures).
3. En arrivant, nous (*s'installer* dans la chambre).
4. Est-ce que vous me comprenez? Je (*se demander*).
5. Mes parents me demandent de (*se passer* d'auto).
6. Les touristes viennent à Paris pour (*s'amuser*).
7. Nous sommes allés à la pharmacie pour (*se procurer* des médicaments).
8. Le monsieur se lève et il (*s'approcher* du bâtiment).

Exercice 18C   Impératif des verbes pronominaux [18.03 – 18.04]

Employez l'impératif indiqué.

MODÈLE: *Dites à un inconnu de:* se rendre au bureau
          Rendez-vous au bureau.

1. *Dites à un inconnu de:* se lever / s'adresser à l'agent
2. *Dites à un inconnu de:* se dépêcher / se reposer un peu
3. *Dites à un inconnu de ne pas:* se fâcher / se dépêcher
4. *Dites à un bon ami de:* se contenter d'un repas par jour
5. *Dites à un bon ami de:* se lever / se coucher / se rendre au bureau
6. *Dites à un bon ami de ne pas:* se fâcher / se décourager
7. *Suggérez à tout le monde (vous-même y compris) de:* s'approcher du feu / se lever / s'occuper de la cuisine

8. *Suggérez à tout le monde (vous-même y compris) de ne pas:* se décourager / se tromper d'étage / se contenter de peu

9. *Dites aux autres de:* s'éloigner / s'installer au salon / rester plus longtemps

10. *Dites aux autres de ne pas:* s'occuper de la vaisselle / se presser / partir si tôt / se mettre en colère

Exercice 18D   Interrogatif des verbes pronominaux [8.07]

Mettez les phrases suivantes à la forme interrogative (a) en employant **est-ce que** et (b) en employant l'inversion.

MODÈLE: Jean se lève à six heures du matin.
(a) **Est-ce que** Jean **se lève** à six heures du matin?
(b) Jean **se lève-t-il** à six heures du matin?

1. Jean se dépêche de finir ses devoirs.
2. Nous nous rendons à l'école vers neuf heures.
3. Jeanne se met à étudier après le dîner.
4. Les jeunes gens s'amusent bien à la plage.
5. Le professeur ne se fâche jamais.
6. Vous vous occupez de la cuisine.
7. Tu te passes de voiture sans te plaindre.
8. Nous nous réunissons dans la salle 206.
9. Les Smith s'installent dans un petit appartement du quartier.
10. Tu te contentes d'un traitement [*salary*] de 200 F par semaine.

Révision lexicale

Le bureau

1. L'**ameublement** (*m.*) du bureau. Les meubles d'un bureau ne sont pas si nombreux que ceux d'une maison particulière. Dans le bureau du directeur de cette entreprise il y a deux bureaux, deux sièges, trois **classeurs** à quatre tiroirs, une table téléphone et une table pour **le duplicateur à alcool.**

2. Le bureau du directeur est plus grand et plus impressionnant que la table de travail de sa secrétaire. Monsieur a un fauteuil extrêmement confortable, tandis que la dactylo n'a qu'**une chaise tournante.**

3. Les **accessoires** (*m.*). Les bureaux ont tous les deux **un sous-main** en plastique vert, une **lampe de travail** flourescente, **une corbeille à courrier,** et, par terre, **une corbeille à papier.** Le directeur a **un répertoire téléphonique** qui le permet de trouver instantanément le numéro de téléphone de son correspondant. Il a **une calculatrice électronique** dans un tiroir.

4. La dactylo a un bureau moins élégant mais plus pratique. Elle s'occupe des **dossiers** et de la correspondance commerciale. Dans un tiroir elle a quantité de **papier à lettres** et d'enveloppes, des **trombones,** des **anneaux caoutchouc, une agrafeuse** et **un dateur** à encrage automatique. À côté se trouve **sa machine à écrire** électrique.

Identifiez les objets ci-dessous:

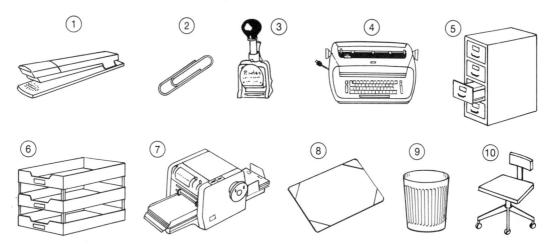

Exercice 18T   Thème français

1. Those gentlemen are talking to each other about [*au sujet de*] public transportation.
2. We content ourselves with earning very little money, but we have a good time.
3. My father asked me to do without a typewriter, so I am using a secretary.
4. What is happening in the street in front of that shop? An accident?
5. My name is Jean-Paul Poisson. What's your name?
6. The director's office is on the fifth floor. You are on the sixth.
7. Excuse me. I have the wrong floor. I wonder whether I have the correct address.
8. Little Gérard is in the bathroom. He is washing his hands and face [*la figure*].
9. Get up and go over to the secretary's desk; don't forget to tell her that you need a job application [*une demande d'emploi*].
10. Do you express yourself precisely? One must always speak softly and politely.

Exercice 18F   Sujet de conversation ou de causerie

Décrivez chronologiquement vos occupations quotidiennes habituelles. Servez-vous de plusieurs verbes pronominaux. Repassez la chronologie [10.11]. Employez (entre autres verbes): **se réveiller, se lever°, s'habiller, se laver, prendre* le petit déjeuner, sortir*, aller* à l'université, déjeuner, faire* (du sport), se reposer, dîner, s'amuser** (comment?), **étudier, se coucher.**

Révision systématique

1. My family has only one car. It's a Renault. [10.04] [5.09]
2. Nobody gets the wrong floor in this building; there's only one floor. [10.05] [18.01] [3.14]
3. I have not yet finished my homework for Tuesday. [10.03]
4. Our concierge told those little boys not to open that door. [14.04]
5. The first showing of the new Italian play takes place next week. [3.15]

La place de l'Opéra (*French Government Tourist Office*)

19

VERBES PRONOMINAUX: PASSÉ COMPOSÉ

VOIX PASSIVE ET PRONOM **ON**

PASSÉ COMPOSÉ DES VERBES PRONOMINAUX tpc

19.01 FORMATION. The *passé composé* of reflexive verbs is formed using the auxiliary *être**, preceded by the dual pronouns (subject and reflexive):

tpc **se laver**   to get washed   *pp.* **lavé** (être*)

je **me suis lavé**(e)	nous **nous sommes lavé**(e)s
tu **t'es lavé**(e)	vous **vous êtes lavé**(e)(s)
il **s'est lavé**	ils **se sont lavés**
elle **s'est lavée**	elles **se sont lavées**

Throughout the *passé composé* of reflexive verbs the pattern is the same: dual pronouns always in the same configuration:

je me suis	**nous nous sommes**
tu t'es } + *pp.*	**vous vous êtes** } + *pp.*
il s'est	**ils se sont**

ag **19.02** AGREEMENT OF THE PAST PARTICIPLE. The past participle of a reflexive verb agrees in gender and number with a preceding direct object

(PDO). This is the same as the agreement for verbs compounded with *avoir**
[15.04]. If a direct object *follows* the verb, therefore, there is *no* agreement.

Elle s'est ⬚lavée⬚.	s' is DO. She washed *what*? (herself)
Elle s'est ⬚lavé⬚ **les mains.**	DO follows *pp*. She washed *what*? (her hands)
Elle s'est ⬚acheté⬚ **une voiture.**	DO follows *pp*. She bought *what*? (a car)

It is not always easy to tell whether the reflexive pronoun represents a
direct or indirect object. The following lists provide guidance when in doubt.
The following reflexive verbs *always* have agreement of the past participle
with a PDO:

s'apercevoir* de [N]	to notice, to perceive [N]
s'approcher (de [N])	to approach (*sthg*)
s'arrêter (de [I])	to stop (*doing sthg*)
se douter (de [N]) or (**que** [C][1])	to suspect (*sthg*) *or* (that [C])
s'écrier	to exclaim
s'en aller*	to go away
s'endormir*	to fall asleep; to go to sleep
se lever°	to get up
se servir* de	to use, to make use of
se souvenir* de [N]	to remember (*sbdy*, *sthg*)
se tromper (de [N])	to be mistaken; to have the wrong [N]

The following reflexive verbs *never* have agreement of the past participle:

se plaire*	to be pleased
se parler	to talk to one another
se ressembler	to resemble one another
se sourire*	to smile at each other
se succéder°	to follow one another
Ils se sont parlé.	They spoke to each other.

Agreement of the past participle with the PDO (i.e., reflexive pronoun) should
be made with other verbs.

EXAMPLES

Elle **s'est** serv*ie* d'un stylo.	(**se servir** always agrees)
Elles **se sont** souri.	(**se sourire** never agrees)
Elle **s'est demandée** s'il venait.	(not listed: make agreement)
Elle **s'est** pass*ée* de voiture.	(not listed: make agreement)

[1]The symbol [C] indicates that a clause would appear at this position.

19.03 INTERROGATION: INVERSION METHOD. The verb unit [10.01] consists of the reflexive pronoun plus the auxiliary verb (for example, **me suis, s'est**). Reverse the order of subject and verb unit for interrogation. (Note that the past participle is not involved.)

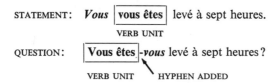

STATEMENT: *Vous* | vous êtes | levé à sept heures.

VERB UNIT

QUESTION: | Vous êtes | *-vous* levé à sept heures?

VERB UNIT   HYPHEN ADDED

Noun Subject: Supplied Pronoun. If the subject is a noun instead of a pronoun, leave the sentence in *normal order*, and supply the appropriate subject pronoun (corresponding to the subject noun) after the verb unit, joining them with a hyphen.

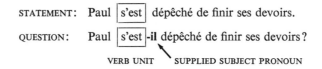

STATEMENT: Paul | s'est | dépêché de finir ses devoirs.

QUESTION: Paul | s'est | *-il* dépêché de finir ses devoirs?

VERB UNIT   SUPPLIED SUBJECT PRONOUN

INTERROGATION: **Est-ce que** METHOD. The **Est-ce que** method may be used, placing this expression in front of the statement in normal order:

Est-ce que | vous vous êtes levé à sept heures |?

NORMAL ORDER

When the subject is *je*, **est-ce que** is mandatory.

19.04 NEGATION. Place the verb unit between **ne . . . pas** (or other negative expression):

VERB UNIT

Vous **ne** | **vous êtes** | **pas** levé à sept heures ce matin.

Paul **ne** | **s'est** | **pas** dépêché de finir ses devoirs.

19.05 NEGATIVE QUESTION. In making a negative question, first create the question by inversion [19.03], then place the new expanded verb unit (now including the hyphenated subject pronoun) between **ne . . . pas**:

EXPANDED VERB UNIT

(a) | **Vous êtes-*vous*** | levé à sept heures ce matin?

(b) **Ne** | **vous êtes-*vous*** | **pas** levé à sept heures ce matin?

   Didn't you get up at seven o'clock this morning?

Exercice 19A   Passé composé

Mettez les phrases suivantes au passé composé.

MODÈLES :   Paul se couche à minuit.
Paul **s'est couché** à minuit.
Il dort bien.
Il **a** bien **dormi**. [7.01A]

1. Paul se réveille à six heures et demie.
2. Il se lève tout de suite.
3. Il s'habille en hâte.
4. Il se lave les mains et la figure.
5. Il prend son petit déjeuner.
6. Il sort pour aller à l'université.
7. Il arrive en classe à huit heures.
8. Il s'installe à sa place.
9. Après la classe il se repose un peu.
10. Il déjeune à midi.
11. Il fait du tennis avec un ami.
12. Il se repose après le match.
13. Il dîne avec sa famille à sept heures.
14. Il s'occupe de ses leçons.
15. Il se couche vers onze heures.

Exercice 19B   Accord du participe passé [19.02]

Mettez les phrases suivantes au passé composé, en faisant attention à l'accord du participe passé.

MODÈLE :   Marie se lave avant le petit déjeuner.
Marie **s'est lavée** avant le petit déjeuner.

1. Marie se lève de bonne heure.
2. Elle se lave les mains.
3. Elle se dépêche de faire la vaisselle.
4. Voilà la voiture que Robert s'achète.
5. Jeanne se procure une boîte en bois.
6. Nous nous occupons de la leçon.
7. La famille se réveille vers sept heures.
8. Cette belle jeune fille se marie avec Jean-Paul Masson.
9. Les étudiants s'installent dans la bibliothèque.
10. Ils se demandent si le professeur se fâche.

Exercice 19C   Interrogation [19.03]

Mettez à l'interrogatif vos réponses à l'exercice précédent (à l'exception du numéro 4), (a) en vous servant de **est-ce que** et (b) en utilisant l'inversion.

MODÈLE :   Marie s'est lavée avant le petit déjeuner.
(a) **Est-ce que** Marie s'est lavée avant le petit déjeuner?
(b) Marie **s'est-elle lavée** avant le petit déjeuner?

Exercice 19D   Négation [19.04]

Mettez les phrases suivantes à la forme négative.

MODÈLE :   Nous nous sommes découragés.
Nous **ne nous sommes pas** découragés.

1. Ce monsieur s'est approché du bureau.
2. Le poids-lourd s'est arrêté au feu rouge.
3. Le pilote s'est occupé du débarquement des passagers.
4. La concierge s'est contentée de bavarder.
5. Vous vous êtes trompé de vol.

Exercice 19E   Interrogation négative [19.05]

Mettez les phrases suivantes (a) à la forme interrogative en utilisant l'inversion, et ensuite (b) à la forme négative de l'interrogation.

MODÈLE :   Ils se sont réveillés à six heures.
(a) **Se sont-ils** réveillés à six heures?
(b) **Ne se sont-ils pas** réveillés à six heures?

1. Georges s'est dépêché d'aller à Roissy.
2. Vous vous êtes demandés si l'avion est en retard.
3. Tu peux te passer de voiture.
4. Nous nous sommes trompés de gare.
5. Les étudiantes se sont réunies dans la grande salle.

VOIX PASSIVE ET PRONOM on

19.06   IDENTIFICATION OF THE PASSIVE.   The passive is much more frequently used in English than in French. In speaking and writing French, avoid passive constructions by rephrasing your thought. In the *passive*, the subject is acted upon. In *active* constructions, the subject is the *doer* of the action indicated by the verb.

PASSIVE   Our dog was killed by a car.
ACTIVE   A car killed our dog.   *Une voiture a tué notre chien.*

PASSIVE   French is spoken in Canada.
ACTIVE   They speak French in Canada.   *On parle français au Canada.*

PASSIVE   He is admired by everybody.
ACTIVE   Everybody admires him.   *Tout le monde l'admire.*

176

19.07 Use of pronoun **on** to avoid a passive. Most sentences which occur to the English mind in the passive form can be recast into the active form. If the agent (doer of the action) is not mentioned, the pronoun **on** can be used as a subject.

The house is seen in the distance.	PASSIVE
= One sees the house in the distance.	ACTIVE
On voit la maison dans le lointain.	
The doors were closed at 1:30.	PASSIVE
= One closed the doors at 1:30.	ACTIVE
On a fermé les portes à 1 h 30.	
The teacher was given a prize.	PASSIVE
= They gave the teacher a prize.	ACTIVE
On a offert un prix au professeur.	

If the agent *is* mentioned, simply use that agent as the subject and recast the sentence into active construction. (**On** is not needed.)

John was given a book *by the teacher.*
= *The teacher* gave John a book.
Le professeur a donné un livre à Jean.

19.08 Reflexive verbs replacing the passive. Certain verbs are sometimes used reflexively to avoid the passive. Among these are **se composer de** [*to be composed of*], **se diviser en** [*to be divided into*], **se dire** [*to be said*], **se vendre** [*to be sold*].

La symphonie **se divise en** quatre mouvements.
   The symphony *is divided into* four movements.
Cela ne **se dit** pas.
   That *is* not *said.*
Le livre **se compose de** douze chapitres.
   The book *is composed of* twelve chapters.
Les portes **se ferment** à midi.
   The doors *are closed* at noon.
Le tabac **se vend** ici.
   Tobacco *is sold* here.
L'électricité **s'utilise** partout.
   Electricity *is used* everywhere.

The last three examples could just as well be made active by using **on**:

On ferme les portes à midi.
On vend le tabac ici.
On utilise l'électricité partout.

19.09 TRUE PASSIVE VOICE. The passive may be formed (as in English) by using any tense of **être** + [PAST PARTICIPLE]. The past participle agrees in gender and number with the subject. [Review 16.02]

> **être** + *pp.*

> Il **a été puni** par son père.
> Elles **ont été punies** par leur père.
> La maison **a été bâtie** en 1976.

19.10 USE OF **de** OR **par** AS AGENT WITH THE PASSIVE. When the passive voice is used, **de** + [AGENT] usually indicates a static situation; **par** + [ACTIVE AGENT] indicates action.

> Notre chien **a été écrasé par** un camion. (*action*)
> Our dog was run over by a truck.
> M. Leclerc **est admiré de** tout le monde. (*static*)
> Mr. Leclerc is admired by everybody.
> La maison **était entourée d'**un mur. (*static*)
> The house was surrounded by a wall.
> Les voitures **sont examinées par** leur propriétaire. (*action*)
> The cars are examined by their owner.
> Les arbres **ont été couverts de** neige. (*static*)
> The trees have been covered with snow.

Exercice 19F   Pour éviter la voix passive [19.06 – 19.10]

Mettez les phrases suivantes à la voix active.

MODÈLES: M. Leclerc est admiré.
On admire M. Leclerc.
Notre maison a été bâtie en 1974.
On a bâti notre maison en 1974.

1. Ma voiture a été réparée.
2. Mon stylo a été perdu par mon frère.
3. Les portes ont été fermées avant neuf heures.
4. Cette symphonie a été composée au dix-neuvième siècle.
5. Ma bicyclette a été volée [*stolen*].
6. Notre voiture a été réparée par le mécanicien.
7. Cette pièce a été représentée pour la première fois à Paris.
8. Cette pièce a été représentée par la Comédie-Française.
9. Ma composition a été corrigée par le professeur.
10. Ma composition a été corrigée.
11. Les phrases anglaises ont été répétées.
12. Les phrases italiennes ont été répétées par les étudiants.
13. La machine à écrire a été vendue.
14. Le tabac est vendu ici.
15. Cette fenêtre a été ouverte ce matin.

16. Le petit Jean a été puni.
17. Les boutiques sont fermées au mois d'août.
18. Un livre a été offert au meilleur élève.
19. La ville est divisée en vingt arrondissements.
20. L'heure de la réunion a été fixée.

Exercice 19G   Sujet de composition ou de causerie

Racontez une journée passée de votre vie, en imitant à peu près les événements de la vie de Paul (Exercice 19A). Développez un peu en donnant quelques détails intéressants. Servez-vous également de quelques idiotismes et du pronom *on*.

Révision
systématique

1. Does your connecting flight leave from Roissy? [12.01] [16.07]
2. Why does the postman complain about our dog so often? [12.02] [18.08]
3. At what time does your plane arrive in Geneva? [12.02]
4. It's a question of doing without luxuries [**le superflu** *s.*], isn't it? [18.01] [12.07]
5. What are you reading? What's going on? [12.09] [18.01]

Intérieur de la Maison Guerlain (*Photo Almasy-Gerlain*)

20

Imparfait Plus-que-parfait

IMPARFAIT (IMPERFECT TENSE) *ti*

~~~~~~

20.01 GENERAL. The *imparfait* is a past tense. It indicates continuing action (or state of being) in the past, action that was *habitual* or occurred time and again. A key to deciding whether to use this tense is that there is *no clear indication of the time of beginning or ending* of the action described. (The word "imperfect" means not completed.)

In narration the imperfect is used to describe *background* information, while the *passé composé* indicates specific actions and events carried out against the background [20.05].

20.02 FORMATION. The imperfect is the most regularly formed tense. Both regular and irregular verbs (except *être*) follow the same system. For the stem (*le radical*), use the *nous*-form of the present tense, dropping the **-ons** ending, and add the following endings of the imperfect:

-ais	**-ions**
-ais	**-iez**
-ait	**-aient**

In the imperfect the verb **travailler** uses the stem **travaill-** (from **nous travaill-ons** *tp*). This is a typical example of the formation of the imperfect:

je travaill**ais**	nous travaill**ions** ⎫	*was/were working*
tu travaill**ais**	vous travaill**iez** ⎬	*used to work*
il travaill**ait**	ils travaill**aient** ⎭	*worked*

The regularity of the formation of the imperfect is shown in the examples below.

VERB	STEM DERIVED FROM	IMPERFECT
travailler	nous **travaill**ons	je travaill**ais**
finir	nous **finiss**ons	je finiss**ais**
rendre	nous **rend**ons	je rend**ais**
venir*	nous **ven**ons	je ven**ais**
prendre*	nous **pren**ons	je pren**ais**
lire*	nous **lis**ons	je lis**ais**

20.03 ENGLISH EQUIVALENTS. In giving English equivalents for the imperfect there are three possible choices. They should be tried out in the order given below to determine which one is most appropriate in the context.

(a) **was (do)ing** something	il finissait	he **was** finish**ing**
(b) **used to (do)** something	il arrivait	he **used to** arrive
(c) [**did**] something	il prenait	he **took**

For certain verbs such as the following, English requires the one-word equivalent (c).

il était	he was	(never *he was being*)
il savait	he knew	(never *he was knowing*)
il comprenait	he understood	(never *he was understanding*)

20.04 HABITUAL ACTION IN THE PAST. Actions or situations that were habitual or usual in the past (*used to* happen) are easily identified because of the frequent inclusion of such adverbials as **souvent, toujours, tous les jours, parfois, quelquefois, rarement, jamais.**

Nous **allions souvent** au théâtre quand nous étions à Paris.
    We often went (used to go, would go) to the theater when we were in Paris.
Jeanne **prenait toujours** le métro.
    Jean always used to take (would take) the subway.
Je **ne finissais jamais** avant midi.
    I never used to finish (finished) before noon.

Notice that the English word *would* is sometimes used with the meaning *used to*. The word *would* is also an important indicator of the conditional tense (*tc*) [22.01]. You should test English sentences containing *would* to see if *used to* means the same thing. If so, the imperfect is correct for French. But, for example, in the sentence "I *would* like to go downtown tomorrow," the test fails, and the imperfect cannot be used.

20.05 NARRATION: INTERPLAY OF IMPERFECT AND PASSÉ COMPOSÉ. Narration of past events consists of two main parts: *actions* and *background descriptions*. In French, use the *passé composé* for the actions, and the imperfect for the background descriptions, which correspond to stage settings in the theater.

In setting a scene, the imperfect is used to tell of the *size, shape, color,* and *other physical attributes* of *buildings, people, clothing, the weather,* and even *habitual mental attitudes* ("mental stage settings"). These things are "habitual" for the duration of a scene, as opposed to the movements of the actors (*passé composé*).

> La fenêtre **était** ouverte, parce qu'il **faisait** très chaud. J'ai ouvert doucement les persiennes et j'ai entendu une voix. J'ai saisi mes clefs et j'ai descendu l'escalier en hâte. Jacques **était** là devant la porte. Il **avait l'air** fatigué et découragé. J'ai ouvert la porte.

In this passage you can distinguish between "background" in the imperfect, and actions in the *passé composé*.

TEST YOURSELF

Select the *imparfait* or the *passé composé* for each verb in italics in the left-hand column. (Cover the answers in the right-hand column until you have decided.)

1.	Last week the weather *was* fine.	1. (*ti*)	Weather: "durable" condition
2.	Mr. Dupont *was sleeping*.	2. (*ti*)	No time indicator
3.	Suddenly the alarm clock *sounded*.	3, (*tpc*)	Sudden action
4.	Mr. Dupont *woke up*.	4. (*tpc*)	Sudden action
5.	He *got out* of bed.	5. (*tpc*)	Sudden action
6.	He *was* in a good mood.	6. (*ti*)	Mental background
7.	He *took* a shirt out of the drawer.	7. (*tpc*)	Action
8.	It *was* a blue shirt.	8. (*ti*)	Clothing: durable condition
9.	He *liked* that shirt very much.	9. (*ti*)	Mental attitude
10.	He *put it on*.	10. (*tpc*)	Action
11.	He *finished* dressing.	11. (*tpc*)	Action
12.	He *went* downstairs.	12. (*tpc*)	Action

20.06 Action in progress when another event occurred. In the sentence "I was reading when Alain came in," the imperfect is used for the ongoing event (*was reading*), and the *passé composé* for the spontaneous event (*came in*) occurring during the ongoing event. This combination of imperfect and *passé composé* is very frequent.

In the diagram below representing time, the head of the arrow is the present moment (*present tense*, and the idiom **être en train de**). On the shaft of the arrow the ⊗ represents an event at a *specific* (or specifically understood) *time*, conveyed by the *passé composé*. The wavy lines on the arrow shaft, joined by a bracket, represent the *indistinct times of beginning and ending* of an action, typical of the imperfect.

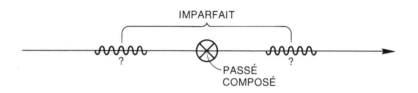

(1) Je **lisais** quand Marie **est entrée** dans la salle.

I *was reading* [⌁] when Marie *came into* [⊗] the room.

(2) Robert **regardait** la télévision quand vous **avez téléphoné**.

Robert *was looking at* television [⌁] when you *telephoned* [⊗].

Sometimes both verbs may be in the imperfect:

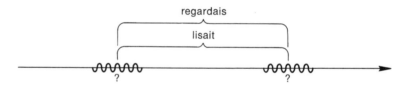

(3) Je **regardais** la télévision pendant que Paul **lisait** le journal.

I *was watching* television [⌁] while Paul *was reading* the paper [⌁].

20.07 Depuis-Construction with the imperfect. We have already seen the use of the present tense with **depuis** [9.04]. The only other tense that can be used with **depuis** is the imperfect, meaning *had been* [DOING SOMETHING] *for* [TIME].

Georges **lisait** le journal **depuis dix minutes** [*but is no longer doing it*].

Georges $\boxed{had}$ *been reading* the newspaper *for ten minutes*.

Compare this with the present tense in the *depuis*-construction:

Georges **lit** le journal **depuis dix minutes.**

George $\boxed{has}$ *been* reading the paper *for ten minutes* [*and is still reading it*].

With the present tense, the action is still going on. With the imperfect (**had been**) the action is over, and the relationship of that action to another is expressed (in the *passé composé*) or implied:

Georges **lisait** (*ti*) le journal depuis dix minutes **quand Jean est arrivé** (*tpc*).
George *had been reading* the paper for ten minutes *when John arrived*.

Exercice 20A Formation de l'imparfait [20.02]

Mettez les phrases suivantes à l'imparfait en ajoutant à la phrase la locution *quand je suis parti.* (Vous êtes libre d'inventer une autre locution pour remplacer celle-ci.)

MODÈLE : Jean-Paul **lit** un roman.
Jean-Paul **lisait** un roman quand je suis parti.

1. J'ai soif.
2. Il fait chaud.
3. Tu te reposes.
4. Je m'amuse bien.
5. Vous mettez la table.
6. Je sais la vérité.
7. Nous finissons de déjeuner.
8. Édouard a envie de sortir.
9. Maurice est de mauvaise humeur.
10. Les jeunes filles écoutent des disques.

Exercice 20B Action en train de se faire [20.06]

Combinez les deux phrases de sorte que le premier verbe se trouve à l'imparfait et le second au passé composé ou à l'imparfait.

MODÈLE : Georges lit. / J'arrive.
Georges **lisait** quand je **suis arrivé**.

1. Maman se repose. / Je sors.
2. Antoinette met la table. / Pierre arrive.
3. Charles écrit une poésie. / Il entend un bruit.
4. Le général de Gaulle est dans le salon. / Il meurt.
5. Il fait très froid. / Napoléon est à Moscou.
6. Le président est à Paris. / Il fait la connaissance du premier ministre.
7. Mon père est à la maison. / On attaque Pearl Harbor.
8. Le pilote est dans le désert. / Le petit prince se fait voir.
9. Emma habite à la campagne. / Charles Bovary la trouve.
10. Ces deux hommes attendent Godot. / Pozzo et Lucky arrivent.

PLUS-QUE-PARFAIT (PLUPERFECT)

tpp   **20.08**   GENERAL.   The pluperfect is a compound tense indicating action or situation in the past *prior to another past event*. The auxiliary verb is in the imperfect and always means *had*:

> **J'avais fini** ma composition quand vous **êtes arrivée.**
> I *had finished* my composition when you *arrived.*

ANTERIOR EVENT (*tpp*) ☒   PASSÉ COMPOSÉ ⊗

Represented schematically on the "time" arrow:

20.09   FORMATION.   The auxiliary verb is in the imperfect, followed by the past participle. Agreement of past participles remains as before: for **avoir***, agreement is with the PDO [15.04]; and for **être***, agreement is with the subject [16.02].

finir [to finish]

j'	avais	fini		nous	avions	fini
tu	avais	fini		vous	aviez	fini
il	avait	fini		ils	avaient	fini

└——————AUXILIARY VERB IN IMPERFECT——————┘

VERB	EXAMPLE	MEANING
parler	**J'avais parlé** au professeur.	I *had spoken* to the teacher.
bâtir	Il **avait bâti** la maison.	He *had built* the house.
répondre	Ils **avaient répondu** à la lettre.	They *had answered* the letter.
aller*	Elle **était allée** en ville.	She *had gone* downtown.
venir*	Ils **étaient venus** nous voir.	They *had come* to see us.
mettre*	**J'avais mis** la table.	I *had set* the table.
avoir*	Nous **avions eu besoin** d'un stylo.	We *had needed* a pen.
être*	**J'avais été** devant la gare.	I *had been* in front of the station.

Exercice 20C   Plus-que-parfait [20.08 – 20.09]

Combinez en une seule phrase les paires suivantes, en mettant la première phrase au plus-que-parfait selon le modèle. Remplacez le nom superflu de la seconde phrase par un pronom, s'il y a lieu.

MODÈLE :   (a) J'ai vu cette pièce.
            (b) J'ai rencontré l'auteur *de cette pièce.*
            J'avais (déjà) **vu** cette pièce *quand* j'*en* ai rencontré l'auteur. [13.07A]

1. (a) Jacques a écrit la lettre au maire.
   (b) Vous avez téléphoné.
2. (a) Nous avons pris les billets.
   (b) On a annoncé le départ.
3. (a) Vous n'avez pas encore mis la table.
   (b) Les invités sont entrés dans la salle à manger.
4. (a) Marie s'est mariée avec Jean-Paul.
   (b) J'ai vu Marie à Saint-Tropez.
5. (a) Le patron est déjà sorti.
   (b) Vous êtes venu chercher le patron.
6. (a) Nous avons déjà dressé la liste.
   (b) Le patron nous a demandé d'ajouter un nom.
7. (a) L'avion a décollé.
   (b) Ce passager est arrivé.
8. (a) J'ai acheté une machine à écrire.
   (b) Mon oncle m'a donné une machine à écrire. [13.08]
9. (a) Ils ont fini leur travail.
   (b) Ils se sont mis en route.
10. (a) Nous avons retenu une chambre à l'hôtel.
    (b) Nous sommes arrivés à Paris.

Exercice 20T   Thème français

1. John came in and told me that he had already mailed the letter.
2. My brother asked me whether I liked Italian movies.
3. I explained to him that I was going to see a French play.
4. My old roommate asked me if I had noticed the large number of foreign cars on the streets.
5. We had been living in London for three years when war broke out. [*éclater*]
6. Lucien Recamier always wore a dark blue suit when he went to church.
7. Last week the weather was so nice that we drove to the seashore.
8. I was taking a French test, so my friend went to the library to study.
9. The Duponts used to have a small house in the mountains, but they sold it.
10. I had been having a good time at the party when the police knocked at the door of the apartment.

Exercice 20D   Sujet de composition ou de causerie

Racontez un événement intéressant de votre vie en employant le passé composé, l'imparfait, et le plus-que-parfait. [20.05]

Révision
systématique

1. I feel like resting a little before I study. [3.12] [18.01] [11.06]
2. How did Maigret find the passenger who had killed the postman? [12.02] [12.04]
3. Has your grandfather sold his little cottage in the country? [12.04]
4. You are going to take the 4 P.M. flight for Stockholm, aren't you? [12.07]
5. What did the policeman say to the driver of the red car? [12.09B]

Le Château de Chenonceaux, sur le Cher (*Bernard Silberstein/Monkmeyer*)

21

FUTUR,
FUTUR
ANTÉRIEUR

INTERROGATIFS
QUEL,
LEQUEL

POUVOIR*

FUTUR, FUTUR ANTÉRIEUR

21.01 Use. The future tense is used to designate actions expected to occur in the future (**à l'avenir**). It is also used in the following cases:

A.   After **quand, lorsque, dès que** when the action indicated after these words is actually *in the future* [21.02].

B.   In the result clause of conditional sentences when the **si**-clause is in present tense [21.03].

21.02 After **quand, lorsque, dès que, aussitôt que**.   When the action indicated after these words is actually in the future (although in English it is in the present tense), the French verb following these conjunctions *must* be in the future tense.

> J'irai à Paris **quand** je **serai** riche.
>> I will go to Paris when I *am* (will be) rich.
> Je donnerai la lettre à Pierre **dès que** je le **verrai**.
>> I will give the letter to Pierre as soon as I *see* him.

An easy rule of thumb is that if *one verb* in a sentence containing **quand** (**lorsque, dès que, aussitôt que**) is in the future, *both* must be in the future.

21.03 Conditional sentences: present-future combination. A conditional sentence is one containing a proviso (**si**-clause) and a result clause. If the **si**-clause is in the present tense, the result clause is in the future.

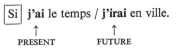

If I *have* time / I *will go* downtown.

Si j'ai le temps / j'irai en ville.

⬆ PRESENT   ⬆ FUTURE

The order of clauses is immaterial. **Si** is always followed by the present in this combination:

J'irai en ville **si j'ai** le temps.

21.04 Formation of the future: regular verbs. The future tense of regular verbs is formed by adding future endings to the FC stem (future and conditional stem). The stem for all **-er** and **-ir** verbs is the *whole infinitive*. The stem for **-re** verbs is the infinitive minus the final **-e**. The endings (which resemble the present tense of *avoir** in several places) are as follows:

-ai	-ons
-as	-ez
-a	-ont

EXAMPLES

arriver   FC stem: **arriver-** [will arrive]

j'arriver**ai**	nous arriver**ons**
tu arriver**as**	vous arriver**ez**
il arriver**a**	ils arriver**ont**

finir   FC stem: **finir-** [will finish]

je finir**ai**	nous finir**ons**
tu finir**as**	vous finir**ez**
il finir**a**	ils finir**ont**

vendre   FC stem: **vendr-** [will sell]

je vendr**ai**	nous vendr**ons**
tu vendr**as**	vous vendr**ez**
il vendr**a**	ils vendr**ont**

s'amuser   FC stem: **s'amuser-** [will have a good time]

je m'amuser**ai**	nous nous amuser**ons**
tu t'amuser**as**	vous vous amuser**ez**
il s'amuser**a**	ils s'amuser**ont**

21.05 Future tense of irregular verbs. Some irregular verbs have special future (FC) stems, while others form the FC stem in the regular way. When in doubt, check Appendix C for irregular verbs in the future. Learn the FC stems for the irregular verbs thus far reviewed. Those having special stems are as follows:

INFINITIVE	FC-STEM	EXAMPLE
aller*	ir-	Il **ir**a en France demain.
être*	ser-	Elle **ser**a heureuse.
avoir*	aur-	Il **aur**a une voiture.
faire*	fer-	Vous **fer**ez la cuisine.
venir*	viendr-	Il **viendr**a demain.
tenir*	tiendr-	Tu **tiendr**as un livre.

Other irregular verbs form their future tense in a regular manner, using the whole infinitive, or (for *-re* verbs) dropping the final **-e**:

lire*	lir-	Il **lir**a ce roman.
écrire*	écrir-	Elle **écrir**a une poésie.
mettre*	mettr-	Je **mettr**ai la table.
prendre*	prendr-	Il **prendr**a les billets.
ouvrir*	ouvrir-	Nous **ouvrir**ons la porte.
partir*	partir-	Il **partir**a demain.

The FC stem will be included in the review sections for further irregular verbs.

tfa **21.06** FUTURE PERFECT (*le futur antérieur*).   The future perfect is a compound tense formed with the future of the auxiliary verb, plus the past participle of the main verb. The meaning always includes the words *will have* [DONE SOMETHING].

EXAMPLES

travailler [to work] *pp.* **travaillé** (avoir*)

j'**aurai travaillé**	nous **aurons travaillé**
tu **auras travaillé**	vous **aurez travaillé**
il **aura travaillé**	ils **auront travaillé**

I (you, he, we, you, they) **will have** worked

aller* [to go] *pp.* **allé** (être*)

je **serai allé**(e)	nous **serons allé**(e)s
tu **seras allé**(e)	vous **serez allé**(e)(s)
il **sera allé**	ils **seront allés**
elle **sera allée**	elles **seront allées**

I (you, he, she, we, you, they) **will have** gone

À cinq heures j'**aurai travaillé** pendant huit heures.
  At five o'clock I *will have worked* eight hours.
Quand vous arriverez j'**aurai fini** ma composition.
  When you arrive I *will have finished* my composition.

Temps futur [21.04]

Remplacez les mots en italique par le futur.

1. Je *vais traverser* la rue malgré la circulation intense.
2. Nous *allons laver* la vaisselle après le repas.
3. M. Bertin *va bâtir* une maison.
4. M. Bertin *va faire* bâtir une maison.
5. Le chauffeur *va arrêter* le camion au feu rouge [red light].
6. Paul et René *vont s'approcher* du guichet.
7. Enfin vous *allez me dire* la vérité.
8. Mes parents *vont lire* la nouvelle ce soir.
9. Nous *allons être* de retour avant minuit.
10. Tu *vas avoir* le temps de m'aider à laver la vaisselle.

Exercice 21B Choix de temps

Terminez la phrase en y ajoutant les mots entre parenthèses et en mettant le verbe au *futur*, à *l'imparfait* ou au *passé composé*, selon le cas.

MODÈLE: (je reviens tout de suite) Si je ne trouve pas le professeur, . . .
Si je ne trouve pas le professeur, je **reviendrai** tout de suite.

1. (il se repose) Si François est fatigué, . . .
2. (nous parlons français) S'il ne comprend pas l'anglais, . . .
3. (ses parents le punissent) Si l'enfant n'est pas sage . . .
4. (Jean prend les billets) Si vous n'avez pas d'argent, . . .
5. (il est de retour à 6 h.) Si papa prend le rapide [*express*], . . .
6. (je viens vous voir) Si je reste longtemps en ville, . . .
7. (vous venez nous voir) Quand vous serez en ville, . . .
8. (vous venez nous voir) Quand vous avez été en ville, . . .
9. (vous venez nous voir) [*you used to come . . .*] Quand vous étiez en ville, . . .
10. (je vais en Amérique) Quand je serai riche, . . .
11. (ils se reposent) Quand mes parents seront vieux, . . .
12. (nous nous amusons) Quand nous étions jeunes, . . .

INTERROGATIFS quel, lequel

21.07 INTERROGATIVE ADJECTIVE **quel**. The interrogative adjective **quel** [*which, what*] has four forms; use the form which agrees in gender and number with the noun that follows.

m.s. **Quel roman** as-tu lu?

f.s. **Quelle pièce** as-tu vue?

m.pl. **Quels devoirs** as-tu faits?

f.pl. **Quelles leçons** as-tu étudiées?

If a verb comes directly after a form of **quel**, agreement with the *noun* must still be made.

> **Quel** est **le prix** de ce dictionnaire?
> **Quelle** est **votre adresse**?

In indirect questions, **quel** is used in such expressions as:

> Dites-moi **quelle pièce** tu as vue.
> Tell me what play you saw.

21.08 INTERROGATIVE PRONOUN **lequel**. The interrogative pronoun **lequel** [*which one*] has four forms. Select the proper form to agree in gender and number with the noun you have in mind.

	SINGULAR	PLURAL
MASCULINE	**lequel**	**lesquels**
FEMININE	**laquelle**	**lesquelles**
Meaning	*which one*	*which ones*

If you expect a singular noun as an answer, the singular form is used; if you expect a plural noun as an answer, use the plural form.

> Vous pouvez prendre **un** de ces livres. **Lequel** voulez-vous?
> You can take one of these books. Which *one* do you want?
> Vous pouvez prendre **deux** de ces livres. **Lesquels** voulez-vous?
> You can take two of these books. Which *ones* do you want?
> Voilà trois voitures neuves. **Laquelle** préférez-vous?
> There are three new cars. Which *one* do you prefer?

Notice that **lequel** (being a pronoun) can be used alone, while **quel** (being an adjective) must be followed by a noun.

> Un de ces livres est à vous. **Lequel**?
> One of these books is yours. Which? (Which one?)

To ask *which one of* [N *pl.*] add **de** plus the article or adjective accompanying the plural noun:

> **Lequel de ces** romans as-tu lu?
> Which [one] of these novels have you read?
> **Laquelle de ces** pièces préférez-vous?
> Which [one] of these plays do you prefer?
> **Lesquels de mes** chats aimez-vous mieux?
> Which [ones] of my cats do you like best?

21.09 AFTER A PREPOSITION (**dans laquelle...?**). For the interrogatives *with which, to which, in which,* etc., use the appropriate form of **lequel** after the preposition:

> **Dans laquelle** de ces maisons habitez-vous?
>> In which [one] of these houses do you live?
> **Avec lesquels** des étudiants avez-vous parlé?
>> With which [ones] of the students did you speak?

Contractions of **à** and **de** occur in the usual way with the *le / les* part of **lequel, lesquels,** and **lesquelles** [1.03]. Thus **à** + **lequel** results in **auquel** (*to which*); **de** + **lesquels** becomes **desquels** (*of which*), etc.

> **Auquel de ces** romans pensez-vous?
>> Which one of these novels are you thinking about?
> **Auxquelles de ces** dames avez-vous répondu?
>> Which ones of those ladies did you answer?

Remember that there is no contraction with *la,* hence none with *laquelle:*

> **À laquelle des** pièces de Molière penses-tu?

Exercice 21 C Interrogatifs *quel, lequel* [21.06 – 21.09]

Complétez les questions suivantes en ajoutant la forme appropriée de **quel** ou de **lequel.**

MODÈLE: —— de vos tantes sont à Paris?
Lesquelles de vos tantes sont à Paris?

1. —— de vos cours à l'université sont les plus difficiles?
2. —— est le prix de cette revue?
3. —— de vos amies est la plus jolie?
4. —— scène de Shakespeare est entièrement en français?
5. —— des scènes de Shakespeare sont situées à Venise?
6. À —— des poèmes de Charles Baudelaire pensez-vous? "Le Voyage"?
7. De —— des dictionnaires as-tu besoin? *Le Petit Robert?*
8. Dans —— des pièces avez-vous installé votre téléviseur?
9. —— symphonies (*f.*) de Haydn trouvez-vous les plus belles?
10. —— s'appelle "la Symphonie Militaire"?

Exercice 21 D *quel, lequel* [21.07 – 21.09]

Donnez l'équivalent français.

1. Which book did you read last week?
2. Which ones will you read next week?
3. What is the price of a round-trip ticket for Rouen?
4. There are three express trains. Which one do you want to take?

5. Which of your friends did you go to the shore with?
6. Which one of Molière's comedies are you speaking of?
7. Which of these novels were written by Balzac?
8. Which airport does this bus go to?
9. In which room in your apartment do you study the best?
10. What is your best course at the university currently?

VERBE IRRÉGULIER pouvoir*

21.10 Review the verb **pouvoir*** in Appendix C, verb table 22, paying special attention to the present, passé composé, imperfect and future tenses.

tp	Il **peut** sortir maintenant.	He *may* go out now. (PERMISSION)
	Il **peut** ouvrir cette fenêtre.	He *can* open that window. (PHYSICAL ABILITY)
tpc	Il **a pu** ouvrir cette boîte.	He *succeeded in* opening that box.
	Il **n'a pas pu** la fermer.	He *was not able to* close it.
ti	Il **pouvait** voir le bateau.	He *could* see the boat.
tf	Il **pourra** venir demain.	He *will be able* to come tomorrow.

NOTE THE FORMS: *pp.* **pu** (avoir)

FC **pourr-**

21.11 REMARKS ON **pouvoir***. · The verb **pouvoir*** is usually followed by an infinitive, with the meaning *to be able* [to do something]. However, notice above the special meaning for the passé composé, *to succeed in*. In French there are two verbs for expressing "can," and they cannot be used interchangeably:

A. **pouvoir*** [I] is used for *physical ability* or *permission*.

Pouvez-vous ouvrir cette porte?	*Can you* open this door?
Vous **pouvez partir** demain.	You *may* leave now.

B. **savoir*** [I] is used for *can* [do something] when *learned ability* or *skill* is implied: it means *to know how*.

Jean **sait parler** russe.	John can speak Russian.
Je **sais taper** à la machine.·	I can type.
Savez-vous jouer au tennis?	Can you play tennis?

Exercice 21E   Emploi de *pouvoir** [21.10 – 21.11]

Remplacez le verbe en italique par l'infinitif précédé de la forme appropriée de **pouvoir** ou de **savoir**, selon le cas.

197

Marie *accompagnera* sa mère en ville.
Marie **pourra** ACCOMPAGNER sa mère en ville.

Verbe irrégulier
pouvoir

1. Marguerite *sortira* ce soir.
2. Boris *parle* russe.
3. Je *tape* ma composition à la machine.
4. Robert *arrivera* demain.
5. Nous *ouvrons* cette porte facilement.
6. Vous *conduisez* un camion.
7. Elle *téléphonera* au directeur avant midi, n'est-ce pas?
8. Quand nous serons à Paris nous *visiterons* le Louvre.
9. Si j'arrive à l'heure, j'*aiderai* ma mère.
10. M. Machin *porte* cette boîte.
11. Suzanne *fait* la cuisine.
12. Jean *lit* très bien.

Exercice 21T   Thème français

1. Next week I will be on vacation; I will be able to drive to Cannes.
2. If I have enough money, I will be able to go there by boat.
3. When I arrive in Geneva, I will telephone your cousin.
4. I will have enough time at the airport to buy a ticket for the connecting flight.
5. I am sure that your aunt and uncle will be glad to hear your voice when you call them.
6. Where will you go when you leave Italy?
7. John promised to write me a long letter when he arrives in Nice.
8. As soon as I get back from the post office I will read all the magazines.
9. During the summer I will be in Switzerland for five weeks.
10. I will do some skiing and some sightseeing. I am sure I will have spent most of my money when I return.

Révision
systématique

1. Close the windows—don't open them now. When John arrives we will open them. [13.02]
2. When you came in I was listening to a symphony. Did you hear it? [13.05]
3. "Are you tired today?" "I am. I just returned from a tennis match." [13.04] [11.10]
4. We are waiting for the bus because we are going to attend a lecture. [13.05]
5. We have been waiting for it [*the bus*] for fifteen minutes. [9.06]

Bureau de poste automatique (*Photo PTT*)

22

Conditionnel | Conditionnel passé | vouloir*

CONDITIONNEL *tc*

22.01 USES. The conditional tense (usually including the word *would* in English)[1] is used for:

A. POLITE REQUESTS, STATEMENTS, AND QUESTIONS. The use of the conditional (especially of *vouloir* and *devoir*) softens a statement that might be harsh or brusque. Compare *I want a ticket* with *I would like a ticket.*

Je **voudrais** une chemise bleue.	I *would like* a blue shirt.
Pierre **voudrait** partir à midi.	Pierre *would like* to leave at noon.
Je **devrais** étudier.	I *should* (*ought to*) study.

B. FUTURE ACTIONS WITH RELATION TO A PAST TIME. When a past time has been established as a base of reference, a future action relative to it is in the conditional:

Je savais qu'elle **comprendrait**.	I knew that she would understand.
Il m'a dit qu'il **viendrait**.	He told me that he would come.

[1] When the English "would" is used with the meaning "used to," the *imparfait* is required in French [20.04].

When we lived in Paris we *would go* to the beach every summer.
Quand nous habitions à Paris, nous **allions** au bord de la mer tous les étés.

C. Conditional sentences: imperfect-conditional combination. In a conditional sentence, the result clause must be in the conditional tense when the si-clause is in the imperfect [20.02].

> Si **j'avais** le temps, **j'irais** en ville.
>
> IMPERFECT   CONDITIONAL
>
> If I had time, I would go downtown.
>
> Tu **comprendrais** si tu **faisais** attention.
>
> You would understand if you paid attention.

D. Hypothetical, potential, or imaginary information. When a "fact" of unverified or dubious accuracy is passed on, the conditional is often used to indicate that the speaker does not take responsibility for its accuracy:

> On propose de construire une fusée qui **atteindrait** Vénus.
>
> A rocket that *would reach* Venus is being proposed.
>
> C'est Michel qui **serait** malade?
>
> Is it Michel who is *supposed to be* (said to be) sick?

22.02 Formation: regular verbs. The conditional tense of regular verbs is formed by adding the conditional endings (same as the imperfect endings) to the FC stem. As indicated previously [21.04], the FC stem is the whole infinitive of **-er** and **-ir** verbs, and the infinitive of **-re** verbs minus the final **-e**. All FC stems, regular and irregular, end in **-r**. The conditional endings are:

-ais	**-ions**
-ais	**-iez**
-ait	**-aient**

EXAMPLES

arriver FC stem: **arriver-** [would arrive]

j'arriver**ais**	nous arriver**ions**
tu arriver**ais**	vous arriver**iez**
il arriver**ait**	ils arriver**aient**

finir FC stem: **finir-** [would finish]

je finir**ais**	nous finir**ions**
tu finir**ais**	vous finir**iez**
il finir**ait**	ils finir**aient**

rendre FC stem: **rendr-** [would give]

je rendr**ais**	nous rendr**ions**
tu rendr**ais**	vous rendr**iez**
il rendr**ait**	ils rendr**aient**

se lever° FC stem: **se lever-** [would get up]

je me lèver**ais**	nous nous lèver**ions**
tu te lèver**ais**	vous vous lèver**iez**
il se lèver**ait**	ils se lèver**aient**

22.03 FORMATION: IRREGULAR VERBS. The same special FC stems which you learned for the future tense of certain irregular verbs [21.05] are also used for the conditional tense. The conditional endings are added to those special stems.

aller FC stem: **ir-** [would go]

j'irais	nous irions
tu irais	vous iriez
il irait	ils iraient

CONDITIONNEL PASSÉ

22.04 PAST CONDITIONAL. The past conditional is formed by using the conditional of the appropriate auxiliary verb (always meaning "would have") plus the past participle. Agreement of past participles must be made as usual for all compound tenses [15.04] [16.02].

travailler *pp.* **travaillé** (avoir*) [would have worked]

j'**aurais** travaillé	nous **aurions** travaillé
tu **aurais** travaillé	vous **auriez** travaillé
il **aurait** travaillé	ils **auraient** travaillé

venir* *pp.* **venu** (être*) [would have come]

je **serais** venu(e)	nous **serions** venu(e)s
tu **serais** venu(e)	nous **seriez** venu(e)(s)
il **serait** venu	ils **seraient** venus
elle **serait** venue	elles **seraient** venues

se dépêcher *pp.* **se dépêché** (être*) [would have hurried]

je **me serais** dépêché(e)	nous **nous serions** dépêché(e)s
tu **te serais** dépêché(e)	vous **vous seriez** dépêché(e)(s)
il **se serait** dépêché	ils **se seraient** dépêchés
elle **se serait** dépêchée	elles **se seraient** dépêchées

EXAMPLES

Si j'avais eu le temps j'**aurais travaillé** à la bibliothèque.
    If I had had the time, I *would have worked* in the library.
Si Jean avait su que le temps lui manquait, il **se serait dépêché**.
    If John had known that he lacked time, he *would have hurried*.

22.05 CONDITIONAL SENTENCES. The conditional sentence occurs in three standard combinations, just as in English:

(a) Si Jean **a** le temps, il **ira** en ville.
        PRESENT-FUTURE COMBINATION [21.03]
(b) Si Jean **avait** le temps, il **irait** en ville.
        IMPARFAIT-CONDITIONAL COMBINATION [22.01C]

(c)   Si Jean **avait eu** le temps, il **serait allé** en ville.

PLUPERFECT-PAST CONDITIONAL COMBINATION [22.04 Examples]

Combination (c) is really a variety of (b), with the addition of a past participle in both halves of the sentence. The auxiliary verbs conform to the imperfect-conditional system.

The combinations are summarized in the following table:

si-CLAUSE	RESULT CLAUSE	EXAMPLE
Present	Future	Si Paul **est** fatigué, il **se reposera.** [21.03]
Imparfait	Conditional	Si Paul **était** fatigué, il **se reposerait.** [22.01C]
Pluperfect	Past Conditional	Si Paul **avait été** fatigué, il **se serait reposé.** [22.05]

The clauses may be in either order: the **si**-clause may be used at the end rather than at the beginning if desired.

Paul **se reposerait** s'il **était** fatigué.

Exercice 22A   Conditionnel [22.01B]

Recommencez chaque phrase par *Il m'a dit que . . .* suivi du conditionnel.

MODÈLE: René *est* en retard.
Il m'a dit que René **serait** en retard.

1.   M. Dupont arrive demain.
2.   Les Smith viennent nous voir.
3.   Suzanne met la table.
4.   Jeanne va au marché.
5.   Mon oncle a besoin de trois billets.
6.   Le professeur lit ma poésie.
7.   Il écrit une lettre au ministère.
8.   Il fait une promenade à motocyclette avec moi.
9.   Vous prenez une décision.
10.   Il se passe de voiture.

Exercice 22B   Phrases conditionnelles [22.01 C]

Faites une phrase conditionnelle sur les remarques suivantes, selon le modèle.

MODÈLE: Jean n'*étudie* pas; il ne *réussira* pas.
Si Jean **étudiait**, il **réussirait**.

1.   Il n'écoute pas le professeur; il ne comprend pas les leçons.
2.   Elle n'a pas le temps; elle ne visite pas le Louvre.

3. Nous n'avons pas de voiture; nous n'allons pas à la campagne.
4. Hans n'a rien à dire; il ne parle pas. (S'il avait quelque chose à dire . . .)
5. Hélène ne sait pas danser; elle n'a pas beaucoup d'amis.
6. Cecil n'a pas besoin d'argent; il ne travaille pas.
7. L'enfant n'est pas fatigué; il ne se couche pas.
8. Paul n'a pas d'argent sur lui; il ne prend pas les billets.
9. Le chauffeur n'a pas vu le feu rouge; il ne s'est pas arrêté.
10. Il n'est pas allé au Moulin Rouge; il ne s'est pas amusé.

VERBE IRRÉGULIER vouloir*

22.06 Review the irregular verb **vouloir*** in Appendix C, verb table 33, paying special attention to the present, passé composé, imperfect, future, and conditional tenses. **Vouloir*** is usually followed directly by an infinitive, sometimes by a noun.

tp	Jean **veut** partir.	John *wants to* leave.
tpc	Jean **a voulu** partir.	John *tried to* leave.
	J'ai **voulu** faire la vaisselle.	I *offered to* wash the dishes.
ti	Jean **voulait** voir ce film.	John *wanted to* see that movie.
tf	Jean **voudra** vous revoir.	John *will want to* see you again.
tc	Jean **voudrait** lui parler.	John *would like to* speak to her (him).

FC-STEM: **voudr-**

22.07 REMARKS ON **vouloir***. This verb resembles **pouvoir*** in the present tense singular forms: *je* **v**eux, *tu* **v**eux, *il* **v**eut. **Vouloir*** has various meanings and uses:

A. PRESENT TENSE. The present tense of **vouloir*** is used for very strong expressions of will; to the French ear it is brusque and often impolite. It is preferable to use the conditional to express desires and polite requests.

Je **veux** partir.	*(tp)*	I insist on leaving.
Je **voudrais** partir.	*(tc)*	I would like to leave.

Que **voudriez-vous** faire maintenant?
Je **voudrais** voir des montres-bracelets, s'il vous plait.

B. PASSÉ COMPOSÉ TENSE. In the passé composé the meanings of **vouloir*** are different from what one might expect:

J'ai **voulu** lui parler.	I *tried to* speak to him.
Je **n'ai pas voulu** lui parler.	I *refused to* speak to him.
J'ai **voulu** l'aider.	I *offered to* help him.

C. IDIOMS WITH **vouloir***.

Verbe irrégulier
vouloir*

vouloir bien ([I])   to be willing
vouloir dire ([N])   to mean
en vouloir à [P]   to hold a grudge against

EXAMPLES

Je **voulais bien** l'accompagner.
   I was willing to go with him.
Voulez-vous m'accompagner? **Je veux bien.**
   Do you want to go with me? Sure.
Que **voulez-vous dire**?
   What do you mean?
Que **veut dire** le mot "berline"?
   What does the word "berline" mean?
Jean **en veut à** cet agent de police.
   John is holding a grudge against that policeman.

The imperative form **veuillez** is a rather formal way of saying *please*:

Veuillez fermer la porte.
   Kindly close the door.

Exercice 22C   *vouloir** [22.06–22.07]

Remplacez les mots en italique par l'équivalent approximatif avec **vouloir***.

MODÈLE: Paul *accepte de* nous accompagner.
           Paul **veut bien** nous accompagner.

1. J'*accepte de* faire la vaisselle.
2. Je *désire* acheter un dictionnaire russe.
3. Roger *a essayé de* lui parler.
4. Qu'est-ce que cela *signifie*?
5. Cet étudiant *a du ressentiment contre* le répétiteur.
6. J'*ai envie d'*aller au cinéma ce soir.
7. J'étais en ville hier soir; j'*avais envie de* dîner chez Henri.
8. Le général insiste: il *commande* une Cadillac, sans contredit.
9. Qu'est-ce que vous *tâchez de me communiquer* par là?
10. Nous *avons refusé de* travailler le dimanche.

Exercice 22T   Thème français

1. I would like to avoid getting up too early. [11.05] [18.08]
2. I would get up late if I didn't need to work.
3. If I had lots of money I would take a trip to Switzerland.
4. If I went to Germany, I would go to Berlin.
5. My friend told me that she would like to ski in the Alps.

6. If we buy our tickets now, we will be able to leave the house late.
7. If we had bought our tickets early, we would have been able to leave late.
8. If you came to our apartment before going to the theater, we would have a bite to eat.
9. If I were rich, I would go to England and the United States.
10. When I am rich, I will go to Venice and Vienna.
11. What does this sentence mean? Are you willing to read it?
12. According to this article, the prime minister is supposed to be ill.

Révision
lexicale

Noms dérivés de l'infinitif

1. **être** se transforme en **un être**. *Un être humain.* On désire quelque chose de *tout son être*.

2. **pouvoir** devient le nom **le pouvoir**. Un étudiant a *un grand pouvoir* de concentration. *Le pouvoir législatif, le pouvoir exécutif, le pouvoir judiciare.* Il y a *la séparation des pouvoirs* de la constitution des États-Unis.

3. **devoir.** Tous les étudiants reconnaissent **le devoir** qu'il faut faire à l'université. Le soldat *fait son devoir* dans le combat. Le devoir, c'est une obligation morale.

4. **déjeuner, dîner** existent également sous forme de nom: **le déjeuner**, c'est le repas de midi; **le dîner**, le repas du soir. On déjeune, on *fait un bon déjeuner*.

5. **aller** se transforme en nom quand il s'agit d'un billet. On demande **un aller** [*one-way ticket*] ou **un aller** (et) **retour** [*round-trip ticket*] pour un voyage.

6. **sourire** devient **le sourire**, l'expression du visage heureux. Un large sourire [*a grin*]. Gardez le sourire [*Keep smiling*].

7. **se souvenir de** produit le nom **le souvenir**, la mémoire qu'on garde du passé. On a *des souvenirs d'enfance*.

Exercice 22D   Sujet de composition ou de causerie

1. Racontez une journée de votre vie telle qu'elle serait si vous étiez milliardaire. (Employez le conditionnel autant que possible.)
2. Dites ce que vous feriez si vous étiez chef d'État (ou président).

Révision
systématique

1. We gave our teacher our compositions. We gave them to him last week, but he has not corrected them yet. [14.02] [14.05] [10.03]
2. The students asked the lecturer some difficult questions about economics, and he answered them carefully. [14.04] [14.10] [7.08]
3. I took the history examination yesterday. I passed it, but John failed his. [14.10] [12.11]
4. Those girls that you saw at the movies arrived in Paris very recently. [15.04] [16.02]
5. Your brother and mine have some interesting machines; I saw some of them in your garage. [12.11] [5.01] [15.05]

La Place Clichy animée le soir (*WHO-Almasy/Monkmeyer*)

23

Pronoms relatifs qui, que

devoir*

PRONOMS RELATIFS qui, que   *rel*

～～～～～～～～～～～～～～～～～～～～～～～～～～～～～～～～～～～

23.01 Use. A relative pronoun is used to join two sentences dealing with the same subject. In the second of the two sentences, the relative pronoun replaces a noun already used in the first sentence. (We shall call this the *repetitious noun*, or RN.) For example:

TWO SENTENCES   I am looking for | **my pen. My pen** | was on the table.
                       REPETITIOUS NOUN

TWO CLAUSES   I am looking for my pen, **which** was on the table.
                MAIN CLAUSE   SUBORDINATE CLAUSE

In this example, both original sentences deal with the same topic, "my pen." In the new sentence, "my pen" was replaced by the relative pronoun "which." This joins the two sentences into a single one. Each of the original sentences became a *clause*: the first is the *main clause*; the second, containing the relative pronoun, is the *subordinate clause*.

In French the same system applies, and using the same example, we have:

TWO SENTENCES   Je cherche **mon stylo. Mon stylo** était sur la table.

TWO CLAUSES   Je cherche mon stylo   **qui**   était sur la table.
                                 RELATIVE PRONOUN

207

In order to select the proper French relative pronoun, you must know whether the repetitious noun in the subordinate clause is used as a *subject*, *direct object*, or *object of a preposition* (dealt with in Chapter 24).

23.02 SUBJECT OF A CLAUSE: **qui**. The relative pronoun **qui** replaces a repetitious noun used as subject of the sentence to become a subordinate clause.

> Voilà le professeur. **Le professeur** arrive en ce moment.
> Voilà le professeur   **qui**   arrive en ce moment.
>   ↑   ↑
>   SUBJECT   VERB

> Voici un devoir. **Le devoir** est difficile.
> Voici un devoir   **qui**   est difficile.

The RN may equally well be a *pronoun* representing a noun in the main clause.

> Je cherche un monsieur. **Il** parle chinois.   [il = **un monsieur**]
> Je cherche un monsieur **qui** parle chinois.

23.03 DIRECT OBJECT RELATIVE PRONOUN **que**. When the repetitious noun of the second clause is used as direct object, substitute **que** and move it to the beginning of the clause:

(1)   Voici <u>une voiture neuve</u>. J'aime **cette voiture**.   D.O.

> | J'aime   **que**   SUBSTITUTION |
>   **que**   j'aime.   CORRECT ORDER

Voici une **voiture** neuve **que** j'aime.
Here's a new car that I like.

(2)   Où est <u>ce livre</u>? J'ai perdu **le livre**.   D.O.

> | J'ai perdu   **que**   SUBSTITUTION |
>   **que** j'ai perdu.   CORRECT ORDER

Où est **le livre que** j'ai perdu?
Where is the book (that) I lost?

If the noun replaced is plural or feminine singular, and a compound tense is being used in the subordinate clause, the past participle must now agree in gender and number with the noun. By placing the direct object **que** at the head of the subordinate clause, you are creating a PDO [15.04].

(3)   J'aime beaucoup <u>la pièce</u>. J'ai vu **cette pièce** hier soir.

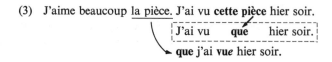

>   **que** j'ai **vue** hier soir.

(4)   Voilà la faute de grammaire. Jean a fait **cette faute.**

> Jean a fait   **que**

que Jean a **faite.**

ATTENTION! Look out for the missing "that".

English sentences often omit the direct object relative pronoun *that*; but in French the word **que** cannot be left out. Be alert for such sentences. The empty brackets below show the location of the missing *that*:

> There is the man [   ] my father employed.
> Voilà l'homme **que** mon père a employé.
> The girls [   ] you saw are students.
> Les jeunes filles **que** vous avez vues sont des étudiantes.

23.04   POSITION OF THE SUBORDINATE CLAUSE.   The subordinate clause fits into the main clause directly after the repetitious noun. (You could place a caret mark after the repetitious noun in the main clause to remind yourself of this.)

COMBINE: $\begin{cases} \textbf{Le livre} \wedge \textbf{est sur la table.} & \text{MAIN CLAUSE} \\ \text{Vous cherchez } \textbf{le livre.} & \text{BECOMES SUBORDINATE} \\ \qquad\qquad\quad \text{RN} \end{cases}$

le livre replaced by *que*: *que* **vous cherchez**

SOLUTION: **Le livre** | que vous cherchez | **est sur la table.**

23.05   SIMPLIFIED RULE: **qui** or **que**?   Although the following is not strictly a grammatical rule, it is helpful to many students. Knowing that the subject usually is in the initial position in a sentence, and that the direct object tends to be towards the end, use this guide:

> Initial word, use **quI**
> End word,   use **quE**

Thus in examining the sentence to be made subordinate *Jean a fait cette faute*, if *faute* is the RN, it would be replaced by *que* because it is at the end: *que* **Jean a faite.** (Note agreement required with PDO.)

Exercice 23A   Pronoms relatifs [23.01 – 23.03]

Répétez (ensuite écrivez) les phrases suivantes en les faisant commencer par *Voilà* suivi du nom en italique. Employez le pronom relatif **qui** ou **que** et faites les changements nécessaires.

MODÈLE : *Ce livre* m'intéresse.

Voilà *le livre* **qui** m'intéresse.

1. *Le train* part toujours à l'heure.
2. Nous achèterons *une lampe*.
3. *Ce monsieur* est vraiment intelligent.
4. J'ai pris *une décision importante*. (Attention : PDO)
5. *La grammaire* était sur la table hier.
6. Paul a apporté *la tasse* à son père.
7. M. Durand a acheté *une voiture*.
8. Pierre a trouvé *la clé* dans le tiroir.
9. Je dois lire *ce roman*.
10. Nous avons visité *le musée*.

Exercice 23B   Pronoms relatifs [23.01 – 23.05]

Combinez les deux phrases en employant un pronom relatif (**qui** ou **que**). La première phrase deviendra toujours la proposition principale (*main clause*).

MODÈLE :   (a) Jean a une auto.

(b) L'auto a coûté cher.

Jean a une auto **qui** a coûté cher.

1. (a) Marie est une étudiante extraordinaire.
   (b) Marie est absente aujourd'hui.
2. (a) La machine est dans cette boîte.
   (b) Vous cherchez la machine.
3. (a) J'ai déjà lu ce roman.
   (b) Vous m'avez prêté ce roman.
4. (a) Lucien prépare son devoir.
   (b) Lucien a l'air hostile.
5. (a) J'ai besoin d'argent.
   (b) Mon père m'a promis cet argent.
6. (a) Les questions sont très difficiles.
   (b) Notre professeur pose les questions.
7. (a) La machine est dans cette boîte.
   (b) Vous cherchiez cette machine hier.
8. (a) Les Lebrun ont une maison à la campagne.
   (b) Nous avons vu leur maison l'été passé.
9. (a) L'avion part de l'aéroport Charles de Gaulle.
   (b) Nous prenons cet avion.
10. (a) La pièce sera jouée à la Comédie-Française.
    (b) Nous allons voir cette pièce demain soir.

VERBE IRRÉGULIER **devoir***

23.06   Review the verb **devoir*** in Appendix C, verb table 9, paying special attention to the tenses already reviewed. Notice that this verb is nearly always

Verbe irrégulier devoir*

followed directly by an infinitive, and that it has special meanings that must be learned for each tense.

tp	Je **dois** partir.	I *must* leave.
	Paul **doit être** riche.	Paul *must be* rich.
	Paul me **doit** dix francs.	Paul *owes* me ten francs.
tpc	Marie **a dû** partir.	{ Marie *had to* leave. { Marie *must have* left.
	Elle **a dû** oublier son billet.	She *must have* forgotten her ticket.
ti	Je **devais** l'accompagner.	I *was* (*supposed*) *to* go with her.
tf	Je **devrai** étudier demain.	I *will have to* study tomorrow.
tc	Je **devrais** étudier, mais . . .	I *ought to* study, but . . .

NOTE THE FORMS: *pp.* **dû** (avoir)

FC **devr-**

23.07 REMARKS ON **devoir***. Learn the special uses and meanings of the various tenses with this verb.

A. PRÉSENT. **must** [I], **owe(s)** [N]. Indicates obligation, and when the following infinitive is *être*, probability. (See *tp* examples above.)

B. PASSÉ COMPOSÉ. **had to** [I], **must have** [I]. Indicates obligation in the past on one occasion; or probability of something having happened.

C. IMPARFAIT. **was to, was supposed to** [I]. Indication of something planned for the past that was not done.

D. FUTUR. **will have to** [I]. Indication of strong obligation for the future.

E. CONDITIONNEL. **ought to** [I], **should** [I] (but probably won't). Indication of a consciousness of obligation, but lack of certainty that it will be carried out; hence the implied or expressed *mais*. . . .

Exercice 23C *devoir** [23.06 – 23.07]

Donnez l'équivalent approximatif des phrases suivantes, en employant le verbe **devoir**.

MODÈLE: Jacques *est obligé d'*étudier maintenant.
Jacques **doit** étudier maintenant.

1. Jean-Paul était obligé de travailler hier.
2. Je suis obligé de payer dix francs à mon ami.
3. Cette dame a l'air riche.
4. Il est probable que vous parents sont allés au cinéma.
5. Demain je serai obligé de travailler.
6. Hier j'ai été obligé d'aller à l'aéroport.
7. Je sais qu'il faut étudier, mais je t'accompagne au cinéma quand même.
8. J'avais l'intention de visiter Vienne, mais je n'avais pas le temps.
9. Il semble que j'ai oublié mon parapluie (*umbrella*).
10. On m'a obligé de passer un examen en sociologie.

Exercice 23D   Pronoms relatifs *qui* et *que* [23.01 – 23.05]

Joignez les deux phrases l'une à l'autre au moyen d'un pronom relatif.

MODÈLE: L'avion est en retard. **Il vient d'atterrir.**
L'avion **qui vient d'atterrir** est en retard.

1. La voiture est bleue. Jean a pris cette voiture.
2. Cette lettre est longue. Vous avez tapé la lettre.
3. L'aéroport est énorme. L'aéroport se trouve au nord de Paris.
4. L'aéroport est gigantesque. Nous avons visité cet aéroport.
5. Ma mère a trois chats. Ils ont toujours faim.
6. Le car arrive devant l'hôtel. Vous attendez le car depuis un quart d'heure.
7. Notre chauffeur a doublé un poids-lourd. Ce poids-lourd roulait très vite.
8. Le camion était chargé de marchandises. Vous voyez le camion là-bas.
9. Le livre traite de l'imprimerie. Je cherche ce livre.
10. Alexandre s'est marié avec une Italienne. Elle doit être riche.

Exercice 23T   Thème français

1. The gentleman who got the wrong address is an architect.
2. The young ladies you saw at the department store are stenographers.
3. Tourists who come to Paris always have a good time on the Left Bank.
4. Étienne owes me the ten dollars that I lent him last week.
5. The secretary hurried to type the letters that the director had written.
6. You must have seen the books Professor Foulet wrote when he was in Paris.
7. We have just come from the lecture that took place at the university.
8. I was supposed to go to the bookstore with my former roommate this afternoon.
9. Which one of these cars is the Citroën your father bought?
10. You will be amazed when you see the watch I gave [to] my father.
11. The teacher must have been astonished when he read my composition.
12. I was watching the program you recommended when there was an electrical failure [*une panne d'électricité*].
13. In three weeks I will have to take my English examination.
14. Tuesday evening my father had to stay at the office.
15. I ought to visit my aunt and uncle in Rouen, but I have too much homework to do.

Exercice 23E   Sujet de composition ou de causerie

Imaginez un professeur qui fait toujours ce qui plaît aux étudiants. Parlez de sa façon de faire les conférences, d'expliquer la leçon, de se comporter. Employez autant de pronoms relatifs que possible.

Révision systématique

1. John's mother had a small black cat and mine had three. [2.07] [6.02] [12.11] [15.05]
2. Those windows had been opened before we arrived. [19.07] [15.06] [11.06]

3. Several old ladies went into that shop and stayed there for two hours. [3.10] [16.03] [14.07]
4. Mr. Dupont took a book out of the drawer and began to write in it. [16.05] [6.05] [19.01] [14.08]
5. The Smiths had Mr. Levitt build a new house; they had it built on a hill. [1.04D] [17.01 – 17.02]

L'Île de la Cité avec Notre-Dame (*Sodel-M. Brigaud/Interphotothèque*)

24

Pronoms relatifs après une préposition

voir*

PRONOMS RELATIFS APRÈS UNE PRÉPOSITION `rel`

24.01 OBJECT OF A PREPOSITION. If the repetitious noun (RN) in a subordinate clause follows a preposition, use the relative pronoun **qui** for *persons*, or a form of **lequel** for *things*. Move the whole resulting prepositional phrase to the head of the subordinate clause.

<table>
<tr><td></td><td colspan="2">RN</td><td></td></tr>
<tr><td>PERSON</td><td>Voilà la dame.</td><td>J'ai parlé avec la dame.</td><td></td></tr>
<tr><td></td><td>∧</td><td>avec qui</td><td>REPLACEMENT</td></tr>
<tr><td></td><td></td><td>avec qui j'ai parlé.</td><td>CORRECT ORDER</td></tr>
<tr><td></td><td colspan="2">Voilà la dame avec qui j'ai parlé.</td><td></td></tr>
</table>

<table>
<tr><td></td><td colspan="2">RN</td></tr>
<tr><td>THING</td><td>La table est ronde.</td><td>J'ai mis la lettre sur la table.</td></tr>
<tr><td></td><td>∧</td><td>sur laquelle</td></tr>
<tr><td></td><td></td><td>sur laquelle j'ai mis la lettre</td></tr>
<tr><td></td><td>La table</td><td>| sur laquelle j'ai mis la lettre | est ronde.</td></tr>
</table>

Notice that the subordinate clause must follow the RN directly [23.04].

215

REMEMBER: After a preposition, **QUI** for PERSONS,
a form of **LEQUEL** for THINGS

24.02 **dont** REPLACING **de** [N]. If the prepositional phrase begins with **de** or a form of **de** (**du, des, de la, de l'**), use **dont** instead of *qui* or a form of *lequel*. This is a simplification always preferred.

> Voilà la dame. J'ai parlé **de la dame.**   PERSON
> **dont**
> **dont** j'ai parlé.
> *of whom*
> Voilà la dame **dont j'ai parlé**.
> *There is the lady I spoke of.*

> Voilà le livre. Paul parlait **de ce livre.**   THING
> **dont** Paul parlait
> *about which*
> Voilà le livre **dont Paul parlait**.
> *There is the book Paul was talking about.*

24.03 FORMS OF **lequel**. The pronoun **lequel** has two components (**le/quel**), both of which must agree in gender and number with the noun replaced in a prepositional phrase. The forms are:

	MASCULINE	FEMININE
Singular	*le*quel	*la*quelle
Plural	*les*quels	*les*quelles

When the preposition **à** precedes, contraction occurs [1.03]. Thus **à** + **lequel** becomes **auquel**. The forms involved are:

m.s.	*m.pl.*	*(f.s.)*	*f.pl.*
*au*quel	*aux*quels	à laquelle NO CONTRACTION	*aux*quelles

> Voilà la maison **dans laquelle** Victor Hugo est né.
> *There is the house Victor Hugo was born in.*
> Voici le roman **auquel** je pensais.
> *Here is the novel I was thinking about.*

24.04 Use of **lequel** in reference to persons. After the prepositions **entre** [*between*], **parmi** [*among*], and **sans** [*without*], **lequel** may be used rather than **qui**:

> Voilà un professeur **sans lequel** je ne réussirais pas.
> *There is a teacher without whom I would not pass.*

24.05 Use of the antecedent **ce** (**ce qui**, **ce que**, **ce dont**). Relative pronouns follow a noun (the RN) in the main clause. This is the *antecedent*, telling us just what noun is involved.

> Voilà ‖la voiture‖ **dont** tu as parlé.   There is the car you spoke about.
>   ANTECEDENT

Here, **dont** has the noun antecedent **la voiture**. Sometimes the antecedent is missing or unspecified, and the word **ce** then is supplied (for *things only*):

>   ANTECEDENT
> Voilà ‖**ce**‖ **dont** tu as parlé.   There is *what* you spoke about.
> Je sais ‖**ce**‖ **qui** arrive.   I know *what* is happening.
> Je sais ‖**ce**‖ **que** vous voulez.   I know *what* you want.

If the relative pronoun referring to a thing is at the *beginning* of a sentence, the sentence will begin with **Ce qui**, **Ce que**, or **Ce dont**.

> **Ce que** vous dites est vrai.   *What* you say is true.
> **Ce qui** se passe est un désastre.   *What* is happening is a disaster.
> **Ce dont** j'ai besoin est un stylo.   *What* I need is a pen.

The forms with **ce** refer only to things, never to persons. Notice the contrast between the following:

> Je sais **ce qui** arrive.   I know *what* is happening.
> Je sais **qui** arrive.   I know *who* is arriving.

When a sentence begins with **ce qui**, **ce que**, or **ce dont**, an additional (redundant) **ce** may be used in the second half of the sentence, optionally:

> **Ce qui** se passe, [**c'**]est un désastre.
> **Ce que** vous faites, [**c'**]est votre affaire.

But the redundant **ce** is mandatory if the second clause contains **être** plus a *personal pronoun* or a *plural noun*:

Ce qui m'agace, **c'est lui** et sa vanité.   PERSONAL PRONOUN lui
    What infuriates me is he and his vanity.

Ce que je cherche, **c'est [ce sont] des livres espagnols.**   PLURAL NOUN
    What I am looking for is some Spanish books.

24.06   USE OF **où** FOR LOCATION OR TIME.   When a prepositional phrase
containing the RN expresses a location or a time, **où** may be used to replace the
entire phrase.

Voilà **la maison.** Mon père est né **dans cette maison.**   PREPOSITIONAL PHRASE
                                         indicating location

     Voilà la maison **dans laquelle** mon père est né.
or Voilà la maison   **où**   mon père est né.

Prepositions such as **à, chez, dans, sous, sur, devant, derrière** and others
introduce phrases indicating location that may be replaced by **où**:

Voilà la boutique. Paul a stationné la voiture **devant cette boutique.**

Voilà la boutique $\begin{Bmatrix} \textbf{devant laquelle} \\ \textbf{où} \end{Bmatrix}$ Paul a stationné la voiture.

To indicate *from where*, use **d'où**:

Voilà le musée. Alain revient **du musée.**
Voilà le musée **d'où** revient Alain.

Notice the inversion of subject and verb in the prepositional phrase of the
last sentence. Inversion often occurs after a relative pronoun when the
subject is a noun rather than a personal pronoun.

    TIME.   The word *when* is conveyed by **où** (not *quand*) directly after a
noun:

          NOUN
Il pleuvait | **le jour** | où je suis allé à Chantilly.

    It was raining on the day (when) I went to Chantilly.

When there is no noun antecedent, **quand** may be used:

          VERB
Il | **pleuvait** | **quand** je suis allé à Chantilly.

24.07 TABLE OF RELATIVE PRONOUNS.

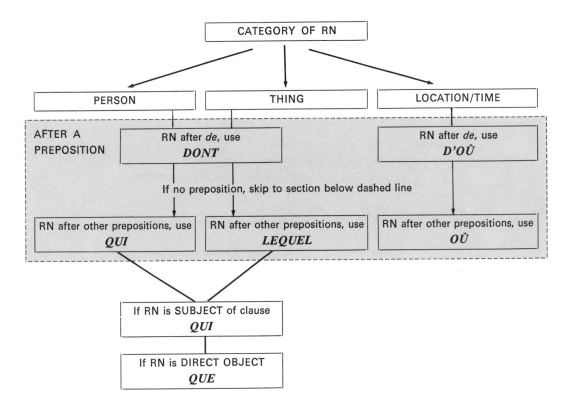

VERBE IRRÉGULIER voir*

24.08 Review the verb **voir*** [*to see*] in Appendix C, verb table 32, paying special attention to the present, passé composé, imperfect, future, and conditional tenses.

tp   Je **vois** l'autobus qui vient.

tpc Hier j'**ai vu** mon avocat.

ti   À Paris je **voyais** souvent mon oncle Jules.

tf   Demain je **verrai** un film italien.

tc   Si j'avais le temps, je **verrais** ce film avec vous.

NOTE THE FORMS: *pp.* **vu** (avoir)

                      FC **verr-**

The compound of this verb, conjugated the same way, is **revoir***, *to see again.*

J'ai revu Pierre l'année suivante.	I *saw* Pierre *again* the following year.
Au revoir!	Goodbye! (*Until we see each other again*)

Exercice 24A   Pronoms relatifs et prépositions [24.01 – 24.07]

Combinez les deux phrases au moyen d'un pronom relatif (**qui, lequel, dont, où**). Phrase (a) est toujours la proposition principale.

MODÈLE: (a) Le stylo est rouge.
            (b) J'ai écrit cette lettre *avec ce stylo.*
            Le stylo **avec lequel** j'ai écrit cette lettre est rouge.

1. (a) Voilà la jeune fille.
   (b) J'ai dîné *avec cette jeune fille* hier soir.
2. (a) L'école est grande.
   (b) Robert a garé la voiture *derrière cette école.*
3. (a) Jacques a acheté un dictionnaire.
   (b) Il a besoin *de ce dictionnaire* pour ses cours.
4. (a) La maison se trouve rue Royale.
   (b) Mme Legrand demeurait *dans cette maison.*
5. (a) Le théâtre est près d'ici.
   (b) Vous pensez *à ce théâtre.*
6. (a) Le professeur se trouve devant la bibliothèque.
   (b) Nous avons parlé *avec ce professeur* la semaine dernière.
7. (a) Donnez-moi le stylo, s'il vous plaît.
   (b) Vous avez écrit vos devoirs avec ce stylo.
8. (a) La rue est étroite.
   (b) La maison du médecin se trouve dans cette rue.
9. (a) Voilà la valise.
   (b) J'ai oublié la clef de cette valise.
10. (a) Voilà le professeur.
    (b) Nous avons vu la femme de ce professeur à Monaco.

Exercice 24B   Pronoms relatifs: Révision [23.01 – 23.05] [24.01 – 24.07]

Combinez les phrases au moyen du pronom relatif approprié.

1. (a) Voilà un monsieur distingué.
   (b) *Ce monsieur* travaille au ministère.
2. (a) Robert cherche la lettre.
   (b) Il a perdu *cette lettre* ce matin. [Attention: accord du *pp.*]
3. (a) Voilà le patron.
   (b) La femme *du patron* est actrice.
4. (a) Lucien a lu une fable.
   (b) Il aime beaucoup *cette fable.*
5. (a) Voilà quelques-uns de mes amis.
   (b) *Sans ces amis* je ne parlerais jamais français.

6. (a) Alexandre est un étudiant sérieux.
   (b) Les problèmes *d'Alexandre* ne sont pas graves.
7. (a) Ce bruit est désagréable.
   (b) Mes voisins font *ce bruit.* [*inversion needed*]
8. (a) Voilà le car.
   (b) *Ce car* part de la Porte Maillot à midi.
9. (a) Le directeur est dans son bureau.
   (b) Nous admirons le talent du directeur.
10. (a) Voilà le théâtre.
    (b) Monsieur Porra est le gérant de ce théâtre.
11. (a) Je connais cette dame.
    (b) La dame est assise près de la fenêtre.
12. (a) Nous cherchons le chien marron.
    (b) Mon voisin a perdu le chien.
13. (a) L'orchestre vient de commencer la symphonie.
    (b) Schubert a composé cette symphonie en 1828.
14. (a) Voilà le chien.
    (b) Le chien vous déteste.
15. (a) Voilà le chien.
    (b) Vous détestez le chien.

Exercice 24C Pronoms relatifs (Facultatif)

Remplacez les tirets par le pronom relatif approprié.

MODÈLES: Voilà la dame avec — vous avez parlé.
Voilà la dame **avec qui** vous avez parlé.
Le chien — vous a mordu est marron.
Le chien **qui** vous a mordu est marron.

1. La jeune fille — arrive en retard s'appelle Jeanne.
2. Le professeur — nous aimons bien enseigne la chimie.
3. La voiture — mon père a achetée est une Peugeot.
4. Voilà la tour — Georges a souvent parlé.
5. Le livre — j'ai besoin est une grammaire.
6. Voilà la voiture — je voudrais acheter.
7. Voilà — je voudrais acheter.
8. Je regarde — se passe dans la rue.
9. — je voudrais, c'est une motocyclette.
10. Le jeune homme avec — le patron parlait est un avocat.
11. La maison devant — se tient la concierge est l'immeuble de Jean.
12. La musique — vous écoutez est la symphonie de César Franck.

Exercice 24T Thème français

1. Yesterday I attended a good lecture. The lecture I attended took place at the Lycée Louis le Grand.
2. Your friends were listening to some music when I arrived at their apartment. The music they were listening to was a symphony by Mozart.

3. I saw that gentleman again. He is the man whose car was parked behind mine on the Boulevard Haussmann.
4. The lawyer you saw in the bookstore is one of my father's customers.
5. I saw the beautiful book you bought yesterday. It's a novel whose author I have forgotten.
6. When I arrive in England I will visit the museum you spoke about.
7. The day I arrive in London I will see the publisher of your book.
8. Do you know where that truck came from?
9. The table you put your watch on used to belong to Louis XIV.
10. Do you know what Jean-Paul is doing? He is having his car repaired. It's the car he bought during the summer.

Exercice 24D   Sujet de composition ou de causerie

Décrivez les curiosités de la ville où demeurent vos parents en employant des pronoms relatifs. Identifiez la ville dont vous parlerez, ensuite indiquez le nombre d'habitants et les industries principales. Puis vous pouvez parler des monuments tels que l'hôtel de ville, la bibliothèque, les parcs, les musées, les écoles, les théâtres, etc.

Révision systématique

1. I heard the plane approaching the airport. What a noise! [17.03] [18.08] [16.05]
2. The policeman near the main door allowed the visitors to pass. [17.03]
3. John went up to the second floor, where he is washing his hands and face. [18.06] (*Attention au numéro de l'étage.* Voir Chapitre 6, Révision lexicale.)
4. Our club [*le cercle*] will meet Monday at the Dupont's. What an interesting club! [18.01] [16.05]
5. After the tennis match, the boys went back to the dormitory to rest. [18.08]

Arrêt d'autobus, boulevard Raspail (*Helena Kolda/Monkmeyer*)

25

Emploi du subjonctif

Présent du subjonctif

EMPLOI DU SUBJONCTIF *sj*

25.01 USE. The subjunctive mood consists of two tenses, present and past subjunctive. These forms are used mainly in subordinate clauses beginning with **que** (and certain other conjunctions) when the main clause contains verbs of *wishing*, *doubting*, or *emotion*. The decision to use the subjunctive in the **que**-clause depends upon the content of the *main clause*, not upon the information contained in the subordinate clause.

25.02 CLASSES OF SUBORDINATE CLAUSES. For purposes of learning the use of the subjunctive, main clauses may be divided into three classes:

CLASS	MAIN CLAUSE INDICATES	AFTER **que** USE:
A	A **fact** will follow [25.03]	INDICATIVE (any tense)
B	What follows is *not a fact*, but rather **desirable, possible, doubtful** [25.04]	SUBJUNCTIVE
C	**Emotional content** expressed before *que* [25.05]	

25.03 CLASS A: MAIN CLAUSE INDICATING FACT. If the main clause states or indicates that what is to follow is an undisputed *fact* (or so considered by the speaker), use the indicative after **que**. Any tense of the indicative may be appropriate, depending upon the time expressed (present, passé composé, future, etc.).

> Je **sais que** Marie *est* malade.
> > I know that Mary is ill.
> **Il est probable que** Marie *est* malade.
> > It is likely that Mary is ill.

MAIN CLAUSE INDICATES FACT:

Je **sais** que	
Je **suis sûr(e)** que	
Il est **vrai** que	
Il est **probable** que	Marie **est** malade.
Il **dit** que	INDICATIVE
Il **paraît** que	
Je **pense** que	
Je **crois** que	

Notice that **Il est probable** is in Class A, while **Il est possible** is in Class B and requires the subjunctive. For an explanation of the cases of **penser** and **croire*** see 25.06.

25.04 CLASS B: MAIN CLAUSE INDICATING NON-FACT. If the main clause indicates that what is to follow is not yet a fact, but is only *desirable* (not yet fulfilled), *possible, hypothetical,* or even *doubtful* or *false,* then the subordinate clause will contain a verb in the subjunctive.

MAIN CLAUSE INDICATES NON-FACT

(1) DESIRABILITY

Il **faut** que	
Il **est bon** que	
Il **est juste** que	
Il **vaut mieux** que	Marie **soit** absente.
Je **veux** que	SUBJUNCTIVE
Je **ne veux pas** que	
Je **désire** que	
Je **ne désire pas** que	

Other main clauses implying that what is to follow is desirable, though not yet a fact, include:

Il est **essentiel** que	Il **préfère** que
Il est **important** que	Il **demande** que

Il est **nécessaire** que
Il est **préférable** que
Il est **temps** que
Il **aime mieux** que

Il **tient à** *ce que*[1]
Il **insiste** *pour que*[1]
Il **souhaite** que

(2) POSSIBILITY

Il est **possible** que ⎫ Marie **soit** malade.
Il **se peut** que ⎭ SUBJUNCTIVE

It is possible that Mary is ill.

(3) DOUBTFUL OR CONTRARY TO FACT

Je **doute** que ⎫
Il **ne paraît pas** que
Il **ne semble pas** que
Il **ne dit pas** que
Êtes-vous sûr(e) que ⎬ Marie **soit** malade
Je **ne crois pas** que   SUBJUNCTIVE
Je **ne pense pas** que
Croyez-vous que
Pensez-vous que ⎭

Notice that this category includes the negative and interrogative forms of some verbs from Class A (**penser, croire***, **paraître***). When such verbs are used to contradict (*Je ne crois pas*) or to express doubt or uncertainty (*croyez-vous*) the subjunctive is called for in the **que**-clause.

Among other main clauses implying doubt or lack of factuality with regard to the following **que**-clause are:

Il est **faux** que
Il est **impossible** que
Il est **incroyable** que

Il **n'est pas vrai** que
Il **n'est pas probable** que
Il **n'est pas certain** que
Je **ne suis pas certain**(e) que

25.05 CLASS C: MAIN CLAUSE HAVING EMOTIONAL CONTENT. If the main clause contains an impression of emotional content such as *surprise*, *regret*, *fear*, *anxiety*, *embarrassment*, the **que**-clause should contain a verb in the subjunctive.

MAIN CLAUSE HAS EMOTIONAL CONTENT

Je **regrette** que ⎫
Je **suis désolé(e)** que
Je **suis content(e)** que
Je **suis heureux (-se)** que ⎬ les soldats **soient** ici.
Je **suis surpris(e)** que   SUBJUNCTIVE
Je **suis étonné(e)** que
Je **suis fâché(e)** que ⎭

[1]Notice the special antecedent for *que* in these structures.

J'ai peur que⎫
Je crains que⎭ Marie ne parte.[2]

25.06 **Penser, croire*, espérer°.** These verbs are followed by the indicative when used positively, and by the subjunctive when used *negatively* or *interrogatively*. When a French speaker says **je pense** or **je crois**, he is reflecting factuality so far as he is concerned, hence the indicative follows.

Je **pense que** Marie **est** malade.	I think Mary is ill.
Je **crois que** vous **comprenez.**	I believe you understand.
J'**espère que** Charles **viendra.**	I hope Charles will come.

However, if these verbs are used in the *negative* or *interrogative* forms, the subjunctive is used after **que.**

Je **ne pense pas que** Marie **soit** malade.	I don't think Mary is ill.
Je **ne crois pas que** vous **compreniez.**	I don't believe you understand.
Espérez-vous que Charles **vienne?**	Do you hope Charles is coming?

conj

25.07 CONJUNCTION **que** MANDATORY. The conjunction **que** ("that") is required in French, although often omitted in English. Observe the English equivalents in the foregoing examples. Notice that the conjunction "that" is omitted (or may be added without changing the meaning); in French, the conjunction **que** is always present.

25.08 FORMATION OF THE PRESENT SUBJUNCTIVE. For most verbs, the **ils**-form of the present indicative, stripped of its *-ent* ending, is the stem of the present subjunctive. All verbs, both regular and irregular, (except *avoir** and *être**), add the following endings:

-e	-ions
-es	-iez
-e	-ent

VERB	INDICATIVE (*tp: ILS*-FORM)	SUBJUNCTIVE
parler	ils **parlent**	que je parle
finir	ils **finissent**	que je finisse
vendre	ils **vendent**	que je vende
dire*	ils **disent**	que je dise

---

[2]**Avoir peur** and **craindre* que** require **ne** before the verb in the **que**-clause. It has *no negative meaning* unless **pas** is also used.

J'**ai peur que** vous **ne** tombiez.	I am afraid you *will fall*.
Il **craint que** Marie **ne** parte.	He is afraid Mary *will leave*.

The negative meaning takes effect if both **ne** and **pas** are present:

J'**ai peur que** Marie **ne** vienne **pas.**	I am afraid that Mary *will not* come.

VERB	INDICATIVE (*tp: ILS*-FORM)	SUBJUNCTIVE
écrire*	ils **écriv**ent	que j'écrive
mettre*	ils **mett**ent	que je mette
partir*	ils **part**ent	que je parte
offrir*	ils **offr**ent	que j'offre
conduire*	ils **conduis**ent	que je conduise
connaître*	ils **connaiss**ent	que je connaisse
paraître*	ils **paraiss**ent	que je paraisse

MODEL CONJUGATIONS IN THE PRESENT SUBJUNCTIVE

regarder [to look at]

Il faut que je **regarde** que nous **regardions**
que tu **regardes** que vous **regardiez**
qu'il **regarde** qu'ils **regardent**

Notice the similarity with the present indicative of the **-er** verbs:

tp je **regarde** nous regard*ons*
tu **regardes** vous regard*ez*
il **regarde** ils **regardent**

finir [to finish]

Il se peut que je **finisse** que nous **finissions**
que tu **finisses** que vous **finissiez**
qu'il **finisse** qu'ils **finissent**

répondre [to answer]

Je doute que je **réponde** que nous **répondions**
que tu **répondes** que vous **répondiez**
qu'il **réponde** qu'ils **répondent**

dire* [to say]

Croit-on que je **dise** cela? que nous **disions** cela?
que tu **dises** cela? que vous **disiez** cela?
qu'il **dise** cela? qu'ils **disent** cela?

25.09 avoir* AND **être***. These two verbs have irregular endings in the present subjunctive:

avoir* [to have]

que j'**aie** que nous **ayons**
que tu **aies** que vous **ayez**
qu'il **ait** qu'ils **aient**

être* [to be]

que je **sois** que nous **soyons**
que tu **sois** que vous **soyez**
qu'il **soit** qu'ils **soient**

25.10 TIME INDICATION, PRESENT SUBJUNCTIVE. The present subjunctive indicates either *present* or *future* meaning. Thus the verb **que je finisse** in the present subjunctive may mean either *that I am finishing* (present) or *that I will finish* (future). The context of the conversation or text, and/or the presence of an adverb of time (**maintenant, demain**) indicate which is meant.

PRESENT TIME   Il se peut que nous **comprenions** maintenant.
It is possible that we *understand* now.

FUTURE TIME   Il se peut que nous **comprenions** plus tard.
It is possible that we *will understand* later.

Compare the following sentences in which the future time of the subordinate clause is conveyed in different ways:

INDICATIVE   Je sais que   je **finirai** le travail demain.
SUBJUNCTIVE   Je doute que je **finisse** le travail demain.
            . . . *I will finish the work tomorrow.*

Exercice 25A   Emploi du subjonctif [25.01 – 25.06]

Complétez chaque phrase par *Marie est malade* ou par *Marie soit malade*, selon le cas.

MODÈLES: Je suis sûr que . . .
          Je suis sûr que *Marie **est** malade,*
          Je doute que . . .
          Je doute que *Marie **soit** malade.*

1. Il est vrai que . . .
2. Je pense que . . .
3. Je ne pense pas que . . .
4. Il est possible que . . .
5. Paul dit que . . .
6. Nous regrettons que . . .
7. Croyez-vous que . . .
8. Il paraît que . . .
9. Je crains que . . .
10. Le professeur doute que . . .

Exercice 25B   Emploi et formation du subjonctif [25.01 – 25.06]

Ajoutez à la proposition principale la phrase entre parenthèses; mettez le verbe au subjonctif ou à l'indicatif selon le cas.

MODÈLE: (Lucien est content.) Je veux que . . .
         Je veux que Lucien **soit** content.

1. (Vous parlerez français.) Il faut que . . .
2. (Robert finit son travail.) Il vaut mieux que . . .

3. (Nous vendrons notre voiture.) Il se peut que . . .
4. (Il dit la vérité.) Il est essentiel que . . .
5. (Tu écris une lettre à Marie.) Je tiens à ce que . . .
6. (Marie met la table.) Maman désire que . . .
7. (Il part à midi.) Je doute que . . .
8. (Il finit à midi.) Pensez-vous que . . .
9. (Nous arriverons demain.) Il faut que . . .
10. (Je partirai demain.) Mes amis sont étonnés que . . .
11. (Je conduirai la voiture). Maman demande que . . .
12. (Jacques finit ses devoirs.) Le professeur est surpris que . . .
13. (Nous visitons la France.) Voulez-vous que . . .
14. (Je finirai le travail demain.) Il faut que . . .
15. (Je finirai le travail demain.) Il est probable que . . .

Exercice 25T   Thème français

1. I am sure that you will tell the truth.
2. We are glad that you will tell the truth.
3. It is necessary that I mail these letters immediately.
4. My father was astonished that you are selling your car.
5. It is possible that we will arrive in Lyons late.
6. I am glad that you are answering the letter.
7. Alexandre is anxious for you to look at his stamp collection.
8. We would like our son to attend the lecture this evening.
9. I am astonished that Paul is reading German poetry.
10. My parents want me to drive my little brother to school.

Exercice 25C   Sujet de composition ou de causerie

Décrivez un individu ou un bureau dont les qualités vous semblent étonnantes ou douteuses. Employez des phrases qui contiennent des verbes au subjonctif. («Je connais un avocat qui gagne beaucoup d'argent. Je doute qu'il soit malhonnête, mais il a des clients douteux. Il est possible qu'il connaisse des gangsters» . . . etc.)

Révision systématique

1. When we lived in London we often used to take walks in Green Park. [8.11B] [20.04]
2. Last week the weather was bad, so (*therefore*) we went to the library to read. [20.05] [7.05] [11.01]
3. While I was reading a volume of the encyclopedia, one of my friends came into the reading room. [20.06]
4. I had been writing a French composition for half an hour when she left the building. [20.07]
5. John had already bought some apples when I saw him at the market. He gave me three. [20.08] [13.03] [14.03] [13.08]

Le nouveau visage de Paris au-delà de Montparnasse (*Helena Kolda/Monkmeyer*)

26

Subjonctif
(suite)

Subjonctif
des verbes
irréguliers

SAVOIR*

SUBJONCTIF (suite)   *sj*

~~~~~~

26.01 ADDITIONAL USES OF THE SUBJUNCTIVE. The subjunctive is used automatically after certain *conjunctions* [26.02], after *superlatives* [26.03], and after verbs expressing *purpose*, *wish*, or *expectation* when the specifications are merely theoretical [26.04].

26.02 CONJUNCTIONS REQUIRING SUBJUNCTIVE. The following conjunctions automatically require the subjunctive in the subordinate clause that follows them:

avant que	before
pour que, afin que	so that, in order that
en attendant que	until [**if** *a future action*]
jusqu'à ce que	until [**if** *a future action*]
pourvu que	provided that
bien que, quoique	although
à moins que . . . ne	unless

Il fera son travail **avant que** vous **reveniez.**
   He will do his work before you come back.

Il travaille **pour que** je **devienne** médecin.

He is working so that I may become a doctor.

Nous regarderons la télévision **jusqu'à ce que** Marie **revienne**.

We will watch television until Mary comes back.

Nous partons maintenant, **à moins que** vous **ne soyez** trop fatigué.

We are leaving now, unless you are too tired.

26.03 SUPERLATIVES REQUIRE SUBJUNCTIVE. When a **que**-clause follows a superlative or the equivalent (**le seul, l'unique, le premier, le dernier**, etc.), the verb of the subordinate clause should be in the subjunctive:

L'Étranger est **le meilleur roman** *que* nous **ayons lu.**

L'Étranger is the *best* novel that we have read.

Georges est le garçon **le plus intelligent** *que* je **connaisse.**

George is the *most intelligent* boy I know.

C'est la pièce **la plus passionnante** *que* je **connaisse.**

It's the *most exciting* play I know.

C'est **le seul dictionnaire** *qu'*on **puisse** obtenir en ce moment.

It's the *only dictionary* that can be obtained at present.

The effect of the use of the subjunctive here is to soften the statement, to avoid sounding too dogmatic or certain of the fact, and to allow for a differing opinion that may be held by others.

26.04 QUEST FOR A THEORETICAL OBJECT. When a verb of purpose, wish, or expectation such as **chercher** (*to look for*) is followed by a subordinate clause indicating theoretically desirable qualities of the object sought, use the subjunctive to express the desirability and lack of factuality.

Je cherche **une** dactylo **qui comprenne** l'arabe.

I am looking for *a* stenographer who understands Arabic.

Nous cherchons **une** voiture **qui ait** huit cylindres.

We are looking for *an* eight-cylinder car.

In the event the thing sought is *not* merely theoretical but an actual identifiable person or thing, use the indicative:

Je cherche **le monsieur qui est arrivé** hier soir.

I am looking for *the* gentleman who arrived yesterday evening.

Je cherche **la** dactylo **qui comprend** l'arabe. Est-elle occupée?

I am looking for *the* stenographer who understands Arabic. Is she busy?

26.05 REPLACEMENT OF THE SUBJUNCTIVE BY OTHER STRUCTURES. When possible, avoid the subjunctive. This is particularly desirable when the subject of both the main and subordinate clauses is the same.

She is glad that she is in France.

IDENTICAL SUBJECT

The infinitive structure may easily replace the subjunctive otherwise indicated for the subordinate clause:

> Elle est contente **d'être** en France.
> She is glad *to be* in France.

A. EMOTIONAL CONTENT OF MAIN CLAUSE. When the main clause involves emotional content, and the subject of both clauses is identical, use **de** + INFINITIVE instead of a **que**-clause.

> Nous **regrettons de ne pas pouvoir** assister à la conférence.
> We are sorry that we cannot attend the lecture.
> Il est **étonné de voir** son ancien professeur.
> He is astonished to see his former teacher.
> Je suis **fâché d'avoir** oublié le nom de cette dame.
> I am embarrassed to have forgotten that lady's name.

B. CONJUNCTIONS USING **de** + INFINITIVE. The conjunctions **avant que** and **afin que**, which normally require the subjunctive [26.02], may be changed: **que** is replaced by **de** + INFINITIVE when the subject of both clauses is identical.

> **avant de** [I] Il fait ses devoirs **avant de regarder** la télévision.
> **afin de** [I] Il étudie **afin de réussir** aux cours.

The conjunction **pour que** may be reduced to **pour** [I]:

> **pour** [I] Il parle lentement **pour être** compris.

C. **Bien que** + PRESENT PARTICIPLE [31.01]. When the subject of both clauses is identical, **bien que** may be followed by a present participle. If the verb after **bien que** is *être** (*ps.p.* **étant**), it may be omitted.

> **Bien que jouant** mal de la guitare, je peux accompagner des chansons.
> Although I play the guitar poorly, I can accompany songs.
> **Bien que fatigué**, j'assiste aux cours aujourd'hui. (Bien qu'**étant** fatigué)
> Although I am tired, I am attending classes today.

D. WISHING, DESIRING, PREFERRING. A main clause containing **désirer**, **vouloir***, **preferer**°, **aimer**, **aimer mieux** may be followed immediately by an infinitive when the subject is the same for both the main verb and the infinitive.

> Il **aime mieux** PRENDRE l'avion.
> Je **préfère** DÎNER au restaurant.
> Nous **voudrions** FAIRE un match de tennis.

However, if the subjects are different, the subjunctive cannot be avoided:

Il **aime mieux que** vous **preniez** l'avion.

He prefers that you take the plane.

Nous **voudrions que** vous **lisiez** cette lettre.

We would like you to read this letter.

E. REPLACEMENT OF **jusqu'à ce que**. The conjunction **jusqu'à ce que** [*until*] (which requires the subjunctive) may be replaced by **jusqu'à** [N] or **jusqu'au moment où** [INDICATIVE CLAUSE] to avoid the subjunctive.

SUBJUNCTIVE Nous avons parlé **jusqu'à ce que** ta mère **soit arrivée**.

INDICATIVE Nous avons parlé **jusqu'à l'arrivée** de ta mère.

$$\underset{\text{NOUN}}{\rule{2cm}{0.4pt}}$$

Gilbert a étudié **jusqu'au moment où** le professeur **est parti**.

Gilbert studied until (the moment when) the teacher left.

F. **Il faut que** [C, *sj*] REPLACED BY **Il faut** + INFINITIVE. The expression **il faut** may be followed directly by an infinitive if the *speaker* is the person required to do something:

SUBJUNCTIVE Il faut **que j'étudie** ce soir.

INFINITIVE Il (me) faut ÉTUDIER ce soir.

The insertion of an indirect object pronoun before **faut** makes it possible to indicate obligation on the part of any specific person:

Il **vous** faut étudier.   *You* must study.

Il **leur** faut étudier.   *They* must study.

SUBJONCTIF DES VERBES IRRÉGULIERS

26.06 PRESENT SUBJUNCTIVE OF **faire***, **savoir***, **pouvoir***. Learn the present subjunctive of these three important verbs.

VERB	STEM	PRESENT SUBJUNCTIVE	
faire*	**fass-**	que je fasse	que nous fassions
		que tu fasses	que vous fassiez
		qu'il fasse	qu'ils fassent
savoir*	**sach-**	que je sache	que nous sachions
		que tu saches	que vous sachiez
		qu'il sache	qu'ils sachent
pouvoir*	**puiss-**	que je puisse	que nous puissions
		que tu puisses	que vous puissiez
		qu'il puisse	qu'ils puissent

Il faut que je **fasse** mes devoirs.

    I must do my homework.

Je veux que tu **saches** la vérité.

    I insist that you know the truth.

Je doute que Paul **puisse** ouvrir cette fenêtre.

    I doubt that Paul can open that window.

26.07 Two-stem irregular verbs. Some irregular verbs use a stem derived from the *ils*-form (present indicative) for the "L-area" (silent ending) forms of the subjunctive, and use a different stem for the *nous*- and *vous*-forms.

The stem of the *nous*- and *vous*-forms of the present subjunctive usually conforms to the spelling of the infinitive stem. For example, **prendre*** has the following forms in the present subjunctive:

que je **prenne**	que nous **prenions**
que tu **prennes**	que vous **preniez** } **pren-** STEM
qu'il **prenne**	qu'ils **prennent**

prenn- STEM

Verbs which have two stems in the subjunctive are listed below.

VERB	STEM FOR je, tu, il, ils	STEM FOR nous, vous
aller*	que j'**aill**-e	que nous **all**-ions
prendre*	que je **prenn**-e	que nous **pren**-ions
tenir*	que je **tienn**-e	que nous **ten**-ions
venir*	que je **vienn**-e	que nous **ven**-ions
vouloir*	que je **veuill**-e	que nous **voul**-ions
voir*	que je **voi**-e	que nous **voy**-ions
devoir*	que je **doiv**-e	que nous **dev**-ions

26.08 Imperatives of **avoir***, **être***, **savoir***. The imperative forms of these verbs are derived from the present subjunctive.

avoir*	**aie**	N'aie pas peur.	Don't be afraid.
	ayez	N'ayez pas peur.	Don't be afraid.
	ayons	N'ayons pas peur.	Let's not be afraid.
être*	**sois**	Sois sage.	Be good. Behave yourself.
	soyez	Soyez tranquille.	Be quiet.
	soyons	Soyons calmes.	Let's be calm.
savoir*	**sache**	Sache la vérité.	Know the truth.
	sachez	Sachez la vérité.	Know the truth.
	sachons	Sachons la vérité.	Let's know the truth.

VERBE IRRÉGULIER savoir*

26.09 REVIEW **savoir*** [*to know*] in Appendix C, verb table 25.

tp	Il **sait** la date.	He *knows* the date.
	Il **sait** nager.	He *knows how* to swim.
tpc	Il **a su** que Pierre est parti.	He *found out* that Pierre has left.
ti	Il **savait** que nous allions en Espagne.	He *knew* that we were going to Spain.
tf	Il **saura** ce que nous faisons.	He *will know* what we are doing.
tc	Il **saurait** les faits.	He *would know* the facts.
sj	Je doute qu'il **sache** les faits.	I doubt that he *knows* the facts.

NOTE THE FORMS: *pp.* **su** (avoir*) *found out*
FC **saur-**

26.10 REMARKS ON **savoir***. The verb **savoir*** has various meanings and uses.

A. Followed by a NOUN, **savoir*** means *to know* [*a fact*].

Jacques **sait** LA DATE de la prise de la Bastille.
Albert **sait** LA LEÇON pour aujourd'hui.

Carefully distinguish between this and **connaître***, which means *to know* only if it is the same as *to be acquainted with*.

Je **connais** le directeur de notre société.
Nous **connaissons** bien la France.

B. Followed by an INFINITIVE, **savoir*** means *to know how* [*to do something*].

Mes amis **savent** JOUER aux échecs.
My friends can (*know how to*) play chess.
Nous ne **savons** pas DANSER.
We can't (*don't know how to*) dance.

Notice these idiomatic uses:

Je ne sais que faire.	I don't know what to do.
Il en sait plus long que moi.	He knows more about it than I.

C. In the passé composé, **savoir*** sometimes has the idiomatic meaning *found out*:

J'**ai su** que mes parents allaient acheter une voiture.
I found out that my parents were going to buy a car.

Exercice 26A   Emploi du subjonctif [26.01 – 26.03]

Combinez le fragment entre parenthèses avec la phrase incomplète, en mettant le verbe de la proposition subordonée au subjonctif s'il le faut.

MODÈLE: Vous réussirez pourvu que . . . (vous ne faites pas de fautes)
Vous réussirez pourvu que vous ne **fassiez** pas de fautes.

1. J'attendrai ici jusqu'à ce que . . . (tu finis tes devoirs)
2. Il faut que . . . (j'écris une composition)
3. Ils viendront pourvu que . . . (vous leur dites la nouvelle)
4. Je parle lentement afin que . . . (vous me comprenez)
5. Elle fait beaucoup de fautes bien que . . . (elle est intelligente)
6. Nous étudierons en attendant que . . . (le professeur revient)
7. Vous réussirez à moins que . . . (vous faites trop de fautes)
8. Ne parlez pas avant que . . . (les faits sont connus)
9. Il a apporté son cahier pour que . . . (je vois son travail)
10. Il fermera la porte avant que . . . (nous pouvons sortir)
11. C'est le meilleur dictionnaire que . . . (je connais)
12. C'est le seul fait historique que . . . (Philippe sait)
13. C'est la plus longue promenade que . . . (nous avons fait)
14. Ce roman est la plus court que . . . (vous avez dans votre collection)
15. Ce match était le plus passionnant que . . . (on peut imaginer)

Exercice 26B   Moyen d'éviter le subjonctif [26.05]

Combinez les deux phrases au moyen d'un infinitif.

MODÈLE: Jean est content. Il visite Chartres.
Jean est **content de visiter** Chartres.

1. Nous sommes heureux. Nous allons au ballet.
2. Je suis fâché. Je fais des fautes d'orthographe.
3. Les étudiantes voudraient le faire. Elles vont au centre.
4. Le docteur Broussard est content. Il possède une voiture neuve.
5. Pierre regrette. Il nous quitte.

Exercice 26C   Remplacement du subjonctif [26.05B]

Combinez les deux phrases au moyen du mot entre parenthèses.

MODÈLE: Il déjeune. Il va au cinéma. (*avant*)
Il déjeune **avant d'aller** au cinéma.

1. On travaille. On gagne de l'argent. (*afin*)
2. J'ai travaillé. J'ai gagné de l'argent. (*pour*)
3. Nous étudions. Nous sortons. (*avant*)
4. Je finis mes devoirs. Je joue au tennis. (*avant*)
5. Marie met la table. Elle s'occupe de la cuisine. (*avant*)

Exercice 26D Subjonctif des verbes irréguliers [26.06 – 26.07]

Refaites les phrases en commençant par le fragment entre parenthèses.

MODÈLE: Je fais mes devoirs. (Il faut que . . .)
Il faut **que je fasse** mes devoirs.

1. Tu sais tes leçons. (Il vaut mieux que . . .)
2. Je puis finir ce travail. (Je doute que . . .)
3. Nous ferons une promenade à bicyclette. (Il est possible que . . .)
4. Le patron prendra une décision demain. (Croyez-vous que . . .)
5. Nous verrons la Tour Eiffel. (Il est temps que . . .)

Exercice 26T Thème français

1. Please read this note before the director returns.
2. Write your name and address on this card before you go into Mr. Lefort's office.
3. I agree to go get the tickets, provided you take care of the transportation.
4. I can take my father's car unless he goes to the airport.
5. The boss is looking for a sociologist who knows how to organize a public opinion poll [*un sondage d'opinion*].
6. I found out that there are three plans [*le formule*] for purchasing a car abroad. Here is the best plan that one can imagine.
7. Although Charles writes German well, he can't speak it.
8. A fellow who used to work with me [*a former colleague*] found out that IBM is looking for an engineer who knows computers well.
9. Do you think that we can move (= transport) this heavy table into the living room? I'm afraid it is too big.
10. If I knew how to do it, I would move it without asking for help.

Exercice 26E Sujet de composition ou de causerie

Parlez d'une profession ou d'un métier qui vous intéresse, en signalant les buts [*purposes, goals*] de cet emploi, aussi bien que les avantages et les inconvénients que vous y prévoyez. (Servez-vous des conjonctions et des structures enseignées dans ce chapitre.)

Révision systématique

1. We left the apartment house at eight-thirty: we have been on the way for two and a half hours. [9.06]
2. Do you feel like a game of tennis? [3.12] [8.11E]
3. You are lucky that you succeed in everything you do. No matter how hard I try, I can't learn Russian. [3.12]
4. Roger's father had him clean out his garage. He had him clean it before he left for the office. [2.07] [17.01] [17.02] [26.05]
5. I heard Jacques singing in the bathroom. [17.03]

Le Cisalpin, Trans-Europ Express entre Paris et Milan (*Y. Broncard/SNCF*)

27

Passé
du subjonctif

MENER°

PASSÉ DU SUBJONCTIF   *sj.p.*

27.01   USE OF THE PAST SUBJUNCTIVE.   This tense is used in subordinate clauses requiring the subjunctive when the *time is in the past*. The present subjunctive expresses present and future times [25.10]; the past subjunctive expresses any past time.

PRESENT TIME:	Il est possible que	Robert **arrive** aujourd'hui. ⎫ *sj.*
FUTURE TIME:	Il est possible que	Robert **arrive** demain. ⎬
PAST TIME:	Il est possible que	Robert **soit arrivé** hier. *sj.p.*

The past subjunctive (**soit arrivé**) is a compound tense corresponding in formation to the passé composé: it consists of the auxiliary verb in the present subjunctive, plus the past participle:

INDICATIVE (passé composé)   elle *est* **arrivée**
SUBJUNCTIVE (passé)   qu'elle *soit* **arrivée**

The past subjunctive is used in subordinate clauses (1) after main clauses expressing *doubt, possibility, desirability,* or *emotional content* [Classes

B and C, 25.04–25.06], (2) after certain *conjunctions* [26.02], and (3) after *superlatives* [26.03], when the time is in the *past* in the **que**-clause.

27.02 FORMATION OF THE PAST SUBJUNCTIVE. The past subjunctive consists of the appropriate auxiliary verb in the present subjunctive plus the past participle. There is no change in the list of verbs using the auxiliary *être** [16.03] nor in the rules for agreement of past participles. Review the present subjunctive of the auxiliaries *avoir** and *être** [25.09], since they are a part of every verb in the past subjunctive.

Compare the passé composé with the past subjunctive on the following chart:

AUXILIARY VERB	INDICATIVE PASSÉ COMPOSÉ	SUBJUNCTIVE PASSÉ DU SUBJONCTIF	MEANINGS (IDENTICAL)
avoir*	il **a fini**	qu'il **ait fini**	he finished
	vous **avez lu**	que vous **ayez lu**	you read
	ils **ont fait**	qu'ils **aient fait**	they did
	j' **ai trouvé**	que j' **aie trouvé**	I found
	il **a eu**	qu'il **ait eu**	he had
être*	elle **est arrivée**	qu'elle **soit arrivée**	she arrived
	ils **sont partis**	qu'ils **soient partis**	they left
	je me **suis reposé**	que je me **sois reposé**	I rested
	il s' **est levé**	qu'il se **soit levé**	he got up

MODEL CONJUGATIONS IN THE PAST SUBJUNCTIVE

parler (avoir*)

que j'**aie parlé**	que nous **ayons parlé**
que tu **aies parlé**	que vous **ayez parlé**
qu'il **ait parlé**	qu'ils **aient parlé**

finir (avoir*)

que j'**aie fini**	que nous **ayons fini**
que tu **aies fini**	que vous **ayez fini**
qu'il **ait fini**	qu'ils **aient fini**

entrer (être*)—typical of verbs using auxiliary *être**

que je **sois entré(e)**	que nous **soyons entré(e)s**
que tu **sois entré(e)**	que vous **soyez entré(e)(s)**
qu'il **soit entré**	qu'ils **soient entrés**
qu'elle **soit entrée**	qu'elles **soient entrées**

s'amuser (être*)—typical of reflexive verbs

que je me **sois amusé(e)**	que nous nous **soyons amusé(e)s**
que tu te **sois amusé(e)**	que vous vous **soyez amusé(e)(s)**
qu'il se **soit amusé**	qu'ils se **soient amusés**
qu'elle se **soit amusée**	qu'elles se **soient amusées**

Meanings are identical with the *passé composé*. Thus:

Passé du subjonctif	

que nous ayons parlé	that we spoke, that we have spoken
qu'il ait fini	that he finished, that he has finished
que je sois entré	that I entered, that I have entered
qu'il se soit amusé	that he had a good time

Exercice 27A Formation du passé du subjonctif [27.02]

Mettez les verbes au passé du subjonctif. Commencez chaque phrase par **Il est possible que . . .**

MODÈLE: Il a parlé au professeur
Il est possible qu'il **ait parlé** au professeur.

1. Il a travaillé hier.
2. Il a dîné avec Suzanne.
3. Il a fini la leçon.
4. Il a vendu son auto.
5. Il a lu ce roman.
6. Vous avez perdu la lettre.
7. Vous avez oublié son adresse.
8. J'ai posé trop de questions.
9. J'ai mal compris.
10. Mme Dupont est venue nous voir.
11. Elle est déjà partie.
12. Les jeunes filles sont allées au cinéma.
13. Mes parents sont retournés à Londres.
14. Jacques et Francine ont fait du tennis.
15. Paul s'est réveillé tôt.
16. Le docteur Petit s'est acheté une télévision couleur.
17. Le poids-lourd s'est arrêté au feu rouge.
18. Le commis s'est trompé d'étage.
19. Nous avons réussi à l'examen.
20. Le concert a eu lieu au Palais de Chaillot.

Exercice 27B Emploi du subjonctif [27.01 – 27.02]

Commencez la phrase par le fragment entre parenthèses et mettez le verbe au subjonctif s'il y a lieu.

MODÈLE: Marie est arrivée. (Il se peut que . . .)
Il se peut que Marie **soit arrivée.**

1. La concierge a fermé la porte. (Je sais que . . .)
2. La concierge a ouvert la porte. (Je ne suis pas sûr que . . .)
3. Le petit Jean s'est lavé les mains. (J'espère que . . .)
4. Ma mère est descendue. (Je ne crois pas que . . .)
5. Le directeur est parti. (Je crains que . . .)

6. Nous avons eu de la chance. (Il est vrai que . . .)
7. Tu n'as pas eu de chance. (Nous regrettons que . . .)
8. Lucien a déjà fini ses devoirs. (Je suis étonné que . . .)
9. Son ami Poirot l'a aidé. (Je me doute que . . .)
10. L'Américaine est descendue à l'Hôtel du Louvre. (Je me demande si . . .)
11. Elle a rendu visite à une amie à Saint-Cloud. (Il est possible que . . .)
12. Vous avez réussi au cours. (Le professeur est heureux que . . .)
13. L'avocat est parti en vacances. (Je regrette que . . .)
14. Le ministre a proposé une nouvelle formule. (Il est bon que . . .)
15. Vous avez fait trop de fautes. (Vous réussirez à moins que . . .)
16. Nous l'avons vue. (C'est la plus belle voiture que . . .)
17. Paul l'a écrite. (C'est la lettre la plus intéressante que . . .)
18. Les jeunes filles sont rentrées. (Il ne semble pas que . . .)
19. Nous avons vu une pièce de Giraudoux. (Le professeur est content que . . .)
20. Vous avez dit la vérité. (L'agent ne croit pas que . . .)

VERBE IRRÉGULIER **mener°**

The verb **mener°** [*to lead*] is irregular only in the present, present subjunctive, and FC-stem.

27.03 PRESENT. There are two stems for the present tense of **mener°**. The *nous-* and *vous-*forms are regular, using **men-** as the stem derived in the usual way from the infinitive. The irregularity consists only of a grave accent added in the "L-AREA," making the stem **mèn-** for these four forms. The endings are the same as for regular *-er* verbs in the present: *-e, -es, -e, -ons, -ez, -ent.*

je **mène**	nous **menons**	} Regular
tu **mènes**	vous **menez**	
il **mène**	ils **mènent**	

L-AREA: Stem Change

27.04 FUTURE AND CONDITIONAL. The FC-stem is **mèner-** (notice the grave accent), to which is added the endings of the future [21.04] or conditional [22.02].

tf: will lead

je **mène**rai	nous **mène**rons
tu **mène**ras	vous **mène**rez
il **mène**ra	ils **mène**ront

tc: would lead

je **mène**rais	nous **mène**rions
tu **mène**rais	vous **mène**riez
il **mène**rait	ils **mène**raient

27.05 OTHER TENSES. Other tenses are regularly formed.

A. IMPARFAIT.

Je **menais** une vie tranquille.	I used to lead a quiet life.
Elle **menait** l'enfant à l'école.	She used to take the child to school.

B. COMPOUND TENSES (*les temps composés*). The past participle is formed from the infinitive in the regular way: **mené** (*avoir*):

tpc   Il **a mené** une vie exemplaire.
tpp   Il **avait mené** une vie exemplaire.
sj.p. Je doute qu'il **ait mené** une vie exemplaire.

C. PRESENT SUBJUNCTIVE. The same orthographic change occurs in the present subjunctive as occurred in the present indicative: the stem acquires a grave accent in the L-AREA:

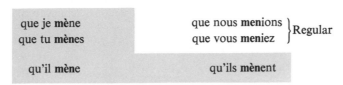

que je **mène**	que nous **menions** } Regular
que tu **mènes**	que vous **meniez** }
qu'il **mène**	qu'ils **mènent**

L-AREA: Stem Change

27.06 RELATED VERBS. Four verbs conjugated in the same way are the compounds **amener**° *to bring* [PERSON], **emmener**° *to take* [PERSON], **ramener**° *to bring back* [PERSON], and **se promener**° *to take a walk*.

A. **amener**° means *to bring* (someone) *to* the location of the speaker.

Amenez votre amie chez moi ce soir.
   Bring your friend to my house this evening.

B. **emmener**° means *to take* (someone) *to* another place, away from the speaker.

Tu vas au cinéma? **Emmène** les enfants.
   You're going to the movies? *Take* the children *along*.
J'ai **emmené** Marguerite à la soirée.
   I *took* Marguerite to the party.

C. **ramener**° (= re-mener) *to bring* (someone) *back again*.

— **Ramenez** le malade demain, dit le médecin.
   "*Bring* the patient *back again* tomorrow," said the doctor.

D. **se promener**° *to take a (walk)(ride)* [8.10B]

Il **se promène** avec son chien.

Nous **nous promenons** en auto cet après-midi.

Ils **se sont promenés** en bateau.

Exercice 27C *emmener*° ou *amener*° [27.06]

Choisissez le mot juste. Employez la forme appropriée dans votre réponse.

1. Vous êtes à l'appareil. Vous invitez un ami à venir chez vous. Vous dites : — (Amenez) (Emmenez) votre camarade de chambre.
2. Vous sortez pour aller faire des commissions en ville. Votre frère vous accompagnera. Vous dites : — Je vais (amener) (emmener) mon frère.
3. Vous êtes à la porte de votre habitation. Vous voyez venir Paul, accompagné de son oncle Jules. Vous vous dites : — Tiens ! Paul (amène) (emmène) son oncle Jules !
4. Paul vous dit en arrivant avec son oncle : — Salut ! J'ai (amené) (emmené) mon oncle Jules.
5. Quand nous quittons Paris pour les grandes vacances, nous allons au bord de la mer. Nous (amenons) (emmenons) toujours notre chien Tonton.

Révision lexicale

Les trains

1. La Société nationale des chemins de fer français (la S.N.C.F.) est un **réseau** [*system*, *network*] nationalisé d'une grande importance dans la vie économique française.

2. Il y a plusieurs **gares** à Paris. Les plus importantes sont la Gare du Nord (pour des trains à destination de Calais et de Bruxelles), la Gare de l'Est (à destination de Bâle), la Gare Saint-Lazare (à destination du Havre), la Gare de Lyon (pour Dijon et Nice), la Gare d'Austerlitz, la Gare Montparnasse, et d'autres.

3. On offre deux classes de train, dont la première coûte plus cher. Les trains de luxe comme *le Mistral* entre Paris et Nice sont entièrement composés de voitures de la première classe. Ce train est un des T.E.E. (**Trans-Europ Express**) ; il faut une réservation pour prendre un T.E.E.

4. Les trains européens marchent toujours à l'heure. On les classe ainsi : le plus rapide s'appelle **un rapide** [*express*], qui ne s'arrête qu'aux plus grandes gares. Ensuite il y a l'**express**, train ordinaire qui s'arrête aux grandes villes. Un train **omnibus** [*local*] s'arrête à toutes les gares.

5. Au **guichet** [*ticket-window*] on peut demander **un billet simple** [*one-way ticket*] (**pour** Rouen, par exemple), un billet **aller** (**et**) **retour** [*round-trip ticket*]. Il faut indiquer tout de suite la classe : — Un aller-retour première pour Rouen, s'il vous plaît.

6. Les bagages. Dans la gare on peut laisser ses bagages **à la consigne** [*check-room*], ou **à la consigne automatique** [*coin-operated lockers*].

Exercice 27T   Thème français

1. There comes Maurice! (There is Maurice who is coming.) He has brought some students along with him. Great!
2. Do you think that Maurice has brought his girl friend Geneviève along?
3. "Don't forget. You must bring your father back here Monday," said the lawyer.
4. Do you believe that Gérard has finished his research?
5. I do. It is possible that he has written his final report, and that he has handed it in to the director.
6. We must make an important decision tomorrow. We will have made it when the lawyer arrives day after tomorrow.
7. Mounier is anxious for me to go camping with him; I am sorry that I promised to do it.
8. I am not sure you understood the problem that I explained to you. It's complicated.
9. It's a complicated problem, so I am looking for a scientist who knows nuclear physics [*la physique nucléaire*] well.
10. John brought along my old history teacher, but I am afraid that he got the wrong apartment.

Exercice 27D   Sujets de composition ou de causerie

1. L'influence des détails sans importance sur les grands événements du monde. Pascal a dit: «Le nez de Cléopâtre: s'il eut été plus court, toute la face de la terre aurait changé.»

Choisissez un événement; imaginez les changements possibles dans d'autres circonstances. Employez les tournures de phrase suggérées par les chapitres sur le subjonctif pour exprimer vos doutes, vos regrets, vos opinions à cet égard.

2. Décrivez un voyage en chemin de fer.

Révision systématique

1. Wake up! Get up! Don't lie down! Get dressed! Wash your face and hands! Comb your hair! [18.03]
2. Don't hurry to finish the work. Take care of it later. [18.01] [13.07]
3. I am not satisfied with Maurice's report. I doubt that you have read it. [18.05] [27.01]
4. John and I have just played tennis, and we have returned to the dormitory to rest. [11.10] [18.08]
5. Do you take care of the cooking when your parents are in Switzerland? [18.07]

Cabines téléphoniques à l'intérieur d'un bureau de poste (*Photo SIRP—PTT*)

28

Pronom démonstratif celui

Pronoms toniques

PRONOM celui

~~~~~~

28.01 USE. The pronoun **celui** [*the one*] enables you to avoid repeating a noun just mentioned. There are four forms of this pronoun and the one selected must match the gender and number of the replaced noun. A form of **celui** is always followed by either (1) a *relative pronoun*, (2) **de** + [N] to show possession, or (3) **-ci** or **-là**.

(1) le livre	Voici **celui que** j'ai acheté. [28.03]	
	Here's *the one* I bought.	
(2) la montre	**Celle de Robert** est sur la table. [28.04]	
	Robert's [= *the one of Robert*] is on the table.	
(3) le stylo	**Celui-ci** est rouge. [28.05]	
	This one is red.	

28.02 AGREEMENT. The four forms of **celui** are shown below. The form selected must agree in gender and number with the noun replaced.

	MASCULINE	FEMININE	MEANING
Singular	**celui**	**celle**	the one
Plural	**ceux**	**celles**	the ones ('those')

EXAMPLES

Je cherche mon	**livre**	et	**celui**	de Robert.
J'ai lavé ma	**chemise**	et	**celle**	de mon frère.
J'ai mes	**livres**	et	**ceux**	de Marie.
J'ai lavé mes	**chemises**	et	**celles**	de mon frère.

⤷REPRESENTING⤶

28.03 **celui** + RELATIVE PRONOUN.

J'ai trouvé mon billet et **celui que** vous avez pris.

I found my ticket and *the one* you bought.

(. . . les étudiants) **Ceux qui** ont passé l'examen sont partis.

(. . . the students) *Those who* took the exam have left.

(. . . la jeune fille) C'est **celle dont** je vous ai parlé.

(. . . the girl) She's *the one* I spoke to you about.

28.04 **celui** FOLLOWED BY **de** (OR OTHER PREPOSITION) + NOUN.

J'ai ma clef et **celle de** Robert.

I have my key and *Robert's.*

Marie apporte mon dictionnaire et **celui de** Francine.

Mary is bringing my dictionary and *Francine's.*

Jacques a vu vos parents et **ceux de** Lucien.

Jacques saw your parents and *Lucien's.*

Voilà mon livre et **celui auquel** vous pensiez.

There is my book and *the one* you were thinking about.

28.05 **celui** + **-ci** OR **-là** [*this one*, *that one*]. By adding the suffix **-ci** to any form of **celui**, the meaning is changed from *the one* to *this one*; in the plural, to *these*. By adding **-là** the meaning is changed to *that one, those*. The following table shows all the forms using suffixes.

		SINGULAR		PLURAL	
-ci	MASCULINE	**celui-ci**	{this one,	**ceux-ci**	{these,
	FEMININE	**celle-ci**	the latter	**celles-ci**	the latter
-là	MASCULINE	**celui-là**	{that one,	**ceux-là**	{those,
	FEMININE	**celle-là**	the former	**celles-là**	the former

Ce livre-**ci** est neuf; **celui-là** est vieux.

This book is new; that one is old.

Ces maisons-**là** sont belles; **celles-ci** ne le sont pas.

Those houses are beautiful; these are not.

Notice that by adding **-ci** or **-là** to a noun, the meaning of **ce** can be specified:

ce livre	this *or* that book	**ce livre-ci**	*this* book
		ce livre-là	*that* book

28.06 **celui-ci** [*the latter*]/ **celui-là** [*the former*]. When two nouns have been mentioned, the next clause or sentence may refer to them as *the former . . . the latter*. In French, however, the order of reference is reversed: *the latter* (**celui-ci**) . . . *the former* (**celui-là**). Use the form of **celui** that agrees in gender and number with the nouns referred to.

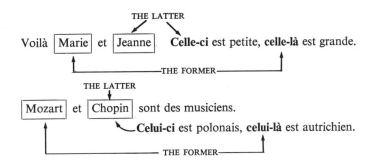

Exercice 28A   Pronom *celui* [28.01 – 28.06]

Évitez la répétition d'un nom en remplaçant les mots en italique par la forme appropriée de **celui**.

MODÈLE: J'ai vu ma voiture et *la voiture* de Jean dans le parking.
J'ai vu ma voiture et **celle** de Jean dans le parking.

1. Voilà un stylo. C'est *le stylo* que j'ai trouvé hier.
2. J'ai une machine à écrire. C'est *la machine* que nous avons vue hier aux Galeries Lafayette.
3. Les fables de La Fontaine sont *les fables* (*f.*) que nous allons expliquer en classe.
4. Il se peut que vous pensiez aux pièces de Beaumarchais. Moi, je pensais *aux pièces* de Molière.
5. —De quels livres as-tu besoin?
   —J'ai besoin *des livres* qui sont au troisième rayon [*shelf*].
6. Cette auto-là est trop longue; *cette auto*-ci est trop courte.
7. Ce chien-ci est très jeune; *ce chien*-là est très vieux.
8. J'aime les philosophes du dix-septième siècle, surtout Pascal et La Rochefoucauld. *La Rochefoucauld* était soldat; *Pascal* était physicien.
9. Voilà le doyen et le professeur qui arrivent au restaurant. *Le doyen* a soif; *le professeur* ne veut qu'un sandwich au fromage.

10. Mes parents font un voyage en Espagne; *les parents* de Pierre visitent l'Angleterre.

Exercice 28B   Pronom *celui* ou Pronom possessif [28.01] [12.11]

Remplacez les mots en italique par **celui** ou par le pronom possessif approprié. Par exemple, on peut remplacer *le livre* par **celui**; mais *votre livre* doit être remplacé par le pronom possessif **le vôtre**.

1. Voici mon livre à moi. C'est *votre livre* qui est perdu.
2. Voici ma montre. C'est *la montre* que vous m'avez vendue.
3. Paul a pris mon billet et *votre billet à vous*.
4. Paul a apporté mon sandwich et *le sandwich* que vous avez commandé.
5. Je cherche les disques (*m.*) de Johnny Hallyday et *les disques* d'Edith Piaf.
6. Je cherche mes disques et *tes disques à toi*.
7. Mes parents et *les parents* de Robert assisteront au concert ce soir.
8. Mes parents et *les parents de Robert* assisteront au concert ce soir.
9. Ma valise est usée, mais *la valise de René* est neuve.
10. Ma valise est usée, mais *la valise* de René est neuve.

PRONOMS TONIQUES

d,j   **28.07** TABLE OF DISJUNCTIVE PRONOUNS.   The following table shows the personal pronouns called *disjunctive* or stressed (**pronoms toniques**). Their uses are described in sections 28.08 and 28.09.

DISJUNCTIVE PRONOUN	MEANING	CORRESPONDS TO SUBJECT PRONOUN
moi	I, me	je
toi	you	te
lui	him	il
elle	her	elle
(soi)	(oneself, himself, herself, itself)	
nous	us	nous
vous	you	vous
eux	them (*m.pl.*)	ils
elles	them (*f.pl.*)	elles

When plural nouns of mixed genders are used, the masculine plural form **eux** applies:

Voilà **Paul** et **Marie**. Je vais au cinéma **avec eux**.

28.08 SUMMARY OF USES OF DISJUNCTIVE PRONOUNS. The disjunctive pronouns are separated from the verb, unlike all other pronouns which cling to the verb. Disjunctive pronouns have the following uses:

A.	Alone or after **C'est (Ce sont)**	**Lui.** C'est **lui.**
B.	After a preposition	avec **moi**
C.	Part of a compound subject	**Lui et moi,** nous . . .
D.	Emphasis on subject	**Moi, je** comprends.
E.	After **que** in comparisons	plus fort **que moi**
F.	To clarify or emphasize possessive adjectives	sa maison **à lui**
G.	With **C'est** [*dj*] **qui** . . .	**C'est moi qui** ai parlé.

28.09 APPLICATION OF DISJUNCTIVE PRONOUNS.

A. ALONE OR AFTER **C'est** (or **Ce sont**).

—Qui a écrit cette lettre? —**Moi.** or —**C'est moi.** —**Ce sont eux.**

B. AFTER A PREPOSITION.

Nous allons au cinéma **avec eux.**	We are going to the movies with them.
Je me souviens **de lui.**	I remember him.
M. Dupont va **chez lui.**	Mr. Dupont is going home.
Chacun **pour soi.**	Everyone for himself.

Certain verbal structures using the régime à [P] may *not* replace this régime by an indirect object pronoun. Instead, the preposition à is retained, and a disjunctive pronoun is used in place of the name of the person.

Je pense **à Robert.**	Je pense **à lui.** NOT Je lui pense.
Il s'intéresse **à ses élèves.**	Il s'intéresse **à eux.**
Faites attention **au professeur.**	Faites attention **à lui.**

If a *thing*, rather than a person, follows the preposition à, you may replace à [N]:

Il s'intéresse **à la musique.**	Il s'**y** intéresse. [14.07]

The following verbs (there are others) require a disjunctive pronoun in the régime à [P] (see [14.10]):

penser à	**faire attention à**
songer à	**s'habituer à**
s'intéresser à	

Use a disjunctive pronoun for persons after **de**:

Le soldat s'est **approché de Jean**. Le soldat s'est **approché de lui**.

C. PART OF A COMPOUND SUBJECT. When there are two subjects, either one or both may be disjunctive pronouns (no regular subject pronoun can be used at the same time).

Lui et elle parlent français. He and she speak French.
Mon père et moi allons en ville. My father and I are going downtown.

Marie et lui vont an cinéma. He and Mary are going to the movies.

If **moi** is part of the compound subject, use the *nous*-form of the verb; otherwise use the third person plural form (*ils*-form).

D. EMPHASIS OF THE SUBJECT. In French, emphasis is placed on the subject by adding a disjunctive pronoun at the beginning or end of the sentence, separated from the rest of the sentence by a comma. (In English emphasis is conveyed by oral stress on the subject, and in writing by use of italics.)

Moi, je comprends le russe. *I* understand Russian.
Il est riche, **lui**. *He* is rich.
Hélène est intelligente, **elle**. *Helen* is intelligent.

When the subject is a noun, place the disjunctive pronoun at the end of the sentence.

E. AFTER **que** IN COMPARISONS [8.01].

Lucien écrit **mieux que moi**.
  Lucien writes better than I.
J'ai **plus** de disques **que lui**.
  I have more records than he (does).

F. TO CLARIFY OR EMPHASIZE POSSESSIVE ADJECTIVES: **à** + [*dj*].

The possessive adjectives **son** and **sa** can mean either *his* or *her*. If you need to distinguish between them (although context usually makes it clear), add **à** and the disjunctive pronoun **lui** (*his*) or **elle** (*her*).

Voilà Jean et Marie; et voilà **sa maison à lui**.
  There are John and Mary; and there is *his* house.
Voici **son livre à elle**.
  Here is *her* book.

Similarly, **à nous** or **à vous** may be added for emphatic use of *our* or *your*, and **à eux (elles)** for *their*.

> Votre école est grande, mais **notre école à nous** est plus grande.
> Your school is big, but *our* school is bigger.

G.   **C'est** [*dj*] **qui** [VERB]. The verb of the **qui**-clause must agree in person and number with the disjunctive pronoun.

> —Qui a dit cela?
> —C'est **moi** qui **ai** dit cela.

"I'm the one who said that." ("*I* said that.")

> —Qui a pris les billets?
> —C'est **vous** qui **avez** pris les billets.

"You're the one who bought the tickets."
"*You* bought the tickets."

> —Qui a visité le Louvre hier?
> —C'est **nous** qui **avons** visité le Louvre hier.

"*We* visited the Louvre yesterday."

Exercice 28C   Pronoms toniques [28.07 – 28.09]

Répondez aux questions par **C'est** [*dj*] ou **Ce sont** [*dj*]:

MODÈLE: Qui arrive? Georges?
C'est **lui**.

1.   Qui parle français?
     Albert? / Marie? / mes parents? / les étudiantes?
2.   Qui a fini le devoir?
     Albert? / Albert et Georges? / Marie et Jeanne?
3.   Qui est là?
     Mme Dubois? / les soldats? / le facteur? / M. et Mme Smith?

Répondez aux questions en vous servant d'une proposition avec **qui**.

MODÈLE: Est-ce vous qui avez fermé la porte?
Oui, c'est **moi**. C'est *moi* qui *ai* fermé la porte.

4.   Est-ce Albert qui a cherché le dictionnaire?
5.   Est-ce Mme Jacotin qui me cherche?

6. Est-ce le patron qui a téléphoné?
7. Est-ce vous qui avez emprunté l'annuaire? (C'est **moi** qui . . .)
8. Est-ce moi qu'on demande au bureau?
9. Est-ce votre famille qui dîne au restaurant?
10. Est-ce moi qui ai fait trop de bruit?
11. Est-ce vous qui avez mis la lettre à la poste?
12. Est-ce vous qui avez vu la nouvelle pièce?
13. Est-ce vos amis qui ont l'air timide?
14. Est-ce Marie qui joue si bien du violon?
15. Est-ce votre camarade de chambre qui a joué au poker hier?
16. Est-ce Roger qui a gagné tout l'argent?
17. Est-ce nous qui avons fait tant de bruit?
18. Est-ce moi qui doit prendre les billets?
19. Est-ce l'avocat qui s'est acheté une Rolls?
20. Est-ce vous qui vous occupez de la cuisine?
21. Est-ce que la locution «est-ce» est une forme de «c'est»? [5.12]

Insistez sur le sujet au moyen d'un pronom tonique.

MODÈLE: Je parle français.
      Moi, je parle français. *ou* Je parle français, **moi**.

22. Jean-Paul comprend l'arabe.
23. Mes amis ont visité l'Australie.
24. Pierre déteste les chats.
25. Tu es toujours à l'heure.
26. Marguerite est vraiment très belle.
27. J'aime bien les mathématiques.

Remplacez les mots en italique par un pronom [28.09C].

28. Voilà le médecin. Sa femme et *le médecin* vont à Genève en auto.
29. *Mlle Fontenay* et *M. Leclerc* viennent d'entrer.
30. Gérard et [*la personne qui parle*] allons en ville.

Exercice 28T   Thème français

1. Is your car in front of *our* apartment house or Robert's?
2. *I* am the one who knows how to type.
3. Are you sure that this table is the one Mrs. Masson wants? Is it possible she wants that one?
4. She and I drove to Calais, where we were to have lunch with a famous scientist.
5. Roosevelt and Churchill were both great men; the former was American and the latter was English.
6. This apartment house is a skyscraper; that one is rather small.
7. I took my watch and my father's downtown to have them repaired.
8. There are two cars over there. This one is a Ford and that one is a Renault. It's easy to see the difference.

9. There is the lady we saw at the theater and the one we saw later in the restaurant. I was thinking about them this morning.
10. I doubt that that girl is the one that we saw on [*dans*] the train to Rouen.

Exercice 28D   Sujet de composition ou de causerie

Comparez deux objects ou deux personnes, en vous servant de *celui* et des pronoms toniques.

Révision
systématique

1. I wondered whether René had sold his typewriter. [19.01]
2. When she heard the postman coming, Marie got up and went to the door. [19.01]
3. Did you and he have a good time at the party? [19.03]
4. Luckily Robert didn't marry that stenographer; he got rid of her. [18.01] [19.04]
5. Breakfast had been prepared when we got up this morning. [19.07]

Place de la Concorde avec l'Obélisque (*French Government Tourist Office*)

29

Verbes à radical variable

CRAINDRE*

VERBES À RADICAL VARIABLE

~~~~~~

sc **29.01** STEM-CHANGING VERBS. Certain -*er* verbs (verbs of the first conjugation) have a slight spelling irregularity in the L-AREA of the present indicative, present subjunctive, future, and conditional. This irregularity has already been noted in the verb **mener**° [27.03]. Since the irregularity is a change in spelling, these verbs are also called *orthographic-changing* verbs.

The three types of stem change in the L-AREA are:
- (a) **è** replaces **e** in the stem: **men**/er, je **mène** [29.02]
- (b) **è** replaces last **é** in the stem: **préfér**/er, je **préfère** [29.03]
- (c) **ll** replaces **l**, or **tt** replaces **t** in the stem: **appel**/er, j'**appelle**; **jet**/er, je **jette** [29.04]

Learn the specific verbs listed in each category.

29.02 VERBS CHANGING **e** TO **è** IN THE STEM. The verb **acheter**° (like **mener**° previously studied in 27.03) is an example of this type of stem-changing verb.

*Verbes à radical
variable*

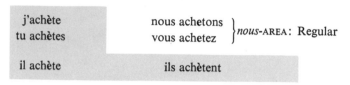

PRESENT TENSE

j'achète	nous achetons
tu achètes	vous achetez
il achète	ils achètent

}*nous*-AREA: Regular

e BECOMES è

FUTURE TENSE
FC-STEM: **achèter-**

j'ach**è**terai	nous ach**è**terons
tu ach**è**teras	vous ach**è**terez
il ach**è**tera	ils ach**è**teront

STEM CHANGE THROUGHOUT

The FC-stem incorporates the spelling change of the present indicative into the infinitive, that is, an accent is added throughout the future and conditional tenses. The present subjunctive has the same L-AREA configuration as the present indicative.

IMPERFECT: Regularly formed from present tense of *nous*-form, dropping -*ons*. No accent is added. The imperfect stem is therefore **achet-**: *il achetait, nous achetions*.

COMPOUND TENSES: Regular. *j'ai acheté, j'avais acheté, j'aurai acheté*.

Verbs in this category of stem-changing verbs:

INFINITIVE	L-AREA (*tp*)	FUTURE	MEANING
acheter°	il achète	il achètera	to buy
achever°	il achève	il achèvera	to finish, to complete
crever°	il crève	il crèvera	to burst; to die
geler°	il gèle	il gèlera	to freeze
lever°	il lève	il lèvera	to raise, to lift
se lever°	il se lève	il se lèvera	to get up
mener° [27.03]	il mène	il mènera	to lead
amener°	il amène	il amènera	to bring [P]
emmener°	il emmène	il emmènera	to take [P]
se promener°	il se promène	il se promènera	to go for a walk (ride)

29.03 VERBS CHANGING é TO è IN THE STEM.   Two- and three-syllable stems whose last vowel is **é** change the **é** to **è** in the L-AREA.

préférer [to prefer]

PRESENT TENSE

je préfère	nous préférons
tu préfères	vous préférez

}*nous*-AREA: Regular

il préfère   ils préfèrent

é becomes è

FUTURE TENSE (Regular throughout)

je préférerai	nous préférerons
tu préféreras	vous préférerez
il préférera	ils préféreront

The spelling change in the present tense of these verbs does *not* affect the future or conditional tenses. Verbs in this category include:

INFINITIVE	L-AREA	FUTURE (stem-infinitive)	MEANING
compléter°	il complète	il complétera	to complete
espérer°	il espère	il espérera	to hope
exagérer°	il exagère	il exagérera	to exaggerate
posséder°	il possède	il possédera	to possess
préférer°	il préfère	il préférera	to prefer
protéger°	il protège	il protégera	to protect
répéter°	il répète	il répétera	to repeat
révéler°	il révèle	il révélera	to reveal
succéder°	il succède	il succédera	to follow
suggérer°	il suggère	il suggérera	to suggest

29.04 VERBS DOUBLING **l** OR **t** IN THE STEM. Verbs such as **appeler**° (or **s'appeler**°) and **jeter**° double the final stem consonant to retain the sound [ε] in the L-AREA; this change also occurs throughout the future and conditional.

appeler° [to call]

PRESENT TENSE

j'appelle	nous appelons
tu appelles	vous appelez

}One **l** as in the infinitive

il appelle   ils appellent

DOUBLE **l**

Verbes à radical   j'appellerai   nous appellerons
variable   tu appelleras   vous appellerez
                       il appellera   ils appelleront

The verb **se rappeler**° [N] (*to remember* [N]) follows the stem change for
appeler°:

Je me rappelle l'histoire.   I remember the story.
Nous nous rappelons cette photo.   We remember this photo.
Nous nous la rappelons.   We remember it.

Exercice 29A   Verbes à radical variable

Écrivez vos réponses aux questions suivantes. Faites des phrases complètes
et vérifiez soigneusement l'orthographe.

MODÈLE: Nous **achetons** des livres de classe. Et vous?
            Moi aussi, **j'achète** des livres de classe.

1. Nous amenons des amies au théâtre. Et vous?
2. Nous crevons de faim. Et vous?
3. Vous n'exagérez jamais. Et votre camarade de chambre?
4. Appelez-vous le médecin quand vous avez mal à la tête?
5. Gelez-vous en hiver?
6. Espérez-vous réussir à l'examen?
7. Jetez-vous vos livres.par terre?
8. Comment vous appelez-vous? Comment s'appellent vos meilleurs amis?
9. Comment s'appellent vos professeurs?
10. Qui emmenez-vous au cinéma?
11. À quelle heure vous levez-vous d'habitude?
12. Vous promenez-vous souvent en avion?
13. Répétez-vous toujours ce que le professeur dit?
14. Complétez-vous votre travail à l'heure?
15. Suggérez-vous souvent de bonnes solutions aux problèmes?
16. Lequel préférez-vous: un président qui joue au golf ou un président qui
    joue du piano?
17. Combien de dictionnaires possédez-vous?

Toujours par écrit, remplacez le futur immédiat par le temps futur.

18. Je *vais achever* mes devoirs avant cinq heures et demie.
19. Nous *allons compléter* notre collection de timbres.
20. Robert *va posséder* une collection magnifique de timbres-poste.
21. Le professeur *va préférer* une composition bien écrite.
22. Les Dupont *vont acheter* une nouvelle maison dans la banlieue.
23. Ils *vont appeler* un avocat pour les aider.
24. Ce vendeur *va exagérer* les qualités de sa marchandise.
25. J'espère que François *va amener* sa femme chez nous.

VERBE IRRÉGULIER craindre*

~~~~~~

29.05   Review the forms of **craindre*** [*to fear*] in Appendix C, verb table 7. Other verbs ending in **-indre** that are conjugated in the same way are:

atteindre*	to reach, to attain
éteindre*	to extinguish; to put out (the lights)
peindre*	to paint
repeindre*	to repaint
plaindre*	to pity
se plaindre* de	to complain (about)

29.06   PRESENT INDICATIVE.   Notice that all these verbs drop **-dre** from the infinitive for singular forms; in the plural forms the stem *-n* becomes **-gn** before the ending.

	crain|dre	attein|dre	étein|dre	pein|dre	plain|dre
je	crain|s	atteins	éteins	peins	plains
tu	crain|s	atteins	éteins	peins	plains
il	crain|t	atteint	éteint	peint	plaint
nous	crai|gn|ons	atteignons	éteignons	peignons	plaignons
vous	crai|gn|ez	atteignez	éteignez	peignez	plaignez
ils	crai|gn|ent	atteignent	éteignent	peignent	plaignent
pp.	**craint**	**atteint**	**éteint**	**peint**	**plaint**

Nous **atteignons** notre but.
Éteignez l'électricité, s'il vous plaît.
Je vous **plains**.
Il **se plaint** du bruit.

We are attaining our goal.
Turn off the lights, please.
I pity you.
He is complaining about the noise.

29.07   COMPOUND TENSES.   The past participles are formed by dropping **-dre** from the infinitive and adding **-t**. The auxiliary is **avoir** (except for the reflexive verb **se plaindre***).

Il **a atteint** son but.
Nous **avons éteint** la lumière.
Il **s'est plaint** du bruit.

He attained his goal.
We turned out the lights.
He complained about the noise.

Exercice 29B   *craindre** et verbes apparentés

Complétez les phrases suivantes en employant le verbe entre parenthèses.

MODÈLE :   (se plaindre)   Quand je suis la victime d'une injustice, je . . .
Quand je suis la victime d'une injustice, **je me plains**.

1. Pour conserver l'énergie électrique, je . . . (éteindre les lumières)
2. Pour protéger l'extérieur, je . . . (peindre la maison)
3. Quand nous recevons de mauvaise notes, nous . . . (se plaindre)
4. Quand vous êtes malheureux, je . . . (vous plaindre)
5. Si l'on fait trop de bruit, mes voisins . . . (se plaindre)
6. Si la circulation est intense dans la rue, je . . . (craindre de la traverser)
7. Pour guider les voitures sur la route, on y . . . (peindre des lignes jaunes)
8. En partant de bonne heure le matin, je . . . (atteindre Paris avant midi)
9. En sortant d'un tunnel, les chauffeurs . . . (éteindre les phares)
10. Si l'on n'est pas satisfait de la couleur de la maison, on . . . (la repeindre)

Exercice 29T   Thème français

1. Can you reach the big red book on top of the bookcase?
2. My father always complains about the color of our house, so we are repainting it this summer.
3. It is essential that we make a trip to Rouen next week. If we start early, we will reach the city before the stores close (the closing of the stores).
4. My mother bought this book and the one you see on the desk. She is interested in Jean Giraudoux, and I am interested in him, too.
5. Tomorrow I will get up early and (I will) go for a bicycle ride. I will take my brother along.
6. Turn off the lights before you leave the room. The principal [*le proviseur*] complained about the waste of energy yesterday.
7. You paint very well, but I prefer still-life [*la nature morte*]. You exaggerate some of the details, whereas Antoine never exaggerates them.
8. I am afraid that we are not attaining our professional goals. The boss suggests that we study more.
9. I am dying of hunger! I suggest we take a taxi to the Tour d'Argent. I will call a taxi immediately.
10. I pity that poor woman in front of the restaurant. The weather is cold and she is freezing.

Révision systématique

1. When I worked in an office of the Ministry of Education, I used to have lunch every day around two o'clock. [20.04] [10.11]
2. I was writing my English composition when my cousin came in and asked me to go to the department store with her. [20.06] [16.03] [14.04]
3. Jacques, who is the most timid boy in our class, had been washing his car for twenty minutes when a big black dog approached him. [20.07] [18.01]
4. Our lawyer missed the train for Calais because he had stayed too long in the restaurant. [20.08]
5. Yves will come to get me at the library as soon as I telephone (to) him to tell him that I need a ride [*le transport*] [21.04] [21.02]

Vue aérienne du Château de Chenonceaux (*Delvert/Secrétariat d'Etat au Tourisme*)

30

Verbes à radical variable (suite)

ceci, cela

VERBES À RADICAL VARIABLE (suite)

sc **30.01** VERBS CHANGING **c** TO **ç** BEFORE **a, o, u**. Verbs ending in **-cer** change the **c** to **ç** in every form where the next letter is **a, o,** or **u**. This occurs in the *nous*-form of the present indicative and in the L-AREA of the imperfect. It also occurs in the passé simple [32.03].

commencer° [*to begin*]

PRESENT TENSE

je commence	nous commençons [c + o]
tu commences	vous commencez
il commence	ils commencent

IMPERFECT TENSE

je commençais	nous commencions
tu commençais	vous commenciez
il commençait	ils commençaient

Verbs in this category include:

agacer°	j'agace, nous agaçons	to infuriate
commencer°	je commence, nous commençons	to begin
déplacer°	je déplace, nous déplaçons	to displace
exercer°	j'exerce, nous exerçons	to exercise, to exert
menacer° (**de** [ɪ])	je menace, nous menaçons	to threaten (to)
renoncer° (**à**)	je renonce, nous renonçons	to renounce, to give up
remplacer°	je remplace, nous remplaçons	to replace

The reason for this spelling change is to retain the [s] sound of the letter -**c**- throughout the conjugation. Since **c** becomes the hard [k] sound when followed by **a**, **o**, or **u**, the cedilla is added because **ç** is always pronounced [s].

COMBINATION	PRONOUNCED [k]	PRONOUNCED [s]
c + **a** [ka]	**c**afé, **c**atholique	**ç**a, commen**ç**a
c + **o** [ko]	**c**ousin, **c**ommander	le**ç**on, gar**ç**on
c + **u** [ky]	**c**uisine, **c**ulture	re**ç**u, dé**ç**u

30.02 VERBS CHANGING **g** TO **ge** BEFORE **a**, **o**, **u**. Verbs ending in -**ger** have a stem ending in -**g**. If the personal ending begins with **a**, **o**, or **u**, the letter **e** is added to the **g**. This change occurs in the present and imperfect (also in the passé simple [32.03]).

manger° [to eat]

PRESENT TENSE

je mange	nous mang**e**ons [g + o]
tu manges	vous mangez
il mange	ils mangent

IMPERFECT TENSE

je mangeais	nous mangions
tu mangeais	vous mangiez
il mangeait	ils mangeaient

Verbs in this category include:

changer° (**de** [N])	je change, nous changeons	to change
charger° [N] **de** [N]	je charge, nous chargeons	to load (with)
corriger°	je corrige, nous corrigeons	to correct
exiger°	j'exige, nous exigeons	to require, to oblige
manger°	je mange, nous mangeons	to eat

obliger°	j'oblige, nous obligeons	to oblige, to require
nager°	je nage, nous nageons	to swim
voyager°	je voyage, nous·voyageons	to travel

30.03 VERBS CHANGING y TO i. Verbs ending in **-oyer** and **-uyer** change the **y** to **i** when there is a silent ending. This occurs in the L-AREA of the present indicative and present subjunctive. The change is also made throughout the future and conditional tenses.

employer° [to employ, to use]

PRESENT TENSE

j'emploie	nous employons
tu emploies	vous employez
il emploie	ils emploient

IMPERFECT (NOT AFFECTED)

j'employais	nous employions
tu employais	vous employiez
il employait	ils employaient

FUTURE (MODIFIED INFINITIVE)
FC-Stem: **emploier-**

j'emploierai	nous emploierons
tu emploieras	vous emploierez
il emploiera	ils emploieront

Verbs in this category include:

s'appuyer° (sur)	je m'appuie, nous nous appuyons	to lean (on)
appuyer° (sur)	j'appuie, nous appuyons	to press (on), to support
employer°	j'emploie, nous employons	to employ, to use
envoyer°	j'envoie, nous envoyons	to send [FC-stem: **enverr-**]
essuyer°	j'essuie, nous essuyons	to wipe
nettoyer°	je nettoie, nous nettoyons	to clean
se noyer°	je me noie, nous nous noyons	to drown
renvoyer°	je renvoie, nous renvoyons	to send away, to dismiss; to refer [FC-stem: **renverr-**]

30.04 VERBS ENDING IN **-ayer**: OPTIONAL CHANGES. Verbs ending in **-ayer** may follow the rule for verbs ending in **-uyer** and **-oyer**, changing **y** to **i** in the present, future, and conditional. However, they may also be used as entirely regular verbs retaining the **y** throughout.

essayer [to try]

Verbes à radical
variable (suite)

PRESENT TENSE

j'essaie (j'essaye)   nous essayons
tu essaies (tu essayes)   vous essayez
il essaie (il essaye)   ils essaient (ils essayent)

Verbs in this category include:

payer   je paie, je paye   to pay (for)
rayer   je raie, je raye   to cross out, to strike out

Exercice 30A   Verbes à radical variable [30.01 – 30.04]

Récrivez les phrases suivantes en remplaçant le sujet de la phrase par celui indiqué entre parenthèses. Retenez le temps du verbe. Attention aux changements d'orthographe.

MODÈLE: Robert **commence** la leçon vers huit heures. (*Nous*)
           Nous commençons la leçon vers huit heures.

1. Renée **déplace** des meubles dans son appartement. (*Nous*)
2. Nous **appelons** la police en cas d'urgence. (*Je*)
3. Je **renonce** aux cigarettes. (*Nous*)
4. Nous **commencions** à lire le journal. (*Il*)
5. Nous **remplacions** toujours les livres perdus. (*Paul*)
6. Jacques **agace** parfois les agents. (*Nous*)
7. Le professeur **corrige** nos fautes de grammaire. (*Nous*)
8. Les touristes **changent** leur argent à l'aéroport. (*Nous*)
9. Vous **exigiez** toujours une action immédiate. (*Pierre*)
10. Le concierge **oblige** les touristes à attendre. (*Nous*)
11. Quand vous **étiez** à la plage vous **nagiez** tous les jours. (*je*)
12. Mon père **voyage** souvent. (*Nous*)
13. Nous **employons** une machine à écrire. (*Je*)
14. Le professeur **essuie** le tableau noir. (*Nous*)
15. Nous nous **ennuyons** à la maison. (*Françoise*)
16. Nous **essayons** de réparer cette machine. (*Paul*)
17. Je **paie** toutes mes dettes. (*Nous*)
18. Nous **rayons** ces mots pour les annuler. (*Je*)
19. Mes parents **renvoient** la bonne. (*Vous*)
20. Vous **exigez** que les enfants se lavent les mains. (*Nous*)

Exercice 30B   Thème [30.01 – 30.04]

1. Napoléon began his march to Moscow in 1812.
2. He was beginning his campaign when Victor Hugo was ten years old.
3. A bookcase that is too high is in danger of falling [threatens to fall].
4. My uncle used to travel to Berlin every summer.
5. I will use my electric typewriter to write my homework.

ceci [this], cela [that]

30.05 GENERAL.   **Ceci** and **cela** are demonstrative pronouns. **Cela** refers to something already mentioned: *that, the foregoing*; **ceci** refers to something that *will be* mentioned:

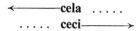

These pronouns refer to a statement or general idea already expressed (**cela**) or about to be expressed (**ceci**). They should not be confused with the adjectives *this* or *that* (**ce, cette**) used to modify a noun (as in *that house*).

30.06 USES OF **ceci** [*this, the following*].   **Ceci** may be used to refer to a statement about to be made.

> Écoutez **ceci**: je pars demain à midi.
> Listen to *this*: I am leaving tomorrow at noon.

It is also used in contrast with **cela**.

> J'aime **ceci**, mais ne n'aime pas **cela**.
> I like *this*, but I don't like *that*.

In this case the meaning of the two pronouns would be clarified by the speaker's gestures, pointing to "this" and "that."

30.07 USES OF **cela** [*that, the foregoing*].   The pronoun **cela** may be used as a subject, direct object, object of a preposition, or for emphasis of a subject. It refers to a whole idea already mentioned (the *antecedent*).

(1) Subject

> Robert a réussi. ⟵————————**Cela** me plaît.

(2) Direct object

> Georges est parti. ⟵————————Je ne comprends pas **cela**.

(3) Object of a preposition

> Paul a vu le directeur. ⟵————————Il est venue **pour cela**.

ceci, cela

(4) Emphasis of subject

| Allons au cinéma! | ◄———————Cela, c'est une bonne idée! |

The shortened form of **cela** is **ça**, frequently used in conversation:

Ça m'est égal.	It's all the same to me. (I don't care.)
Ça, c'est une bonne idée.	That's a good idea.
Comment ça va?	How goes it? (How are things going?)
Je lui ai parlé de ça.	I spoke to him (her) about that.

30.08 FOUR FORMS OF "THAT": **ce** [N] / **que** [C] / **celui** / **cela**. In English, four different uses of the word "that" call for different words in French.

A. | that [NOUN] | ADJECTIVE **ce, cet, cette** [N] [5.07].

Cet HOMME parle anglais.   *That man* speaks English.

B. | that [CLAUSE] | CONJUNCTION **que** [C] [25.07]

Je sais **que** PAUL PART.   I know *that Paul is leaving.*

C. | that (of [N]) | PRONOUN **celui, celle** (= the one) [28.01]

J'ai ma clef et **celle de Robert.**   I have my key and *Robert's.*

D. | that | (*alone*)   PRONOUN **cela** [30.07]

Cela me plaît.	*That* pleases me.
Je sais **cela.**	I know *that.*
Je vous ai parlé **de cela.**	I spoke to you *about that.*

Exercice 30C *ceci* ou *cela* [30.05 – 30.07]

Répétez (et écrivez) les phrases en remplaçant les mots en italique par **ceci** ou par **cela**, selon le cas.

1. Il est venu pour *nous voir.*
2. *Le fait que René a bien travaillé* me plaît.
3. Je vais vous dire *un fait important*: le roi est mort.
4. *Nous vous dirons ce qui* est évident: vous manquez de talent.
5. Avez-vous lu *l'article dans le journal* hier?

6. Voici une revue que tu n'as pas vue. Lisons *cette revue*.
7. *Que vous partiez demain* m'est tout à fait égal.
8. *Robert a réussi à l'examen. C'est une chose qui* plaît à sa mère.
9. Voilà deux tableaux: j'aime *ce tableau-ci*, mais je n'aime pas *celui-là*.
10. Voilà deux phrases: *cette phrase-là* est claire, mais *celle-ci* ne l'est pas.

Exercice 30T Thème français

1. I gave up smoking because it is bad for the health. Did you know that?
2. Listen to this: according to the paper, they are beginning to build a skyscraper beside the library! That annoys me.
3. I was beginning to be discouraged until you told me that the plan is going to be canceled [*annuler*] [19.07: use *on*]
4. The Duponts have settled down in their new apartment. They like that. [That is pleasing to them.]
5. Mr. Dupont told me this: it is very difficult to move, and he is sorry that he left our neighborhood.
6. That constant noise in the apartment next to ours used to annoy me.
7. Janine married a young doctor who has just arrived from Sweden.
8. This is certain: they must content themselves with a very small apartment at first, at least until they can find another that is larger.
9. Doctor Swenson will require an office [*un cabinet*] in a building near the center of the city. He will employ two nurses and a secretary.
10. He will take the subway until he can buy a small economical car.

Exercice 30D Sujet de composition ou de causerie

Quels sont les problèmes de logement, de transport, de nourriture, et d'emploi d'un jeune couple qui veut se marier?

Révision systématique

1. When I see your father I will tell him that you're having a good time. [21.02] [18.01]
2. If I see your mother, I will tell her you are bored. [21.03] [30.03]
3. I would have gone to the zoo if I had finished my work early. [22.04] [20.10] [22.05C]
4. What plays did you see in London? Tell me what actors you saw. [21.07]
5. You attended several plays—I know that. Which ones did you like best? [21.08]

Quai de la Gare de Lyon, Paris (*Mackay/Monkmeyer*)

31

Participe présent | Correspondance usuelle

PARTICIPE PRÉSENT   *ps.p.*

31.01 GENERAL. The present participle in French always ends in **-ant** (corresponding to *-ing* in English). It is used after **en** or **tout en** to indicate *method* of doing something, or to show that its action is *simultaneous* with another.

> J'ai appris le français **en étudiant**.
>> I learned French *by studying*. (METHOD)
> Il a dit bonjour **en nous regardant**.
>> He said hello *while looking at us*. (SIMULTANEITY)

REMINDER: The French present participle *cannot be used* for some English forms ending in *-ing*, notably the present tense, and *-ing* forms following prepositions (where the infinitive is required in French):

> Il **arrive** à la gare.
>> He *is arriving* at the station. [English: present progressive tense]
> Nous avons dîné **avant de quitter** la maison.
>> We dined *before leaving* the house. [English: after a preposition]

31.02 FORMATION OF PRESENT PARTICIPLE. Using the present indicative *nous*-form, drop the *-ons* and add *-ant* to form the present participle. (This is the same stem used for forming the imperfect tense.)

VERB	*NOUS*-FORM	PRESENT PARTICIPLE	MEANING
travailler	nous **travaill**ons	en travaill**ant**	by working
finir	nous **finiss**ons	en finiss**ant**	by finishing
rendre	nous **rend**ons	en rendant	by giving
aller*	nous **all**ons	en allant	by going
faire*	nous **fais**ons	en faisant	by doing
mettre*	nous **mett**ons	en mettant	by putting
prendre*	nous **pren**ons	en prenant	by taking
avoir*	*Irregular*	**ayant***	having
être*	*Irregular*	**étant***	being
savoir*	*Irregular*	**sachant***	knowing

31.03 USES OF THE PRESENT PARTICIPLE.

A. METHOD: **en** + [*ps.p.*]. This structure indicates the method by which something is done (*by doing something*). When **en** + [*ps.p.*] is used, emphasis is upon the *means* or *method* by which the action of the main verb is accomplished. The question "by doing what?" is answered by **en** + [*ps.p.*].

J'ai réussi **en travaillant** dur.
> I passed (succeeded) *by working* hard.

Paul a appris sa leçon **en étudiant** toute la nuit.
> Paul learned his lesson *by studying* all night.

B. SIMULTANEOUS EVENTS: **en** + [*ps.p.*]. This structure indicates simultaneity (*while doing something*). The events indicated by both the main verb and the present participle are happening at the same time.

Je suis tombé **en descendant**.
> I fell *while coming downstairs*.

Gaston écoutait la radio **en jouant** aux dames.
> Gaston was listening to the radio *while playing* checkers.

C. CONCURRENT EVENTS: **tout en** + [*ps.p.*]. This structure is used if two events occur at the same time, and it is considered unusual for them to do so.

Gaston parlait **tout en écoutant** la radio.
> Gaston was talking *while listening to* the radio.

Elle lisait un livre **tout en regardant** la télévision.
> She was reading a book (even) *while watching* television.

D. PARTICIPLE WITHOUT **en.** The present participle used alone indicates simultaneous events, action just prior to the main verb, or *cause* of the action indicated by the main verb.

Ouvrant les yeux, elle a dit bonjour.	SIMULTANEOUS EVENTS
Ouvrant la porte, il a vu sa femme.	JUST PRIOR (to *il a vu*)
Ne **sachant** que faire, il n'a rien fait.	CAUSE
Étant bien fatiguée, elle s'est couchée.	CAUSE

E. **ayant** + [*pp.*] / **étant** + [*pp.*] When followed by a past participle, **ayant** and **étant** indicate a marked priority of event (*having done something*). In English this structure is often expressed as "after he finished (doing something) he (did something else)." The structure in French uses **ayant** plus the past participle of the main verb (for verbs using **avoir*** as auxiliary), or **étant** plus the past participle (for verbs using **être***).

ayant travaillé	having worked
étant arrivé	having arrived

EXAMPLES

Ayant travaillé dur, nous sommes retournés à la maison.
    Having worked hard, we went back to the house.
Ayant dîné, nous sommes allés au théâtre.
    Having dined, we went to the theater.
    (= After *we* dined, *we* went to the theater.)
Ayant trouvé un stylo, elle a commencé à écrire.
    Having found a pen, she began to write.
    (= After *she* found a pen, *she* began to write.)
Étant entrés dans l'appartement, ils ont fermé la porte à clef.
    Having gone into the apartment, they locked the door.
    (= After *they* went into the apartment, *they* locked the door.)

Exercice 31A   Formation du participe présent [31.02]

Remplacez l'infinitif entre parenthèses par la forme appropriée du verbe.

1. En (*chercher*) mon stylo, j'ai trouvé un billet de banque.
2. (*Savoir*) les faits, l'inspecteur a pu arrêter le jeune homme.
3. Bien que (*jouer*) mal de la guitare, je peux accompagner des chansons.
4. (*Être*) très intelligent, le directeur a résolu le problème.
5. (*Avoir*) besoin d'argent, Monique est passée par la banque pour toucher un chèque.
6. Il s'était endormi en (*écrire*) sa composition.
7. En (*entendre*) ces mots, l'avocat a quitté la salle en hâte.
8. Ne (*être*) pas amateur de musique, Lucie s'est endormie au concert.

9. Il lisait un roman tout en (*écouter*) la radio.
10. (*Fermer*) le livre avec soin, Henri l'a remis sur la table.

Exercice 31 B Emploi du participe présent [31.03]

Combinez les deux phrases en remplaçant le verbe en italique par la forme appropriée.

MODÈLE :   J'ai réussi à l'examen. J'*ai* beaucoup *étudié*.
En étudiant beaucoup, j'ai réussi à l'examen.

1. Paul a fini sa composition. Il *a écrit* toute la nuit.
2. Marie est tombée. Elle *descendait* l'escalier.
3. L'agent n'a rien fait. Il ne *savait* que faire.
4. Georges *a salué* le professeur. Il lui a donné sa composition.
5. J'ai acheté un stylo à la librairie. J'en *avais* besoin.
6. Mme Renault est rentrée à la maison. Elle *était* bien fatiguée.
7. Renée a appris la nouvelle. Elle *écoutait* la radio.
8. Cet auteur a fait grand plaisir au public. Il *a écrit* un roman passionnant.
9. Il a posé son chapeau sur une table. Il *est entré* dans le salon.
10. François *avait* très faim. Il est entré dans un restaurant tout près.

Révision lexicale

Noms dérivés du participe présent

Plusieurs noms sont dérivés du participe présent. En voici quelques exemples :

1. le **remplaçant** (*v.* **remplacer**, *to replace*)
   Une personne qui remplace une autre s'appelle **un remplaçant**.
2. le **passant** (*v.* **passer**, *to pass by*)
   Une personne qui passe dans la rue s'appelle **un passant**.
3. le **commandant** (*v.* **commander**, *to command*)
   Un officier supérieur s'appelle **un commandant**.

Maintenant complétez les phrases suivantes en vous servant du nom dérivé du verbe indiqué.

4. **assister** [*to attend*]
   Ceux qui assistent à un meeting s'appellent des . . .
5. **survivre** [*to survive*]
   Une personne qui survit à un catastrophe s'appelle un . . .
6. **correspondre** [*to correspond*]
   Un journaliste qui écrit des reportages s'appelle . . .
7. **gagner** [*to win*]
   Celui (Celle) qui gagne à la loterie s'appelle . . .
8. **représenter** [*to represent*]
   Une personne qui représente une autre s'appelle . . .
9. **négocier** [*to negotiate, to do business*]
   Une personne qui fait le commerce en grand s'appelle . . .

10. **débuter** [*to begin*]

Une personne qui fait son début s'appelle . . .

LA CORRESPONDANCE USUELLE

This section deals with social and business correspondence and related matters.

31.04 RETURN ADDRESS [*l'expéditeur*]. Put your own address and the date in the upper right-hand corner of the stationery [*le papier à lettres*]. (Do not change your address into a different form, because the recipient will use it to answer you, and the post office may not recognize it in altered form.)

3920 Arrow Drive	96, quai du Maréchal Joffre
Raleigh, North Carolina 27612	92 Courbevoie
le 23 avril 1979	France
	le 17 mars 1978

31.05 SALUTATION [*l'en-tête*]. For business letters the last name of the addressee is not used in the salutation, but simply *Monsieur*, *Messieurs*, *Mademoiselle*, or *Madame* followed by a comma. Some variations:

Dear Sir:	Monsieur,
Dear Madam:	Madame,
Dear Miss Burton:	Mademoiselle,
Dear Mr. Dubois:	Monsieur,
Gentlemen:	Messieurs,
Dear Professor Lebon:	Monsieur,
	Monsieur le Professeur,

Personal letters may have a less formal salutation, including the first name:

Dear Albert,	Cher Ami, / Cher Albert,
	Mon cher Albert,
Dear Jacqueline,	Chère Amie, / Chère Jacqueline,
	Ma chère Jacqueline,
Dear Friends,	Mes chers Amis,

31.06 Tutoiement OR **vouvoiement**? The degree of friendship already established will indicate whether to use the familiar *tu*-form (*tutoyer* is the verb meaning to use this form) or the *vous*-form in the letter. Business letters, of course, will always use the *vous*-form. Personal letters should be consistent throughout, and not switch from *tu-* to *vous-*forms once you have settled that question.

Current trend is towards greater usage of *tutoiement*, especially between students (even though they may not have established a firm friendship as yet), and among members of the armed forces, of equal rank. *Vouvoiement* is proper in addressing superiors, older people, and strangers in general.

31.07 COMPLIMENTARY CLOSING [*formule finale*]. Complimentary closings such as those below are used verbatim in French letters as the final paragraph. They are the equivalent of *Yours very truly*, *Sincerely yours*, etc. Notice that the same title of address used in the salutation is repeated as part of the complimentary closing.

> VERY FORMAL AND RESPECTFUL:
> Veuillez agréer, Monsieur (Madame, Monsieur le Directeur, etc.) l'expression de mes salutations distinguées.
>
> TO A BUSINESS FIRM:
> Recevez, Messieurs, mes meilleurs salutations.
>
> TO A PROFESSIONAL COLLEAGUE (*semi-formal*):
> Recevez, Monsieur, l'expression de mes sentiments distingués.
> (As the bond of friendship becomes closer, *distingués* may be modulated to *sympathiques* and later to *affectueux*.)

In correspondence between students or close friends, typical complimentary closings for letters are:

> Je vous envoie (Je t'envoie), mon cher Ami, mes souvenirs les plus cordiaux.
> Je t'envoie, mon cher Jacques, mes souvenirs les plus sympathiques.
> Bien amicalement,

31.08 ABBREVIATIONS. Do not abbreviate any part of a title on the envelope or in the salutation: spell out *Monsieur*, *Madame*, or *Mademoiselle*. Within the body of the letter, it is more respectful to spell out all titles of persons mentioned, in case they at some time may read the letter or see a copy.

31.09 NUMBERS. Spell out numbers under a hundred; use figures for dates and longer numbers:

> En **1976** il y avait **dix-huit** étudiants dans la classe.

Exercice 31 C   Composition

Vous venez de recevoir la lettre suivante d'un ami qui habite la banlieue de Paris. Composez une réponse à cette lettre (voir les suggestions qui la suivent).

> 23, rue de l'Église
> Kremlin-Bicêtre
> le 19 juin

Mon cher Ami (Ma chère Amie),

J'ai bien reçu ta lettre du 18 mai, dont je te remercie. Je te prie de m'excuser de ce long délai. J'ai eu beaucoup de travail cette année et j'ai en ce moment beaucoup de concours et d'examens. Je profite donc d'un moment libre pour t'écrire une petite lettre qui, j'espère, te trouvera en bonne santé.

Les cours se terminent le 5 juillet. J'ai passé mon baccalauréat technique le 12, 13 juin et j'attends les résultats avec beaucoup d'impatience. Je pars pour Nantes (à l'est de la France) dans trois jours, pour passer un concours d'entrée aux écoles d'ingénieurs de l'Armement de la Marine Française. Pendant ces quatre jours à Nantes j'essaierai de t'envoyer de jolies cartes de cette partie de la France.

Ensuite je travaille du 7 juillet au 31 août à l'hôtel Ambassador. Si tu passes par Paris pendant les vacances, viens me voir à Kremlin-Bicêtre où tu pourras passer quelques jours chez moi.

Je me suis fiancé le 6 avril: ma fiancée s'appelle Françoise et elle est infirmière à l'Hôpital. Dans ma prochaine lettre je t'enverrai des photos de nous deux.

Tu me demandes ce que je compte faire cet été. Je travaille jusqu'au 31 août, et serai donc en vacances entre le 1er septembre et le 15 septembre. Si tu te trouves encore en France au mois de septembre nous pourrions visiter un peu la France (surtout l'Est) et descendre le Rhin ensemble.

En attendant de tes nouvelles et le plaisir de te revoir,

Bien amicalement,

Gérard

En composant votre réponse, parlez de ce que vous faites et de ce que vous comptez faire à l'avenir. Demandez à Gérard s'il a réussi à ses examens. Dites-lui si vous avez bien reçu les cartes postales qu'il a promis de vous envoyer; félicitez-le d'être fiancé, et demandez-lui la date de son mariage. Dites-lui s'il peut compter sur vous pour la visite chez lui, et pour la descente du Rhin. Si vous ne pouvez pas accepter son invitation, faites vos excuses et donnez les raisons de votre refus.

Exercice 31T   Thème français

1. I thank you for your letter of November 7th, and hope you will be able to make the trip to Switzerland.
2. Next week Pierre will take a competitive examination for admission to medical school.
3. My parents are leaving for Italy in five days; during these five days I will take advantage of some free moments to help them make arrangements.
4. I will be on vacation for two weeks in September, so I will be able to take a trip down the Rhine with my fiancée.

5. Could you spend a few days with us before you leave the city?
6. I don't think that I will make the trip to Moscow because the weather is too cold in Russia.
7. Knowing that I must be back in the United States before September 15th, I would like to buy my tickets before I return to Paris from Nice.
8. I found out that Kremlin-Bicêtre is a suburb of Paris by looking at a map of the city.
9. I have been writing these sentences for ten minutes. It is possible that I will finish them before my roommate returns.
10. What I need is a glass of beer. When Robert comes back I will ask him to go get some.

Révision systématique

1. Dominique would like to play tennis this afternoon after her sister arrives. [22.01] [26.05C]
2. Mr. Leblanc told me that he would mail my letter before he goes to the office. [22.01] [26.05]
3. If the driver had seen the red light he would have stopped the truck immediately. [22.05]
4. What the officer means is that it is not your fault. [24.05] [22.07C] [5.09]
5. I am willing to lend you the dictionary that you need. [22.07C] [24.02]

Notre-Dame au coucher du soleil (*Silberstein/Monkmeyer*)

32

Passé
simple

Imparfait
du subjonctif

32.01 Uses. The *passé simple* (called in English the past definite) is found in literary works and historical texts. It is never used colloquially. The passé simple is generally used under the same circumstances as those calling for the passé composé [15.02]: the action is fully completed in the past, and the time of happening is specified or strongly implied.

The passé simple corresponds in meaning with the passé composé:

PASSÉ SIMPLE	PASSÉ COMPOSÉ	MEANING
il **travailla**	il a travaillé	he worked
il **arriva**	il est arrivé	he arrived
elle **se leva**	elle s'est levée	she got up
il **écouta**	il a écouté	he listened

In narration, the passé simple is used for actions in the past, and the imperfect for background descriptions. (The arrangement in 20.05 for the interplay of passé composé and imperfect also pertains here, with the passé simple substituted for the passé composé.)

32.02 Non-use of the passé simple. Even under circumstances allowing the passé simple (literary and historical use), do not use the passé simple for the following:

A. Recent past. **Hier j'ai vu** le professeur Jolivet.

B. Past related to the present.

Voici le livre que j'**ai acheté**. Here is the book I bought.

C. **Depuis** structure. The **depuis** structure may be used with the passé composé but not with the passé simple:

Je ne vous **ai** pas **vu depuis** longtemps.
I have not seen you for a long time.

32.03 Formation. The passé simple is formed by dropping the infinitive ending of a regular verb, and adding the appropriate tense endings. The following chart shows the three ending systems: the **-ai** system for regular **-er** verbs like *parler*; the **-is** system for regular **-ir** and **-re** verbs. A third system using the **-us** endings is for certain irregular verbs only.

Below the double line you will find the irregular verbs using each system.

	REGULAR VERBS		SOME IRREGULAR VERBS
	-er	**-ir and -re**	
je	-ai	-is	-us
tu	-as	-is	-us
il	-a	-it	-ut
nous	-âmes	-îmes	-ûmes
vous	-âtes	-îtes	-ûtes
ils	-èrent	-irent	-urent

IRREGULAR VERBS USING THE ABOVE SYSTEMS		
-ai System	**-is** System	**-us** System
all- (aller*)	**d-** (dire*)	**d-** (devoir*)
	f- (faire*)	**f-** (être*)
	m- (mettre*)	**e-** (avoir*)
	v- (voir*)	**p-** (pouvoir*)
	pr- (prendre*)	**s-** (savoir*)
	naqu- (naître*)	**voul-** (vouloir*)
	écriv- (écrire*)	**véc-** (vivre*)
		mour- (mourir*)

Passé simple

je parlai	je finis	je vendis
tu parlas	tu finis	tu vendis
il parla	il finit	il vendit
nous parlâmes	nous finîmes	nous vendîmes
vous parlâtes	vous finîtes	vous vendîtes
ils parlèrent	ils finirent	ils vendirent

MODEL IRREGULAR VERBS

(-**ai** System)	(-**is** System)	(-**us** System)
aller*	*dire**	*pouvoir**
j'allai	je dis	je pus
tu allas	tu dis	tu pus
il alla	il dit	il put
nous allâmes	nous dîmes	nous pûmes
vous allâtes	vous dîtes	vous pûtes
ils allèrent	ils dirent	ils purent

In practice, the third person is more often seen than other forms. The *il-* and *ils*-forms of the verbs on the above table are shown for recognition here:

faire*	il **fit**	ils **firent**	did, made, caused
mettre*	il **mit**	ils **mirent**	put
voir*	il **vit**	ils **virent**	saw
prendre*	il **prit**	ils **prirent**	took
naître*	il **naquit**	ils **naquirent**	was (were) born
écrire*	il **écrivit**	ils **écrivirent**	wrote
devoir*	il **dut**	ils **durent**	had to
être*	il **fut**	ils **furent**	was (were)
avoir*	il **eut**	ils **eurent**	had
savoir*	il **sut**	ils **surent**	knew
vouloir*	il **voulut**	ils **voulurent**	wanted (to)
vivre*	il **vécut**	ils **vécurent**	lived
mourir*	il **mourut**	ils **moururent**	died

Elle **entra** dans la salle.	= Elle **est entrée** dans la salle.
Il **finit** de travailler.	= Il **a fini** de travailler.
Nous **vendîmes** la voiture.	= Nous **avons vendu** la voiture.
J'allai voir mon ami.	= Je **suis allé(e)** voir mon ami.
Ils me **dirent** bonjour.	= Ils m'**ont dit** bonjour.
Ils **durent** partir.	= Ils **ont dû** partir.

The passé simple of **venir*** and **tenir*** have unusual forms in that they use the **-is** system of endings, omitting the **-i** of the ending.

venir* Stem: **vin-**	tenir* Stem: **tin-**
je vins [*came*]	je tins [*held*]
tu vins	tu tins
il vint	il tint
nous vin**mes**	nous tinmes
vous vin**tes**	vous tintes
ils vin**rent**	ils tin**rent**

32.04 PAST ANTERIOR (passé antérieur). The past anterior is a compound tense formed by using the passé simple of the auxiliary (**avoir*** or **être***) plus the past participle. This tense is presented for recognition only, as it is occasionally encountered in reading.

EXAMPLES

chercher [*to look for*]	**aller*** [*to go*]
j'**eus cherché** [*had looked for*]	je **fus allé(e)** [*had gone*]
tu **eus cherché**	tu **fus allé(e)**
il **eut cherché**	il **fut allé**
elle **eut cherché**	elle **fut allée**
nous **eûmes cherché**	nous **fûmes allé(e)s**
vous **eûtes cherché**	vous **fûtes allé(e)(s)**
ils **eurent cherché**	ils **furent allés**
elles **eurent cherché**	elles **furent allées**

Exercice 32A   Passé simple

The following historical passage is taken from Chateaubriand's *Mémoires d'Outre-Tombe* (ca. 1811), describing his interview with George Washington in Philadelphia in 1791.

Identify the verbs used in the passé simple. Rewrite the passage or passages assigned, replacing the passé simple with the passé composé.

1. Lorsque j'*arrivai* à Philadelphie, le général Washington n'y était pas; je *fus* obligé de l'attendre une huitaine de jours. Je le *vis* passer dans une voiture que tiraient quatre chevaux fringants, conduits à grandes guides.... Quand j'*allai* lui porter ma lettre de recommandation, je *retrouvai* la simplicité du vieux Romain.

2. Une petite maison, ressemblant aux maisons voisines, était le palais du président des États-Unis: point de gardes, pas même de valets. Je frappai; une jeune servante ouvrit. Je lui demandai si le général était chez lui; elle me répondit qu'il y était. Je répliquai que j'avais une lettre à lui remettre.

3. La servante me demanda mon nom, difficile à prononcer en anglais et qu'elle ne put retenir. Elle me dit alors doucement: «*Walk in, sir*; entrez, monsieur» et elle marcha devant moi dans un de ces étroits corridors qui servent de vestibule aux maisons anglaises. Elle m'introduisit dans un parloir où elle me pria d'attendre le général. . . .

4.   Au bout de quelques minutes, le général entra: d'une grande taille, d'un air calme et froid plutôt que noble, il est ressemblant dans ses gravures. Je lui présentai ma lettre en silence; il l'ouvrit, courut à la signature qu'il lut tout haut avec exclamation: «Le colonel Armand!» C'est ainsi qu'il l'appelait et qu'avait signé le marquis de la Rouërie.

5.   Nous nous assîmes. Je lui expliquai tant bien que mal le motif de mon voyage. Il me répondait par monosyllabes anglais et français, et m'écoutait avec une sorte d'étonnement; je m'en aperçus, et je lui dis avec un peu de vivacité: «Mais il est moins difficile de découvrir le passage du nord-ouest que de créer un peuple comme vous l'avez fait. — *Well, well, young man*! Bien, bien, jeune homme,» s'écria-t-il en me tendant la main. Il m'invita à dîner pour le jour suivant, et nous nous quittâmes.

IMPARFAIT DU SUBJONCTIF

32.05   USE OF THE IMPERFECT SUBJUNCTIVE.   The imperfect subjunctive is rarely used in present-day French, and practically limited to the third-person. Most French speakers substitute the present subjunctive.

After a main clause, superlative, or conjunction calling for the subjunctive [25.02, 25.06, 26.03], the verb of the subordinate clause is in the imperfect subjunctive *if the main clause is in the past.*

PRESENT	Je doute qu'il **vienne.**	I doubt that he *will come.*
PAST	Je doutais qu'il **vînt.**	I doubted that he *would come.*

In spoken French the last sentence would nevertheless use the present subjunctive:

WRITTEN	Je doutais qu'il **vînt.**	Imperfect Subjunctive
SPOKEN	Je doutais qu'il **vienne.**	Present Subjunctive

32.06   MEANING.   The imperfect subjunctive, like the imperfect indicative, indicates action in progress in the past (*was doing something*) or habitual action in the past (*used to do something*). In addition, the imperfect subjunctive often means *would do something*; yet note the various ways of giving English equivalents:

Il voulait **qu'elle lui donnât** de l'argent.
    He wanted her to give him some money. [He wanted that she give him some money.]
L'agent a ordonné plusieurs fois **qu'on ne le laissât pas** entrer.
    The policeman several times ordered that he should not be admitted.
Elle serait partie sans **que vous le sussiez.**
    She must have left without your knowing it. [22.01D]

Je n'ai rien bu, **quoique j'eusse soif.**

    I didn't drink anything, although I was thirsty.

Je ne croyais pas **qu'il prît** les billets.

    I didn't believe that he would buy the tickets.

32.07 FORMATION OF THE IMPERFECT SUBJUNCTIVE. The stem is derived from the infinitive (regular verbs). For irregular verbs the stem is the same as for the passé simple [32.03].

There are three ending systems:

-asse system for **-er** verbs
-isse system for **-ir** verbs
-usse system for some irregular verbs

These rarely used forms are included in the verb tables of Appendix B (regular verbs) and Appendix C (irregular verbs) for recognition purposes only.

Appendix A   NUMBERS AND DATES

A. CARDINAL AND ORDINAL NUMBERS.

	CARDINAL	ORDINAL
1	un, une	premier, première (1er, 1re)
2	deux	deuxième, second, -e (2e)
3	trois	troisième (3e)
4	quatre	quatrième (4e)
5	cinq	cinquième (5e)
6	six	sixième (6e)
7	sept	septième (7e)
8	huit	huitième (8e)
9	neuf	neuvième (9e)
10	dix	dixième (10e)
11	onze	onzième (11e)
12	douze	douzième (12e)
13	treize	treizième (13e)
14	quatorze	quatorzième (14e)
15	quinze	quinzième (15e)
16	seize	seizième (16e)
17	dix-sept	dix-septième (17e)
18	dix-huit	dix-huitième (18e)
19	dix-neuf	dix-neuvième (19e)
20	vingt	vingtième (20e)
21	vingt et un[1] (une)	vingt et unième (21e)
22	vingt-deux	vingt-deuxième (22e)
23	vingt-trois	vingt-troisième (23e)
30	trente	trentième (30e)
40	quarante	quarantième (40e)
50	cinquante	cinquantième (50e)
60	soixante	soixantième (60e)
70	soixante-dix	soixante-dixième (70e)
71	soixante et onze	soixante et onzième (71e)
72	soixante-douze	soixante-douzième (72e)
80	quatre-vingts[2]	quatre-vingtième (80e)
81	quatre-vingt-un	quatre-vingt-unième (81e)
90	quatre-vingt-dix	quatre-vingt-dixième (90e)
91	quatre-vingt-**onze**	quatre-vingt-onzième (91e)
92	quatre-vingt-**douze**	quatre-vingt-douzième (92e)
93	quatre-vingt-**treize**	quatre-vingt-treizième (93e)

[1]No hyphens are used in 21, 31, 41, 51, 61, or 71, in which the word *et* is used.
[2]The final *-s* is omitted in all other forms of the 80 series: *quatre-vingt-un*, etc.

CARDINAL		ORDINAL
94	quatre-vingt-**quatorze**	quatre-vingt-quatorzième (94e)
95	quatre-vingt-**quinze**	quatre-vingt-quinzième (95e)
96	quatre-vingt-**seize**	quatre-vingt-seizième (96e)
97	quatre-vingt-**dix-sept**	quatre-vingt-dix-septième (97e)
98	quatre-vingt-**dix-huit**	quatre-vingt-dix-huitième (98e)
99	quatre-vingt-**dix-neuf**	quatre-vingt-dix-neuvième (99e)
100	cent	centième (100e)
101	cent un	cent unième (101e)
102	cent deux	cent deuxième (102e)
200	deux cents	deux centième (200e)
201	deux cent un	deux cent unième (201e)
1.000	mille	millième (1.000e)
1.000.000	million	millionième (1.000.000e)

NOTE: A period is used to separate number groups (thousands, ten thousands, etc.). A comma is used for the decimal mark; for example, the metric equivalent of an inch would be 2,54 cm.

B. APROXIMATE NUMBERS. The suffix *-aine* indicates "about" the number mentioned. It makes a feminine noun of the number.

une diz**aine** de soldats	about ten soldiers
une cent**aine** de francs	about a hundred francs

NOTE: *une douzaine* means exactly 12 (a dozen).

C. *Mille* vs. *milles*. The invariable form without a final *-s* is the word for *thousand;* with the *-s* it means *miles*. Use *mil* in dates.

cinq **mille** soldats	5000 soldiers
cinq **milles**	five miles
en l'an **mil** neuf cent soixante-dix-sept	in 1977

D. THE USE of *million* REQUIRES *de*.

Paris a plus de six **millions d'**habitants.
Cet avion a coûté plus de trois **millions de** dollars.

A billion is **un milliard (de).**

E. DIMENSIONS AND STATISTICS: *sur = by* or *of*. Notice the use of *sur* in the following statements:

Neuf **sur** dix de nos étudiants parlent anglais.
Nine out of ten of our students speak English.

Cette pièce **a** huit mètres **de long sur** quatre **de large.**

This room is 8 meters long by 4 [meters] wide.

NOTE: *Avoir** rather than *être** is used in dimensions.

F. DATES AND TITLES. In dates and titles, use cardinal numbers except for "the first" (*premier*):

	le 20 février	SPOKEN: le *vingt* février
	le 17 mars	le *dix-sept* mars
BUT	**le 1ᵉʳ avril**	le *premier* avril

Dates including A.D. and B.C. use the following French abbreviations, which stand for *après Jésus-Christ* and *avant Jésus-Christ.*

apr. J.-C.	A.D.
av. J.-C.	B.C.
En 853 av. J.-C.	In 853 B.C.

Notice the use of cardinal numbers for rulers:

	Louis XIV	Louis *quatorze*
	Henri IV	Henri *quatre*
BUT	**François 1ᵉʳ**	François *premier*

G. FRACTIONAL PARTS.

la moitié de [N]	half of [N]
le quart ($\frac{1}{4}$) (0,250)	a quarter
le tiers ($\frac{1}{3}$) (0,333)	a third
deux tiers ($\frac{2}{3}$) (0,666)	two-thirds
un dix-septième ($\frac{1}{17}$)	one seventeenth

Demi is invariable when placed before a noun. It agrees when it follows.

demi, -e ($\frac{1}{2}$) (0,5)	half
une heure et demie	an hour and a half
une demi-heure	a half-hour
une demi-tasse	a demitasse

H. WRITTEN FORMS. In writing (but not in printing), the number 7 is usually barred: 7. The number 5 is often written 5, the combination 75 may be 75 . The number 1 is written with a long beginning, like this 1.

I. COMBINATION CARDINAL-ORDINAL. The cardinal number precedes the ordinal when both are used.

Les **deux premières** maisons sont blanches.
The first two houses are white.

Appendix B   MODEL REGULAR VERBS

SUMMARY OF VERB TENSES

INDICATIF

Temps simples

Présent [9.01]
  il travaille
  il va

Imparfait [20.01]
  il travaillait
  il allait

Passé simple (Passé défini) [32.01]
  il travailla
  il alla

Futur [21.01]
  il travaillera
  il ira

Conditionnel [22.01]
  il travaillerait
  il irait

Temps composés

Passé composé
  il a travaillé [15.03]
  il est allé [16.01]

Plus-que-parfait [20.08]
  il avait travaillé
  il était allé

Passé antérieur [32.04]
  il eut travaillé
  il fut allé

Futur antérieur [21.06]
  il aura travaillé
  il sera allé

Conditionnel passé [22.04]
  il aurait travaillé
  il serait allé

SUBJONCTIF

Présent du subjonctif [25.08]
  qu'il travaille
  qu'il aille

Imparfait du subjonctif [32.05]
  qu'il travaillât
  qu'il allât

Passé du subjonctif [27.01]
  qu'il ait travaillé
  qu'il soit allé

Présent *tp* [9.01]	Imparfait *ti* [20.01]	Passé Simple *tps* [32.01]	Futur *tf* [21.01]	Conditionnel *tc* [22.01]	Présent du Subjonctif *tp sj* [25.08]
1 travailler Model *-er* verb					
je travaille	travaillais	travaillai	travaillerai	travaillerais	travaille
tu travailles	travaillais	travaillas	travailleras	travaillerais	travailles
il travaille	travaillait	travailla	travaillera	travaillerait	travaille
nous **travaill**ons*	travaillions	travaillâmes	travaillerons	travaillerions	travaillions
vous travaillez	travailliez	travaillâtes	travaillerez	travailleriez	travailliez
ils travaillent	travaillaient	travaillèrent	travailleront	travailleraient	travaillent
2 entrer Model verb requiring auxiliary *être**					
entre	entrais	entrai	entrerai	entrerais	entre
entres	entrais	entras	entreras	entrerais	entres
entre	entrait	entra	entrera	entrerait	entre
entrons*	entrions	entrâmes	entrerons	entrerions	entrions
entrez	entriez	entrâtes	entrerez	entreriez	entriez
entrent	entraient	entrèrent	entreront	entreraient	entrent
3 se trouver Model reflexive verb					
je me trouve	me trouvais	me trouvai	me trouverai	me trouverais	me trouve
tu te trouves	te trouvais	te trouvas	te trouveras	te trouverais	te trouves
il se trouve	se trouvait	se trouva	se trouvera	se trouverait	se trouve
nous nous **trouv**ons*	nous trouvions	nous trouvâmes	nous trouverons	nous trouverions	nous trouvions
vous vous trouvez	vous trouviez	vous trouvâtes	vous trouverez	vous trouveriez	vous trouviez
ils se trouvent	se trouvaient	se trouvèrent	se trouveront	se trouveraient	se trouvent
4 remplir Model *-ir* verb					
remplis	remplissais	remplis	remplirai	remplirais	remplisse
remplis	remplissais	remplis	rempliras	remplirais	remplisses
remplit	remplissait	remplit	remplira	remplirait	remplisse
remplissons*	remplissions	remplîmes	remplirons	remplirions	remplissions
remplissez	remplissiez	remplîtes	remplirez	rempliriez	remplissiez
remplissent	remplissaient	remplirent	rempliront	rempliraient	remplissent
5 vendre Model *-re* verb					
vends	vendais	vendis	vendrai	vendrais	vende
vends	vendais	vendis	vendras	vendrais	vendes
vend	vendait	vendit	vendra	vendrait	vende
vendons*	vendions	vendîmes	vendrons	vendrions	vendions
vendez	vendiez	vendîtes	vendrez	vendriez	vendiez
vendent	vendaient	vendirent	vendront	vendraient	vendent

*The boldface portion is the stem for the imperfect [20.01] and present participle [31.01].

Imparfait du Subjonctif ti sj [32.05]	Passé Composé tpc [15.03][16.01]	Plus-que-parfait tpp [20.08]	Passé Antérieur tpa [32.04]
travaillasse	j'ai travaillé	j'avais travaillé	j'eus travaillé
travaillasses	tu as travaillé	tu avais travaillé	tu eus travaillé
travaillât	il a travaillé	il avait travaillé	il eut travaillé
travaillassions	nous avons travaillé	nous avions travaillé	nous eûmes travaillé
travaillassiez	vous avez travaillé	vous aviez travaillé	vous eûtes travaillé
travaillassent	ils ont travaillé	ils avaient travaillé	ils eurent travaillé
entrasse	je suis entré(e)	j'étais entré(e)	je fus entré(e)
entrasses	tu es entré(e)	tu étais entré(e)	tu fus entré(e)
entrât	il est entré	il était entré	il fut entré
	elle est entrée	elle était entrée	elle fut entrée
entrassions	nous sommes entré(e)s	nous étions entré(e)s	nous fûmes entré(e)s
entrassiez	vous êtes entré(e)(s)	vous étiez entré(e)(s)	vous fûtes entré(e)(s)
entrassent	ils sont entrés	ils étaient entrés	ils furent entrés
	elles sont entrées	elles étaient entrées	elles furent entrées
me trouvasse	je me suis trouvé(e)	je m'étais trouvé(e)	je me fus trouvé(e)
te trouvasses	tu t'es trouvé(e)	tu t'étais trouvé(e)	tu te fus trouvé(e)
se trouvât	il s'est trouvé	il s'était trouvé	il se fut trouvé
	elle s'est trouvée	elle s'était trouvée	elle se fut trouvée
nous trouvassions	nous nous sommes trouvé(e)s	nous nous étions trouvé(e)s	nous nous fûmes trouvé(e)s
vous trouvassiez	vous vous êtes trouvé(e)(s)	vous vous étiez trouvé(e)(s)	vous vous fûtes trouvé(e)(s)
se trouvassent	ils se sont trouvés	ils s'étaient trouvés	ils se furent trouvés
	elles se sont trouvées	elles s'étaient trouvées	elles se furent trouvées
remplisse	j'ai rempli	j'avais rempli	j'eus rempli
remplisses	tu as rempli	tu avais rempli	tu eus rempli
remplît	il a rempli	il avait rempli	il eut rempli
remplissions	nous avons rempli	nous avions rempli	nous eûmes rempli
remplissiez	vous avez rempli	vous aviez rempli	vous eûtes rempli
remplissent	ils ont rempli	ils avaient rempli	ils eurent rempli
vendisse	j'ai vendu	j'avais vendu	j'eus vendu
vendisses	tu as vendu	tu avais vendu	tu eus vendu
vendît	il a vendu	il avait vendu	il eut vendu
vendissions	nous avons vendu	nous avions vendu	nous eûmes vendu
vendissiez	vous avez vendu	vous aviez vendu	vous eûtes vendu
vendissent	ils ont vendu	ils avaient vendu	ils eurent vendu

(Continued on next page)

Futur Antérieur *tfa* [21.05]	Conditionnel Passé [22.04]	Passé du Subjonctif *sjp* [27.01]	Impératif *imp* [9.10]
travailler			
j'aurai travaillé	j'aurais travaillé	j'aie travaillé	
tu auras travaillé	tu aurais travaillé	tu aies travaillé	travaille
il aura travaillé	il aurait travaillé	il ait travaillé	
nous aurons travaillé	nous aurions travaillé	nous ayons travaillé	travaillons
vous aurez travaillé	vous auriez travaillé	vous ayez travaillé	travaillez
ils auront travaillé	ils auraient travaillé	ils aient travaillé	
entrer			
je serai éntré(e)	je serais entré(e)	je sois entré(e)	
tu seras entré(e)	tu serais entré(e)	tu sois entré(e)	entre
il sera entré	il serait entré	il soit entré	
elle sera entrée	elle serait entrée	elle soit entrée	
nous serons entré(e)s	nous serions entré(e)s	nous soyons entré(e)s	entrons
vous serez entré(e)(s)	vous seriez entré(e)(s)	vous soyez entré(e)(s)	entrez
ils seront entrés	ils seraient entrés	ils soient entrés	
elles seront entrées	elles seraient entrées	elles soient entrées	
se trouver			
je me serai trouvé(e)	je me serais trouvé(e)	je me sois trouvé(e)	
tu te seras trouvé(e)	tu te serais trouvé(e)	tu te sois trouvé(e)	trouve-toi
il se sera trouvé	il se serait trouvé	il se soit trouvé	
elle se sera trouvée	elle se serait trouvée	elle se soit trouvée	
nous nous serons trouvé(e)s	nous nous serions trouvé(e)s	nous nous soyons trouvé(e)s	trouvons-nous
vous vous serez trouvé(e)(s)	vous vous seriez trouvé(e)(s)	vous vous soyez trouvé(e)(s)	trouvez-vous
ils se seront trouvés	ils se seraient trouvés	ils se soient trouvés	
elles se seront trouvées	elles se seraient trouvées	elles se soient trouvées	
remplir			
j'aurai rempli	j'aurais rempli	j'aie rempli	
tu auras rempli	tu aurais rempli	tu aies rempli	remplis
il aura rempli	il aurait rempli	il ait rempli	
nous aurons rempli	nous aurions rempli	nous ayons rempli	remplissons
vous aurez rempli	vous auriez rempli	vous ayez rempli	remplissez
ils auront rempli	ils auraient rempli	ils aient rempli	
vendre			
j'aurai vendu	j'aurais vendu	j'aie vendu	
tu auras vendu	tu aurais vendu	tu aies vendu	vends
il aura vendu	il aurait vendu	il ait vendu	
nous aurons vendu	nous aurions vendu	nous ayons vendu	vendons
vous aurez vendu	vous auriez vendu	vous ayez vendu	vendez
ils auront vendu	ils auraient vendu	ils aient vendu	

Appendix C   irregular verbs

VERB	TABLE NUMBER
aller* *to go*	1
apercevoir* *to perceive*	24
apparaître* *to appear*	19
appartenir* *to belong to*	29
apprendre* *to learn*	23
s'asseoir* *to sit down*	3
atteindre* *to attain*	7
avoir* *to have*	2
commettre* *to commit*	17
comprendre* *to understand*	23
conduire* *to drive, to conduct*	5
connaître* *to be acquainted with*	4
construire* *to build*	5
contenir* *to contain*	29
convenir* *to agree*	30
courir* *to run*	6
couvrir* *to cover*	18
craindre* *to fear*	7
croire* *to believe*	8
découvrir* *to uncover, to discover*	18
décrire* *to describe*	11
détruire* *to destroy*	5
devenir* *to become*	30
devoir* *to owe, to be obliged to*	9
dire* *to say*	10
disparaître* *to disappear*	19
dormir* *to sleep*	27
écrire* *to write*	11
entreprendre* *to undertake*	23
envoyer° *to send*	12
éteindre* *to put out (the lights)*	7
être* *to be*	13
faire* *to make, to do, to cause*	14
falloir* *to be necessary*	15
s'inscrire* *to register*	11
interdire* *to forbid*	10
introduire* *to introduce*	5
lire* *to read*	16
maintenir* *to maintain*	29
mentir* *to lie*	27
mettre* *to put*	17
obtenir* *to obtain*	29
offrir* *to offer*	18
omettre* *to omit*	17
ouvrir* *to open*	18

VERB	TABLE NUMBER
paraître* *to appear*	19
partir* *to depart, to leave*	20
peindre* *to paint*	7
permettre* *to permit*	17
plaindre* *to pity*	7
plaire* *to please*	21
pouvoir* *to be able to*	22
prendre* *to take*	23
produire* *to produce*	5
promettre* *to promise*	17
recevoir* *to receive*	24
reconnaître* *to recognize*	4
reprendre* *to take back; to resume*	23
retenir* *to retain*	29
revenir* *to come back (again)*	30
savoir* *to know*	25
sentir* *to feel*	27
servir* *to serve*	26
sortir* *to go out*	27
souffrir* *to suffer*	18
se souvenir* (de) *to remember*	30
suivre* *to follow; to take (a course)*	28
surprendre* *to surprise*	23
survivre* *to survive*	31
tenir* *to hold*	29
traduire* *to translate*	5
venir* *to come*	30
vivre* *to live*	31
voir* *to see*	32
vouloir* *to want*	33

Présent tp [9.01]	Imparfait ti [20.01]	Passé Composé tpc [15.03][16.01]	Passé Simple tps [32.01]	Futur tf [21.01]	Conditionnel tc [22.01]

1 aller* [to go] pp. allé (Aux. être) ps.p. allant

Présent	Imparfait	Passé Composé	Passé Simple	Futur	Conditionnel
je vais	allais	je suis allé(e)	allai	irai	irais
tu vas	allais	tu es allé(e)	allas	iras	irais
il va	allait	il est allé	alla	ira	irait
nous allons	allions	nous sommes allé(e)s	allâmes	irons	irions
vous allez	alliez	vous êtes allé(e)(s)	allâtes	irez	iriez
ils vont	allaient	ils sont allés	allèrent	iront	iraient

2 avoir* [to have] pp. eu (Aux. avoir) ps.p. ayant

Présent	Imparfait	Passé Composé	Passé Simple	Futur	Conditionnel
j'ai	avais	j'ai eu	eus	aurai	aurais
tu as	avais	tu as eu	eus	auras	aurais
il a	avait	il a eu	eut	aura	aurait
nous avons	avions	nous avons eu	eûmes	aurons	aurions
vous avez	aviez	vous avez eu	eûtes	aurez	auriez
ils ont	avaient	ils ont eu	eurent	auront	auraient

3 s'asseoir* [to sit down] pp. assis (Aux. être) ps.p. s'asseyant

Présent	Imparfait	Passé Composé	Passé Simple	Futur	Conditionnel
je m'assieds	m'asseyais	je me suis assis(e)	m'assis	m'assiérai	m'assiérais
tu t'assieds	t'asseyais	tu t'es assis(e)	t'assis	t'assiéras	t'assiérais
il s'assied	s'asseyait	il s'est assis	s'assit	s'assiéra	s'assiérait
elle s'assied	s'asseyait	elles s'est assise	s'assit	s'assiéra	s'assiérait
nous nous asseyons	nous asseyions	nous nous sommes assis(es)	nous assîmes	nous assiérons	nous assiérions
vous vous asseyez	vous asseyiez	vous vous êtes assis(es)	vous assîtes	vous assiérez	vous assiériez
ils s'asseyent	s'asseyaient	ils se sont assis	ils assirent	ils assiéront	s'assiéraient
elles s'asseyent	s'asseyaient	elles se sont assises	elles assirent	elles assiéront	s'assiéraient

4 connaître* [to be acquainted with] pp. connu (Aux. avoir) ps.p. connaissant

Présent	Imparfait	Passé Composé	Passé Simple	Futur	Conditionnel
je connais	connaissais	j'ai connu	connus	connaîtrai	connaîtrais
tu connais	connaissais	tu as connu	connus	connaîtras	connaîtrais
il connaît	connaissait	il a connu	connut	connaîtra	connaîtrait
nous connaissons	connaissions	nous avons connu	connûmes	connaîtrons	connaîtrions
vous connaissez	connaissiez	vous avez connu	connûtes	connaîtrez	connaîtriez
ils connaissent	connaissaient	ils ont connu	connurent	connaîtront	connaîtraient

5 construire* [to construct] pp. construit (Aux. avoir) ps.p. construisant

Présent	Imparfait	Passé Composé	Passé Simple	Futur	Conditionnel
je construis	construisais	j'ai construit	construisis	construirai	construirais
tu construis	construisais	tu as construit	construisis	construiras	construirais
il construit	construisait	il a construit	construisit	construira	construirait
nous construisons	construisions	nous avons construit	construisîmes	construirons	construirions
vous construisez	construisiez	vous avez construit	construisîtes	construirez	construiriez
ils construisent	construisaient	ils ont construit	construisirent	construiront	construiraient

NOTE: In the present subjunctive, a stem change in the *nous*- and *vous*-forms is shown by boldface.

Plus-que-parfait *tpp* [20.08]	Présent du Subjonctif *tp sj* [25.08]	Imparfait du Subjonctif *ti sj* [32.05]	Impératif *imp* [9.10]
j'étais allé(e)	que j'aille	*que j'* allasse	
tu étais allé(e)	que tu ailles	allasses	va
il était allé	qu'il aille	allât	
nous étions allé(e)s	que nous **allions**	allassions	allons
vous étiez allé(e)(s)	que vous **alliez**	allassiez	allez
ils étaient allés	qu'ils aillent	allassent	
j'avais eu	*que j'* aie	*que j'* eusse	
tu avais eu	aies	eusses	aie
il avait eu	ait	eût	
nous avions eu	**ay**ons	eussions	ayons
vous aviez eu	**ay**ez	eussiez	ayez
ils avaient eu	aient	eussent	
je m'étais assis(e)	que je m'asseye	*que je* m'assise	
tu t'étais assis(e)	que tu t'asseyes	t'assisses	assieds-toi
il s'était assis	qu'il s'asseye	s'assît	
elle s'était assise	qu'elle s'asseye	s'assît	
nous nous étions assis(es)	que nous nous asseyions	nous assissions	asseyons-nous
vous vous étiez assis(es)	que vous vous asseyiez	vous assissiez	asseyez-vous
ils s'étaient assis	qu'ils s'asseyent	s' assissent	
elles s'étaient assises	qu'elles s'asseyent	s' assissent	

Also : **reconnaître*** *to recognize*

j'avais connu	*que je* connaisse	*que je* connusse	
tu avais connu	connaisses	connusses	connais
il avait connu	connaisse	connût	
nous avions connu	connaissions	connussions	connaissons
vous aviez connu	connaissiez	connussiez	connaissez
ils avaient connu	connaissent	connussent	

Also : **conduire*** *to drive*   **produire*** *to produce*
détruire* *to destroy*   **traduire*** *to translate*
introduire* *to introduce*

j'avais construit	*que je* construise	*que je* construisisse	
tu avais construit	construises	construisisses	construis
il avait construit	construise	construisît	
nous avions construit	construisions	construisissions	construisons
vous aviez construit	construisiez	construisissiez	construisez
ils avaient construit	construisent	construisissent	

Présent tp [9.01]	Imparfait ti [20.01]	Passé Composé tpc [15.03][16.01]	Passé Simple tps [32.01]	Futur tf [21.01]	Conditionnel tc [22.01]

6 courir* [to run] pp. couru (Aux. avoir) ps.p. courant

je cours	courais	j'ai couru	courus	courrai	courrais
tu cours	courais	tu as couru	courus	courras	courrais
il court	courait	il a couru	courut	courra	courrait
nous courons	courions	nous avons couru	courûmes	courrons	courrions
vous courez	couriez	vous avez couru	courûtes	courrez	courriez
ils courent	couraient	ils ont couru	coururent	courront	courraient

7 crain/dre* [to fear] pp. craint (Aux. avoir) ps.p. craignant

je crains	craignais	j'ai craint	craignis	craindrai	craindrais
tu crains	craignais	tu as craint	craignis	craindras	craindrais
il craint	craignait	il a craint	craignit	craindra	craindrait
nous craignons	craignions	nous avons craint	craignîmes	craindrons	craindrions
vous craignez	craigniez	vous avez craint	craignîtes	craindrez	craindriez
ils craignent	craignaient	ils ont craint	craignirent	craindront	craindraient

8 croire* [to believe] pp. cru (Aux. avoir) ps.p. croyant

je crois	croyais	j'ai cru	crus	croirai	croirais
tu crois	croyais	tu as cru	crus	croiras	croirais
il croit	croyait	il a cru	crut	croira	croirait
nous croyons	croyions	nous avons cru	crûmes	croirons	croirions
vous croyez	croyiez	vous avez cru	crûtes	croirez	croiriez
ils croient	croyaient	ils ont cru	crurent	croiront	croiraient

9 devoir* [to be obliged to; to owe] pp. dû (Aux. avoir) ps.p. devant

je dois	devais	j'ai dû	dus	devrai	devrais
tu dois	devais	tu as dû	dus	devras	devrais
il doit	devait	il a dû	dut	devra	devrait
nous devons	devions	nous avons dû	dûmes	devrons	devrions
vous devez	deviez	vous avez dû	dûtes	devrez	devriez
ils doivent	devaient	ils ont dû	durent	devront	devraient

10 dire* [to say] pp. dit (Aux. avoir) ps.p. disant

je dis	disais	j'ai dit	dis	dirai	dirais
tu dis	disais	tu as dit	dis	diras	dirais
il dit	disait	il a dit	dit	dira	dirait
nous disons	disions	nous avons dit	dîmes	dirons	dirions
vous dites	disiez	vous avez dit	dîtes	direz	diriez
ils disent	disaient	ils ont dit	dirent	diront	diraient

Plus-que-parfait *tpp* [20.08]	Présent du Subjonctif *tp sj* [25.08]	Imparfait du Subjonctif *ti sj* [32.05]	Impératif *imp* [9.10]
j'avais couru	*que je* coure	*que je* courusse	
tu avais couru	coures	courusses	cours
il avait couru	coure	courût	
nous avions couru	courions	courussions	courons
vous aviez couru	couriez	courussiez	courez
ils avaient couru	courent	courussent	

Also: **atteindre*** *to reach*   **plaindre*** *to pity*

        éteindre* *to extinguish*   **se plaindre*** *to complain*

        peindre* *to paint*

j'avais craint	*que je* craigne	*que je* craignisse	
tu avais craint	craignes	craignisses	crains
il avait craint	craigne	craignît	
nous avions craint	craignions	craignissions	craignons
vous aviez craint	craigniez	craignissiez	craignez
ils avaient craint	craignent	craignissent	

j'avais cru	*que je* croie	*que je* crusse	
tu avais cru	croies	crusses	crois
il avait cru	croie	crût	
nous avions cru	**croy**ions	crussions	croyons
vous aviez cru	**croy**iez	crussiez	croyez
ils avaient cru	croient	crussent	

j'avais dû	*que je* doive	*que je* dusse	
tu avais dû	doives	dusses	
il avait dû	doive	dût	—
nous avions dû	**dev**ions	dussions	
vous aviez dû	**dev**iez	dussiez	
ils avaient dû	doivent	dussent	

Also: **interdire*** *to forbid*

j'avais dit	*que je* dise	*que je* disse	
tu avais dit	dises	disses	dis
il avait dit	dise	dît	
nous avions dit	disions	dissions	disons
vous aviez dit	disiez	dissiez	dites
ils avaient dit	disent	dissent	

Présent tp [9.01]	Imparfait ti [20.01]	Passé Composé tpc [15.03][16.01]	Passé Simple tps [32.01]	Futur tf [21.01]	Conditionnel tc [22.01]

11 écrire* [to write] pp. écrit (Aux. avoir) ps.p. écrivant

j'écris	écrivais	j'ai écrit	écrivis	écrirai	écrirais
tu écris	écrivais	tu as écrit	écrivis	écriras	écrirais
il écrit	écrivait	il a écrit	écrivit	écrira	écrirait
nous écrivons	écrivions	nous avons écrit	écrivîmes	écrirons	écririons
vous écrivez	écriviez	vous avez écrit	écrivîtes	ecrirez	écririez
ils écrivent	écrivaient	ils ont écrit	écrivirent	écriront	écriraient

12 envoyer* [to send] pp. envoyé (Aux. avoir) ps.p. envoyant

j'envoie	envoyais	j'ai envoyé	envoyai	enverrai	enverrais
tu envoies	envoyais	tu as envoyé	envoyas	enverras	enverrais
il envoie	envoyait	il a envoyé	envoya	enverra	enverrait
nous envoyons	envoyions	nous avons envoyé	envoyâmes	enverrons	enverrions
vous envoyez	envoyiez	vous avez envoyé	envoyâtes	enverrez	enverriez
ils envoient	envoyaient	ils ont envoyé	envoyèrent	enverront	enverraient

13 être* [to be] pp. été (Aux. avoir) ps.p. étant

je suis	étais	j'ai été	fus	serai	serais
tu es	étais	tu as été	fus	seras	serais
il est	était	il a été	fut	sera	serait
nous sommes	étions	nous avons été	fûmes	serons	serions
vous êtes	étiez	vous avez été	fûtes	serez	seriez
ils sont	étaient	ils ont été	furent	seront	seraient

14 faire* [to make, to do] pp. fait (Aux. avoir) ps.p. faisant

je fais	faisais	j'ai fait	fis	ferai	ferais
tu fais	faisais	tu as fait	fis	feras	ferais
il fait	faisait	il a fait	fit	fera	ferait
nous faisons	faisions	nous avons fait	fîmes	ferons	ferions
vous faites	faisiez	vous avez fait	fîtes	ferez	feriez
ils font	faisaient	ils ont fait	firent	feront	feraient

15 falloir* [to be necessary (to)] pp. fallu (Aux. avoir)

il faut	il fallait	il a fallu	il fallut	il faudra	il faudrait

Plus-que-parfait tpp [20.08]	Présent du Subjonctif tp sj [25.08]	Imparfait du Subjonctif ti sj [32.05]	Impératif imp [9.10]

Also: **décrire*** *to describe*
s'inscrire* *to register*

j'avais écrit	*que j'* écrive	*que j'* écrivisse	
tu avais écrit	écrives	écrivisses	écris
il avait écrit	écrive	écrivît	
nous avions écrit	écrivions	écrivissions	écrivons
vous aviez écrit	écriviez	écrivissiez	écrivez
ils avaient écrit	écrivent	écrivissent	

Also: **renvoyer*** *to dismiss*

j'avais envoyé	*que j'* envoie	*que j'* envoyasse	
tu avais envoyé	envoies	envoyasses	envoie
il avait envoyé	envoie	envoyât	
nous avions envoyé	**envoy**ions	envoyassions	envoyons
vous aviez envoyé	**envoy**iez	envoyassiez	envoyez
ils avaient envoyé	envoient	envoyassent	

j'avais été	*que je* sois	*que je* fusse	
tu avais été	sois	fusses	sois
il avait été	soit	fût	
nous avions été	**soy**ons	fussions	soyons
vous aviez été	**soy**ez	fussiez	soyez
ils avaient été	soient ·	fussent	

j'avais fait	*que je* fasse	*que je* fisse	
tu avais fait	fasses	fisses	fais
il avait fait	fasse	fît	
nous avions fait	fassions	fissions	faisons
vous aviez fait	fassiez	fissiez	faites
ils avaient fait	fassent	fissent	

il avait fallu	qu'il faille	qu'il fallût	—

Présent tp [9.01]	Imparfait ti [20.01]	Passé Composé tpc [15.03][16.01]	Passé Simple tps [32.01]	Futur tf [21.01]	Conditionnel tc [21.01]

16 lire* [to read] pp. lu (Aux. avoir) ps.p. lisant

je lis	lisais	j'ai lu	lus	lirai	lirais
tu lis	lisais	tu as lu	lus	liras	lirais
il lit	lisait	il a lu	lut	lira	lirait
nous lisons	lisions	nous avons lu	lûmes	lirons	lirions
vous lisez	lisiez	vous avez lu	lûtes	lirez	liriez
ils lisent	lisaient	il ont lu	lurent	liront	liraient

17 mettre* [to put] pp. mis (Aux. avoir) ps.p. mettant

je mets	mettais	j'ai mis	mis	mettrai	mettrais
tu mets	mettais	tu as mis	mis	mettras	mettrais
il met	mettait	il a mis	mit	mettra	mettrait
nous mettons	mettions	nous avons mis	mîmes	mettrons	mettrions
vous mettez	mettiez	vous avez mis	mîtes	mettrez	mettriez
ils mettent	mettaient	ils ont mis	mirent	mettront	mettraient

18 ouvrir* [to open] pp. ouvert (Aux. avoir) ps.p. ouvrant

j'ouvre	ouvrais	j'ai ouvert	ouvris	ouvrirai	ouvrirais
tu ouvres	ouvrais	tu as ouvert	ouvris	ouvriras	ouvrirais
il ouvre	ouvrait	il a ouvert	ouvrit	ouvrira	ouvrirait
nous ouvrons	ouvrions	nous avons ouvert	ouvrîmes	ouvrirons	ouvririons
vous ouvrez	ouvriez	vous avez ouvert	ouvrîtes	ouvrirez	ouvririez
ils ouvrent	ouvraient	ils ont ouvert	ouvrirent	ouvriront	ouvriraient

19 paraître* [to appear] pp. paru (Aux. avoir) ps.p. paraissant

je parais	paraissais	j'ai paru	parus	paraîtrai	paraîtrais
tu parais	paraissais	tu as paru	parus	paraîtras	paraîtrais
il paraît	paraissait	il a paru	parut	paraîtra	paraîtrait
nous paraissons	paraissions	nous avons paru	parûmes	paraîtrons	paraîtrions
vous paraissez	paraissiez	vous avez paru	parûtes	paraîtrez	paraîtriez
ils paraissent	paraissaient	ils ont paru	parurent	paraîtront	paraîtraient

20 partir* [to depart] pp. parti (Aux. être) ps.p. partant

je pars	partais	je suis parti(e)	partis	partirai	partirais
tu pars	partais	tu es parti(e)	partis	partiras	partirais
il part	partait	il est parti	partit	partira	partirait
nous partons	partions	nous sommes parti(e)s	partîmes	partirons	partirions
vous partez	partiez	vous êtes parti(e)(s)	partîtes	partirez	partiriez
ils partent	partaient	il sont partis	partirent	partiront	partiraient

Plus-que-parfait *tpp* [20.08]	Présent du Subjonctif *tp sj* [25.08]	Imparfait du Subjonctif *ti sj* [32.05]	Impératif *imp* [9.10]
j'avais lu	*que je* lise	*que je* lusse	
tu avais lu	lises	lusses	lis
il avait lu	lise	lût	
nous avions lu	lisions	lussions	lisons
vous aviez lu	lisiez	lussiez	lisez
ils avaient lu	lisent	lussent	

Also : **commettre*** *to commit*   **permettre*** *to permit*
     omettre* *to omit*   **promettre*** *to promise*

j'avais mis	*que je* mette	*que je* misse	
tu avais mis	mettes	misses	mets
il avait mis	mette	mît	
nous avions mis	mettions	missions	mettons
vous aviez mis	mettiez	missiez	mettez
ils avaient mis	mettent	missent	

Also : **couvrir*** *to cover*   **offrir*** *to offer*
     découvrir* *to discover*   **souffrir*** *to suffer*

j'avais ouvert	*que j'* ouvre	*que j'* ouvrisse	
tu avais ouvert	ouvres	ouvrisses	ouvre
il avait ouvert	ouvre	ouvrît	
nous avions ouvert	ouvrions	ouvrissions	ouvrons
vous aviez ouvert	ouvriez	ouvrissiez	ouvrez
ils avaient ouvert	ouvrent	ouvrissent	

Also : **apparaître*** *to appear*
     disparaître* *to disappear*

j'avais paru	*que je* paraisse	*que je* parusse	
tu avais paru	paraisses	parusses	parais
il avait paru	paraisse	parût	
nous avions paru	paraissions	parussions	paraissons
vous aviez paru	paraissiez	parussiez	paraissez
ils avaient paru	paraissent	parussent	

Also : **dormir*** *to sleep*
     sentir* *to feel*

j'étais parti(e)	*que je* parte	*que je* partisse	
tu étais parti(e)	partes	partisses	pars
il était parti	parte	partît	
nous étions parti(e)s	partions	partissions	partons
vous étiez parti(e)(s)	partiez	partissiez	partez
ils étaient partis	partent	partissent	

21 plaire* [to please] pp. plu (Aux. avoir) ps.p. plaisant

Présent	Imparfait	Passé Composé	Passé Simple	Futur	Conditionnel
je plais	je plaisais	j'ai plu	plus	plairai	plairais
tu plais	tu plaisais	tu as plu	plus	plairas	plairais
il plaît	il plaisait	il a plu	plut	plaira	plairait
nous plaisons	nous plaisions	nous avons plu	plûmes	plairons	plairions
vous plaisez	vous plaisiez	vous avez plu	plûtes	plairez	plairiez
ils plaisent	ils plaisaient	ils ont plu	plurent	plairont	plairaient

22 pouvoir* [to be able] pp. pu (Aux. avoir) ps.p. pouvant

Présent	Imparfait	Passé Composé	Passé Simple	Futur	Conditionnel
je peux (puis)	pouvais	j'ai pu	pus	pourrai	pourrais
tu peux (puis)	pouvais	tu as pu	pus	pourras	pourrais
il peut	pouvait	il a pu	put	pourra	pourrait
nous pouvons	pouvions	nous avons pu	pûmes	pourrons	pourrions
vous pouvez	pouviez	vous avez pu	pûtes	pourrez	pourriez
ils peuvent	pouvaient	ils ont pu	purent	pourront	pourraient

23 prendre* [to take] pp. pris (Aux. avoir) ps.p. prenant

Présent	Imparfait	Passé Composé	Passé Simple	Futur	Conditionnel
je prends	prenais	j'ai pris	pris	prendrai	prendrais
tu prends	prenais	tu as pris	pris	prendras	prendrais
il prend	prenait	il a pris	prit	prendra	prendrait
nous prenons	prenions	nous avons pris	prîmes	prendrons	prendrions
vous prenez	preniez	vous avez pris	prîtes	prendrez	prendriez
ils prennent	prenaient	ils ont pris	prirent	prendront	prendraient

24 recevoir* [to receive] pp. reçu (Aux. avoir) ps.p. recevant

Présent	Imparfait	Passé Composé	Passé Simple	Futur	Conditionnel
je reçois	recevais	j'ai reçu	reçus	recevrai	recevrais
tu reçois	recevais	tu as reçu	reçus	recevras	recevrais
il reçoit	recevait	il a reçu	reçut	recevra	recevrait
nous recevons	recevions	nous avons reçu	reçûmes	recevrons	recevrions
vous recevez	receviez	vous avez reçu	reçûtes	recevrez	recevriez
ils reçoivent	recevaient	ils ont reçu	reçurent	recevront	recevraient

25 savoir* [to know] pp. su (Aux. avoir) ps.p. sachant

Présent	Imparfait	Passé Composé	Passé Simple	Futur	Conditionnel
je sais	savais	j'ai su	sus	saurai	saurais
tu sais	savais	tu as su	sus	sauras	saurais
il sait	savait	il a su	sut	saura	saurait
nous savons	savions	nous avons su	sûmes	saurons	saurions
vous savez	saviez	vous avez su	sûtes saurez	saurez	sauriez
ils savent	savaient	ils ont su	surent	sauront	sauraient

Plus-que-parfait tpp [20.08]	Présent du Subjonctif tp sj [25.08]	Imparfait du Subjonctif ti sj [32.05]	Impératif imp [9.10]
j'avais plu	*que je* plaise	*que je* plusse	
tu avais plu	plaises	plusses	plais
il avait plu	plaise	plût	
nous avions plu	plaisions	plussions	plaisons
vous aviez plu	plaisiez	plussiez	plaisez
ils avaient plu	plaisent	plussent	
j'avais pu	*que je* puisse	*que je* pusse	
tu avais pu	puisses	pusses	
il avait pu	puisse	pût	—
nous avions pu	puissions	pussions	
vous aviez pu	puissiez	pussiez	
ils avaient pu	puissent	pussent	

Also : **apprendre*** *to learn; to teach*   **reprendre*** *to take back;*
          comprendre* *to understand*   *to resume*
          entreprendre* *to undertake*   **surprendre*** *to surprise*

j'avais pris	*que je* prenne	*que je* prisse	
tu avais pris	prennes	prisses	prends
il avait pris	prenne	prît	
nous avions pris	**pren**ions	prissions	prenons
vous aviez pris	**pren**iez	prissiez	prenez
ils avaient pris	prennent	prissent	

Also : **apercevoir*** *to perceive*

j'avais reçu	*que je* reçoive	*que je* reçusse	
tu avais reçu	reçoives	reçusses	reçois
il avait reçu	reçoive	reçût	
nous avions reçu	**recev**ions	reçussions	recevons
vous aviez reçu	**recev**iez	reçussiez	recevez
ils avaient reçu	reçoivent	reçussent	
j'avais su	*que je* sache	*que je* susse	
tu avais su	saches	susses	sache
il avait su	sache	sût	
nous avions su	sachions	sussions	sachons
vous aviez su	sachiez	sussiez	sachez
ils avaient su	sachent	sussent	

Présent tp [9.01]	Imparfait ti [20.01]	Passé Composé tpc [15.03][16.01]	Passé Simple tps [32.01]	Futur tf [21.01]	Conditionnel tc [22.01]

26 servir* [to serve] pp. servi (Aux. avoir) ps.p. servant

je sers	servais	j'ai servi	servis	servirai	servirais
tu sers	servais	tu as servi	servis	serviras	servirais
il sert	servait	il a servi	servit	servira	servirait
nous servons	servions	nous avons servi	servîmes	servirons	servirions
vous servez	serviez	vous avez servi	servîtes	servirez	serviriez
ils servent	servaient	ils ont servi	servirent	serviront	serviraient

27 sortir* [to go out] pp. sorti (Aux. être) ps.p. sortant

je sors	sortais	je suis sorti(e)	sortis	sortirai	sortirais
tu sors	sortais	tu es sorti(e)	sortis	sortiras	sortirais
il sort	sortait	il est sorti	sortit	sortira	sortirait
nous sortons	sortions	nous sommes sorti(e)s	sortîmes	sortirons	sortirions
vous sortez	sortiez	vous êtes sorti(e)(s)	sortîtes	sortirez	sortiriez
ils sortent	sortaient	ils sont sortis	sortirent	sortiront	sortiraient

28 suivre* [to follow] pp. suivi (Aux. avoir) ps.p. suivant

je suis	suivais	j'ai suivi	suivis	suivrai	suivrais
tu suis	suivais	tu as suivi	suivis	suivras	suivrais
il suit	suivait	il a suivi	suivit	suivra	suivrait
nous suivons	suivions	nous avons suivi	suivîmes	suivrons	suivrions
vous suivez	suiviez	vous avez suivi	suivîtes	suivrez	suivriez
ils suivent	suivaient	ils ont suivi	suivirent	suivront	suivraient

29 tenir* [to hold] pp. tenu (Aux. avoir) ps.p. tenant

je tiens	tenais	j'ai tenu	tins	tiendrai	tiendrais
tu tiens	tenais	tu as tenu	tins	tiendras	tiendrais
il tient	tenait	il a tenu	tint	tiendra	tiendrait
nous tenons	tenions	nous avons tenu	tînmes	tiendrons	tiendrions
vous tenez	teniez	vous avez tenu	tîntes	tiendrez	tiendriez
ils tiennent	tenaient	ils ont tenu	tinrent	tiendront	tiendraient

Plus-que-Parfait *tpp* [20.08]	Présent du Subjonctif *tp sj* [25.08]	Imparfait du Subjonctif *ti sj* [32.05]	Impératif *imp* [9.10]
	Also: **courir*** *to run* **partir*** *to depart*		
	dormir* *to sleep* **sentir*** *to feel* **sortir*** *to go out*		
j'avais servi	*que je* serve	*que je* servisse	
tu avais servi	serves	servisses	sers
il avait servi	serve	servît	
nous avions servi	servions	servissions	servons
vous aviez servi	serviez	servissiez	servez
ils avaient servi	servent	servissent	
	Also: **dormir*** *to sleep*		
	mentir* *to lie*		
	sentir* *to feel*		
j'étais sorti(e)	*que je* sorte	*que je* sortisse	
tu étais sorti(e)	sortes	sortisses	sors
il était sorti	sorte	sortît	
nous étions sorti(e)s	sortions	sortissions	sortons
vous étiez sorti(e)(s)	sortiez	sortissiez	sortez
ils étaient sortis	sortent	sortissent	
j'avais suivi	*que je* suive	*que je* suivisse	
tu avais suivi	suives	suivisses	suis
il avait suivi	suive	suivît	
nous avions suivi	suivions	suivissions	suivons
vous aviez suivi	suiviez	suivissiez	suivez
ils avaient suivi	suivent	suivissent	
	Also: **appartenir*** *to belong to* **maintenir*** *to maintain*		
	contenir* *to contain* **retenir*** *to retain*		
	obtenir* *to obtain*		
j'avais tenu	*que je* tienne	*que je* tinsse	
tu avais tenu	tiennes	tinsses	tiens
il avait tenu	tienne	tînt	
nous avions tenu	**ten**ions	tinssions	tenons
vous aviez tenu	**ten**iez	tinssiez	tenez
ils avaient tenu	tiennent	tinssent	

Présent tp [9.01]	Imparfait ti [20.01]	Passé Composé tpc [15.03][16.01]	Passé Simple tps [32.01]	Futur tf [21.01]	Conditionnel tc [22.01]

30 venir* [to come] pp. venu (Aux. être) ps.p. venant

je viens	venais	je suis venu(e)	vins	viendrai	viendrais
tu viens	venais	tu es venu(e)	vins	viendras	viendrais
il vient	venait	il est venu	vint	viendra	viendrait
nous venons	venions	nous sommes venu(e)s	vînmes	viendrons	viendrions
vous venez	veniez	vous êtes venu(e)(s)	vîntes	viendrez	viendriez
ils viennent	venaient	ils sont venus	vinrent	viendront	viendraient

31 vivre* [to live] pp. vécu (Aux. avoir) ps.p. vivant

je vis	vivais	j'ai vécu	vécus	vivrai	vivrais
tu vis	vivais	tu as vécu	vécus	vivras	vivrais
il vit	vivait	il a vécu	vécut	vivra	vivrait
nous vivons	vivions	nous avons vécu	vécûmes	vivrons	vivrions
vous vivez	viviez	vous avez vécu	vécûtes	vivrez	vivriez
ils vivent	vivaient	ils ont vécu	vécurent	vivront	vivraient

32 voir* [to see] pp. vu (Aux. avoir) ps.p. voyant

je vois	voyais	j'ai vu	vis	verrai	verrais
tu vois	voyais	tu as vu	vis	verras	verrais
il voit	voyait	il a vu	vit	verra	verrait
nous voyons	voyions	nous avons vu	vîmes	verrons	verrions
vous voyez	voyiez	vous avez vu	vîtes	verrez	verriez
ils voient	voyaient	ils ont vu	virent	verront	verraient

33 vouloir* [to want] pp. voulu (Aux. avoir) ps.p. voulant

je veux	voulais	j'ai voulu	voulus	voudrai	voudrais
tu veux	voulais	tu as voulu	voulus	voudras	voudrais
il veut	voulait	il a voulu	voulut	voudra	voudrait
nous voulons	voulions	nous avons voulu	voulûmes	voudrons	voudrions
vous voulez	vouliez	vous avez voulu	voulûtes	voudrez	voudriez
ils veulent	voulaient	ils ont voulu	voulurent	voudront	voudraient

Plus-que-parfait *tpp* [20.08]	Présent du Subjonctif *tp sj* [25.08]	Imparfait du Subjonctif *ti sj* [32.05]	Impératif *imp* [9.10]

Also : **convenir*** *to agree* **revenir*** *to come back*
  devenir* *to become* **se souvenir*** **(de)** *to remember*

j'étais venu(e)	*que je* vienne	*que je* vinsse	
tu étais venu(e)	viennes	vinsses	viens
il était venu	vienne	vînt	
nous étions venu(e)s	venions	vinssions	venons
vous étiez venu(e)(s)	veniez	vinssiez	venez
ils étaient venus	viennent	vinssent	

Also : **survivre*** *to survive*

j'avais vécu	*que je* vive	*que je* vécusse	
tu avais vécu	vives	vécusses	vis
il avait vécu	vive	vécût	
nous avions vécu	vivions	vécussions	vivons
vous aviez vécu	viviez	vécussiez	vivez
ils avaient vécu	vivent	vécussent	

Also : **revoir*** *to see again*

j'avais vu	*que je* voie	*que je* visse	
tu avais vu	voies	visses	vois
il avait vu	voie	vît	
nous avions vu	voyions	vissions	voyons
vous aviez vu	voyiez	vissiez	voyez
ils avaient vu	voient	vissent	

j'avais voulu	*que je* veuille	*que je* voulusse	
tu avais voulu	veuilles	voulusses	veuille
il avait voulu	veuille	voulût	
nous avions voulu	voulions	voulussions	
vous aviez voulu	vouliez	voulussiez	veuillez
ils avaient voulu	veuillent	voulussent	

Appendix D   GOVERNMENT of iNfiNiTivES

A. VERBS FOLLOWED DIRECTLY BY AN INFINITIVE

aimer	to like to
aimer mieux	to prefer to
aller*	to be going to
compter	to expect to
courir*	to run to
croire*	to believe [*one is doing*]
daigner	to condescend to
descendre	to go downstairs to
désirer	to want to
détester	to hate to
devoir*	to have to, to be obliged to
écouter	to listen [*to sthg being done*]
entendre	to hear (*sthg being done*)
envoyer°	to send
envoyer° chercher	to send for
espérer°	to hope to
faillir* (j'ai failli [ɪ])	to nearly [*do sthg*]
faire*	to cause [*sthg to be done*]
falloir* (il faut only form)	to be necessary [*to do sthg*]
laisser	to allow [*sthg to be done*]
oser	to dare to
paraître*	to appear to
penser	to plan to
pouvoir*	to be able to
préférer°	to prefer to
prétendre	to claim to
regarder	to watch [*sthg being done*]
rentrer	to return home to
retourner	to go back (in order) to
revenir*	to come back (in order) to
savoir*	to know how to
sembler	to seem to
sentir*	to feel [*sthg happening*]
souhaiter	to wish to
valoir* mieux	to be preferable to
venir*	to come to [*do sthg*]
voir*	to see [*sthg being done*]
vouloir*	to want to

B. VERBS REQUIRING **à** BEFORE A FOLLOWING INFINITIVE

aimer à	to like to
s'amuser à	to have fun [*doing sthg*]
s'appliquer à	to apply oneself to

apprendre* à	to learn to
avoir* à	to have to
avoir* [N] à	to have [*sthg*] to [*do*]
se borner à	to limit oneself to
chercher à	to seek to
commencer° à	to begin to
consentir* à	to consent to
consister à	to consist of [*doing sthg*]
continuer à	to continue to
se décider à	to decide to
se déterminer à	to determine to
déterminer [P] à [I]	to persuade [P] to
se disposer à	to prepare to
employer° [N] à	to use [N] to [*do sthg*]
enseigner [N] à	to teach [N] to
exciter [N] à	to instigate [N] to
s'exercer° à	to practice [*doing sthg*]
se fatiguer à	to wear oneself out [*doing sthg*]
forcer° [N] à	to force [N] to
s'habituer à	to become accustomed to
hésiter à	to hesitate to
inviter [N] à	to invite [N] to [*do sthg*]
se mettre* à	to begin to
obliger° [N] à	to oblige, force [N] to
s'occuper à	to busy oneself in [*doing sthg*]
parvenir* à	to succeed in
pencher à	to be inclined to
penser à	to consider [*doing sthg*]
persister à	to persist in [*doing sthg*]
se plaire* à	to take pleasure in
se préparer à	to prepare to
procéder° à	to proceed to
provoquer [N] à	to provoke [N] to
recommencer° à	to begin [*doing sthg*] again
réduire* [N] à	to reduce [N] to [*doing sthg*]
renoncer° à	to give up [*doing sthg*]
se résigner à	to resign oneself to
se résoudre* à	to resolve to
réussir à	to succeed in
servir* à	to serve to
songer° à	to consider [*doing sthg*]
tarder à	to delay in
tenir* à	to be anxious to
travailler à	to work to
viser à	to aim to

Appendix D

achever° de	to finish [*doing sthg*]
s'arrêter de	to stop [*doing sthg*]
avertir [P] de	to warn [P] to
cesser de	to stop [*doing sthg*]
choisir de	to choose to
commander [N] de	to order [N] to
conseiller [P] de	to advise [P] to
se contenter de	to be content to
convaincre* [P] de	to convince [P] to
convenir* de	to agree to
craindre* de	to fear to
crier de	to shout to
décider de	to decide to
défendre [à P] de	to forbid [P] to
demander [à P] de	to ask [P] to
se dépêcher de	to hurry to
déterminer de	to determine to
dire* [à P] de	to tell [P] to
écrire* [à P] de	to write [P] to
s'efforcer° de	to make an effort to
empêcher [N] de	to prevent [N] from [*doing sthg*]
s'empresser de	to make haste to
essayer° de	to try to
éviter de	to avoid [*doing sthg*]
(s') excuser [P] de	to excuse [P] from [*doing sthg*]
finir de	to finish [*doing sthg*]
forcer° [N] de	to force [N] to
inspirer [N] de	to inspire [N] to
interdire* [à N] de	to forbid [N] to
jouir de	to enjoy [*doing sthg*]
jurer de	to swear to
manquer de	to fail to
menacer° de	to threaten to
mériter de	to deserve to
négliger° de	to neglect to
obtenir* de	to obtain permission to
offrir* de	to offer to
ordonner [à N] de	to command [N] to
oublier de	to forget to
pardonner [à N] de	to pardon [N] for [*doing sthg*]
parler de	to talk about [*doing sthg*]
permettre* [à N] de	to permit [N] to
persuader [N] de	to persuade [N] to

prendre* garde de	to be careful *not* to
prendre* soin de	to take care to
se presser de	to hurry to
prier [N] de	to ask [N] to
promettre* [à P] de	to promise [P] to
proposer de	to propose to
refuser de	to refuse to
regretter de	to regret to
remercier [N] de	to thank [N] for [*doing sthg*]
reprocher [N] de	to reproach [N] for
risquer de	to run the risk of
soupçonner [N] de	to suspect [N] of
se souvenir* de	to remember [*to do sthg*]
tâcher de	to try to
tenter de	to try to
venir* de	to have just [*done sthg*]

Appendix E   NAMES OF COUNTRIES

This list includes the principal countries. The corresponding adjective in the third column, when capitalized, is the name of the inhabitant or native.

EUROPE	EUROPE *f.*	européen, européenne
Austria	l'Autriche *f.*	autrichien, autrichienne
Belgium	la Belgique	belge
Czechoslovakia	la Tchécoslovaquie	tchécoslovaque
Denmark	le Danemark	danois, danoise
England	l'Angleterre *f.*	anglais, anglaise
Finland	la Finlande	finnois, finnoise
France	la France	français, française
Germany	l'Allemagne *f.*	allemand, allemande
(West)	République fédérale d'Allemagne (R.F.A.)	
(East)	République démocratique allemande (R.D.A.)	
Greece	la Grèce	grec, greque
Holland	la Hollande, les Pays-Bas	hollandais, hollandaise
Ireland	l'Irlande *f.*	irlandais, irlandaise
Italy	l'Italie *f.*	italien, italienne
Luxemburg	le Luxembourg	
Monaco	Monaco	monégasque
Netherlands	la Néerlande, les Pays-Bas	hollandais, hollandaise
Norway	la Norvège	norvégien, norvégienne
Poland	la Pologne	polonais, polonaise
Portugal	le Portugal	portugais, portugaise
Rumania	la Roumanie	roumain, roumaine
Russia	la Russie, l'Union soviétique	russe
Scotland	l'Écosse *f.*	écossais, écossaise
Spain	l'Espagne *f.*	espagnol, espagnole
Sweden	la Suède	suédois, suédoise
Switzerland	la Suisse	suisse
Turkey	la Turquie	turc, turque
AFRICA	AFRIQUE *f.*	africain, africaine
Algeria	Algérie *f.*	algérien, algérienne
Congo	la République du Congo	congolais, congolaise
Dahomey	le Dahomey	dahoméen, dahoméenne
Egypt	l'Égypte *f.*	égyptien, égyptienne
Libia	la Libye	libyen, libyenne
Morocco	le Maroc	marocain, marocaine
Tunisia	la Tunisie	tunisien, tunisienne

ASIA	ASIE *f.*	asiatique
China	la Chine	chinois, chinoise
India	l'Inde *f.*	indien, indienne
Japan	le Japon	japonais, japonaise
AUSTRALIA	AUSTRALIE *f.*	australien, australienne
NORTH AMERICA		
Canada	le Canada	canadien, canadienne
Mexico	le Mexique	mexicain, mexicaine
United States	les États-Unis *m.pl.*	américain, américaine
SOUTH AMERICA		
Argentina	l'Argentine *f.*	argentin, argentine
Bolivia	la Bolivie	bolivien, bolivienne
Brazil	le Brésil	brésilien, brésilienne
Chili	le Chili	chilien, chilienne
Ecuador	l'Équateur *f.*	équatorien, équatorienne
Nicaragua	le Nicaragua	nicaraguayen, nicaraguayenne
Paraguay	le Paraguay	paraguayen, paraguayenne
Peru	le Pérou	péruvien, péruvienne
MIDDLE EAST		
Iran	l'Iran	iranien, iranienne
Israel	Israël	israélien, israélienne
Saudi Arabia	l'Arabie Saoudite *f.*	arabe
United Arab Republic	la République Arabe Unie	arabe

Appendix E

ENTITY	CONDITIONS	*in, to*	EXAMPLES
A. Continent	All (*except below*)	**en**	en Europe, en Asie en Amérique (du Sud) (du Nord)
	With non-geographical determinant	**dans**	dans l'Amérique de Cortez dans l'Asie des steppes
B. Country, State	FEMININE NAMES (All European countries except le Portugal, le Danemark, le Luxembourg)	**en**	en France, en Italie, en Suisse, en Russie, en Pologne, en Espagne, en Chine, en Californie, en Virginie, en Floride, en Louisiane, en Inde, en Caroline du Nord
	MASCULINE SING. Names with initial vowel	**en**	en Israël en Équateur (*Ecuador*) en Arkansas, en Ohio
	MASCULINE SING. Names with initial consonant	**au**	au Portugal, au Danemark au Canada, au Brésil au Texas, au Dakota du Nord
	PLURAL NAMES Name followed by determinant	**aux** **dans +** [article]	aux États-Unis (U.S.A.) aux Pays-Bas (Holland) dans l'État de New York dans l'Inde d'aujourd'hui
C. Provinces (France)	All	**en**	en Normandie, en Bretagne, en Poitou, en Provence
D. Cities	[see 1.05] Name followed by determinant	**à** **dans le**	à Paris, à Londres au Havre [1.04B] dans le Paris de ma jeunesse [1.04C]

Appendix F

A. Punctuation

B. Capitalization

C. Division of words

D. Common abbreviations

A. Punctuation

1. Punctuation Marks (les signes de la ponctuation)

. le point [*period, full stop*]

, la virgule [*comma*] (is also used as decimal mark)

: les deux points [*colon*]

; le point et virgule [*semicolon*]

! le point d'exclamation [*exclamation point*]

? le point d'interrogation [*question mark*]

... les points de suspension marquent l'omission ou l'interruption.

- le trait d'union [*hyphen*] sert à lier les parties d'un mot composé tel que *la porte-fenêtre*, et à marquer la division d'un mot.

— le tiret [*dash*] marque un changement d'interlocuteur dans un dialogue.

« » les guillemets. On met un guillemet [«] au commencement d'une citation, et un autre [»] à la fin.

( ) les parenthèses

[ ] les crochets

' une apostrophe marque l'elision: *l'ami; peu d'arbres; qu'une.*

2. Punctuation of Quotations

(a) After a form of **dire*** use a colon, then a dash before the quotation:

Le professeur a dit:—Donnez-moi votre livre, s'il vous plaît.

(b) In an extended block of conversation, place an opening guillemet [«] at the beginning of the passage consisting of dialogue, and at the end of the passage place a closing guillemet [»].

Each speaker's part begins with a dash. Explanatory remarks inserted into the speech are marked only by separating commas.

«—Comment va Pierre?
—Bien, dit Eve. Veux-tu le voir?
—Mais certainement, dit M. Darbédat avec gaieté, je vais lui faire une petite visite.»

(c) Explanatory phrases (such as "said he," "he replied," "she thought") require inversion of subject and verb. No special punctuation is used to show that this is not part of the quotation, except for setting the phrase apart by commas.

—Bien, **dit Eve.** Veux-tu le voir?
—Tu te trompes, **dit Jean avec effort,** je sais très bien que tu pars.

B. Capitalization

1. Days of the week, months, and names of languages are not capitalized in French. The pronoun **je** is not capitalized unless it is the first word in a sentence.

Il est arrivé **lundi**, le 21 **octobre**.
En Espagne on parle **espagnol**.
Il sait que **je** pars aujourd'hui.

2. Adjectives derived from proper nouns are not capitalized.

C'est une auto **américaine**. (*from* Amérique)
C'est un livre **parisien**. (*from* Paris)

Notice the use of capital letters to designate *persons*:

Il est **Français**.	He's a Frenchman.
	(= He's French.)
Il parle français.	He speaks French.

Compare three forms of "French":

un **Français**	a Frenchman
une **Française**	a French woman
le **français**	French (*language*)

3. The words **rue**, **boulevard**, and **place** are not capitalized.

23, **rue** Jasmin
la **place** des Vosges
le **boulevard** Saint-Germain

4. Geographical names: only the modifier is capitalized.

la mer **Méditerranée**	the Mediterranean Sea
le pas de **Calais**	the Straits of Dover
le massif **Central**	the Massif Central

5. Names of institutions capitalize only the first noun unless the name is hyphenated.

la **Bibliothèque** nationale
l'**Assemblée** nationale
l'**Académie** française
BUT La **Comédie-Française** (*hyphenated*)

6. Names of buildings are fully capitalized.

le Palais du Louvre
l'Hôtel des Invalides
la Gare du Nord

C. DIVISION OF WORDS. Avoid dividing words. It is not necessary in handwritten or typewritten work, and it does not improve comprehension or appearance of your work. (In printing, word division is sometimes unavoidable.) If you must divide, be sure to follow the French rules of division.

1. Divide between syllables, beginning each syllable with a consonant if possible. (Syllables in French *end* with a vowel, a diphthong [**ou**, **au**, **oi**, etc.], or a nasal vowel [**on**, **en**, **an**, **in**, **ain**].)

bou-quet	soi-xante
ca-pi-tale	plu-ri-el
ta-bleau	dou-ter
loi-sir	é-taient
en-fant	é-di-f*i*ce
in-croy-a-ble	joue-rai

2. Divide between two consecutive consonants (except if one is **r** or **l**, see paragraph 3). Do not divide **ch**, **th**, or **gn**.

détes-ter	pois-son
ob-jet	travail-**ler**
ha-**che**	biblio-**th**èque
igno-rant	

3. When **r** or **l** combine with another consonant, keep both consonants together to start the following syllable:

qua-**tre**	é-**cr**ivain
li-**bre**	a-**dr**esser
re-**gr**et	dis-po-ni-**ble**

However, the combinations **rl** and **lr** may be divided:

par-**l**er	Mal-**r**aux

4. Do not divide after an apostrophe:

au-jour-d'hui

5. Three consecutive consonants. The first stays with the preceding syllable, and the other two move to the following syllable:

es-prit   **com-pte**

6. Do not subdivide prefixes such as **in-**, **dés-**, **dis-**:

in-croyable   **dés-**agréable   **dis-**paraître

7. Do not divide one-syllable words:

le   **les**   **des**   **une**   **ces**

8. Mute *e* (or a silent ending) does not form a separate syllable:

ca-pi-**tale**   é-di-**fice**   **é-taient**

The boldface portions of these words contain a mute *e*, and cannot be further divided. In **étaient**, the ending **-aient** is a silent ending which cannot be divided.

D. COMMON ABBREVIATIONS (*abbréviations usuelles*). French abbreviations do not end in a period if the abbreviation ends in the same letter as the word fully spelled out. Some of the common abbreviations without periods are:

Cie	compagnie	**St, Ste**	Saint, Sainte
Dr	docteur	**N°**	numéro
Mgr	Monseigneur	**1er**	premier
Mme	Madame	**1ère**	première
Mlle	Mademoiselle	**h**	heure(s) [*o'clock*]

Other frequently-encountered French abbreviations are listed below. (Special abbreviations used in this text are listed at the beginning of the Vocabularies.)

c.-à-d.	c'est-à-dire (= *that is, i.e.*)
C.A.P.E.S.	Certificat d'Aptitude Pédagogique pour l'Enseignement du Second Degré
E.N.A.	École Nationale d'Administration
E.S.S.E.C.	École Supérieure des Sciences Économiques et Commerciales
E.-U.	États-Unis (*also* U.S.A.)
f., fr.	francs
M.	Monsieur
MM.	Messieurs
O.N.U.	Organisation des Nations Unies
O.T.A.N.	Organisation du Traité de l'Atlantique du Nord
P. et T.	Postes et Télécommunications ("les P. et T.")
P.D.G.	Président-Directeur Général (*also written* P.d.g.)
S.N.C.F.	Société nationale des chemins de fer français (French National Railways)
S.A.	Société anonyme (*Incorporated*)
s.v.p.	s'il vous plaît
R.S.V.P.	Répondez, s'il vous plaît (*Please reply*)
T.S.V.P.	tournez, s.v.p. (*over; see other side*)
U.R.S.S.	Union des Républiques Socialistes Soviétiques (U.S.S.R.)

Recently there has been a tendency in some French publications to capitalize only the first letter of an abbreviation. Thus you may come across:

O.t.a.n.   C.i.a.   I.b.m.   F.b.i.   C.b.s

Abbreviations and Symbols Used in the Vocabularies

adj.	Adjective	[P]	Person appears here
adj.p.	Adjective precedes noun	*pl.*	Plural
adv.	Adverb	*pn.*	Pronoun
[C]	Clause appears here	*poss.*	Possessive
[C + *sj.*]	Clause with subjunctive verb	*pp.*	Past participle
conj.	Conjunction	*prep.*	Preposition
f.	Feminine noun	*ps.p.*	Present participle
f. pl.	Feminine plural	*rel.*	Relative pronoun
f.s.	Feminine singular	(*sbdy*)	Somebody
[I]	Infinitive appears here	*sj.*	Subjunctive
id.	Idiom	(*sthg*)	Something
imp.	Imperative	[T]	Time indication
interr.	Interrogative	*ti*	Imperfect (tense, imperfect)
invar.	Invariable	*tp*	Present (tense, present)
m.	Masculine noun	*v.*	Verb
m.pl.	Masculine plural	[*vb*]	Verb appears here
m.s.	Masculine singular	*vt* 15	Verb table 15
n.	Noun (English-French vocabulary)	*	Irregular Verb
[N]	Noun appears here	°	Stem-changing verb
neg.	Negation	≠	Unlike

Vocabularies

A

able: to be — (to do sthg) *v.* pouvoir* [29.09] (*vt* 22)

about (=*concerning*) au sujet de [N]; traiter de [N] [to deal with, to be about; il s'agit de [N] or [I] It is a a matter of; (=*approximately*) vers [T]; [N] environ

abroad à l'étranger

absent-minded *adj.* distrait,-e

absolutely *adv.* tout à fait; absolument; complètement

accident *n.* un accident

accompany *v.* accompagner

according to selon [N]

acquaintance: to make the — of faire* la connaissance de [P]

acquainted: to be — with *v.* connaître* [N] [26.10A]

account (=*story, description*) *n.* le récit

action *n.* une action

activity *n.* une occupation

actor *n.* un acteur; une actrice

actually *adv.* en réalité

address *n.* une adresse

address [P] *v.* s'adresser à [P]

admission (=*permission to enter*) *n.* une entrée

afraid: to be — *v.* avoir peur (de [N]) *or* (*que* [C + *sj*])

after *prep.* après

afternoon *n.* un après-midi; **this —** cet après-midi

ago il y a [T]

agree *v.* être d'accord; **— (to do sthg)** accepter (de [I])

airline *n.* la compagnie aérienne

airport *n.* un aéroport

all *adj.* tout [8.07]

allow *v.* permettre* à [P] de [I]; laisser [I] [16.06] [17.03]

almost *adv.* presque

along: to take [P] **—** *v.* emmener° [P] [27.03]

Alps *n.* les Alpes

already *adv.* déjà

also *adv.* aussi; également

although *conj.* quoique, bien que [C + *sj*] [26.02]

always *adv.* toujours

amazed: to be — *v.* être* étonné(e)

America *nf.* l'Amérique; **in, to —** en Amérique

American *adj.* américain,-e

331

and *conj.* et
animal *n.* un animal
annoy, to *v.* agacer° [30.01]
another *adj.* un(e) autre
answer *n.* la réponse
answer *v.* répondre à [N] *or* à [P]
anxious: to be — (*to do sthg*) *v.* tenir* à [I] [11.12]
any: not [VERB] any [N] ne [*vb*] pas de [N]
anything: not — ne [*vb*] rien
apartment *n.* un appartement; — house un immeuble
apple *n.* la pomme
application (*utilization*) *n.* une application
    — for a position *n.* une demande d'emploi
approach [N] *v.* s'approcher (de [N])
architect *n.* un architecte
armoire (= *wardrobe*) *n.* une armoire
around (= *approximately*) [TIME] *adv.* vers [T]
arrangements: to make — *v.* faire* des préparatifs
    (pour [I])
arrival *n.* l'arrivée *f.*
arrive *v.* arriver
article *n.* un article
as many as autant de [N] que
as soon as aussitôt que
ask a question poser une question
ask [P] to do sthg *v.* demander à [P] de [I]
ask for *v.* demander [N]
astonished: to be — *v.* être* étonné(e)
attend (a function) *v.* assister à [N]
aunt *n.* la tante
author *n.* un auteur; un écrivain; un poète; un drama-
    turge
avoid (doing *sthg*) *v.* éviter (de [I])

B

back: to be — *v.* être* de retour
bad *adj.* mauvais,-e; nuisible (à la santé)
baggage *n.* le bagage (*usually plural*)
ball *n.* la balle
bank *n.* la banque
bathroom *n.* la salle de bains
battle *n.* la bataille
beautiful *adj.* beau, belle
because *conj.* parce que; because of à cause de [N]
bed *n.* le lit; to make the — faire* le lit
bedroom *n.* la chambre (à coucher)
beer *n.* la bière
before (in time) *prep.* avant; (in front of) devant;
    — doing sthg avant de [I]
begin *v.* commencer° (à [I]) [30.01]; se mettre* à [I]
behind *prep.* derrière
Belgium *n.* la Belgique
believe *v.* croire* (*vt* 8)

bellhop *n.* le chasseur
belong to *v.* être* à [N]; appartenir* à [N]
beside *prep.* à côté de
best *adj.* le meilleur, la meilleure [N] [8.06]
best *adv.* le mieux [8.06]
better *adv.* mieux [8.06]
big *adj.* grand,-e; important,-e; énorme
bike (bicycle) *n.* la bicyclette; take a — ride faire* une
    promenade à bicyclette
bite: to get a — to eat *v.* prendre* quelque chose
black *adj.* noir,-e
blond *adj.* blond,-e
blue *adj.* bleu,-e (*m. pl.* bleus)
boat: by — en bateau; to take the — prendre* le
    bateau
book *n.* le livre
bookcase *n.* la bibliothèque
bored *adj.* ennuyé,-e
born, to be *v.* naître*
borrow *v.* emprunter
boss *n.* le patron
bottle *n.* la bouteille
boulevard *n.* le boulevard
boy *n.* le garçon
boyfriend *n.* le petit ami
bread *n.* le pain
breakfast *n.* le petit déjeuner
    to have — prendre* le petit déjeuner
bring [P] along with *v.* amener° [P] [27.03]
    — [P] back ramener° [27.03]
    — [N] down descendre [N]
    — [N] in, to apporter [N]
    — [N] up monter [N]
broke *adj.* fauché,-e
    to be broke *v.* être* sans le sou
brother *n.* le frère
brown *adj.* brun,-e; marron
build *v.* bâtir, construire*
building *n.* un édifice, un bâtiment
bus *n.* (city) un autobus; (interurban) un car, un
    autocar
    by — en autobus, en autocar
but *conj.* mais
buy *v.* acheter° [29.02]
    — a ticket *v.* prendre* un billet
by *prep.* par; (author) de

C

Cairo *n.* Le Caire
call *v.* appeler° [29.04]
campaign (*mil.*) *n.* la campagne
camping: to go — *v.* faire* du camping

car *n.* la voiture, une auto
card *n.* (*index*, etc.) la fiche; la carte
care: to take — of *v.* s'occuper de [N]
carefully *adv.* avec soin, soigneusement
castle *n.* le château fort, le château
cat *n.* le chat; la chatte
catastrophe *n.* le catastrophe
cathedral *n.* la cathédrale
cause sthg to be done *v.* [*causative*] faire* [I] [17.01]
center *n.* le centre
central *adj.* central,-e
century *n.* le siècle; in the 17th — au XVIIᵉ siècle
ceremony *n.* la cérémonie
chair *n.* (*straight back*) la chaise; (*armchair*) le fauteuil
chalet *n.* le chalet
charming *adj.* charmant,-e
château *n.* le château
church *n.* une église
cigarette *n.* la cigarette
city *n.* la ville
clean (up, out) *v.* nettoyer° [30.03]
clear (free) *adj.* libre
close *v.* fermer
closing *f.* la fermeture
club *n.* le cercle, le club
coffee *n.* le café
cold *n.* le froid; to be — avoir* froid (*person*); il fait froid (*weather*)
colleague *n.* le collègue
collection *n.* la collection
color *n.* la couleur; — television la télévision couleur
comb (hair) *v.* se peigner*
come *v.* venir* [11.09] (*vt* 30)
comedy *n.* la comédie
comfortable *adj.* (*person*) être* bien; (*furniture*, etc.) confortable
competitive examination *n.* le concours
complain *v.* se plaindre* (about de [N]) [29.05]
completely *adv.* complètement, tout à fait
complicated *adj.* compliqué,-e
composition *n.* la composition
computer *n.* un ordinateur
concerning au sujet de [N]; en ce qui concerne [N]
concert *n.* le concert
concierge *n.* le concierge, la concierge
connecting (flight) *n.* la correspondance
constant *adj.* incessant,-e, continuel,-le
content: to — oneself (with [N]) or ([I]) *v.* se contenter (de)
convenient *adj.* commode
cooking *n.* la cuisine; to do the — faire* la cuisine
corner *n.* le coin
correct *v.* corriger° [30.02]; *adj.* correct,-e, exact,-e
correctly *adv.* correctement
cottage *n.* la chaumière

country *n.* (*political division*) le pays; (*rural*) la campagne
in the — à la campagne
course (academic) *n.* le cours
take a — *v.* suivre* un cours
cousin *n.* le cousin; la cousine
crew *n.* une équipe; (*of a ship*) un équipage
crime *n.* le crime
criminal justice *n.* la police judiciaire
crusade *n.* la croisade
customer *n.* le client

D

dance *v.* danser
dark [COLOR] *invariable adj.* foncé
day *n.* le jour; la journée
— after tomorrow après-demain
— when le jour où
dean *n.* le doyen
decide *v.* décider (de [I])
decision *n.* la décision; to make a — prendre* une décision
defeat *v.* vaincre*
department store *n.* le grand magasin
desk *n.* le bureau; la table de travail
dessert *n.* le dessert; for — comme dessert
detail *n.* le détail
detective novel *n.* le roman policier
diagnosis *n.* le diagnostic
die *v.* mourir* [16.03]
difference *n.* la différence
difficult *adj.* difficile
dinner (*evening meal*) *n.* le dîner
directional signal *n.* le clignotant
director *n.* le directeur
discouraged: to be — *v.* être* découragé,-e
discover *v.* découvrir* [15.06]
discuss *v.* discuter; délibérer
dishes *n.s.* la vaisselle
display *n.* un étalage
do *v.* faire* [8.10] (*vt* 14)
— the dishes *v.* faire* la vaisselle, laver la vaisselle
— research *v.* faire* des recherches (sur)
— without *v.* se passer de [N]
doctor *n.* le médecin; le docteur
dog *n.* le chien, la chienne
dollar *n.* le dollar
door *n.* la porte
dormitory *n.* le dortoir
doubt *v.* douter [N] *or* (que [C])
downtown *adv.* en ville
drawer *n.* le tiroir
dress *n.* la robe

dress *v.* s'habiller
drink *v.* boire*: *pp.* bu (avoir)
drive *v.* conduire*; aller* [*to* DESTINATION' 'en auto
driver *n.* le chauffeur
during *prep.* pendant [9.04 B]

E

early *adv.* (*for a scheduled activity*) de bonne heure, (*absolute sense*) tôt; **quite early** assez tôt
earn *v.* gagner
easy *adj.* facile
eat *v.* manger° [30.02]; **have something to** — prendre* quelque chose
economical *adj.* économique
economics *nf.* l'économie
education: Ministry of — le Ministère de l'Éducation
electric *adj.* électrique
elegant *adj.* élégant,-e
employ *v.* employer* [30.03]
employee *n.* un employé; une employée
empty *adj.* vide
encyclopedia *n.* une encyclopédie
end *n.* le bout; (*conclusion*) la fin
engaged: to be — **in** *v.* être* en train de [I]
engineer *n.* un ingénieur
England *nf.* l'Angleterre
English *nm.* l'anglais
English *adj.* anglais,-e
Englishman *n.* un Anglais; une Anglaise
enormous *adj.* énorme
enough *adv.* assez (de [N])
enthusiast (fan) *n.* un fervent, un enragé; un fanatique ("fana")
entirely *adv.* complètement, entièrement, tout à fait
envelope *n.* une enveloppe
especially *adv.* surtout
essential *adj.* essentiel,-le
   it is — **that** il est essentiel que (+ *sj*)
evening *n.* le soir
every *adj.* tout,-e [N] [8.07]; chaque [N]
   — **day** tous les jours
   — **summer** tous les étés
everybody, everyone tout le monde
everything *nm.* tout
exaggerate *v.* exagérer° [29.03]
examination *n.* un examen
   fail an — échouer à un examen
   pass an — réussir à un examen
   take an — passer un examen
excellent *adj.* excellent,-e
except: nothing ... except ne ... que [10.04]
excuse *v.* excuser; — **me** Excusez-moi. Pardonnez-moi.
exercise *n.* un exercice

expensive *adj.* cher, chère
experiment *n.* une expérience
explain *v.* expliquer
exploration *n.* une exploration
explorer *n.* un explorateur
express oneself *v.* s'exprimer
express (train) *n.* un rapide
eye *n.* un œil; *pl.* les yeux

F

fable *n.* la fable
face *n.* la figure; le visage
fail *v.* échouer à [N]
failure (breakdown) *n.* une panne (d'électricité) (d'essence)
fall *n.* l'automne; **in the** — en automne
fall *v.* tomber
famous *adj.* célèbre; fameux, fameuse; bien connu
farm *n.* la ferme
father *n.* le père
fault *n.* la faute
feel (like doing sthg) *v.* avoir* envie de (faire *qqch.*) [3.12]
fellow *n.* un type
few: a — quelques [N *pl.*]
fifth floor le quatrième (étage); **on the** — au quatrième
fill *v.* remplir; **to** — [N¹] **with** [N²] remplir [N] de [N]
film (movie) *n.* le film
final *adj.* final,-e
find *v.* trouver
   — **out** *v.* savoir* (*tpc*); apprendre* (*tpc*)
finish *v.* finir (de [I]); achever° [29.02]
first *adj.*, *n.* premier, première
   at — *adv.* d'abord
flight *n.* le vol
floor *n.* un étage (*numbered*); le plancher (*footing*)
fluently *adv.* couramment
fly (travel by air) *v.* aller* [*to* DESTINATION] en avion
for *prep.* pour; (*vehicle*) à destination de [LOCALE]; (= during) pendant [T] [9.04 B]; **have been** (**doing sthg**) — depuis [9.04]
foreign *adj.* étranger, étrangère
forget *v.* oublier; — **to do sthg** oublier de [I]
former *adj.* ancien,-ne (*precedes noun*); **the** — celui-là [28.06]
fortnight (two weeks) *n.* quinze jours
France *n.* la France
free *adj.* libre
freeze *v.* geler° [29.02]
French (*language*) *n.* le français
French *adj.* français,-e
Frenchman *n.* le Français; (*a woman*) la Française
Friday *n.* (le) vendredi

friend *n.* un ami; une amie
from *prep.* de; from *countries, see* [7.12]
front: in — of [PLACE] *prep.* devant
furniture (*a piece of*) *n.* un meuble

G

garage *n.* le garage
general *n.* le général
Geneva *n.* Genève
gentleman *n.* le monsieur; *pl.* les messieurs
German (*language*) *nm.* l'allemand
German *adj.* allemand,-e
Germany *nf.* l'Allemagne
get *v.* obtenir*, se procurer; (= *to call for*) aller* chercher [N]
 — back (from) revenir* de; être* de retour de
 — dressed s'habiller
 — tickets prendre* des billets
 — up se lever° [29.02]
girl *n.* la jeune fille
girlfriend *n.* la petite amie
give *v.* donner; (*gift*) offrir* (*vt* 18)
 — up [N] renoncer° à [N] [30.01]
 — permission donner à [P] la permission de [I]
glad *adj.* content,-e; heureux, heureuse
glass *n.* le verre
go *v.* aller* [1.07] (*vt* 1)
 — back retourner
 — in for [ACTIVITY] faire* (du tennis) etc.
 — into [PLACE] entrer dans [N]
 — on (= happen) se passer; arriver
 — out sortir* [16.07] (*vt* 27)
 — over (to [N]) s'approcher (de [N])
 — sightseeing voir* les curiosités (de la ville)
 — up monter
goal *n.* le but; professional — le but professionnel
good *adj. p.* bon, bonne
grade (*school mark*) *n.* la note
grandmother *n.* la grand-mère
great *adj.* grand,-e [P]; a great man un grand homme;
 Great! Formidable!, Chouette!
green *adj.* vert,-e

H

hair *n.* le cheveu; to comb the — se peigner (les cheveux)
half *adj.* demi,-e;
 an hour and a — une heure et demie
 — an hour une demi-heure
hand *n.* la main
hand in *v.* rendre; remettre*

handkerchief *n.* le mouchoir
happen *v.* se passer; arriver
happy *adj.* heureux, heureuse
hard (= difficult) *adj.* difficile (à [I]); (*surface*) dur,-e
 — to believe difficile à croire*
hardly, scarcely *adv.* à peine (+ *inversion*) [7.05]
have *v.* avoir* [3.12] (*vt* 2)
 — a headache avoir* mal à la tête
 — lunch déjeuner
 — something to eat prendre* quelque chose
 — sthg done faire* [I] quelque chose [17.01]
health *n.* la santé; bad for the—nuisible à la santé
heavy *adj.* lourd,-e
help *n.* un aide; to — *v.* aider [P] à [I]
here *adv.* ici
 — is voici [N]
hey! tiens!
high *adj.* haut,-e
hill *n.* la colline
his (= *item belonging to him*) *poss pn.* le sien, *etc.* [12.10]
his *poss. adj.* son, sa, ses [2.05]
history *n.* une histoire
historic *adj.* historique
hitch-like *v.* faire* de l'auto-stop
Holland *n.* la Hollande; les Pays-Bas
home (*house*) *n.* la maison
 at — à la maison; chez (*dj or* name); his home chez lui
homework *n.* les devoirs
hope *v.* espérer° [29.03]
hotel *n.* un hôtel
hour *n.* une heure
 an — and a half une heure et demie
 half an — une demi-heure
house *n.* la maison
how *adv.* comment
 — to do it comment le faire
 — many combien de [N *pl.*]
humour, to be in a good être* de bonne humeur
hundred *adj.* cent; (-*s* is added on even hundreds above 100)
 four — quatre cents; 401 quatre cent un.
hungry: to be — avoir* faim [3.12]
hurry *v.* se dépêcher (de [I]); to be in a hurry être* pressé(e)

I

if *conj.* si
ill *adj.* malade; souffrant,-e
imagine *v.* imaginer
immediately *adv.* tout de suite; immédiatement
important *adj.* important,-e

impressed *adj.* impressionné(e)
impressive *adj.* impressionnant-e
in *prep.* dans; — (CITY) à
information *nm. pl.* les renseignements (**about** sur)
intelligent *adj.* intelligent,-e
intend (to do *sthg*) *v.* avoir* l'intention de [I]
interested (in *sthg*) *v.* s'intéresser (à *qqch*)
interesting *adj.* intéressant,-e
invasion *n.* un envahissement, une invasion
irregular *adj.* irrégulier, irrégulière
— **verb** un verbe irrégulier
Italian (*language*) *nm.* l'italien
Italian *adj.* italien,-ne
Italy *nf.* l'Italie

J

Japan *n.* le Japon
jet liner *n.* un avion à réaction
just: to have — (done *sthg*) venir* de [I] [11.10]
— **as** [*adj.*] **as** [N] (*comparison*) aussi [*adj.*] que [N]
[8.01]
justice *n.* la justice; **criminal** — la police judiciaire

K

kind (= sort) *n.* une espèce; une sorte
kitchen *n.* la cuisine
knock *v.* frapper (à la porte)
know *v.* (*fact*) savoir*; (*be acquainted with*) connaître*; — (*how to do sthg*) savoir* [I] [26.10B]

L

lady *n.* la dame
land *v.* atterrir
last [T] *adj.* [T] dernier, dernière [6.04]
— **week** la semaine dernière, la semaine passée
late *adj.* en retard (*for a scheduled activity*); tard (*absolute sense*)
later *adv.* plus tard
latter *pn.* celui-ci, celle-ci, *etc.* [28.06]
laundry (business) *n.* la blanchisserie
do the — nettoyer° le linge sale; faire* la lessive
law *n.* la loi
— **student** un étudiant en droit
lawyer *n.* un avocat
learn *v.* apprendre*
least: at — au moins
leave *v.* partir* [16.07] (*vt* 20) — (a PLACE) quitter [PLACE] (*the place or person left must be mentioned with* quitter)

lecture *n.* la conférence
lecturer *n.* le conférencier; la conférencière
left: to the — à gauche
Left Bank *n.* la Rive gauche
lend *v.* prêter
letter *n.* la lettre
library *n.* la bibliothèque
lie down, to *v.* se coucher
light *n.* la lumière; (*traffic signal*) le feu (rouge) (vert)
turn off the — éteindre* [29.05] les lumières; fermer l'électricité
like *v.* aimer (bien)
like (= similar to) *adv.* comme
listen (to *sthg*) *v.* écouter [N]
literature *n.* la littérature
little *adj. p.* petit,-e; *adv.* peu
very — [N] *adv.* peu de [N]
live *v.* vivre*; habiter; demeurer
living room *n.* le salon; le living; le living-room
load (with *sthg*) *v.* charger (de [N]) [30.02]
London *n.* Londres
long *adj. p.* long, longue
a — **time** *adv.* longtemps
look (at) *v.* regarder [N]
— **for** [N] chercher [N]
— **out!** Attention!
lots of *adv.* beaucoup de [N *pl.*]
luckily *adv.* heureusement
lucky: to be — *v.* avoir* de la chance
lunch: to have — *v.* déjeuner
luxuries *n.* le superflu

M

machine *n.* la machine
magazine *n.* la revue; le magazine
mail *v.* mettre* [N] à la poste
main *adj.* principal,-e
make *v.* (trip) faire* un voyage; — **a decision** prendre* une décision
— **happy** rendre [P] heureux
man *n.* un homme
manager *n.* le directeur; le gérant; l'administrateur
sales — le directeur commercial
many *adv.* beaucoup de [N]; bien des [N *pl.*]
as — [N] **as** autant de [N] que
map *n.* la carte; (*city*) le plan (de la ville)
march (*mil. movement*) *n.* la marche
market *n.* le marché
marry *v.* se marier (avec [P])
masterpiece *n.* un chef-d'œuvre (*pl.* des chefs-d'œuvre)
match (*sports*) *n.* la match; la partie
mathematician *n.* le mathématicien

mathematics *nf.* les mathématiques; les maths
    good in — fort en math
matter: no — **how much** (*sthg* is done) *id.* avoir* beau
    [I] (*see use of idiom* [3.12])
May *n.* mai
mayor *n.* le maire
me *pn.* me (*precedes verb*)
mean *v.* vouloir* dire (*qqch*)
meat *n.* la viande
medical school *n.* la faculté de médecine
medical student *n.* un étudiant en médecine; **M.D.** le
    docteur en médecine
meet *v.* (*get together*) se réunir; (*by chance*) rencontrer;
    (*oncoming*) croiser; (*become acquainted with*)
    faire* la connaissance de [P]
middle-aged *adj.* d'un certain âge
mine *poss. pn.* le mien, la mienne [12.12]; la mienne;
    to be — être* à moi [2.11]
ministry (*government bureau*) *n.* le ministère
minute *n.* la minute
    just a — ! Moment!
miss (*sthg*) *v.* manquer [N]. Il a manqué le train.
    I — **you.** Tu me manques.
modern *adj.* moderne
moment *n.* le moment
Monday *nm.* lundi; **every** — le lundi
money *nm.* l'argent
month *n.* le mois; **in the** — **of July** au mois de juillet
mood: to be in a good (bad) — *id.* être* de bonne
    (mauvaise) humeur
more *adv.* davantage; **he is working** — Il travaille
    davantage.
morning: in the — le matin; **every** — tous les matins;
    this — ce matin
Moscow *n.* Moscou
most [+ *adj.*], **the** (*comparison*) le (la) (les) plus [+ *adj.*]
    [8.02]
    the — **intelligent** le plus intelligent, la plus intelli-
    gente
most of la plupart de [N. *pl. including art. or modifier*]
mother *n.* la mère
motorcycle *n.* la motocyclette ("moto")
    go for a — **ride** faire* une promenade à moto-
    cyclette
mountain *n.* la montagne; **in the** —**s** à la montagne
move *v.* (*household*) déménager; (*carry, relocate*) trans-
    porter [N]; (*part of the body*) remuer, bouger;
    — **into the country** aller* s'installer à la cam-
    pagne
movies *n.* le cinéma; **a movie** (*film*) le film
music *n.* la musique
must have (*done sthg*) *v* avoir* dû [I] **He must have left**
    Il a dû partir.
my *poss. adj.* mon, ma, mes [2.05]

N

name *n.* le nom; **his** — **is** Il s'appelle; **What's your** —
    Comment vous appelez-vous? Comment
    t'appelles-tu?
narrow *adj.* étroit,-e
near *prep.* près de [N]
necessary *adj.* nécessaire; **it is** — **to** [I] il faut [I], Il est
    nécessaire de [I]; **it is** — **that** [C] Il faut que
    [C + *sj*]
necktie *n.* la cravate
need: to — *id.* avoir* besoin de [N] *or* [I]
neighborhood *n.* le quartier
nephew *n.* le neveu
nervous *adj.* nerveux, nerveuse
never *neg.* ne . . . jamais
new *adj.* nouveau, nouvelle (*precedes noun*) [5.06];
    What's — Quoi de neuf?
    (*brand-new*) neuf, neuve (*follows noun*)
news *n.* la nouvelle
newspaper *n.* le journal
next *adj.* prochain,-e (*follows unit of time*); — **week**
    la semaine prochaine; **the** — **victim** la pro-
    chaine victime
    — **to** (= beside) *prep.* à côté de [N]
nice *adj.* (*person*) sympathique, gentil,-le; **the weather**
    is — Il fait beau
niece *n.* la nièce
nobody *neg.* personne; ne . . . personne [10.03]; (*at*
    beginning of sentence) Personne ne + [*vb*]
    [10.05]
noise *n.* le bruit
noisily *adv.* avec bruit, bruyamment
noon *nm.* midi
note *n.* la note (*also means* school grade)
nothing *neg.* ne . . . rien [10.03]; Rien ne + [*vb*] [10.05]
notice (*sthg*) *v.* remarquer [N]
novel *n.* le roman
now *adv.* maintenant; actuellement; (*immediately*)
    tout de suite
number *n.* le nombre; (*figure, numeral*) le chiffre
    a — **of** [N *pl.*] (une) quantité de [N]
nurse *n.* une infirmière; la garde-malade

O

obey *v.* obéir (à *qqn ou* à *qqch*)
observe *v.* observer
obtain *v.* obtenir*; se procurer
obviously *adv.* évidemment
o'clock heure; **at eight o'clock** à huit heures
of *prep.* de; — **them** en (*See* 13.07)
office *n.* le bureau; — **building** un immeuble

often *adv.* souvent

old *adj.* vieux, vieil, vieille; (= *former*) ancien,-ne (*precedes noun*); **it is a week —** il est vieux d'une semaine

on *prep.* sur; (*street*) dans la rue; (*boulevard*) sur le boulevard

one *adj.* un, une

only *neg.* ne . . . que [10.04]; seulement

open *v.* ouvrir* [15.06] (*vt* 18)

order: in — to (do sthg) pour [ɪ] [11.01]

organize *v.* organiser

ought (to do sthg) (= should) *v.* devoir* (*tc*). **He ought to study** Il devrait étudier.

our *poss. adj.* notre; *pl.* nos [2.05]

ours *poss. pn.* le (la) nôtre; *pl.* les nôtres [12.10]

out: to take (sthg) — of (sthg) *v.* sortir* [N] de [N]

over (= more than [T]) plus de [T]; **over a week** plus d'une semaine

over there là-bas

owe *v.* devoir*

own: his (her) — *adj.* son (sa) propre [N] [6.04]

P

paint *v.* peindre* [29.05]

paper *n.* (*composition*) une composition; une étude; un compte-rendu; (*material*) le papier

newspaper *n.* le journal

parents *n.pl.* les parents

park *n.* le parc

park *v.* stationner; garer

parking area *n.* le parking

party *n.* la soirée

pass *v.* (*a car*) doubler; **— a course** réussir à un cours; **— customs** passer au poste de douane; **— an exam** réussir à un examen

passenger *n.* le passager, la passagère

pay *v.* payer; **— a visit** faire* une visite à [P]; rendre visite à [P]

peas (green) *n.* les petits pois

pencil *n.* le crayon

perhaps *adv.* peut-être (*inversion required if this is the first word in a clause* [7.05])

permission *n.* la permission

person *n.* la personne

physics *n.* la physique; **nuclear —** la physique nucléaire

piece of furniture *n.* un meuble

pilot *n.* le pilote

place *n.* le lieu; un endroit; **to take —** *v.* avoir* lieu

plan *n.* le plan (*strategic*); **commercial —** la formule

plane (*aircraft*) *n.* un avion; **jet —** un avion à réaction; **by —** en avion

play (*dramatic production*) *n.* la pièce

play *v.* jouer; **—** [GAME] jouer à [*art.* + N]; **—** [MUSICAL INSTRUMENT] jouer de [*art.* + N] **— (tennis) (golf)** etc. faire* (du tennis) (du golf)

playwright *n.* le dramaturge

pleasant *adj.* agréable

please s'il vous plaît; Veuillez [REQUEST]

please (someone) *v.* plaire* à [P]

plot (*literary*) *n.* une intrigue

poem *n.* un poème; une poésie

police *n.* la police (*takes a singular verb*)

policeman *n.* un agent (de police)

politely *adv.* poliment; avec politesse

poll (*public opinion*) *n.* un sondage

poor *adj.* (*financially*) [P] pauvre; (*sympathy*) pauvre [P]

poorly *adv.* mal

Portugal *n.* le Portugal

possible *adj.* possible; **it is — that** [C] il se peut que [C + *sj*], il est possible que [C + *sj*]

post office *n.* le bureau de poste

postman *n.* le facteur

precisely *adv.* précisément

prefer *v.* préférer° [29.03]; aimer mieux

preparation *n.* le préparatif

prepare *v.* préparer

present: at — actuellement; en ce moment; à présent

present (*current*) *adj.* actuel,-le

present-day *adj.* actuel,-le

pretend (to do sthg) *v. id.* faire* semblant de [ɪ]

price *n.* le prix; **what is the — of** [N] C'est combien [*art.* + N]?

prime minister *n.* le premier ministre

principal (of a lycée) *n.* le proviseur

probable: it is — that [C] *v.* il est probable que [C, *indicative*]

problem *n.* le problème; **budgetary —s** les problèmes budgétaires

process: in — of (doing *sthg*) *id.* être* en train de [ɪ]

professor *n.* le professeur

program *n.* le programme

promise *v.* promettre* à [P] de [ɪ]

provided that *conj.* pourvu que [C + *sj*] [26.02]

psychology *n.* la psychologie

public *n.* le grand public; *adj.* public, publique

publisher *n.* un éditeur

purchase *v.* acheter° [29.02] **— a ticket** prendre* un billet

put, place *v.* mettre* (*vt* 17)

Q

question *n.* la question; **to ask a —** poser une question; **to answer a —** répondre à une question

quite (= rather) assez; (= very) tout [8.09]

R

rarely *adv.* rarement; pas souvent
rat *n.* le rat
rather *adv.* assez
reach *v.* atteindre* [N] [29.05]
read *v.* lire* [4.07]
reader *n.* (*book*) le livre de lecture; (*person*) le lecteur, la lectrice
reading room *n.* la salle de lecture
ready *adj.* prêt,-e (à [I])
really *adv.* vraiment; en effet; en réalité
recently *adv.* récemment
recommend *v.* recommander
red *adj.* rouge
refuse (to do sthg) *v.* refuser (de [I])
relative (*kin*) *n.* le parent
religious *adj.* religieux, religieuse
repaint *v.* repeindre* [29.05]
repair *v.* réparer
report *n.* le compte-rendu
require *v.* exiger° [N] [30.02]
research *f.pl.* les recherches
reserve *v.* retenir*
rest *v.* se reposer
restaurant *n.* le restaurant
return (from [N]**)** *v.* revenir* (de [N])
Rhine (*river*) *n.* le Rhin
rid: to get — of [N] *v.* se débarrasser de [N]
ride: to go for a — *v.* faire* une promenade (en auto) (a bicyclette) (en bateau) etc.
rig (*truck*) *n.* un poids-lourd
right: to be — *id.* avoir* raison [3.12]
room *n.* (*general*) la salle, la pièce; (*bedroom*) la chambre; (*living-room*) le salon, le living, le living-room
roommate *n.* le camarade de chambre; la compagne de chambre
round *adj.* rond,-e
round-trip (ticket) *n.* un aller (et) retour
run *v.* courir* [16.07] (*vt* 6); (*machinery, watches, etc.*) marcher
runway *n.* la piste
Russia *n.* la Russie
Russian *adj.* russe; soviétique

S

saleslady *n.* la vendeuse
salesman *n.* le vendeur
same *adj.* même (*place between article and noun*)
satellite *n.* le satellite
satisfied: to be — (with *sthg*) *v.* être* satisfait,-e (de [N])
Saturday *n.* (le) samedi
say *v.* dire* (*vt* 9) (*see Appendix F* (2) *for use with quotations*)
scarcely *adv.* ne [vb] guère
scene *n.* la scène
school (*elementary*) *n.* une école; **at —** à l'école **medical —** l'école de médecine
scientist *n.* le savant
seashore *n.* **at the —, to the —** au bord de la mer
season *n.* la saison
secretary *n.* le secrétaire, la secrétaire; (*typist*) la dactylo
section (*of a city*) *n.* le quartier
sedan *n.* la berline
see *v.* voir* (*vt* 32)
sell *v.* vendre
sentence *n.* la phrase
serve *v.* servir* (*vt* 26)
set out for [PLACE] *id.* se mettre* en route pour [PLACE]
settle down *v.* s'installer
several *adv.* plusieurs [N *pl.*]
shirt *n.* la chemise
shop *n.* la boutique
shop *v.* faire* des emplettes
short *adj.* court,-e (*precedes noun*)
short story *n.* la nouvelle
shout *v.* crier*
show (*performance*) *n.* la représentation; **first —** (*theater*) la première représentation; (*movie*) la première séance
sick *adj.* malade, souffrant,-e
sights (*of the city*) *nf.* les curiosités de la ville
silk *n.* la soie; **made of —** de soie
silver *nm.* l'argent
sing *v.* chanter
sister *n.* la sœur
site *n.* un emplacement, le terrain
sixth floor *n.* le cinquième; **on the —** au cinquième (étage)
sixty-three soixante-trois
ski *v.* faire* du ski
skiing: to do (some) — *v.* faire* du ski
skyscraper *n.* le gratte-ciel, *pl.* les gratte-ciel
slightly *adv.* légèrement
slow *adj.* lent,-e; **slower** *adj.* plus lent,-e
slowly *adv.* lentement
smoke *v.* fumer
so (= **therefore**) *conj.* aussi (+ *inversion*)
sociologist *n.* le sociologue
sociology *n.* la sociologie
sock *n.* (*footwear*) la chaussette
soft *adj.* doux, douce

softly *adv.* doucement
soldier *n.* le soldat
some [N] *partitive structure* [4.01] de la, du de, l', des
— of the [N *pl.*] quelques-un(e)s des [N]
— of them en [13.07]
something *n.* quelque chose
— interesting quelque chose *d*'intéressant
— new quelque chose *de* nouveau
sometimes *adv.* quelquefois, parfois
son *n.* le fils
soon *adv.* bientôt
sorry: to be — *v.* regretter* que [c + *sj*]
Spain *nf.* Espagne; in, to — en Espagne
Spanish (*language*) *nm.* l'espagnol
speak *v.* parler; — about, of parler de; — with parler avec
spend [MONEY] *v.* dépenser (de l'argent)
— [TIME] *v.* passer (la journée, une semaine, etc.)
sport *n.* le sport
—s fan *n.* un fanatique ("fana") de sport
spring (*season*) *n.* le printemps; in the — au printemps
square *n.* la place; (*shape*) le carré
stamp (*postage*) *n.* le timbre-poste, *pl.* les timbres-poste
start *v.* commencer [N]; commencer à [I]; se mettre* à [I]
— out (for) *id.* se mettre* en route (pour [PLACE])
station *n.* la gare
stay *v.* rester (*aux.* être)
stenographer *n.* le (la) sténographe
still *adv.* toujours, encore
still-life *n.* la nature morte
stop *v.* arrêter; s'arrêter
store *n.* le magasin; la boutique
street *n.* la rue; on a — dans une rue
struggle *n.* la lutte; political — la lutte politique
student *n.* un étudiant, une étudiante
law — un étudiant en droit
study *v.* étudier
suburb *n.* la banlieue; le faubourg
subway *n.* le métro
succeed (in doing sthg) *v.* réussir à [I];
— (in a thing) réussir à [N]
suffer *v.* souffrir* (*vt* 18)
sugar *n.* le sucre
suggest *v.* suggérer° [29.03]
suit (*clothing*) *n.* le complet
suitcase *n.* la valise
summer *n.* un été; in the — en été; every — tous les étés
supposed: to be — *tc* of être* [*see* 22.01D]
sure *adj.* sûr,-e
Sure! Bien sûr!
surround *sthg* by *sthg* *v.* entourer [N] de [N]
Sweden *n.* la Suède; in — en Suède

Swedish *adj.* suédois,-e
Switzerland *n.* la Suisse; in — en Suisse
symphony *n.* la symphonie

T

table *n.* la table
take *v.* prendre* [9.13] (*vt* 23)
— advantage of [N] (in order to [I]) profiter de [N] (pour [I])
— care of [N] s'occuper de [N] *or* [I]
— a course suivre* un cours; I am taking a course in sociology je suis un cours de sociologie
— an exam passer un examen
— off (*plane*) décoller; (*clothing*) ôter; (*dishes*, etc.) enlever°
— out (of) sortir* [N] (de)
— [PERSON] emmener°
— place *id.* avoir* lieu
— a ride faire* une promenade (en auto, en bateau, etc.)
— [TIME] (to do *sthg*) mettre* [T] à [I]
tall *adj.* grand,-e
taxi *n.* le taxi
taxi (*aircraft*) *v.* rouler au sol
teacher *n.* le professeur; (*elementary school*) un instituteur, une institutrice
telephone *v.* téléphoner à [P]
television set *n.* la télévision; color — la télévision couleur
tell *v.* dire* à [P] que . . .
terminal building *n.* une aérogare
test *n.* une épreuve
than (*in comparisons*) que
thank (*sbdy for sthg*) *v.* remercier [P] (de [N] *or* [I])
theater *n.* le théâtre; movie — le cinéma
them *pn.* les; to — leur
then *adv.* (*at that time*) alors; (*next*) puis, ensuite
there *adv.* y (*before verb*); là (*as in English word order*)
there is (*sthg*) il y a; voilà (*item pointed at*)
therefore *conj.* aussi [+ *inversion*] [7.05]
thick *adj.* épais,-se
things: my — *n.* mes affaires
think *v.* penser; — about penser à [N]
thirst *n.* le soif
thirsty: to be — *id.* avoir* soif [3.12]
this *adj.* ce, cet, cette, ces [5.07]
those *adj.* ces; ces [N *pl.*]-là
threaten (*to do sthg*) *v.* menacer° de [I] [30.01]
ticket *n.* le billet; to buy a — prendre* un billet; (*traffic*) une contravention
time *n.* le temps; (*recurrence of an event*) la fois
at what — à quelle heure
from — to — de temps en temps

have a good — s'amuser bien
have the — (*to do sthg***)** avoir* le temps (de [I])
on — à l'heure
timid *adj.* timide
tired *adj.* fatigué,-e
to *prep.* à; **— him, — her** *indirect object pn.* lui;
— them leur
today *adv.* aujourd'hui
tomorrow *adv.* demain
tonight *adv.* ce soir
too much (many) *adv.* trop (de [N]); [*vb*] trop
top: on — of au haut de [N]
Tour d'Argent (a restaurant) la Tour d'Argent
tourist *n.* le touriste. la touriste
tower *n.* la tour; (*airport*) la tour de contrôle
town *n.* la petite ville
to — en ville
tractor-trailer *n.* le poids-lourd
tragedy *n.* la tragédie
train *n.* le train; **by —** par le train
transportation *n.* le transport
travel *v.* voyager° [30.02]; faire* un voyage
trip: to take a — *v.* faire* un voyage; faire* le trajet
(de *x* à *y*)
truck *n.* le camion; **heavy —** le poids-lourd
truth *n.* la vérité
try (*to do sthg*) *v.* essayer° (de [I]); tâcher de [I]
Tuesday (le) mardi
turn *v.* tourner; **— off** (lights, electricity) fermer,
éteindre* l'électricité; **— on lights** ouvrir* l'électricité [15.06]
— on directional signal mettre* le clignotant
turn signal *n.* le clignotant; **to turn on the —** mettre*
le clignotant
type *v.* taper (à la machine)
typewriter *n.* la machine à écrire
typist *n.* la dactylo

U

uncle *n.* un oncle
understand *v.* comprendre*
unfortunate *adj.* malheureux, malheureuse
unfortunately *adv.* malheureusement
United States *nm. pl.* les États-Unis: **to the —** aux
États-Unis
university *n.* une université
unless *conj.* à moins que . . . ne [*vb*] [26.02]
until *conj.* jusqu'à ce que [+ *sj. if future action*] [26.02]
use *v.* se servir* de [N] [16.07]; employer° [N] [30.03]
used to (do *sthg***)** *imperfect tense* [20.03] **we used to read**
nous lisions
usual: as — comme d'habitude; comme d'ordinaire

V

vacation *nf. pl.* les vacances; **to be on —** être* en
vacances
summer — les grandes vacances
various *adj.* différent,-e
— sorts of de différentes sortes de
vegetable *n.* la légume
Venice *n.* Venise
verb *n.* le verbe
very *adv.* très, fort
Vienna Vienne
villa *n.* la villa
visit *v.* (*person*) faire* une visite à [P]; rendre visite à
[P]; (*place*) visiter [N]
visitor *n.* le visiteur, la visiteuse; (*guest*) un invité
voice *n.* la voix
volume (book) *n.* le volume, le tome

W

wait for *v.* attendre [N]
waiter *n.* le garçon (de café)
wake up *v.* se réveiller
walk *v.* aller (*to* PLACE) à pied; marcher
walk: to take a — *id.* faire* une promenade;
se promener° [29.02]
want *v.* désirer [I]; vouloir* [I]; **we would like** nous
voudrions
war *n.* la guerre; **World War II** la seconde guerre
mondiale;
— broke out la guerre a éclaté
wash *v.* laver; **— onself, — up** se laver
— the dishes *v.* faire* (*or* laver) la vaisselle
waste *n.* le gaspillage; **— of energy** le gaspillage de
l'énergie
watch (*timepiece*) *n.* la montre; **wristwatch** le montre-
bracelet
watch (*sthg*) *v.* regarder [N]; **—** (*sbdy do sthg*) regarder
[P] [I] [17.03]
wear (*clothes*) *v.* porter
weather *n.* le temps
the — is nice (bad) il fait beau (mauvais) [8.10D]
Wednesday (le) mercredi
week *n.* la semaine; huit jours
well *adv.* bien
were to (do *sthg***)** *imperfect of* devoir* [23.07C]
when *conj.* quand, lorsque [+ *tf if a future action*]
[TIME UNIT] **—** où
when *interr.* quand
whereas *conj.* tandis que
which (one) *interr. pn.* lequel [21.08]
white *adj.* blanc, blanche
who, whom *pn.* qui

whole *adj.* the — [N] tout(e) le (la) [N] [8.07]; **a** — [T] tout(e) un(e) [T]

whom *pn.* qui

whose [N] *pn.* dont [*art.* + N] [24.02]

why *interr.* pourquoi

wide *adj.* large

wife *n.* la femme

willing: to be — (*to do sthg*) *id.* vouloir* bien [I] [22.06]

window *n.* la fenêtre

wine *n.* le vin

winter *n.* l'hiver; **in the** — en hiver

with *prep.* avec

without *prep.* sans

wonder: to — (**whether**) *v.* se demander (si)

wooden *adj.* [N] en bois, de bois

work *n.* le travail

work *v.* travailler

write *v.* écrire* (*vt* 11)

wrong: to be — avoir* tort [3.12]

   to have the — [N] se tromper de [N]

Y

yesterday *adv.* hier

yet: not — pas encore

young *adj.* jeune

   — **men** les jeunes gens

younger *adj.* plus jeune; (*brother*) le frère cadet; (*sister*) la sœur cadette

your *poss. adj.* votre, vos; ton, ta, tes [2.05]

yours *poss. pn.* le (la) vôtre; les vôtres; le tien, la tienne, les tiens, les tiennes [12.13]

Z

zoo *n.* le jardin zoologique

FRANÇAIS–ANGLAIS

A

a (avoir*) has
à *prep.* to, at, in
à côté de [N] *prep.* beside
à peu près *adv.* approximately, about
à pied on foot
absent, -e *adj.* absent
accepter (**de** [I]) to agree (to do *sthg*)
accompagner to accompany, to go with
   accompagné (**de** [P]) accompanied (by *sbdy*)
accomplir to accomplish
accord *m.* agreement
   d'accord I agree
   être d'accord to agree
acheter° [29.02] to buy
achever° [29.02] to finish
acte *m.* act
acteur *m.* actor
actif, active *adj.* active
actrice *f.* actress
actuel, -e *adj.* current, present-day
actuellement *adv.* currently, at present

adjectif *m.* adjective
admirer to admire
adorer to like very much, to adore
adresse *f.* address
s'adresser à [N] to address (*sbdy* or *sthg*)
aérogare *f.* air terminal
aéroport *m.* airport
afin de [I]; **afin que** [C + *sj.*] [26.02] *conj.* in order to
   (that)
agacer° [30.01] to infuriate, to annoy
âge *m.* age
   d'un certain — middle-aged
   Quel âge avez-vous? How old are you?
agent (**de police**) *m.* policeman
agrafeuse *f.* stapler
agréable *adj.* pleasant, agreeable
aider [P] (**à** [I]) to help (*sbdy*) (do *sthg*)
aimer to like, to love
ainsi *adv.* thus
   — de suite and so on
air *m.* attitude, appearance
   avoir l' — (+ *m.s. adj.*) to seem, to appear (*adj.*)
     elle a l'air heureux she seems happy

ajouter to add
  en ajoutant adding
allemand *m.* German (*language*)
allemand, -e *adj.* German
aller* [1.07] to go
alors *adv.* then; at that time
amener° [27.06A] to bring [P]
ameublement *m.* furnishings
ami *m.* friend
amie *f.* friend (*female*)
  sa petite — his girlfriend
amoureux, -se *adj.* in love
  tomber — de [P] to fall in love with (*sbdy*)
amusant, -e *adj.* amusing
s'amuser (bien) to have a good time
an *m.* year
anglais *m.* English (*language*)
anglais, -e *adj.* English
Angleterre *f.* England
animal (*pl.* **animaux**) *m.* animal
anneau caoutchouc *m.* rubber band
année *f.* year
anniversaire *m.* birthday; anniversary
annoncer° to announce
annuaire *m.* telephone directory
annuler to cancel
antériorité *f.* priority, anteriority
août *m.* August
s'apercevoir* (**de** [N]) (*vt* 24) to notice (*sthg*); to perceive (*sthg*)
aperçu *pp.* (**apercevoir***) perceived, seen
appareil *m.* telephone (instrument); camera; apparatus
  à l' — on the phone
apparenté, -e *adj.* related
appartement *m.* apartment
appartenir* (**à** [P]) (*vt* 29) to belong (*to sbdy*)
appel: faire* l' — to call the roll
appeler° [29.04] to call
  s'— to be named; **il s'appelle** ... his name is ...
apporter [N] (**à** [P]) to bring (*sthg*) (*to sbdy*)
  Used for things only. For persons, use **amener°**
apprendre* [9.16] (*vt* 23) to learn; to teach
après *prep.* after
  — avoir (*or* **être**) **+** *pp.* [11.07] after (*doing sthg*)
  d'après [N] according to [N]
après-midi *m.* afternoon
appris *pp.* (**apprendre***) learned
s'approcher (**de** [N]) to approach, to come closer (*to sthg*)
approprié, -e *adj.* appropriate
arabe *m.* Arabic (*language*); *adj.* Arabian
arbre *m.* tree
architecte *m.* architect
argent *m.* money; silver
arrêter to stop; to arrest
  s'— to stop (*doing what one is doing*)

arrivée *f.* arrival; ≠ **le départ** departure
arriver to arrive; to happen
arrondissement *m.* arrondissement (*administrative subdivision of Paris*)
ascenseur *m.* elevator
aspect *m.* appearance
s'asseoir* (*vt* 3) to sit down
assez *adv.* enough, rather, quite; **— de** [N] enough [3.07]
assis, -e *adj.* seated; ≠ **debout** *inv.* standing
assistant *m.* member of the audience; assistant; instructor
assister à [*function, ceremony*] to attend
assurer to provide
a-t-il does he have
attaquer to attack
atteindre* [29.05] to reach; to attain
atteint *tp.* **atteindre***
attendant: en — que *conj.* (+ *sj.*) [26.02] until (*something happens*)
attendre [N] to wait *for* (*sthg*) or (*sbdy*)
attente: salle d' — *f.* waiting room
attention: faire* — à to pay attention to
  Attention! Look out!
atterrir to land
attraper to get; to catch
au, aux *contractions* **à + le, les** to the, in the, at the [1.03]
augmentation *f.* increase; rise
aujourd'hui *adv.* today
aussi *adv.* also, too
  — [+ *inverted subject and verb*] therefore [7.05]
  — bien que [N] *conj.* as well as
aussitot que *conj.* as soon as
autant de [N] **que** *adv.* (*comparison*) [3.07] as much [N] as
auteur *m.* author
auto-stop: faire* de l'— to hitch-hike
autobus *m.* bus (*within a city*)
autocar ("car") *m.* bus (*interurban*)
automne *m.* fall, autumn; **en —** in the fall
autre *adj.* other; **un(e) —** another; **les autres** the others
  vous autres Americains you Americans
autrefois *adv.* formerly
Autriche *f.* Austria
avant *prep.* before (*in* TIME)
  — de [I] before (*doing sthg*) [11.06]
  — que [c + *sj.*] before [c] [26.02]
avantage *m.* advantage; ≠ **inconvénient** *m.* disadvantage
avec *prep.* with; ≠ **sans** without
avenir *m.* future
avion *m.* airplane
  en — by plane
avis *m.* notice
  à mon — in my opinion
  donner un — to give an opinion

avocat *m.* lawyer (*addressed as* Maître, *whether man or woman*)

avoir* [3.12] (*vt 2*) to have
— beau [ɪ] [3.12] to do something in vain
— de la chance to be lucky
— envie de [ɪ] to feel like (*doing sthg*)
— faim to be hungry
— honte de [N] to be ashamed of (*sthg*)
— lieu to take place
— mal à [PART OF BODY] to have a pain in (part)
— raison to be right
— soif to be thirsty
— sommeil to be sleepy
— tort to be wrong

avril *m.* April

B

bagages *m.pl.* baggage
Bâle Basle (Switzerland)
banlieue *f.* suburb(s) *collective*
banque *f.* bank
banquier *m.* banker
basket *m.* basketball
bateau *m.* boat; en — by boat
bâtiment *m.* building
— d'habitation *m.* dwelling
bâtir to build
bavarder to gossip; to talk
beau, bel, belle, *adj. p.* beautiful; fine; handsome [6.01]
beaucoup *adv.* much, a lot, a great deal
— de [N] much, many, lots of [N] [3.07]
beau-père *m.* father-in-law
beauté *f.* beauty
bébé *m. or f.* baby
bel (*m. of beau*) *adj.* [5.06] fine, handsome
belle *adj. f.s.* beautiful; fine; handsome
belle-mère *f.* mother-in-law
besoin *m.* need
avoir — de [N] *or* [ɪ] to need (*sthg*) *or* (*to do sthg*)
bibliothèque *f.* library; bookcase
bicyclette *f.* bicycle
— à moteur motorbike
bien *adv.* well; indeed; eh — well (*interjection*)
bière *f.* beer
bille: stylo à — *m.* ball-point pen
billet *m.* ticket; — de banque *m.* banknote
prendre* un — to buy a ticket
bistro (*also* bistrot) *m.* café; small restaurant
blanc, blanche *adj.* white
bleu, -e (*m.pl.* bleus) *adj.* blue
bois *m.* wood; en —, de —, made of wood, wooden
boisson *m.* beverage, drink
boîte *f.* box; can
— de nuit *f.* night club

bon, bonne *adj.p.* good
bonne *f.* maid
bord *m.* edge; au — de la mer at the seashore
bouche *f.* mouth
bouchée *f.* mouthful
bout *m.* end; au — de [T] after [T]
bouteille *f.* bottle
boutique *f.* shop, store
bruit *m.* noise; avec — noisily
bureau *m.* office; desk; — de poste *m.* post office
but *m.* goal; purpose

C

cadeau *m.* gift
café *m.* café (*restaurant*); coffee
cahier *m.* notebook
calculatrice *f.* calculator
camarade de chambre *m.* roommate; (*female:* la compagne de chambre)
camion *m.* truck
campagne *f.* country (*as opp. to* city); à la — in the country
camping: faire* du — to go camping
candidat *m.* candidate
capitale *f.* capital (*of a country, etc.*); (*for capital letters, use* la majuscule)
car *conj.* for, because
car *m.* bus (*interurban*), (*short for* autocar)
— de ramassage scolaire *m.* school bus
carte *f.* card; map
cas *m.* case; en — d'urgence in an emergency
catastrophe *f.* catastrophe
cathédrale *f.* cathedral
catholique *m. or f., adj.* catholic
causerie *f.* informal talk, lecture
cave *f.* basement, cellar
ce, cet, cette *adj. p.* this, that
ceci *pn.* this [30.06]
ce que *rel.* what [24.05]
cela *pn.* that [30.07]
célèbre *adj.* famous
cent one hundred (*See* Appendix A)
centre *m.* center
cercle *m.* circle; club
certainement *adv.* certainly
cesser (de [ɪ]) to stop (*doing sthg*); to cease
c'est he is, she is, it is [5.09]
— que [C] it's because (+ [C])
chaise *f.* chair (*without arms*); (*with arms:* le fauteuil)
— tournante *f.* swivel-base typing chair
chambre (à coucher) *f.* bedroom
chance *f.* luck; avoir de la — to be lucky
(≠ bad luck le malheur, la mauvaise fortune, "la guigne")

changement *m.* change; (*money*: **la monnaie**)

changer° to change; **— de train** to change trains

chanson *f.* song

chanter to sing

chapeau *m.* hat

chaperon *m.* cape; **le Petit Chaperon Rouge** Little Red Riding Hood

chapitre *m.* chapter

chaque *adj.* each, every

charger° [N] **de** [N] to load (*sthg*) with (*sthg*) [30.02]

charmant, -e *adj.* charming

chasseur *m.* bellhop; hunter

chat *m.* cat

château *m.* country estate; castle

chaud: il fait — it is warm (*weather*)

chauffeur *m.* driver

chaumière *f.* cottage

chef *m.* head (*person*); chief; **— d'État** *m.* chief of state

chemin de fer *m.* railroad; **en —** by train

cher, chère *adj.* (*before* N) dear; (*after* N) expensive

chercher [N] to look *for* (*sthg*); **aller —** to go get

cheval *m.* horse

cheveu *m.* hair; **les cheveux** [head of] hair

chez *prep.* at the home of; **— lui** at his home; **— vous** at (your) home

chien *m.* dog

chimie *f.* chemistry

chinois *m.* Chinese (*language*)

choix *m.* choice

ci-dessous *adv.* below

ci-dessus *adv.* above

Cie *abbreviation* (Compagnie) company

ciel *m.* sky

cigarette *f.* cigarette

cinéma *m.* movie theater; [the art of] movies

circonstance *f.* circumstance

circulation *f.* traffic; **— intense** heavy traffic

citron *m.* lemon

clair, -e *adj.* clear; (*color*) light; **bleu clair** light blue (≠ **foncé** dark (*color*) **bleu foncé** dark blue)

classe *f.* class; **en —** in class; to class

classeur *m.* filing cabinet

clef (*also* **clé**) *f.* key

client *m.* customer; patient; client

clou *m.* nail; **le — de la réussite** the key to success

coffre *m.* trunk

coin *m.* corner

colère *f.* anger; **se mettre* en —** to become angry

combien de [N *pl.*] *interr.* how many

comédie *f.* comedy

commandant *m.* commander; major

commander to order (*sthg*)

comme *adv.* like; as

commencer° [30.01] to begin; **— à** [I] to begin to (*do sthg*)

comment *adv.* how; **— allez-vous?** How are you?

commerçant *m.* merchant

commis *m.* clerk

commission: faire* une — to do an errand

commode *adj.* convenient

comparez *imp.* **comparer**

complet, complète *adj.* complete; full

complètement *adv.* completely

compléter° [29.03] to complete

compliqué, -e *adj.* complicated

se comporter to act, to behave

composer to compose; to make up

comprendre* [9.16] (*vt* 23) to understand; to include

comprennent *tp* **comprendre***

compris *pp.* **comprendre*** understood
y — [N] including (*sthg*) [14.11]

compte-rendu *m.* report

compter to count; **— faire** [N] to plan on doing (*sthg*)

concert *m.* concert

concierge *m.* or *f.* doorkeeper, concierge

concours *m.* competition; competitive examination
— d'entrée competitive extrance examination

conducteur *m.* driver

conduire* (*vt* 5) to drive

conduit *pp.* (**conduire***) driven; **il a —** he drove

conduite: examen de — *m.* driving examination, driver's test

conférence *f.* lecture; **faire* une —** to give a lecture

conférencier *m.* lecturer; **conférencière** *f.* lecturer

confortable *adj.* (*things*) comfortable; (*people: use* **bien**)

congé *m.* leave (of absence); **le jour de —** holiday

connaissance *f.* knowledge; **faire* la — de** [P] to make the acquaintance of (*sbdy*)

connaissez: vous — *tp* **connaître***; you are acquainted with

connaître* (*vt* 4) to be acquainted with

connu *pp.* (**connaître***) known; **bien —** well-known

conte *m.* story, tale

corbeille à courrier *f.* desk tray

corbeille à papier *f.* waste basket

content, -e *adj.* contented, happy, satisfied

se contenter de [N] to be satisfied with (*sthg*)

contient: il — *tp* (**contenir***) it contains

continuer to continue

contravention *f.* traffic ticket; **attraper une —** to get a ticket

contre *prep.* against

contredit: sans — unequivocally; without contradiction

contrôler to check (tickets)

convenable *adj.* proper, correct, appropriate

corriger .02] to correct

côté *m.* side; **à — de** *prep.* beside

coucher [P] to put (*sbdy*) to bed
la chambre à — bedroom

se coucher to go to bed

couleur f. color

courant d'air m. draft

courir* [16.07] (vt 6) to run

cours m. course; suivre* un — to take a course

cousin m. cousine f. cousin

coût m. cost; le — de la vie cost of living

coûter to cost; — cher to be expensive

coûteux, coûteuse adj. costly, expensive

couturière f. dressmaker, seamstress

couvercle m. cover

couvert pp. (couvrir*) covered; — de [N] covered with

craie f. chalk

craindre* [29.05] (vt 7) to fear; — que [C + ne + sj.] to fear that (sthg will happen or has happened) [25.05]

crayon m. pencil

créer to create

crever° to die

criminel m. criminal

croire* (vt 8) to believe [25.06]

croix f. cross; la Croix Rouge Red Cross

croyance f. belief

cruel, -le adj. cruel

cuisine f. kitchen; cooking; faire* la — to do the cooking

curiosité f. curiosity; —s de la ville sights of the city

CV (cheval-vapeur, pl. chevaux-vapeur) horsepower

cyclisme m. cycling (sport)

D

d'abord adv. first, first of all

dactylo f. typist

dame f. lady

dans prep. in

dateur à encrage automatique m. self-inking dater

débarquement m. unloading, disembarkation

débit m. retail shop; — de tabac tobacconist's shop

décider to decide

déclarer to declare

décoller to take off (aircraft)

se décourager° [30.02] to become discouraged

découvrir* [15.06] (vt 18) to discover; to reveal

décrit pp. (décrire*) described

décrivez imp. (décrire*) describe

déjà adv. already

déjeuner m. lunch; le petit — breakfast; prendre* le petit — to have breakfast

déjeuner to have lunch

délai m. delay; interval

délicieux, délicieuse adj. delicious; delightful

demain adv. tomorrow

demander [N] to ask for (sthg); — [N] à [P] to ask (sbdy) for (sthg); on nous demande de [I] we are asked to (do sthg)

se demander (si) to wonder (whether)

demeurer to live, to reside (= habiter)

demi, -e adj. half (Agrees when it follows the N; invariable before N); une heure et demie an hour and a half; une demi-heure half an hour

dent f. tooth; avoir* mal aux dents to have a toothache

départ m. departure; (≠ une arrivée arrival)

se dépêcher (de [I]) to hurry (to do sthg)

déplacer° [30.01] to move, to shift (displace)

depuis [T] since, for [T] [9.04 for special grammar]

dériver to derive

dernier, dernière adj. last [effect of word order 6.04]

derrière prep. behind

des of the, from the, some

dès que conj. [21.02] as soon as

désagréable adj. unpleasant

descendre to go downstairs; to get off (vehicle); to take (sthg) downstairs; — à un hôtel to stay at a hotel

désir m. desire

dessert m. dessert; comme — for dessert

desservir* (vt 26) to serve

dessin m. design; pattern; sketch; un — irrégulier an irregular pattern

destination f. destination; à — de bound for

détail m. detail; maison de — retail store

détester to detest

dette f. debt

deux two; tous les — both

devant prep. in front of

devenir* [11.11] (vt 30) to become

devoir m. duty; les devoirs homework

dictée f. dictation

dictionnaire m. dictionary

différent, -e adj. different; (before N) various

difficile adj. difficult; (≠ facile easy)

dimanche m. Sunday

diplomate m. diplomat

directeur m. manager, director

discuter to discuss

disposition f. disposal

disque m. phonograph record; disk

distingué, -e adj. distinguished

dit: il — tp (dire*) he says; ne — pas does not say

dites imp. (dire*) tell, say

divers, -e adj. various

diviser (en) to divide (into)

dois: je — [I] tp (devoir*) I must (do sthg)

donc conj. therefore

donner to give

dormir* [16.07] (vt 27) to sleep

dort: il — tp (dormir*) he is sleeping

dortoir m. dormitory

dossier *m.* file

d'où *rel.* whence; from where

douane *m.* customs

douanier *m.* customs official

doubler to pass (*a vehicle*)

doucement *adv.* softly; gently

douter to doubt; — **que** [C + *sj.*] [25.04] to doubt that

se douter (**de** [N]) or (**que** [C]) to suspect (*sthg*) *or* that (*sthg happens*)

douteux, douteuse *adj.* doubtful

doyen *m.* dean

dramaturge *m.* playwright (*less used than* auteur dramatique)

dresser une liste to draw up a list

du (de + le) of the, from the, some

duplicateur à alcool *m.* spirit duplicator

dur, -e *adj.* hard; (difficult = **difficile**)

E

eau *f.* water

échouer (**à** [N]) to fail (in *sthg*); ≠ **réussir à**

école *f.* school; — **maternelle** *f.* kindergarten; — **de médecine** medical school

économie *f.* economics; **un étudiant en** — economics student

écouter [N] to listen *to* (*sbdy* or *sthg*) [13.05]

écrire* [4.08] (*vt* 11) to write; **la machine à** — typewriter

s'écrier to exclaim

écrit: par — in writing

écrivain *m.* writer

écrivez *imp.* (**écrire***) write

éditeur *m.* publisher

édifice *m.* building

égal, -e *adj.* equal; **cela m'est égal** it doesn't matter to me

également *adv.* also

égard: à cet — in this regard; in that matter

église *f.* church

élève *m. or f.* pupil, student

s'éloigner to go away, to move off

emmener° [27.06B] to take [P] along

emploi *m.* employment; job; use

employé *m.* **employée** *f.* employee

employer° [30.03] to use; to employ

en employant *ps.p.* using

emprunter to borrow

ému, -e *adj.* moved, affected

en *prep.* in [13.07] (*See Index for various applications*)

encore *adv.* again; still; **pas** — not yet

endommager to damage

s'endormir* [16.07] to go to sleep

enfance *f.* childhood

enfin *adv.* finally

s'ennuyer° [30.03] to be bored

énorme *adj.* enormous

énormément *adv.* enormously

enseignement *m.* instruction; teaching
  — **supérieur** higher education

enseigner to teach

ensemble *adv.* together

ensuite *adv.* next; then

entendre to hear
  Bien entendu! Of course!

entourer [N] (**de** [N]) to surround (*sthg*) with (*sthg*)

entre *prep.* between; among

entrée *f.* entrance

entreprise *f.* firm, establishment

entrer (**dans** [N]) to go in (*a place*); to enter (*place*); (dans *must be used if the place is mentioned.*)

envie: avoir* — **de** [I] to feel like (*doing sthg*)

envoyer° [30.03] to send; — **chercher** [P] to send for [P]

épais, -se *adj.* thick

épaisseur *f.* thickness

équipe *f.* team; crew

équivalent *m.*

escalier *m.* stairs; staircase

Espagne *f.* Spain; **en** — in Spain

espagnol *m.* Spanish (*language*)

espagnol, -e *adj.* Spanish

espérer° [29.03] to hope; (*Use of* sj. *after*, 25.06)

espion *m.* spy

essai *m.* essay

essayer° (**de** [I]) [30.04] to try (*to do sthg*)

est *m.* east; **à l'**— in the east, to the east

étage *m.* floor; **au premier** — on the second floor

était *ti* (**être***) was, used to be

étalage *m.* display; show window display

état *m.* state; **chef d'État** chief of state

États-Unis *m.pl.* United States

été *m.* summer; **en** — in the summer

éteindre* [29.05] extinguish; put out (lights)

étonnant, -e *adj.* astonishing, surprising

étonné, -e *adj.* astonished; surprised

étranger, étrangère *adj.* foreign

être *m.* being

être* [2.10] (*vt* 13) to be
  — **à** [P] to belong to (*sbdy*)
  — **d'accord** to agree
  — **bien** to be comfortable (*of persons*)
  — **le bienvenu** to be welcome
  — **de bonne heure** to be early
  — **en retard** to be late
  — **en train de** [I] to be in the process of (*doing sthg*)

étroit, -e *adj.* narrow

étudiant *m.* **étudiante** *f.* student

étudier to study

événement *m.* event

évidemment *adv.* obviously
éviter to avoid; — de [I] to avoid (*doing sthg*)
exagérer° [29.03] to exaggerate
examen *m.* examination; échouer à un — to fail an exam; passer un — to take an exam; réussir à un — to pass an exam
exception *f.*; à l'exception de with the exception of
s'excuser (de [N]) to apologize (*for sthg*)
exemple *m.* example; par — for example
exercice *m.* exercise, drill
exiger° [30.02] to require
expliquer to explain
exprimer to express; s'— to express oneself
extérieur *m.* exterior; (≠ intérieur *m.* interior)

F

face *f.* face; en — de opposite
fâché, -e *adj.* angry; embarrassed
se fâcher (de [N]) to become angry (*about sthg*)
facile *adj.* easy; (≠ difficile difficult)
facteur *m.* postman
faculté *f.* school; college; la — des sciences School of Science
faim *f.* hunger; avoir — to be hungry (*famished*)
faire* [8.10] (*vt* 14) to make; to do; to cause (*sthg*) to be done [17.01]
  — attention to pay attention
  — du camping to go camping
  — la cuisine to cook, to do the cooking
  — partie de [N] to be a member of (*sthg*)
  — la vaisselle to wash the dishes
  — une visite à [P] to visit (*sbdy*)
  il ne sait que — he doesn't know what to do
se faire* to occur; to be accomplished
  en train de — in progress
  — voir to show oneself
fait *m.* fact
  tout à — *adv.* completely, entirely
familier, familière *adj.* familiar; belonging to the family
famille *f.* family
fantastique *adj.* fantastic
fatigué, -e *adj.* tired
faubourg *m.* suburb = banlieue (*f.*)
fauché *adj.* broke, out of money
faut: il faut [I] one must (*do sthg*); il faut que [C + *sj.*] it is necessary that [C]; il ne faut pas [I] you must not (*do sthg*); Que faut-il faire? What must be done?
faute *f.* mistake; fault
fauteuil *m.* armchair
féliciter to congratulate
femme *f.* woman; wife

fenêtre *f.* window
ferme *f.* farm
fermer to close
fête *f.* holiday; feast (*related to festival*)
feu *m.* fire; (traffic) signal; un feu rouge a red light
feuille *f.* sheet (of paper); leaf
se fiancer (avec [P]) to become engaged (*to sbdy*)
fiche *f.* index card
fier, fière *adj.* proud
figure *f.* face
fille *f.* daughter
  jeune fille *f.* girl
film *m.* movie; picture show
fils *m.* son
fin *f.* end
fini *pp.* (finir) finished
finir to finish
fixer to set for [T]; to fix, establish
flatter to flatter
flatteur *m.* flatterer
fleur *f.* flower
fleuve *m.* river (*flowing into the ocean*) (*For rivers flowing into another river, a lake, a canal, etc. use la rivière.*)
fois *f.* time (*recurrence of an event*); par deux — in two steps
font *tp* (faire*) do, make
football *m.* soccer; (*football is le football américain*)
force *f.* strength
formidable *adj.* formidable; enormous; extraordinary; (*exclamation*) great!
formule *f.* formula; plan
Français *m.* Française *f.* Frenchman; French woman
français *m.* French (*language*)
français, -e *adj.* French
frapper to strike; to knock
frère *m.* brother
fringant, -e *adj.* lively; spirited
fromage *m.* cheese
frontière *f.* frontier; border
fruit *m.* (a piece of) fruit; (*use the plural for more than one piece*)
fumer to smoke; Défense de fumer No Smoking

G

gagner to earn; to win (*a game*, etc.)
garçon *m.* boy; waiter
garde *m.* guard
garder to keep; — un ressentiment (contre [P]) to hold a grudge against (*sbdy*)
gare *f.* station
garer to park
gâteau *m.* cake

gazon *m.* lawn
geler° [29.02] to freeze
général *m.* general
généreux, généreuse *adj.* generous
Genève Geneva (Switzerland)
genou *m.* knee
gens *m.pl.* people; les jeunes — young men
gérant *m.* manager
gigantesque *adj.* gigantic
grammaire *f.* grammar
grand, -e *adj.* large, big; un homme grand a tall man; un grand homme a great man [6.04]
grand-mère *f.* grandmother
grandeur *f.* size
gratte-ciel *m.* skyscraper (*pl.* les gratte-ciel)
grave *adj.* serious, grave
gravure *f.* engraving
gros, -se *adj. p.* massive; heavy
guère: ne [vb] — scarcely
guerre *f.* war
guichet *m.* ticket-window
guide *f.* guide; rein (*for horses*)
guitare *f.* guitar

H

The star (⋆) indicates words beginning with *aspirate h*. No elision or linking can occur with these words (e.g. le héros). Words not marked with a star begin with *mute h*.

h *abbreviation for* heure(s) o'clock
habile *adj.* talented
s'habiller to get dressed
habitation *f.* dwelling
habiter to live
⋆hâte *f.* haste; en — hastily
⋆haut, -e *adj.* high; tout — out loud
⋆hauteur *f.* height
⋆héros *m.* hero
hésiter to hesitate; — à [I] hesitate to do (*sthg*)
heure *f.* hour; time; Quelle — est-il? What time is it?; à l'— on time; à quelle — at what time; de bonne — early
heureusement *adv.* fortunately
heureux, heureuse *adj.* happy
hier *adv.* yesterday; — soir yesterday evening
histoire *f.* story; history
historique *adj.* historic, historical
hiver *m.* winter; en — in the winter
homme *m.* man
⋆honte *f.* shame; avoir — (de [N]) to be ashamed (*of sthg*)
hôpital *m.* hospital

hôtel *m.* hotel; — de ville *m.* city hall
hôtesse *f.* hostess; stewardess
⋆huit eight; — jours a week (= une semaime)
⋆huitaine: une — de jours about a week
humeur *f.* mood; être de bonne (mauvaise) — to be in a good (bad) mood

I

ici *adv.* here
idiotisme *m.* idiom
îlot *m.* isle, island
il y a *id.* (avoir*) there is, there are; — une semaine a week ago; *interr.* y a-t-il is there, are there
imaginer to invent, think up
imitant: en — *ps.p.* imitating, by imitating
immédiat, -e *adj.* immediate
immeuble *m.* apartment house; office building
important, -e *adj.* big, large; important
impressionnant, -e *adj.* impressive
impressionné, -e *adj.* impressed
imprimerie *f.* printing
inconnu *m.* inconnue *f.* stranger
inconvénient *m.* disadvantage
incroyable *adj.* unbelievable
indiquant; en — *ps.p.* indicating
indiqué, -e *adj.* indicated
individu *m.* individual (= une personne)
infirmière *f.* nurse
ingénieur *m.* engineer
insister (sur [N]) to emphasize (*sthg*)
s'installer to settle down
intention *f.* intent; avoir* l'— de [I] to intend to (*do sthg*)
intéressant, -e *adj.* interesting
intéresser [P] to interest (*sbdy*); to concern (*sbdy*); s'intéresser à [N] to be interested in (*sthg*)
intérêt *m.* interest
intitulé, -e *adj.* entitled
introduire* (*vt* 5) to introduce
inviter to invite
irrégulier, irregulière *adj.* irregular
Italie *f.* Italy
italien *m.* Italian (*language*)
Italien *m.* Italian (*man*)
italien, -ne *adj.* Italian
italique: en — in italics

J

jamais *neg.* never; ne [vb] jamais never
Japon *m.* Japan
japonais *m.* Japanese (*language*)

jardin *m.* garden; — **zoologique** zoo
jaune *adj.* yellow
jeter° [29.04] to throw
jeu *m.* game
jeudi *m.* Thursday
jeune *adj.* young; — **fille** *f.* girl; **les jeunes gens** *m.pl.* young men
joli, -e *adj.* pretty
jouer to play; — **à** [GAME]; — **de** [INSTRUMENT]
joueur *m.* player
jour *m.* day; **huit jours** a week; **tous les jours** every day
journal *m.* newspaper
journalier, journalière *adj.* daily
journaliste *m.* journalist, newpaper man
journée *f.* day
jugement *m.* judgment
juger to judge
juillet *m.* July
juin *m.* June
jus *m.* juice
jusqu'à *prep.* as far as
jusqu'à ce que *conj.* until [26.02: *sj required*]
jusque *prep.* as far as

K

kilo (= **kilogramme**) *m.* kilogram (1 kg. = 2.2 *pounds approx.*)
kilomètre *m.* kilometer (8 *km.* = 5 *miles approx.*)

L

la *art.* the; *pn.* her, it
là *adv.* there; **par —** by that
　là-bas *adv.* over there
La Haye The Hague
laid, -e *adj.* ugly
laideur *f.* ugliness; (≠ **beauté** *f.* beauty)
laisser to leave (behind); to allow [16.06D]
lait *m.* milk
langue *f.* language; — **étrangère** foreign language; — **vivante** modern language
large *adj. p.* wide
se laver to wash up; get washed
le *art.* the; *pn.* him, it
Le Caire Cairo
leçon *f.* lesson
lecteur *m.* reader; *f.* **lectrice**
lecture *f.* reading; **salle de —** *f.* reading room
léger, légère *adj.* light (*weight*)
légèrement *adv.* slightly
légume *m.* vegetable
lendemain *m.* the next day; ≠ **la veille** the day before

lent, -e *adj.* slow
lentement *adv.* slowly
les *art.* the; *pn.* them
lettre *f.* letter
lettres *f.pl.* humanities
leur [N] *poss. adj.* their; *pn.* to them (*before verb*)
lever° [29.02] to raise; **se —**° to get up
librairie *f.* bookstore; (≠ **la bibliothèque** library)
libre *adj.* free
lieu *m.* place; **avoir —** to take place
se limiter (**à**) to limit oneself (to)
lire* [4.07] (*vt* 16) to read
lit *m.* bed; **faire* le —** to make the bed
littérature *f.* literature
livre *m.* book; *f.* pound (*weight*)
location *f.* rental
locution *f.* phrase
logement *m.* housing; lodging
logiquement *adv.* logically
loi *f.* law; **étudiant en droit** *m.* law student
Londres London
long, -ue *adj. p.* long
longtemps *adv.* for a long time
lorsque *conj.* when; (**quand** *is more frequently used in conversation*)
lu *pp.* (**lire***) read
lune *f.* moon; (≠ **le soleil** sun)
lundi *m.* Monday; **le —** every Monday, on Mondays
lycée *m.* secondary school; (≠ **collège** *m.* privately owned secondary school

M

ma *adj.f.s.* my
machine *f.* machine; — **à écrire** *f.* typewriter
magasin *m.* store; **grand —** *m.* department store
magazine *m.* magazine (*usually illustrated*)
magnifique *adj.* magnificent
main *f.* hand
maintenant *adv.* now; = **à présent, en ce moment**
maire *m.* mayor
mais *conj.* but; — **oui!** Certainly!; — **non!** Certainly not!
maison *f.* house; business firm; **à la —** at home; — **particulière** private house
mal *adv.* badly, poorly; — **compris** misunderstood; **avoir — à la tête** to have a headache; **tant bien que —** somehow or other, after a fashion
malade *adj.* ill; (*cf.* **souffrant, -e** *adj.* not too well, under the weather); *m., f.* patient
malgré *prep.* in spite of
malheureusement *adv.* unfortunately
malhonnête *adj.* dishonest
maman *f.* mama

manger° [30.02] to eat

manquer [N] to miss (*sthg*); **— de** [N] to lack (*sthg*); **Vous me manquez** I miss you; **Il a manqué le train** He missed the train.

marchandise *f.* merchandise

marché *m.* market

marcher to walk

mardi *m.* Tuesday; **le —** every Tuesday, Tuesdays

mari *m.* husband

mariage *m.* marriage

se marier (avec [P]) to marry (*sbdy*)

marque *f.* brand

marron *adj.* brown

mars March

mathématiques (maths) *f.pl.* mathematics

matière *f.* material

matin *m.* morning; **le —** in the morning; **deux heures du —** 2 : 00 A.M.; (≠ **du soir** P.M.)

mauvais, -e *adj. p.* bad

mécanicien *m.* mechanic

médecin *m.* physician, doctor

médecine *f.* (*profession of*) medicine; **étudiant en —** *m.* medical student; **école de —** *f.* medical school

médicament *m.* medicine (*pharmaceutical*)

meilleur, -e *adj. p.* better (*comparative of* **bon, -ne**); **le meilleur, la meilleure** (*superlative*) the best

même *adj.* (*before* N) same; (*after* N) very; (*at beginning of clause*) Even; **quand —** all the same, anyway; [*vb*] **de même** (*do sthg*) in the same way; **— si** even if

mentionner to mention

mentir* to lie (*prevaricate*) [16.07] (*vt* 27)

mer *f.* sea, ocean; **au bord de la —** at the beach, at the seashore

mercredi *m.* Wednesday; **le —** every Wednesday, Wednesdays

mère *f.* mother

mériter to deserve

messieurs *m.pl. of* **Monsieur**; **ces —** these gentlemen

métier *m.* profession; trade

metteur en scène *m.* producer; director (*movie*)

mettre* [6.05] (*vt* 17) to put
  — (*du temps*) **à** [I] to take (*a certain time*) to (*do sthg*)
  — (*une lettre*) **à la poste** to mail (a letter)
  se — à [I] to begin to (*do sthg*)
  se — en route (pour PLACE) to start out for (PLACE)

métro *m.* subway (*abbrev. for* Chemin de fer métropolitain)

meuble *m.* (piece of) furniture

meurt: il — *tp* (**mourir***) he dies, he is dying

midi noon; **après-midi** *m.* afternoon

mieux *adv.* (*comparative of* **bien**) better; **il vaut — que** it is better that

mille one thousand; (in dates **mil**)

milliardaire *m.* billionaire

ministre *m.* minister (*of state*); ≠ **pasteur** *m.* minister (*religious*)

minuit midnight; ≠ **midi** noon

mis, -e *pp.* (**mettre***) put; **Je l'ai mis(e)** I put it

moderne *adj.* modern

moderniser to modernize

moi *dj.* me

moins *adv.* less; **à — que** *conj.* [+ *sj*] unless; **au —** at least; **— de** [N] less than

mois *m.* month; **au — de** in the month of

moment *m.* moment; **au — où** at the moment when; **en ce —** at this moment

mon *adj.* my

monde *m.* world; **beaucoup de —** lots of people; **tout le —** everybody

monsieur [*plus* NAME] Mr.; **le monsieur** *m.* the gentleman; **Bonjour, monsieur.** Good morning, sir.

monter to go up (stairs); to get on (*a vehicle*); to take [N] up (stairs); **— à bicyclette** to get on a bicycle; **le prix monte** the price is rising

montre *f.* watch (*timepiece*); **montre-bracelet** *f.* wristwatch

monument *m.* public building; monument

morceau *m.* piece

mordre to bite

mot *m.* word

motif *m.* purpose

motocyclette (moto) *f.* motorcycle

moyen *m.* means, way; **— de transport** means of transportation; **au — de** by means of

mur *m.* wall

musée *m.* museum

musique *f.* music; band (*military*)

N

nager° [30.02] to swim

naît: il — tp (**naître***) he is born

naître* to be born (*pp.* **né, -e**) **Il est né (à Paris)** He was born (in Paris)

n'est-ce pas *interr.* isn't it so [12.07]

nettoyer° [30.03] to clean

neuf, neuve *adj.* (brand-)new

neveu *m.* nephew

nez *m.* nose

ni . . . ni *neg.* [10.04] neither . . . nor

nièce *f.* niece

noir, -e *adj.* black; **le tableau —** blackboard

nom *m.* noun; name

nombre *m.* number

nombreux, nombreuse *adj.* numerous

nommer to name

non no; **mais —** certainly not; **ne** [*vb*] **non plus** not (*do sthg*) either

nord *m.* north; **au — de** in, to the north of; **nord-est** northeast

nos *adj. pl.* our

note *f.* grade; note

notre *adj. s.* our

nourriture *f.* food

nouvel (*alternate form of* **nouveau**) *adj. m.s.* new [5.06]

nouvelle *f.* news; **de tes nouvelles** news about yourself

nuit *f.* night; **la —** at night

numéro *m.* number

O

obéir (**à** [P]) to obey (*sbdy*)

obligé *pp.* obliged

obliger° [30.02] to oblige

obtenir* (*vt* 29) to obtain; = **se procurer**

occupation *f* activity

s'occuper de [N] to be busy with (*sthg*), to take care of

odeur *f.* odor

œil (*pl.* **yeux**) *m.* eye

œuvre *f.* work; the collective works of an author, composer, etc.; **—s de référence** reference works

offrir* [15.06] (*vt* 18) to give; to offer

omettant *ps.p.* (**omettre***) omitting

omettre* (*vt* 17) to omit; **n'omettez pas de** [I] don't fail to (*do sthg*)

on *pn.* one [19.07, *use to replace passive*]

oncle *m.* uncle

optimiste *adj.* optimistic

ordinateur *m.* computer

ordonner to order; to command, to ordain

orthographe *f.* spelling

ou *conj.* or; **ou . . . ou** either . . . or

où *adv.* where; **au moment —** at the moment when

oublier to forget; **— de** [I] to forget to (*do sthg*)

oui yes; **mais —** Why, yes. Certainly.

ouvert, -e *pp.* (**ouvrir***) opened; *adj.* open

ouvrage *m.* work; **— littéraire** literary work

ouvrir* [15.06] (*vt* 18) to open

P

page *f.* page

palais *m.* palace

par *prep.* by; through; **— là** by that

paraît: il — que it appears that

parc *m.* park

parenthèses *f.pl.* parentheses; **entre —** in parentheses

parfois *adv.* sometimes

parking *m.* parking lot; parking garage

parler to speak, to talk; ≠ **dire*** to say

parloir *m.* parlor; = **le salon, le living-room**

parmi *prep.* among

pars: je — *tp* (**partir***) I leave; I am leaving

particulier, particulière *adj.* private

partie *f.* part; **une — de** part of

partiellement *adv.* partially

partir* [16.07] (*vt* 20) to leave, to depart

pas *m.* step; pace

passage *m.* passage; **— couvert** covered passageway

passager *m.* passenger

passeport *m.* passport

passer to pass; **— un examen** to take an exam; **— par** [N] to be passing through (*place*); to spend [TIME]

se passer de [N] to get along without (*sthg*)

se passer to happen; = **arriver**

passionnant, -e *adj.* exciting

patiemment *adv.* patiently

patron *m.* 'boss', employer

pauvre *adj.* poor [6.04]; pitiful (*before N*)

payer° [N] [30.04] to pay (*sbdy*); to pay for (*sthg*)

pays *m.* country (*political division*); ≠ **campagne** (*not in urban area*)

paysanne *f.* peasant woman; farm woman

Pays-Bas Netherlands

P.D.G. (**P.d.g.**) *m. invar.* (**Président-directeur général**) President and General Manager

peindre* [29.05] to paint

peine: à — que [7.05] scarcely (*had sthg happened*) than

peinture *f.* painting

pendant *prep.* during; for [9.04 B]

pendant que [C] *conj.* while

pénétrer dans [N] to enter

pensée *f.* thought

penser to think; **— à** [N] to think about (*sthg*)

perdre to lose

perdu *pp.* (**perdre**) lost

père *m.* father

persiennes *f.pl.* venetian blinds

personne *f.* person; **ne . . . personne** *neg.* nobody [10.04]

petit, -e *adj.* small, little; **petit ami** *m.* boyfriend; **petite amie** *f.* girlfriend

peu *adv.* little; **— de** [N *pl.*] very little (*sthg*); **un — de** [N] a little (*sthg*); **— [+ adj.]** *creates an antonym* **peu intelligent** stupid, unintelligent

peuple *m.* people (*nation, race*)

peut: on — one can; **il se peut que** [+ *sj.*] it is possible that [25.04]

peut-être *adv.* perhaps [7.05]

pharmacie *f.* pharmacy; ≠ **drug-store** *m.* (*which sells many items not in the class of drugs*)

philosophe *m.* philosopher

phrase *f.* sentence; ≠ **la locution** phrase

physicien *m.* physicist; ≠ **médecin** *m.* physician

physique *f.* physics

pièce *f.* room (= **la salle**); coin; — **(de théâtre)** play, drama

pied *m.* foot; **à —** on foot

pilote *m.* pilot

piste *f.* path; runway

place *f.* place; square; *Place Vendôme*; — **de l'adjectif** adjective word-order

plage *f.* beach

se plaindre* (de [N]) [29.05] to complain (*about sthg*)

plaire* (à [P]) (*vt* 21) to please (*sbdy*); *pp.* plu (avoir)

plaisir *m.* pleasure

plaît: il — à [P] *tp* (**plaire***) he (it) pleases (*sbdy*); **cela me plaît** I like that

planche *f.* plank; board

plancher *m.* floor (*footing*); ≠ **un étage** (*numbered*) floor

plastique *m. adj.* plastic

plat *m.* dish

plat, -e *adj.* flat

plein, -e *adj.* full (**de** with)

plupart: la — de *adv.* most of

plus *adv.* more; — **de** [N] more [N]; **de plus** in addition

plusieurs [N.*pl.*] *adv.* several

plutôt que *conj.* rather than

pneu (*pl.* **pneus**) *m.* tire

poche *f.* pocket

poème *m.* poem

poésie *f.* poem

poète *m.* poet

point de [N] = **pas de** [N] *neg.* no [N]

pois: petits — *m. pl.* green peas

poli, -e *adj.* polite; **poliment** *adv.* politely

policier *adj.* police; **un roman —** a detective novel

politicien *m.* politician

polonais *m.* Polish (*language*)

polycopier to make copies, reproduce, mimeograph, etc.

pomme *f.* apple; — **de terre** *f.* potato; **pommes frites** french-fries

pont *m.* bridge

port *m.* port

porte *f.* door; gate

porter to carry

portugais *m.* Portuguese (*language*)

poser une question (à [P]) to ask (*sbdy*) a question

possible *adj.* possible; **il est — que** [+ *sj*] [25.04] it is possible that

poste *m.* location; — **de douane** customs desk

pour *prep.* for; — [I] in order to (*do sthg*); — **que** *conj.* so that, in order that (+ *sj.* [26.02])

pourquoi *interr.* why

pourvu que *conj.* provided that (+ *sj.* [26.02])

pouvoir* (*vt* 22) to be able

pouvoir *m.* power

pratique *adj.* practical

précédé de preceded by

précédent, -e *adj.* preceding

précis, -e *adj.* precise; **à deux heures précises** at exactly two o'clock

préfecture de police *f.* police headquarters

préférer° [29.03] to prefer; = **aimer mieux**

premier, première *adj. p.* first

prendre* [9.13] (*vt* 23) to take; — **un billet** to buy a ticket; — **une décision** to make a decision

prends *tp* (**prendre***) **je —** I take, I am taking

préparer to prepare

près: — de [N] *prep.* near, close to (*sthg*); **à peu —** approximately, about

présenter to present

se presser to hurry; = **se dépêcher** (de [I])

prêt, -e *adj.* ready

prêter to lend

prévoir* (*vt* 32) to foresee; *pp.* **prévu, -e** provided for, foreseen

prier [P] **de** [I] to ask (*sbdy*) to (*do sthg*)

printemps *m.* spring; **au —** in the spring

prix *m.* price

problème *m.* problem

prochain, -e *adj.* next; **la semaine prochaine** next week

se procurer [N] to obtain (*sthg*); to get (*sthg*)

professeur *m.* teacher; professor

profiter de [N] to take advantage of (*sthg*)

projet *m.* plan

promenade *f.* walk; ride [8.10B]

promettre* (*vt* 17) to promise; — **à** [P] **de** [I] to promise (*sbdy*) (*to do sthg*)

pronom *m.* pronoun

propre *adj.* (*before noun*) own; (*after noun*) clean [6.04]

protéger° [29.03] to protect

protestant *m.* **protestante** *f.* protestant

protester contre [N] to protest (*sthg*) or (*against sthg*)

provenance *f.* source, origin; **en — de** from

public *m.* public

public, publique *adj.* public

puis *adv.* then, next

puisque *conj.* since; inasmuch as

punir to punish

Q

qualité *f.* good quality; degree of excellence

quand *conj.* when; — **même** anyhow, all the same

quart *m.* quarter; one-fourth

quartier *m.* section; quarter (of a city), neighborhood

quel, -le [N] *interr.* what, which (*item*)?

quelque chose de [+ *m.s. adj.*] something [*adj.*]. **quelque chose de nouveau** something new [3.11]

quelquefois *adv.* sometimes; = **parfois**

quelques [N *pl.*] some [N *pl.*]; **quelques-un(e)s** some

quelqu'un(e) *pn.* someone; — **d'intéressant** someone interesting

question *f.* question; **poser une** — to ask a question; **répondre à une** — to answer a question

qui who; whom

quitter [N] to leave (*sbdy* or *sthg*)

quoi [12.10] what; **avec** — with what; **de** — about what

quoique *conj.* although

quotidien, -ne *adj.* daily

R

raison *f.* reason; **avoir*** — to be right

rarement *adv.* rarely, seldom

rayer° [30.04] to strike out, to cross off

réaliste *adj.* realistic

recherches *f.pl.* research

raconter to tell about (*sthg*); to recount

récrivez *imp.* rewrite

référant: en vous — **à** [N] referring to (*sthg*)

refuser to refuse; — **de** [I] to refuse to (*do sthg*)

regarder [N] to look at (*sthg*)

règle *f.* rule

regretter [P] to miss [P]; — **de** [I] to regret (*to do sthg*); — **que** [+ *sj.*] to regret that [25.05]; **Je regrette** I am sorry

relation *f.* narration, account, report

relier to join, to connect

relisez *imp.* (**lire***) re-read

remercier [P] (**de** [I]) to thank (*sbdy*) for (*doing sthg*); — [P] (**de** [N]) to thank (*sbdy*) for (*sthg*)

remettre* to give; to hand in; to give back (remit)

remplaçant *m.* substitute, replacement; **en remplaçant** *ps.p.* replacing

remplacer° [30.01] to replace

remplir [N] (**de** [N]) to fill (*sthg*) with (*sthg*); **rempli** *pp.* filled

rencontrer to meet [*by chance*]

se rendre à [PLACE] to go to (*a place*)

rendez-vous *m.* meeting; **avoir*** (**un**) — to have an appointment

rendre to give back; to hand in; to make (happy, *etc.*) **Cela me rend** (**heureux**) That makes me (happy) [8.10E *note*]

renoncer° **à** [N] to give (*sthg*) up; to renounce (*sthg*)

renseignements *m.pl.* information (*used in the pl.*)

rentrer to return home

réparer to repair

repas *m.* meal

repasser to review

répertoire téléphonique *m.* telephone index

répéter° [29.03] to repeat

répliquer (**à** [P]) to reply = **répondre à**

répondre (**à** [P] or [N]) to answer (*sbdy*) or (*sthg*)

réponse *f.* answer (response)

se reposer to rest; ≠ **rester** to remain, to stay

representant *m.* representative, agent

représentation *f.* performance, show; (*theater*); ≠ **la séance** (movies)

représenter to represent; to put on (*a play*)

résolu *pp.* (**résoudre***) resolved; solved

ressembler à [N] to resemble (*sthg*) or (*sbdy*)

ressentiment *m.* resentment; **garder un** — **contre** to harbor resentment against; to hold a grudge against

restaurant *m.* restaurant; (*related to* **restaurer**, to restore)

rester to remain; ≠ **se reposer** to rest

résultat *m.* result

retard *m.* delay; **en** — late (*for an appointment*)

retenir* [11.13] (*vt 29*) to retain; to remember; to reserve (a room)

retour *m.* return; **être de** — to be back

retourner to *go back*; ≠ **revenir*** to *come back*

se réunir to meet (*by arrangement*); **la réunion** meeting

réussir (**à** [I]) to succeed (*in doing sthg*); — **à un examen** to pass an examination; ≠ **passer un examen** to take an examination

se réveiller to wake up; ≠ **s'endormir*** to go to sleep

révéler° [29.03] to reveal

revenir* [11.11] (*vt 30*) to come back; ≠ **retourner** to go back

revoir* (*vt 32*) to see (*sthg*) again; to review; **au** — good-by

revue *f.* magazine

rez-de-chaussée *m.* ground floor (lobby)

riche *adj.* rich

ridicule *adj.* ridiculous

rien *neg.* nothing: **ne** [*vb*] **rien** nothing; not anything; — **de** [*adj. m.s.*] **rien d'important** nothing important

robe *f.* dress

roi *m.* king

rôle: à tour de — each person in turn

roman *m.* novel (*genre*)

romancier *m.*, **romancière** *f.* novelist

ronde: à la — in turn, one after the other

rosbif *m.* roast beef

rouge *adj.* red

rouler to roll; — **à bicyclette** to ride a bike; — **au sol** to taxi (*a plane*)

route *f.* highway; **se mettre* en** — **pour** to set out for

rouvert *pp.* (**rouvrir***) re-opened

rouvrir* [15.06] (*vt 18*) to re-open

rue *f.* street; **dans la** — on the street; ≠ **sur le boulevard, la place** on the boulevard, square

ruisseau *m.* stream
russe *m.* Russian (*language*)
Russe *m.* Russian (*person*)
Russie *f.* Russia; l'U.R.S.S. (Union soviétique) U.S.S.R.
rythme *m.* rate; rhythm

S

sa *adj.* his, her, its
sage *adj.* wise; well-behaved; **sois sage** behave yourself
saisir to seize
saison *f.* season
salade *f.* salad
salle *f.* room (= **la pièce**); — **de bains** bathroom; — **de classe** classroom; — **à manger** dining room
salon *m.* living-room
saluer to greet
Salut! Hello! (*used very informally, with close friends*); ≠ **allô** Hello! (*on the phone*); ≠ **Bonjour, monsieur!** Good morning (afternoon, evening) (*normal greeting*)
samedi *m.* Saturday
sans *prep.* without
santé *f.* health
satisfait, -e *adj.* satisfied, contented (**de** with)
savant *m.* scientist, scholar
savoir* (*vt 25*) to know
scène *f.* scene; **sur la** — on stage
science *f.* science
séance *f.* show, performance; **la première** — the first show (movies)
second, -e *adj.* second; **au** — **étage** on the third floor
selon *prep.* according to; — **le cas** as the situation dictates; according to the case
semaine *f.* week; **la** — **passée** *or* **dernière**) last week; **la** — **prochaine** next week
semblant: faire* — **de** [I] to pretend (*to do sthg*)
sembler to seem
sens *m.* meaning; direction
sentir* [16.07] (*vt 27*) to feel; to smell
séparer to separate
sérieux, sérieuse *adj.* serious-minded; serious
servant: en vous — **de** [N] using (*sthg*)
serveuse *f.* waitress; ≠ **le garçon (de café)** waiter
se servir* de [N] [16.07] (*vt 26*) to make use of (*sthg*); to use (*sthg*); = **employer**° [N] [30.03]
seul, -e *adj.* alone; (*before noun*) only
si *conj.* if; **s'il** if he, if it; *adv.* so; **si tôt** so early
siècle *m.* century; **au XXᵉ** — in the 20th century (*use roman numerals for centuries*)
siège *m.* seat
signaler to point out
signifier to mean; to signify

s'il vous plaît please
simple *adj.* simple
situation *f.* location; situation
situé, -e *pp.* located, situated
société *f.* company, corporation
sociologie *f.* sociology
sociologue *m.* sociologist
sœur *f.* sister
soie *f.* silk; **de** — made of silk
soif *f.* thirst; **avoir*** — to be thirsty
soigneusement *adv.* carefully; = **avec soin**
soin *m.* care; **avec** — carefully
soir *m.* evening; ≠ **nuit** *f.* night (*after bedtime*)
soirée *f.* party
soldat *m.* soldier
sommeil *m.* sleep; **avoir*** — to be sleepy
son *adj.* his, her, its
songer° to consider, to muse
sorte *f.* sort, kind
sortir* (**de** [N]) [16.07] (*vt 27*) to go out (*of a place*); — [N] **de** [N] to take (*sthg*) out of (*sthg*)
sou *m.* sou (*smallest coin*); **être sans le** — to be broke (= **être fauché**)
souffrant, -e *adj.* indisposed
souhaiter to wish
souligné, -e underlined
soupe *f.* soup
sourire *m.* smile
sous *prep.* under; **sous-sol** *m.* basement
sous-main *nm. invar.* desk pad
souvent *adv.* often
spacieux, spacieuse *adj.* spacious
spirituel, -le *adj.* witty; (**esprit** *m.* wit)
sport *m.* sport(s); **faire*** **du** — to engage in sports
stationner to park; = **garer**
stylo *m.* (fountain) pen; — **à bille** ball-point pen
su *pp.* (**savoir***) found out; **j'ai** — I found out
succéder° [29.03] to succeed (*in line of succession*); ≠ **réussir** to succeed (*to be successful*)
Suède *f.* Sweden
Suédois *m.* Suédoise *f.* Swede
suédois *m.* Swedish (*language*)
suggérer° [29.03] to suggest
Suisse *f.* Switzerland
suite *f.* continuation; **ainsi de** — and so on; **tout de** — *adv.* immediately
suivant, -e *adj.* following
suivi, -e (**de** [N]) *pp.* followed (*by sthg*)
suivre* (*vt 28*) to follow; to take (*a course*)
sujet *m.* subject; **au** — **de** concerning, on the subject of
sur *prep.* on
sûr, -e *adj.* sure, certain
sûreté *f.* safety; security
surtout *adv.* especially
survivant *m.* survivante *f.* survivor

survivre* to survive
sympathique *adj.* likeable, nice
symphonie *f.* symphony
synonyme *m.* synonym

T

ta *adj.* your (*familiar*)
tabac *m.* tobacco; débit de — (licensed) tobacco shop
table *f.* table; mettre* la — to set the table
tableau *m.* painting; picture; — noir blackboard
tâcher (de [ɪ]) to try (*to do sthg*); = essayer° de [ɪ]
taille *f.* size; stature
tant de [N *pl.*] *adv.* so many (*things*); so much;
   tant bien que mal somehow or other
tante *f.* aunt; ≠ oncle *m.* uncle
taper to type; — à la machine to type
tard *adv.* late; ≠ tôt early
tasse *f.* cup; une — de a cup of
taxi *m.* taxi
technique *adj.* technical
tel, -le que such as
téléviseur *m.* TV set
temps *m.* time; à — on time; de — en — from time to
   time; Quel — fait-il? What's the weather like?;
   — du verbe verb tense
tendre to offer; — la main to hold out one's hand
tenir* [11.09] (*vt* 29) to hold; — à [ɪ] to be eager (*to do
   sthg*) [11.12]; — à [N] to value (*sthg*) highly
tennis *m.* tennis; faire* du — to play tennis (= jouer au
   tennis)
terminer to end, terminate
terre *f.* earth; par — on the ground, on the floor;
   pomme de — *f.* potato
tête *f.* head; avoir* mal à la — to have a headache
thé *m.* tea
théâtre *m.* theater; ≠ cinéma *m.* (movie) theater
thème *m.* translation (*from one's native language into
   another language*) ≠ version
théorie *f.* theory
tiens! well!; tell me more!
timbre-poste *m.* postage stamp; *pl.* timbres-poste
tirer to pull; to fire (*weapon*)
tiret *m.* dash (*punctuation*)
tiroir *m.* drawer
tomber to fall; — amoureux (amoureuse) de to fall in
   love with
ton *adj.* your
tort: avoir* — to be wrong; ≠ avoir* raison to be right
tôt *adv.* early
toujours *adv.* still; always
tour *f.* tower; — de contrôle control tower
touriste *m.,f.* tourist
tournure de phrase *f.* turn of phrase

tous les jours *adv.* every day
tout *adv.* all; every [8.07]; — le monde everybody
traduction *f.* translation
tragédie *f.* tragedy; ≠ la comédie comedy
train *m.* train; par le — by train = en chemin de fer
   être en — de [ɪ] to be in process of (*doing sthg*)
traitement *m.* salary
traiter de [N] to deal with (*sthg*)
trajet *m.* trip
transmettre* to transmit
transport *m.* transportation
travail *m.* work; au — ! get to work!; se mettre* au
   — to start work
travailler to work; — dur to work hard
traverser to cross, to go across (*sthg*)
trente thirty
très *adv.* very
trieur de courrier *m.* stacking desk trays
trombone *m.* paper clip
se tromper to be mistaken; — de [N] to get the wrong
   (*thing*)
trop *adv.* too much; — de [N *pl.*] too much, too many
troubler to trouble
trouver to find; to like; Comment trouvez-vous le
   cours? How do you like (find) the course?
se trouver to be located; Londres se trouve en Angleterre. London is (located) in England.
typique *adj.* typical

U

un, une *art.* a, an; one; un peu de [N] a little (*sthg*)
université *f.* university
usé, -e *adj.* worn, worn-out
utile *adj.* useful
utiliser to use; = se servir* de, employer°

V

va: il — *tp* (aller*) he goes, is going
vacances *f.pl.* vacation; en — on vacation; les grandes
   — summer vacation
vaisselle *f.* dishes; faire* la — to wash the dishes
valet *m.* valet
valise *f.* suitcase
vaut: il — mieux que [+ *sj.*] it is preferable that [25.04],
   it is better that
vedette *f.* star (*performer*)
véhicule *m.* vehicle
veille *f.* the previous day, the day before; la — au soir
   the evening before
vendeur *m.* vendeuse *f.* salesperson
vendre to sell

vendredi *m.* Friday

venir* [11.09] (*vt* 30) to come; — **de** [I] to have just (*done sthg*) [11.10]

Venise Venice

vérifier to verify; = **contrôler**

vérité *f.* truth; **dire* la** — to tell the truth

verre *m.* glass; **un** — **de** a glass of

vers *prep.* towards; about; **vers cinq heures** about five o'clock

vert, -e *adj.* green

version *f.* translation (*into one's native language*)

veut dire: cela — that means; (*from id.* **vouloir* dire**)

viande *f.* meat

vie *f.* life; **le coût de la** — the cost of living

vieil *adj. p.* (*m. of* **vieux,** *before vowel*) old [5.06]

vienne *sj.* (**venir***) will come

Vienne Vienna

vient: il — *tp* (**venir***) comes, is coming

vieux *adj. p.* old

village *m.* village

ville *f.* city; **une petite** — a town; **les curiosités de la** — the sights of the city

vin *m.* wine

vingt twenty; **vingt heures** eight P.M.

violon *m.* violin; **jouer du** — to play the violin

visite *f.* visit; **rendre** — **à** [P], **faire* une** — **à** [P] to visit (*sbdy*); **la visite de la douane** customs inspection

visiter [N] to visit (*place*); (*see* **visite** *for visiting people*)

vite *adv.* fast; quickly

vœu *m.* wish

voilà [N] there is (*sthg*) [*in view*]; **le** — there he (it) is

voir* (*vt* 32) to see

voisin *m.* **voisine** *f.* neighbor

voiture *f.* car; automobile; carriage

vol *m.* flight

volant *m.* steering wheel

vont: ils — *tp* (**aller***) they go, are going

vos *adj.* your

votre *adj.* your

voudrais: je — *tc* I would like

voudriez-vous *interr.* (**vouloir***) would you like

voulez-vous *interr.* (**vouloir***) do you want; **Que** — ? What do you want?

vouloir* (*vt* 33) to wish, to want

vouloir* dire to mean, to signify

vous-même yourself

voyage *m.* trip; **faire* un** — to take a trip

voyager° [30.02] to travel

voyageur *m.* traveler

voyant: en — *ps. p.* (**voir***) upon seeing

vrai, -e *adj.* true; (*cf.* **la vérité** the truth)

vu *pp.* (**voir***) seen

Y

y [14.07] *pn.* there

y a-t-il *interr.* are there

y compris included, including

yeux *m. pl.* eyes (*s.* **un œil**)

Index

360

Demonstrative adjective *ce, cet, cette, ces* [5.07]
depuis:
    equivalent of *il y a : . . que* [9.06]
    imperfect tense with [20.07]
    with passé composé [32.02C]
    passé simplé not used with [32.02C]
    present tense with [9.04]
    vs. *pendant, pour* + time [9.04B]
depuis quand [9.05]
dernier precedes noun [6.01]; follows [6.04]
descendre, transitive use [16.05]
*devenir** [11.11]
*devoir** [23.06]
Direct object, preceding verb, agreement of past participle with [15.04]
Direct object pronoun [13.01]
    precedes infinitive [13.02B]
    required by certain verbs [13.05]
Disjunctive pronoun [28.07]
    compound subject [28.09C]
    emphatic use [28.09D]
Division of words, Appendix F
dont, relative pronoun [24.02]

E

"each," "every" (day of the week) [1.05D]
Elision [1.02]
emmener° [27.06]
Emphasis, use of disjunctive pronoun for [28.09D]
en [13.07]
    academic subject (*en économie*) [2.02]
    expression of quantity or number, with [13.08]
    languages (*en français*) [2.01]
    months (*en avril*) [10.09]
    PDO, no agreement with [15.05A]
    present participle, with [31.01]
    quelques-uns, with [13.09]
    seasons (*en hiver*) [1.06B]
entendre + infinitive [17.03]
espérer que [25.06]
est-ce [2.04]
est-ce que [12.01]
étant + past participle [31.03E]
*être**:
    auxiliary [16.03]
    idioms [2.10]
    imperative forms [26.08]
    possession: *être à* + person [2.08]
    present subjunctive [25.09]
Exclamations [17.04–17.06]

F

*faire**:
    causative [17.01]
    idioms [8.10]
    present subjunctive [26.06]
*falloir**: *il faut* [26.05F] [11.03 note 1]

Family, *révision lexicale*, p. 28
Family name:
    plural does not add *-s* [1.04D]
    possession (*de* + name) [2.07]
    titles include article [1.04D]
"Floor" numbering (first, second, etc.) p. 56
"for (TIME)": *depuis* [9.04] [20.07]
"former . . . latter" [28.06]
"found out": *savoir** in passé composé [26.10C]
"from (COUNTRY)" [7.13]
Future perfect [21.06]
Future tense [21.01]
Future time:
    actions related to past [22.01B]
    *aller** + infinitive: immediate future [1.10]
    in present tenses [9.07]
    present subjunctive [25.10]
    quand, lorsque, with [21.02]

G

General article [1.04A] [4.02]
    unchanged after negative verb [4.06B]
Geographical names:
    article with [1.04B]
    capitalization, Appendix F
    cities [1.06C]
    countries, continents, Appendix E
    "from (COUNTRY)" [7.13]
    mountains [1.04B]
    prepositions with [1.06C]
    rivers [1.04B]
"go" (in, out, etc.), verbs other than *aller** [1.09]
GOVERNMENT OF INFINITIVES: see also Appendix D
    à before infinitive [11.04]
    de before infinitive [11.05]
    no preposition before infinitive [11.03]
grand, -e "tall" vs. "great" [6.04]

H

h, mute and aspirate [1.02]
Habitual or repeated action:
    imperfect tense [20.04]
    present tense [9.02]
    usual day (*every* Saturday) [1.05D]
"had (done something)" [20.08]
"had to (do something)" [23.07B]
"have (person) (do something)": causative *faire**
    [17.01]
"have (something) (done)": causative *faire** [17.01]

I

il est or *c'est* [5.12] [5.13]
il faut + infinitive [25.04]
il faut que + subjunctive [26.05]

O

Object pronoun, word order [14.05]
office, *révision lexicale* p. 169
on replacing passive voice [19.07]
Opinion, subjunctive used [26.03]
Orthographic-changing verbs: see Stem-changing verbs
où, d'où replacing relative pronoun [24.06]
où interrogative [12.02]
*ouvrir** [15.06]

P

par (as agent) [19.10]
parmi (+ *lequel*) for person [24.04]
PARTICIPLE:
    past [15.03] [16.02] [19.02]
    present [31.01–31.03]
*partir** [16.07]
Partitive [4.01]
    de replaces *des* [4.06]
    general article compared [4.02]
    personal ownership or comsumption [4.03]
    table [4.05]
    uncountable (mass) nouns [4.05]
Parts of body, article with [2.09]
Passé composé:
    with *avoir** [15.01]
    with *être** [16.01]
    with imperfect in narration [20.05]
    reflexive verbs [19.01]
Passé simple [32.01]
Passive voice [19.09]
    ways of avoiding [19.07–19.08]
Past anterior [32.04]
Past conditional [22.04]
PAST PARTICIPLE:
    agreement, with *avoir** [15.04]
    agreement, with *être* [16.02]
    agreement, with reflexive verbs [19.02]
    après avoir (être) + past participle [17.07]
    in passive, use [19.09]
    place in negation [10.04]
Past subjunctive [27.01]
pendant, pour ("for TIME") [9.04B]
penser, croire, espérer°*, rule for subjunctive after [25.06]
personne as subject [10.05]
Physical appearance described with imperfect tense [20.05]
*pleuvoir** "to rain" [8.10D]
Pluperfect [20.08]
Plural of nouns [3.01]
plus de + NUMBER [8.05]
plusieurs [3.10]
Plus-que-parfait [20.08]
Polite requests [22.01A]
POSSESSION:
    clothing, parts of body [2.09]

POSSESSION (*cont.*):
    de + noun [2.07]
    *être** à PERSON [2.08]
    possessive adjectives (*mon, ma*) [2.05]
    reflexive verbs [18.06]
Possessive pronouns (*le mien*) [12.11–12.13]
pour "for TIME" [9.04B]; "in order to" [11.01]
pourquoi [12.02]
*pouvoir** [21.10]
    present subjunctive [26.06]
    vs. *savoir** [21.11]
premier, dernier, precede noun [6.01]
*prendre** [9.13–9.15]
PREPOSITION:
    of destination or location [1.06C]; Appendix E
    government of infinitives [11.02]; Appendix D
    required after *entrer, partir*, sortir** [16.04]
PRESENT PARTICIPLE [31.01–31.03]
    replacing subjunctive with *bien que* [26.05C]
Professions [5.13]
PRONOUNS:
    direct object [13.01] [13.05]
    disjunctive [28.07–28.09]
    en [13.07]
    indirect object [14.01]
    multiple, word order [14.05]
    positive imperative, word order [14.06]
    possessive (*le mien*) [12.11–12.13]
    reflexive [18.02]
    relative: see Relative pronouns
    stressed (disjunctive) [28.07–28.09]
    supplied, in interrogative [12.04]
    word order, multiple pronouns [14.05]
    y [14.07–14.08]
Punctuation, Appendix F

Q

quand + future [21.02]
    questions with [12.02]
QUANTITY, EXPRESSIONS OF [3.07] [3.08] [7.10]
que:
    "as," "than" in comparisons [8.01]
    conjunction mandatory [25.07]
    elision of (to *qu'*) [1.02]
    exclamations (*que de livres!*) [17.04]
    que, qu'est-ce que interrogative [12.09]
quel, quelle:
    exclamations (*quelle ville!*) [17.06]
    interrogative [21.07]
quelque chose de + adjective [3.11]
quelques "a few" [3.10]
    quelques-un(e)s, en required before verb [13.09]
Questions: see Interrogation
qui relative pronoun:
    object of preposition [24.01]
    subject of clause [23.02]
quitter requires direct object [16.06C]
quoi object of preposition [12.10]
Quotations, punctuation of, Appendix F

Trains, *révision lexicale*, p. 246
Transitive use of *monter, descendre, sortir** [16.05]

U

Uncountable (mass) nouns, partitive [4.05]
"used to (do something)" [20.03]

V

Vehicles, *révision lexicale* p. 65
venir* [11.09]
   idioms [11.10]
   passé simple [32.03]
Verb-prepositional linkage: see Régimes
Verb unit [10.01]
   reflexive verb [18.05] [19.04] [19.05]
vieil [5.06]
visiter vs. *faire** *une visite à* [1.11] [8.10C]
Voice, passive [19.06] [19.09]
   replaced by *on* [19.07]
voilà, voici [3.14]
   pronoun with, word order [13.02E]
voilà [TIME] *que* [9.06]
voir* [24.08]
   + infinitive [17.03]
vouloir* [22.06] [22.07]

W

Weather [8.10D]
Weeks, days of the [1.05D] [10.08]
"when" (*à quelle heure*) [12.02]
   où replaces *quand* [24.06]
   quand followed by future [21.02]
"which one of" (*lequel* interrogative) [21.08]
Word division: Appendix F
WORD ORDER:
   adjective [6.01]: affects meaning [6.04]
   adverb [7.01] [7.04] [7.06]
   day precedes hour [7.03]
   en [13.07]
   indirect object pronouns [14.01]
   inversion in questions [12.03] [12.04]
   multiple pronouns [14.05]
   possessive pronouns [12.12]
   si-clauses (conditional sentences) [22.05]
   subordinate clause [23.04] [24.01]
"would (do something)": conditional [22.01];
   imperfect [20.04]

Y

y, pronoun [14.07] [14.08]
   idioms [14.11]

Correction Symbols and Abbreviations

ac	Accent: missing, incorrect, or misaligned
adj	Adjective
adj p	Adjective should precede noun
adv	Adverb
ag	Agreement

adjective	[5.01]
celui	[28.02]
disjunctive pronoun	[28.08]
pp (*avoir*)	[15.04]
pp (*être*)	[16.02]
pp (reflexives)	[19.02]

art	Article: required or omitted
aux	Auxiliary verb
c	Contraction [1.03]
cap	Capitalization [Appendix F]
çonj	Conjunction (*que* required)
✐ or ℓ	Delete: not needed
dd	*des* becomes *de*

intervening adjective [6.03]
Partitive after negative verb [4.06]

dj	Disjunctive pronoun [28.07]
do	Direct object required [13.01]
dv	Division of words [Appendix F]
el	Elision [1.02]
ex	Exercise not followed
g	Gender
g inf	Government of infinitives [11.02]
id	Idiom required
inc	Incomplete
ind	Indicative required
inf	Infinitive structure required [11.01]
imp	Imperative error
inv	Inversion

after *aussi, peut-être* [7.05]
questions [12.02-12.04]
quotations [Appendix F]
reflexive verbs [18.07B]
after relative pronoun [24.06]

io	Indirect object [14.01]
lc	Lower case (small letter required)
m	Mood (indicative, subjunctive)
neg	Negation: omitted, incomplete, or wrong meaning [10.01]
om	Omission